ALTYN-DEPE

Gold head of a bull from Excavation 7, priest's tomb, room 7.

University Museum Monograph 55

ALTYN-DEPE

V. M. Masson

Translated by
Henry N. Michael

Published by
THE UNIVERSITY MUSEUM
University of Pennsylvania
Philadelphia
1988

Design, editing, production, typesetting
  Scholarly Publications, The University Museum

Printing
  Science Press
  Ephrata, Pennsylvania

Library of Congress Cataloging-in-Publication Data

Masson, V. M. (Vadim Mikhailovich) , 1929-
    Altyn-Depe.

    (University museum monograph ; 55)
    Translation of: Altyn-Depe.
    1. Altyn-Depe Site (Turkmen S.S.R.)
2. Turkmen S.S.R.--Antiquities. 3. Excavations
(Archaeology)--Turkmen S.S.R. I. Title. II. Series.
DK939.5.A48M3713 1988   958'.5   88-20845
ISBN 0-934718-54-7

The paper in this book meets the guidelines for permanence and
durability of the Committee on Production Guidelines for Book
Longevity of the Council on Library Resources.

AKADEMIYA NAUK TURKMENSKOY SSR

V.M. MASSON

ALTYN-DEPE

LENINGRAD
"NAUKA"
LENINGRADSKOYE OTDELENIYE
1981

Contents

LIST OF ILLUSTRATIONS ix

LIST OF PLATES x

PREFACE xii

FOREWORD xiii

TRANSLATOR'S NOTE xv

AUTHOR'S FOREWORD TO THE ENGLISH EDITION xvi

    INTRODUCTION 1

1. ALTYN-DEPE IN THE ENEOLITHIC AND EARLY BRONZE AGES 6

2. EXCAVATIONS OF THE FORTIFICATIONS 26

3. EXCAVATIONS OF THE LIVING QUARTERS 32

4. INVESTIGATION OF THE CULT CENTER 55

5. ALTYN-DEPE AS AN ARCHAEOLOGICAL COMPLEX
    Questions of Typology and Chronology 81

6. ALTYN-DEPE AS AN URBAN CENTER
    Structural and Functional Characteristics 97

7. ALTYN-DEPE IN THE CULTURAL SYSTEM OF THE ANCIENT EAST . . 111

8. EARLY URBAN CENTERS AND ANCIENT CIVILIZATIONS 123

    CONCLUSION 134

    BIBLIOGRAPHY 138

    LIST OF ABBREVIATIONS 150

    PLATES . . . .

Illustrations

Frontispiece   iv
Figure 1.   Plan of Altyn-Depe   5
Figure 2.   Stratigraphic Transit of Excavation 1   7
Figure 3.   Stratigraphic Representation of Materials from Excavation 1   8-9
Figure 4.   Excavation 11. Profile of the South Wall of Cut   13
Figure 5.   Comparative Stratigraphy of Altyn-Depe   15
Figure 6.   Schematic Representation of Eneolithic Layers at Altyn-Depe   16
Figure 7.   Section of the Eastern Slope of the Wall Mound   18
Figure 8.   Plan of Structures at the Base of the Wall Mound   19
Figure 9.   Plan of Structures in Horizon Altyn 4 of Excavation 1   20
Figure 10.   Excavation 8. Cross-section of Enclosing Walls   28
Figure 11.   Excavation 8. Outer Gate Structures in the Lower Horizon   30
Figure 12.   Excavation 10. Plan of Uncovered Structures   34
Figure 13.   Excavation 5. Plan of Uncovered Structures   38
Figure 14.   Burial 198 (1) and 252 (2, 3)   44
Figure 15.   Excavation 9. Plan of Uncovered Structures . . . . *facing* 46
Figure 16.   Excavation 9. Plan of Burial Chamber 11   52
Figure 17.   Excavation 7. Plan of Uncovered Structures   57
Figure 18.   Excavation 7. Structures   58
Figure 19.   Excavation 7. Plan of Uncovered Buildings at Lower Horizon Level   62
Figure 20.   Excavation 7. Burial Chamber of Priests   63-64
Figure 21.   Excavation 7. Room 7   66
Figure 22.   Excavation 7. Room 7   67
Figure 23.   Excavation 7. Floor Plan of Room 9   69
Figure 24.   Comparison of Signs on Altyn-Depe Statuettes with Early Writings   86
Figure 25.   Distribution of Altyn-Depe Statuettes with Signs   88
Figure 26.   Bronze Age Seals and Motifs on Eneolithic Painted Pottery   90
Figure 27.   The Kelleli and Namazga Variants of Altyn-Depe Culture   92
Figure 28.   General View of Quarters Uncovered in Excavation 9   102
Figure 29.   Histograms of Animal Bone Distribution   104
Figure 30.   Altyn-Depe in the Middle Bronze Age . . . . *facing* 47
Figure 31.   Cultural Influences in the Middle East During the Eneolithic   114
Figure 32.   Cultural Zones and Distribution of Sites with Writing   120
Figure 33.   Typology of Early Civilizations   129
Figure 34.   Schematic Distribution of Urban Cultures in Central Asia   136

Plates

Plate 1   Excavation 5
Plate 2   Excavations 8 and 10
Plate 3   Excavations 9 and 7
Plate 4   Painted Pottery of the Late Eneolithic and Early Bronze Ages
Plate 5   Painted Ceramics of Namazga IV
Plate 6   Namazga V Ceramics
Plate 7   Stone Vessels
Plate 8   Female Terracotta Statuettes
Plate 9   Female Terracotta Statuettes
Plate 10   Female and Male Terracotta Statuettes
Plate 11   Female Terracotta Statuettes
Plate 12   Female and Male Statuettes and Anthropomorphic Figurines
Plate 13   Animal Figurines
Plate 14   Metal Artifacts
Plate 15   Stone Inserts, Flint Arrowheads and Metal Artifacts
Plate 16   Crosslike Seals and Their Impressions
Plate 17   Seals of Geometric and Anthropomorphic Forms
Plate 18   Carved Terracotta Boxes (Reliquaries)
Plate 19   Terracotta Model and Bone Sticks
Plate 20   Stone and Elephant Ivory Beads, Zoomorphic Pourer
Plate 21   Stone Beads and Pendants
Plate 22   Miscellaneous
Plate 23   Bull's Head and Wolf's Head
Plate 24   Namazga I Painted Ceramics
Plate 25   Painted Ceramics
Plate 26   Female and Anthropomorphic Statuettes of the Late Eneolithic
Plate 27   Inventory of Burial 296
Plate 28   Burial 362
Plate 29   Metal Artifacts
Plate 30   Parts of Terracotta Vehicle Models
Plate 31   Namazga V Ceramics
Plate 32   Namazga V Ceramics
Plate 33   Namazga V Ceramics
Plate 34   Namazga V Ceramics
Plate 35   Middle Bronze Age Stone Artifacts, Vessels, and Statuettes
Plate 36   Early Bronze Age Artifacts
Plate 37   Middle Bronze Age Artifacts

Plate 38   Early Bronze Age Artifacts
Plate 39   Late Eneolithic Terracotta Statuettes of Animals and Goddesses
Plate 40   Middle Bronze Age Vessels
Plate 41   Early Bronze Age Stone Lamps
Plate 42   Late Eneolithic and Early Bronze Age Painted Vessels
Plate 43   Miscellaneous Artifacts

Preface

The publication of this Enlgish translation of V.M. Masson's informative report on his excavation at Bronze Age Altyn-Depe in Soviet Turkmenia is a direct outcome of the second Soviet-American Archaeological Exchange in 1983. Eight American scholars, including myself, traveled to Moscow, Leningrad, and Samarkand to read papers, meet Soviet colleagues, and examine archaeological material.

Turkmenistan forms a crossroads between Eastern Iran and Central Asia, and between Siberia and southern Russia and the Indus Valley. It thus has always played an important role in linking cultures in the greater Eurasian land mass in addition to being a center of cultural development in its own right.

This broad role, as we now know from Masson's excavations, had already developed in the third millennium B.C. It is the importance of this development to general cultural history and to the study of the rise of urban centers which makes the details of the excavations at the ancient town of Altyn-Depe especially relevant to the archaeology of other urban areas. Given The University Museum's historical focus on major Bronze Age centers elsewhere in the world, including Iran and the Indus area, it seemed most appropriate for us to undertake the present publication. Professor Masson generously accepted our proposal and provided additional photographs representing significant finds from the excavations of 1981-1983 not included in the original Russian-language publication. These additional photographs are represented in Plates 35-43. While not referred to in the text, their provenience is identified in the captions.

Dr. Henry Michael of our Museum Applied Science Center for Archaeology translated the volume. Professor Philip L. Kohl of Wellesley University kindly reviewed the translation for us. Dr. Masson provided an introduction to the English-language edition. Vincent Pigott defined the metallurgical terms in light of current usage in English. Maurizio Tosi evaluated the illustrations of artifacts excavated in 1983-1984 and recommended several adjustments to the translation of the author's foreword to the English edition. Catherine Ambrose edited the volume and oversaw its production; Leah Reynolds reworked many of the figures; Antonia Montague worked on the layout of the text; Raymond Rorke worked on the final layout of the plates; Anita Liebman designed the plates of objects from recent excavations; and Karen Vellucci, head of our Scholarly Publications department, guided it through the press. We thank them all for their efforts.

Robert H. Dyson, Jr.
Director
The University Museum

Foreword

V. M. Masson's excavation and publication of Altyn-Depe is one of the twentieth century's most significant contributions to our understanding of ancient Asia. In a sense this work added the final dimension to a very large cultural mosaic of the third millennium B.C., knowledge of which had been accumulating since the 1920s.

The excavations of the Royal Graves of Ur, and other sites like Kish and Susa, brought the full richness of Mespotamian civilization to light. At the same time, some 1500 miles to the east, archaeologists unearthed the remains of the contemporary Harappan civilization, a new and totally unexpected civilization of the Indian Bronze Age. It was immediately apparent that the Indus and Mesopotamia were in contact with one another since Harappan artifacts were recovered from a number of places: Ur, Kish, Tell Asmar, Agrab Tepe, to name the more important sites.

Subsequent work on the Iranian plateau at sites like Tepe Sialk and Tepe Hissar uncovered important new material which was clearly a part of the life of the third millennium in "Middle Asia," as we might call this area between the Indus and the Euphrates bounded on the north by the deserts of Central Aisa and on the south by the Arabian Gulf. The picture of interaction between and among these various centers was most incomplete. It was also tantalizingly filled with hints, suggestions, and possibilities. The etched carnelian beads and quantities of lapis lazuli at Hissar and finds like proto-Elamite tablets at Sialk seemed to be "telling" archaeologists something, but it was not at all clear just what that message was.

Renewed archaeological work throughout "Middle Asia" following the hiatus caused by World War II has done much to clarify the early history of this region, revealing an unexpectedly complex mosaic of urban centers and economic vitality. The discovery of the ancient lands of Dilmun and Makkan, now associated with Oman and the island of Bahrein, brought to light other important actors in this set of players. Additional excavation in Iran at Shahr-i Sokhta, Tepe Yahya and the necropolis at Shahdad, and at Mundigak in Afghanistan, have significantly added to our knowledge of the third millennium on the Iranian plateau. Our understanding of these recent discoveries is incomplete, to be sure, and there is a great deal of digging yet to be done: however, a sense of strong economic and political activity in the region has emerged from this work and complements the earlier evidence from Sialk, Hissar, and other sites. Some form of urbanization, if short lived, was clearly a part of the third millennium in the Helmand region. In the greater Indus Valley to the south, excavations at Kot Diji, Sarai Khola, Rehman Dheri, Kalibangan, Banawali, Rangpur, Lothal, and a host of other sites, have added immensely to our understanding of this civilization as well. The Harappan civilization probably remains, in terms of scale, the most enigmatic of these Bronze Age cultures, but new interpretations of this civilization are beginning to clarify some issues. The archaeological work at Mehrgarh, and other surrounding sites at the base of the Bolan Pass, like Nausharo and Sibri, is a very positive case in point. There are numerous and obvious parallels in material culture at these sites which clearly link them with northern "Middle Asia": the northern plain of Afghanistan (also inhabited by Harappans) and Turkmenia.

Altyn-Depe, and the discovery of the Turkmenian Bronze Age civilization, filled the remaining blank in the ancient "Middle Asian" interaction sphere. The urbanization of Turkmenia, best exemplified at Altyn-Depe, brought to closure the third millennium system that had been hinted at with Harappan seals in Mesopotamia and other "stray" finds of uncertain origin on the Iranian plateau.

We now can see that the early centuries of the third millennium throughout "Middle Asia" were a period of cultural change and elaboration on some considerable scale. By 2500 B.C. there was, for reasons that are far from known, a grand conjunction of trade and probably power, of "interconnectedness" to be sure, which ultimately linked Mesopotamia, Dilmun, Makkan, and the Indus overland across Iran and through the Arabian Gulf by sea. We can also see that, taking Turkmenia as our arbitrary starting point, Central Asia was linked west and east via Iranian routes to Mesopotamia and the Indus, as well as south to the Helmund civilization.

Much remains to be done by way of understanding how this conjunction came to be, how and what sustained it, and why, beginning at about 2200 B.C., it seems to have begun a process of cultural disintegration. But, on the positive side, the primary participants in the interaction sphere—Mesopotamia, Dilmun, and Makkan, as well as the Indus, Helmand and Turkmenian civilizations—have been identified. We also have some sense of what items were being traded and we can see the immense changes that this activity brought to the ancient towns and cities.

More challenging perhaps than issues of time/space relationships, as fundamental as such work might be, is the task of trying to assess what this conjunction means within a larger frame of reference. In terms of geographic scale and cultural divesity this was a wholly new kind of human experience, on the cutting edge of cultural innovation, and all such new experiments in human organization deserve our attention.

Gregory L. Possehl
Associate Director
The University Museum

Translator's Note

In this volume the transliteration of names, titles, and place names is based on the system recommended by the United States Board on Geographic Names, with the exception that the Russian "soft sign" is not rendered as an apostrophe. Also, whenever appropriate, the letter "y" is inserted between two vowels.

All words or sentences in brackets, in the text proper, footnotes, and references, are those of the translator. Any words or sentences in parentheses are those of the author.

Henry N. Michael
Senior Fellow
MASCA, The University Museum

Author's Foreword to the English Edition of Altyn-Depe

This volume is dedicated to the results of archaeological excavations in the southwest of Soviet Central Asia where cultures representing the northern limits of the ecumene of the Ancient East developed during the seventh to the second millennia B.C. American archaeology has a longstanding and steadfast tradition of investigating the antiquities of the Middle East, such as excavations of many years standing at Nippur and Jarmo in Iraq, Tepe Hissar and Hasanlu in Iran, and Alishar and Troy in Asia Minor, as well as other sites. The rich collections of the Chicago and Philadelphia museums are among the most valuable for world archaeology. To a lesser degree, the American scientific world is aware of the intensive investigations undertaken in Soviet Central Asia in the 1950s to 1970s, although even here, during the formative period of archaeology, the Carnegie Institute organized the excavation of early Anau settlements in the vicinity of Ashkabad (Pumpelly 1908). Today, it is clear that these were only poor hamlets yielding to the archaeologists lackluster remains of clay-walled cottages and worn sherds sometimes ornamented with inexpressive paintings. Large centers of the urban type were discovered in the area, however, and one of them, Altyn-Depe (which in Turkic means "Golden Hill"), is the subject of the present work. Aside from the real golden objects—golden heads of a bull and a wolf were found here—this site has become the "gold standard" for Central Asiatic archaeology. The almost 30 m thickness of the cultural layers allows us to trace the gradual evolution of the culture of the ancient agriculturalists into an urbanized civilization. The collected materials are widely used in various investigations and have been used, more than once, in the discussion of scientific problems in the course of Soviet-American symposia on the archaeology of early civilizations of the Middle East (Masson 1986). In this brief foreword, I would like to emphasize only two points.

The first deals with the problems concerning the formation of the specifics and internal structure of early urban organisms. American investigators have given much attention to these problems starting with the well-known symposium "City Invincible" held in Chicago in 1958 (Krealing and Adams, eds. 1960). Yet solidly based archaeological material which would characterize the earliest, just forming urban organisms is not so substantial. The famous sites of Mesopotamia, including Uruk, from which the chronology of the earliest process of urbanization was derived, were studied mainly within the confines of the monumental cult centers. The development of these grandiose architectural complexes is significant and representative, but it cannot replace the investigaton of the real structure of the earliest urban centers since these were never extensively excavated. The city quarters of Ur of the Third Dynasty, as documents of the epoch reflect, illustrate the composition of an urban organism which had already undergone a separate evolution in part connected to that of the dominant royal house. At Altyn-Depe extensive, well-documented materials were obtained which characterize the structure and function of an early urban organism taking shape in a natural way on the basis of very early communal structures. In terms of the Mesopotamian periodization, these developments occurred in the times of Late Ubaid-Early Uruk. Hopefully, in Mesopotamia much earlier layers are buried under the many meters of later cultural accumulations. At Altyn-Depe the Bronze Age settlement was abandoned at precisely this fomative stage, thus presenting extensive possibilities for a multi-faceted study.

The second point is tied to the interpretation of the very fact of the finding of yet another early urban or proto-urban civilization in the sociocultural system of the ancient Middle East. Archaeological discoveries in the second half of the twentieth century continue to extend the boundaries of early civilizations. In particular, it is now quite clear that aside form the three great civilizations—Egypt, Mesopotamia, and Harappa—there existed a number of other highly developed organisms, yielding in a number of parameters to those of their older brothers, but adequately distinctive and original. The highly distinctive Ebla civilization discovered in the north of Syria, although in many respects following the Sumerian standards which were the models of the time, is a sufficient index. From the point of view of typology, we can recognize three types of cultures: epochal, regional, and local. Given the special epochal characteristics, all urbanized cultures of the ancient East belong to the first type of civilization. On the next level of analysis, regional traits make their distinct appearance and, in the case of special characteristics for the ancient East, differentiate the regional cultures from the hearths of Mesoamerican and Chinese civilizations. The culture of Altyn-Depe, already representing a third type, without a doubt belongs to the regional type of civilizations of the ancient East. At the same time, investigations of the past decade indicate the existence of a specific subregion which includes a number of areas in the northeast of the ecumene of the ancient East and represents a special cultural world outside of Elam. Thus the Geoksyur assemblage is culturally distinctive and served as an initial foundation for the process of urbanization in this subregion. Tosi and Lamberg-Karlovsky (1973) have noted this. Today, after the finding of Geoksyur sites in the Murghab delta and Sarazm in the upper reaches of the Zeravshan river, the influence of assemblages of the Geoksyur type has grown even more. We have to keep in mind, however, that the boundaries of cultural communities and subregions were mobile. Thus during the fourth and the beginning of the third millennia B.C., the material culture of northern Baluchistan with its expressive painted ceramics clearly gravitated toward the circle of Baluchistan-Indus forms. The Baluchistan-Indus tradition, despite the various links, in general was distinct from the Geoksyur assemblage. Later, as seen in the assemblages of Late Mehrgarh and Sibri, the situation in northwestern Baluchistan changed radically in regard to basic cultural types that

gravitated to the block of cultures which included Altyn-Depe and the early sites of Margiana and Bactria. From this subregion the magnificent artifacts of an artistic culture come forth, and they are brilliantly analyzed by Amiet in his recent work (Amiet 1986). It is pecisely here that we find an original local school of ancient Middle Eastern creativity. In the same work Amiet convincingly shows that imports from this area are extensively represented in early Susa.

The question arises as to what this cluster of civilizations should be called. In a macro-regional setting it manifestly belongs to an early eastern type which, however, has clearly expressed, specific local characteristics, beginning with the types of partitioned metal seals. Since almost all of the striking assemblages of objects of the artistic culture in this subregion are associated with the territory of later Bactria, the cluster of civilizations could be called "proto-Bactrian." On the basis of the accepted stratigraphy for southern Turkmenistan, the civilization of Altyn-Depe in Namazga V times also belongs to this substratum. In Altyn-Depe proper, traits of direct continuity which link the assemblage to the traditions of the Geoksyur circle can be clearly traced. The formation of other local cultures in the proto-Bactrian subregion was apparently different, and in them the strengthening of western ties which lead, in the main, to Elam, but also to Mesopotamia and Syria, played a considerable role. With this strengthening of western contacts, accompanied by a leap into an iconographic variety of art objects, a role could also have been played by the shifting of tribes of the Indo-Iranian or only the Indic linguistic group, which through the process of cultural assimilation could have become one of the components of the proto-Bactrian cultural community.

I hope that the materials presented in this work will further the investigation of the problems included in it as well as a number of other problems associated with the early history and culture of the Middle East. The book practically duplicates the Soviet edition of 1981 with the exception that several plates representing materials from the earliest strata of Altyn-Depe were added. The latter were analyzed after the book was published.

I am grateful to Professor R. Dyson for his efforts toward the publication of this English-language edition. His authority as a scientific investigator and organizer is very high and reaches beyond the circle of specialists. I also want to express my gratitude to H.N. Michael for his careful translation. Let us hope that the cooperation of present-day scientists will promote progress and development in the same measure it did in the early civilizations—an occurrence emphasized more than once in the book.

References Cited

Amiet, P.

1986 L'âge des échanges inter-iraniens 3500-1700 avant J.-Chr. *Notes et Documents des Musées de France, II.* Paris.

Kraeling, C.H., and R.M. Adams, eds.

1960 *City Invincible: Symposium on Urbanization and Cultural Development in the Ancient Near East held at the Oriental Institute of the University of Chicago, December 4-7, 1958.* University of Chicago Press.

Lamberg-Karlovsky, C.C. and M. Tosi

1973 Shahr-i Sokhta and Tepe Yahya: Tracks on the Earliest History of the Iranian Plateau. *East and West,* vol. 23, nos. 1-2, pp. 25-53. Rome.

Masson, V.M., ed.

1986 *Drevniye tsivilizatsii Vostoka. Materialy II sovetsko-amerikanskogo simposiuma* (Ancient Civilizations of the East. Materials presented at the IInd Soviet-American Symposium). Tashkent.

Pumpelly, R.

1908 *Exploration in Turkestan. Expedition of 1904.* Carnegie Institution of Washington. Washington, D.C.

Introduction

In general, this volume describes the results of excavations of Altyn-Depe which were systematically carried out by the South Turkmenistan Archaeological Inter-disciplinary Expedition of the Academy of Sciences of the Turkmen Soviet Socialist Republic (YuTAKE) and the Kara-Kum Expedition of the Leningrad Branch of the Institute of Archaeology, Academy of Sciences of the U.S.S.R. The excavations have provided numerous and varied materials which have been analyzed and published in detail in volumes of TYuTAKE. In this volume a detailed analysis is presented only for the materials of the cult complex (Excavation 7).

The concentration of effort on the excavations of Altyn-Depe was an ordered and natural link in the process of archaeological study of the Turkmen SSR. During 1955-1963 a number of works works were carried out on early agricultural sites of the Neolithic and Eneolithic, among them some which have become standards for Soviet and foreign archaeology, such as Jeitun, Kara-Depe, and Geoksyur. The corresponding materials have been published in full (Masson 1962a, 1964b, 1971b; Khlopin 1963, 1964, 1969; Sarianidi 1965). As a result, an irregularity arose in this field because of a highly visible lag in Bronze Age studies which were carried out episodically and not always on the proper methodological level.

For this reason, the works of YuTAKE were reoriented to Bronze Age sites. In 1964, the excavation of Namazga-Depe was carried out, and in 1965 a systematic study of Altyn-Depe was begun. At that time the site was already known in the literature, and some excavations had already been done there. It was first examined by a specialist in 1929, during the activities of the Khaveran expedition headed by A.A. Semenov (1946). Later, Altyn-Depe not infrequently came to the attention of a number of investigators, but for the most part their results were not published.

Participants in YuTAKE turned their atten-tion to Altyn-Depe early: in 1949 it was examined by Detachment XII. Even then it was observed that the materials from the upper layers of this fortified hill site appeared to be chronologically close to those from the upper layers of Namazga-Depe. In 1952, during the process of broadly conceived excavations for the study of early agricultural sites in southern Turkmenistan, B.A. Kuftin, who headed the XIVth Detachment of YuTAKE, investigated Altyn-Depe and collected important surface materials including terracottas (1954; 1965:263). Later, in 1953, A.F. Ganyalin (1959) sank two small pits to the depth of 3.5 m, which gave an idea of the nature of the archaeological materials in the upper layers.

From 1959 to 1962 the excavations were extended and in addition to Ganyalin, A.A. Marushchenko, D.D. Durdyev, E. Atagarryev, and O.K. Berdyev participated (Berdyev 1971:12-13). Remains of a thick adobe brick wall were found, and a group of structures in the layer were opened; interesting materials were found, including two caches of imports sealed in the walls. Alas, the field documentation was not conducted at the proper level, and the objectivity of the study of the archaeological complexes was now and then substituted with an urge to prove *a priori* this or that proposition. After initiation of the works at Altyn-Depe by YuTAKE, we undertook every effort to publish the results (see Ganyalin 1967).

Nobody suspected that Altyn-Depe was a large center containing uncovered layers of the developed Bronze Age (or that Namazga V, after investigations, would provide a scale for the chronology of southern Turkmenistan). A second large center, Namazga-Depe, even though it exceeds Altyn-Depe in area, was not preserved to the same degree in the upper layers, since these were disturbed over large areas by a later cemetery. This affected the choice of Altyn-Depe as the focus of continuing research for many years. The organization of the research was directed in the first place to the study of the structures of the site correlated in time to Namazga V, and also to the genesis of this archaeological complex.

During the first two seasons the goals of the excavations were to discover the nodal points, investigate in detail the relief of the site, and, on the basis of topography and other criteria, to reconstruct its internal structure. On the basis of precise measurements, the area of Altyn-Depe is 26 hectares, and its height reaches 17-22 m above the surrounding terrain. And, as test pits have shown, the cultural layers extend to at least 8 m and maximally to not less than 30 m. In all, the ruins of Altyn-Depe present a compact mass nearly oval in ground plan. Its slopes are cut by fairly deep draws, partially formed in antiquity and later deepened by meltwaters.

The analysis of the micro-relief of the fortified hill site, based on the character of vegetation and degree of concentration of surface materials, led to the study of its micro-structure. The preliminary determinations, as a rule, were confirmed in the course of excavations. In the south of the site a broad draw indicated the locality of the former entrance, and it was indeed here that the thick-walled gate structures were excavated. Because of the characteristics of the finds on them, the hillocks bordering the draw on both sides received the names "Copper Mound" (in the east) and Mound of Mortars (in the west). The draw proper ends in a widening, flat bottom which was preliminarily named the Central Square. This low feature is filled with clayey sediments and during seasons of abundant precipitation is covered with thick vegetation. A shallow ravine cutting through the center of the lowland, and penetrating to the depth of 1 m, provides evidence of the lack of cultural layers here. The difference in height between the flatland and the surrounding elevated parts reaches 5 m. There were wooden houses here; the foundations are clearly visible after heavy rains. The most visible elevation of Altyn-Depe is in the east of the site and bears the name Tower Mound. It was here that the earliest cultural deposits were concentrated. A traditional continuity made for the important participation of the Tower Mound in the Bronze Age when the Quarters of the Elite were located here, and next to them, the cult center. A Concentration of Living Quarters in the west occupied a major part of Altyn-Depe. Two small elevations on either side of the Tower Mound were named after structures uncovered during the archaeological work: to the southwest the Mound of the Burial Chambers, to the north, clearly set apart in the relief, the Wall Mound.

On the eastern slope of the latter, massive walls of adobe bricks were uncovered, underlining, as confirmed by further excavations, the specific function of this part of the site.

Immediately to the north and east of the Wall Mound there is a flattened area, the Small Square; it separates the northern part of the complex from the major living quarters. Here, on almost 2.5 hectares, there is an abundance of fragmented pottery rejects, slag, and remains of kilns indicated on the surface by oval stains in the burnt soil. Separate kilns were found elsewhere in Altyn-Depe but only this locality seems to have a concentration of them. Here, during the periods of rain, 60 kilns were discovered; during excavations their number had increased by those that did not show signs of presence on the surface. This part of the site was named the Craftsmen's Quarters. Later excavations confirmed the appropriateness of this name. The investigations of Altyn-Depe were conducted with the calculations of data on the internal topography of the site, and every year the new findings were added to indicate more clearly its general characteristics.

In 1965 the principal effort was directed to the investigation of the thick adobe brick wall which had been revealed on the Wall Mound in previous years; during this investigation the complex nature of the various reconstructions was revealed. In Excavation 1, the stratigraphy was determined: three building horizons dating to Namazga V (Altyn 1-3) and one to late Namazga IV (Altyn 4). In Excavation 2, the buildings of the upper cultural layer were investigated, and in Excavations 3 and 4, the burial chambers (Sarianidi 1966). In 1966 the stratigraphic excavations were continued, a pit was sunk in the center of the fortified hill site and the thickness (5 m) of the layer dating to Namazga V was established. In Excavation 5, the section of the upper construction horizon was opened on a large scale, immediately yielding substantive finds (Masson 1967c), and in Excavation 6 (the northern edge of the hill site), burial chambers were studied (Sarianidi 1967). The materials of the first two seasons established the existence in southern Central Asia of a distinctive Bronze Age proto-urban civilization. At the same time, the perspectives and goals, economic, ideological, and social, were charted. Researchers also looked to resolve the problems of chronology, the origin of writing, and the place of the Altyn-Depe culture in the system of early eastern civilizations (Masson 1967d). Later, the goals were reached, and new ones were established, above all, a well-grounded grouping of archaeological assemblages with a firm base of specific types of artifacts, and the evolution of cultures starting with the earliest layers. Correspondingly, the dynamics of the settlement were studied and their role in gradually molding Altyn-Depe into a large habitation center with a complex internal structure was determined.

The years 1967-1969 were quite important for the study of the character of southern Turkmenistan society during the developed Bronze Age, since during those years the monumental cult complex was investigated in detail (Excavation 7). At the same time, the unearthing of buildings in Excavation 5 continued and a dwelling was found below the main street level. Of principle import during 1969 was the discovery of a rectangular house with a specific ground plan which was named the Leader's House (Excavation 9), and also the investigation of the southern entrance to Altyn-Depe, where the bases of massive bastionlike structures were found (Excavation 8). All of this indicated a new level of generalization and suggested that during the Bronze Age, an extensive zone of early urban civilizations existed between Sumer and India, and one of these was Altyn-Depe (Masson 1970f).

In 1970 to 1971, the investigations were conducted in two parallel directions. There were large-scale excavations of specific subdivisions of the early city: the Craftsmen's Quarters (Excavation 10), and the Quarters of the Elite occupying the major part of the Tower Mound (Excavation 9). In addition, the entire 30 m thickness of the cultural deposits of Altyn-Depe was studied in detail. This necessitated the expansion of the labor force, which hitherto numbered 12-15 people. The enlargement of the scope of studies was made possible by the allocation of a bulldozer with an excavation bucket. Together with the unearthing of early structures in Excavations 9 and 10 during 1970-1971, more limited work was carried out in Excavation 5, where structures at the edge of the horizon gradually disappeared, and in Excavation 8, where a number of small structures to the east of the central entrance were cleared. At the same time, eastern limits of the principal dwelling complex were determined, and the much reconstructed surrounding wall, dotted with towers, was uncovered (Excavation 11). The availability of machinery also enabled the extension of the cult complex and Excavation 7. There the buildings of the upper structural horizon were removed, and in the second horizon a separate house with a sub-rectangular ground

plan was uncovered. The investigation of the stratigraphy of the hill site was carried out at two points: on the eastern side of the Craftsmen's Quarters the stratigraphic Excavation 1 was elongated to the form of a transect 4 m wide, and in the depression around Excavation 11 a test pit was sunk to the depth of 14 m before it reached bedrock.

The enlargement of the scale of excavations was furthered by new discoveries. In 1972 during excavations of the cult complex at the third building horizon, a priest's tomb with rich goods was uncovered; the goods included gold heads of a bull and a wolf (Masson 1974b). Also at that time the structures of the upper horizons in Excavations 8-10 were uncovered. After 1972 additional funds were assigned to the project by the Leningrad branch of the Institute of Archaeology and the labor force was increased to between 50 and 60 people.

During 1973 and 1978 extensive investigations were conducted, which turned Altyn-Depe into one of the most studied Bronze Age sites in Central Asia and adjacent regions. Foremost, the large-scale uncovering of the upper building horizon was continued: Excavation 7 was finished, major investigations were carried out in Excavation 9, and the cleaning of part of the urban structures close to the eastern edge of the Central Square was begun (Excavation 13). Sharp differences in the construction and content of tombs distinctly characterized the classes of the urban territory. In 1975, the find in the Elite Quarters (Excavation 9) of a seal with a Harappan type inscription was sensational (Masson 1977e). The other important discovery was the monumental entryway into the town dated to late Namazga IV-early Namazga V (Excavation 8).

The second thrust of the study was to learn the genesis of the culture as represented by the upper layers of the fortified hill site. With this in mind, remains of structures in Excavation 5 were removed and excavations were deepened layer by layer over an area of 500 m^2. The structures of the second and third horizons were seen to belong to Namazga V, and those of the fourth to sixth to Namazga IV. The materials indicate a gradual development of the major elements of Altyn-Depe on a local basis during the Bronze Age.

Such is the brief chronicle of excavations carried out at Altyn-Depe, which demanded the combined efforts of many investigators. During the first years the active participants were I.N. Khlopin, V.I. Sarianidi and A.Ya. Shchetenko.

A.F. Ganyalin conducted excavations in different parts of the site over the period of several years. Invariably, the activities of the expedition became the basis for the training of cadres, a sort of scientific-methodological center. There were regular scientific field sessions and lessons for the participating students of the Leningrad and Ashkabad universities. The result was the formation of the "backbone" cadres of the expedition. Many co-workers started their work at Altyn-Depe as students and continued it as prospective graduate students, doctoral candidates, and later as scientific co-workers. To this number belong V.A. Alekshin, Yu.E. Berezkin, V.A. Zavyalov, L.B. Kircho, G.N. Kurochkin, K. Kurbansakhatov, and N.N. Skakun. Much work in the Altyn-Depe excavations was done by S.B. Gultov, N.A. Lazarevskaya, V.I. Knyshev, and V.I. Osipov. The young co-workers wrote course papers and degree theses on the basis of Altyn-Depe materials, and published articles (Kurochkin 1970; Knyshev 1971; Kircho 1972, 1976, 1979; Skakun 1972, 1977a; Alekshin 1973; Zabyalov 1974, 1977; Kurbansakhatov 1971). Materials from Altyn-Depe were widely utilized in the doctoral dissertations of I.S. Masimov (1973a), V.A. Alekshin (1977), and L.B. Kircho (1980). The methods of field investigation were acquired and mastered by candidates V.A. Sofronov, E. Kadyrov, K. Sabirov, and S.S. Khamrakuliyev; by prospective student and later candidate O. Lollekova, and by prospective student E. Smagulov. The doctoral candidates I.G. Narimanov (AN AzSSR) [Academy of Sciences of the Azerbayzhan SSR], N.M. Shmagliy (AN USSR) [Academy of Sciences at the Uzbek SSR], and V.N. Stanko (Odessa University) visited in order to learn the nature of work on this very large site. The investigations at Altyn-Depe were realized in so large measure thanks to the selfless labor of members of various institutions in Leningrad and Nikolayev, who conducted the ex-

cavations at this early site with enthusiasm during their leaves of absence. The functioning of the camp in a remote and waterless steppe was made possible to no small degree by the managers of the AN TSSR motor depot, A. Mamedov and E. Cheletenov, and of the AN SSSR depot, L. Fakhretdinov and A.G. Zaytsev. To those co-workers who shared the joys of discovery and the hardships of living in the field, I express my profound thanks.

The composition of the participants in the expedition was conditioned by the necessity of a complex approach to the materials obtained during the excavations, that is, the application of various methods of analysis by colleagues in related disciplines. Thus, the paleogeomorphological survey of the region was done by G.N. Lisitsina (1968, 1978), the physical anthropology collections were studied in the field and laboratory by T.P. Kiyatkina (1977a, 1977b; Masson and Kiyatkina 1976), and paleozoology was studied by N.M. Ermolova (1970, 1972, 1976, 1977, 1979). G.F. Korobkova headed a special group which conducted experimental tracewear studies of tools (Korobkova 1974, 1977). The technology of metalworking was analyzed in detail by N.N. Terekhova (1976), and ceramic technology by E.V. Sayko (1972, 1977, 1978). Major work in the investigation of early kilns and hearths, with the goal of establishing their paleomagnetic orientation, was done by G.F. Zagniy. The efforts of this collective labor concerned with a multi-directional study of Altyn-Depe materials are already reflected in many publications. Aside from the works of the expedition leader [Masson], other co-workers have published about 50 scientific articles and reports. Further publications are envisioned as extended works united in thematic collections. The present book should primarily survey the general characteristics of a remarkable Central Asiatic archaeological site.

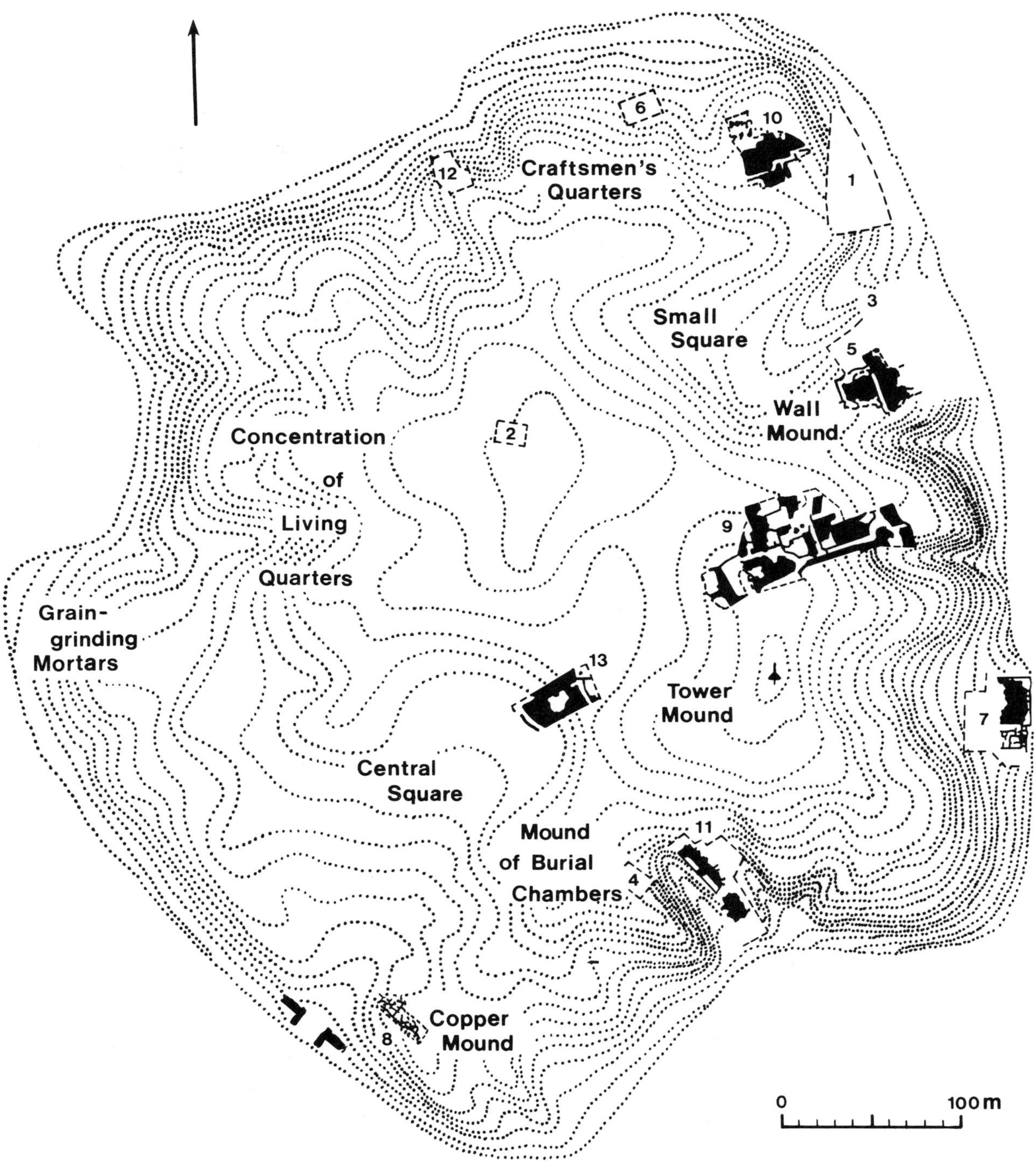

Figure 1. Plan of Altyn-Depe (After A. A. Lyapin).

I

Altyn-Depe in the Eneolithic and Early Bronze Ages

Altyn-Depe spreads over a flatland adjacent to the low southeastern spurs of the Kopet-Dagh, not far from the bed of the fairly large mountain stream of Akmazar or Meana-Chay. To the southeast there is another similar stream, the Chaacha-Chay. During periods of high water, both flood extensive areas. The comparatively secure water supply of the region resulted in its occupation in a rather early period by permanently settled agricultural groups. Here were discovered Jeitun settlements of the 6th millennium B.C.: Chagylly-Depe (Berdyev 1964, 1966), Monzhukly-Depe (Berdyev 1966:29-30; Korobkova 1969:54-57), and Gadymi-Depe (Korobkova and Volovik 1972; Lollekova 1978, 1979:5-6). Materials from Gadymi-Depe and the lower layers of Chagylly-Depe relate to the middle stage of the Jeitun Culture; the complex of Monzhukly-Depe has distinctive traits of the early Jeitun flint industry, according to the conclusions of G. F. Korobkova (1969:58). The Jeitun farmers, who spread over the flatlands, apparently occupied the Meana-Chaacha basin rather early. Judging by the excavations at Gadymi-Depe, a local variant of the Jeitun Culture with specific traits had developed there during its middle stage.

Mondzhukly-Depe is located 1.5 km south of Altyn-Depe. It is possible that somewhere in the depths of this archaeological giant are hidden layers of the Jeitun Culture, although only traces of the Eneolithic have been encountered in the excavations and trenches thus far. Such traces have been obtained in the main as a result of investigations of stratigraphies that allow us to outline the early history of the settlement in general terms. The summary of all the data enabled us to reconstruct an adequate stratigraphic column of Altyn-Depe, well documented by sections and profiles. The latter is particularly important, since the standard excavation of Namazga-Depe, which served as a basis for the new periodization of the Anau Culture, lacked such documentation. In essence, at Namazga-Depe the evidence consisted of archaeological artifacts taken at different recorded depths without affiliation with cultural layers and remains of buildings.

Let us now consider the general characteristics of the major excavations and sections of Altyn-Depe. Very important materials which characterized the Eneolithic deposits were obtained in Excavation 1, located on the eastern edge of the Craftsmen's Quarters. In 1965-1966 three building horizons dated to Namazga V were disclosed here, and correspondingly named Altyn 1 to 3. Horizon Altyn 4, which contained painted ceramics of the type associated with late Namazga IV, was also discovered here. In 1970 the stratigraphic studies were extended in Excavation 1, and a 4 m wide trench was cut into the slope reaching the underlying sterile soil, in the process uncovering horizons Altyn 5 to 15 (Fig. 2). In 1974 the trench was widened at the level of horizons Altyn 9 and 10 with the aim of obtaining materials characteristic of the late Eneolithic complex of the settlement. Stratigraphic excavations at Altyn-Depe were conducted on the building horizons, and after the removal of these, in conventional 50 cm arbitrary levels.

The location of Excavation 1 at the edge of the settlement suggested only partial preservation of the exposed buildings: one of the walls of rooms being excavated, the outside one in relation to the settlement, was unusually disturbed. The Eneolithic layers begin with horizon Altyn 9. Here, at the edge of the trench, a part of a rectangular hearth was seen; its walls were covered with burnt plaster. Next to the hearth there was a trough filled with a considerable amount of pebbles. Judging by the uncovered remains of walls, beyond the hearth was a multi-chambered building, a part of which was a small apartment. In the middle of the apartment was an oval hearth, and in it a vessel fashioned from white, marblelike limestone (Plate VII, item 5). Near the edge of the hearth was a horn of an animal. Also near the edge was the much disturbed burial 278. Apparently the apartment represented an "in-house" sanctuary, common in the

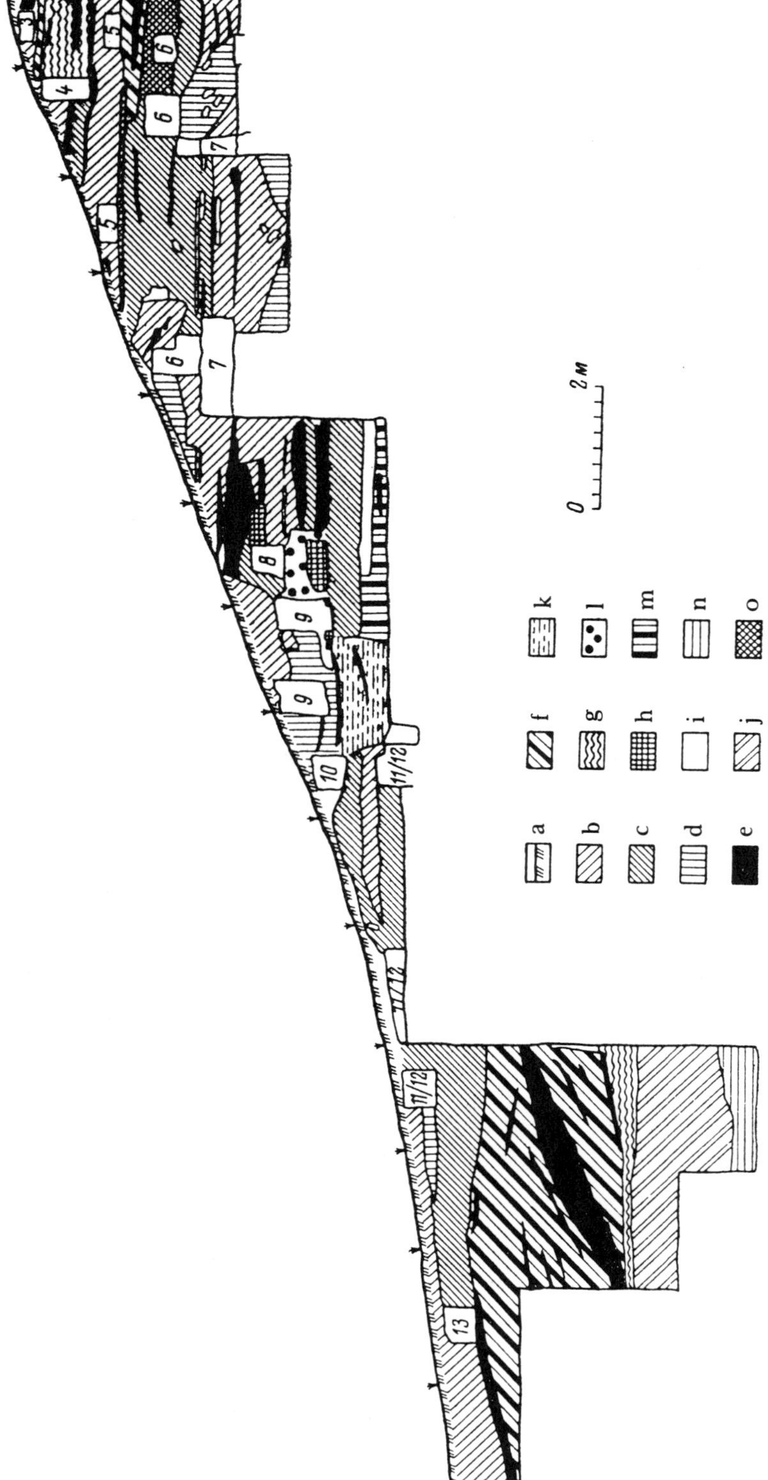

Figure 2. Stratigraphic transit of Excavation 1. Profile of south wall. Numbers indicate Altyn horizons 4 to 13. Key— a: surface accumulations; b: friable layer with pieces of raw material (unbaked clay); c: densely packed raw material; d: layer of debris with pieces of raw material (unbaked clay); e: ash layer; f: debris layer with greenish bands; g: accumulation with greenish bands; h: burnt bricks; i: sun-baked brick walls in cross-section j: layered and lumpy clay; k: a friable layer of brown color; l: burnt plaster of a ceramic kiln; m: clayey fill; n: base clay; o: horizontal clayey band.

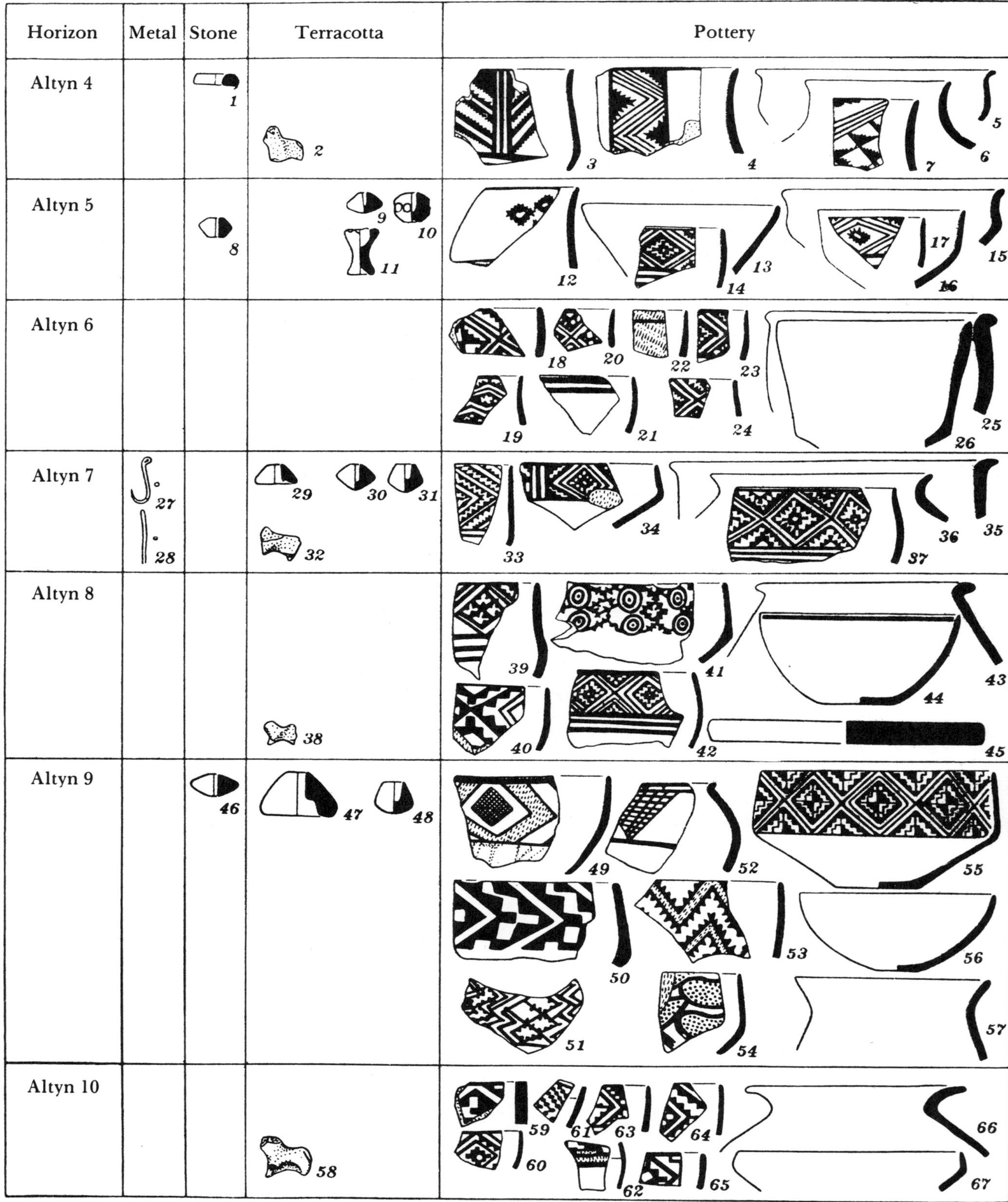

Figure 3. *Stratigraphic representation of materials from Excavation 1. Arabic numerals represent the field numbers of the finds. (Continued on p. 10)*

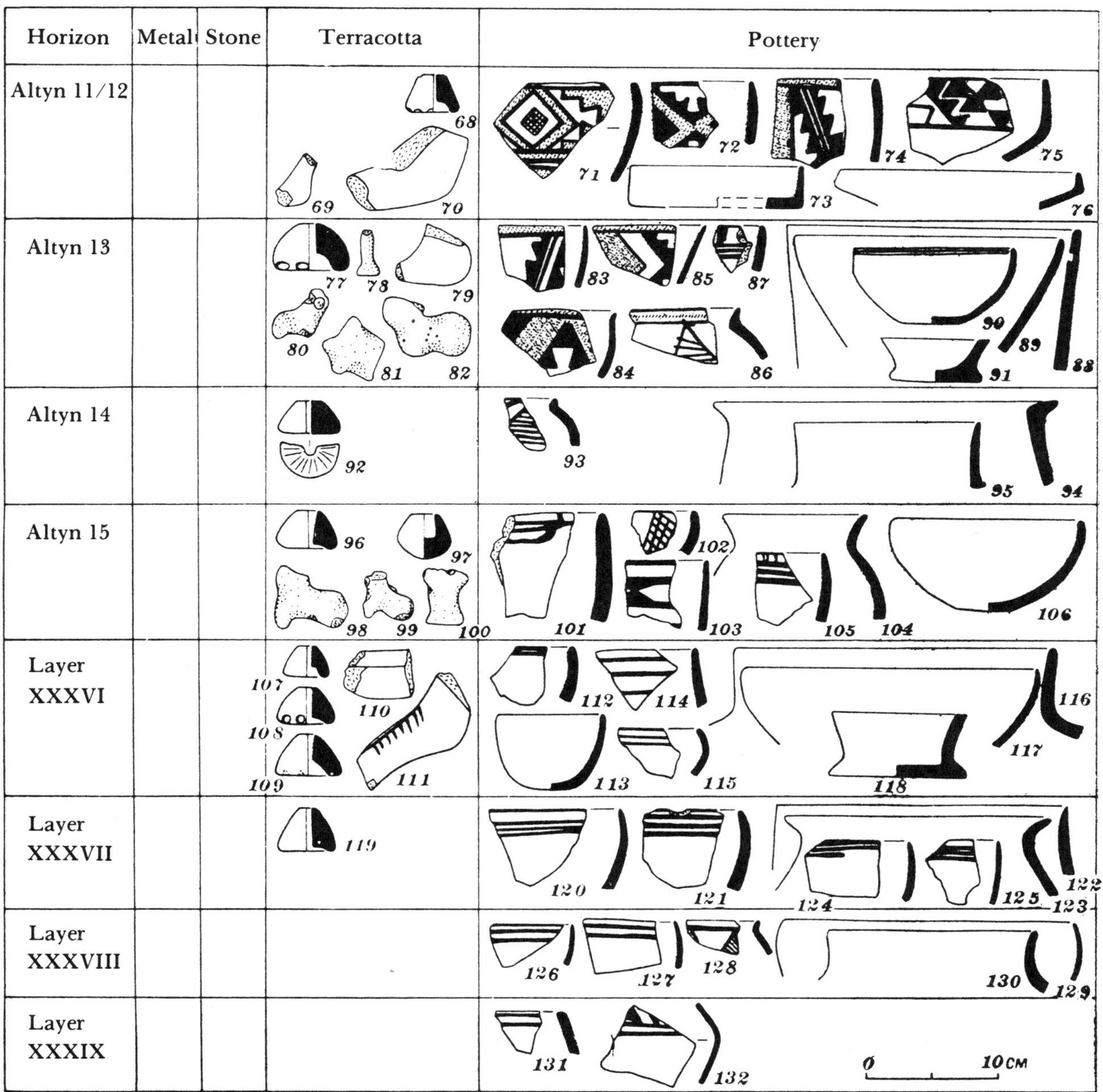

Figure 3. (Continued)   Stratigraphic representation of materials from Excavation 1.

late Eneolithic multi-chambered complexes of Geoksyur 1 and Chong-Depe (Sarianidi 1960:231-235; 1965:10-14). It is of note that in one such sanctuary at Geoksyur disturbed remains of three individuals were found on a layer of burnt brushwood. V. I. Sarianidi is inclined to correlate this find with the cult of body cremation (Sarianidi 1962:51), but in the sanctuary associated with horizon Altyn 9 there were no traces of fire. Yet the fact that human remains were found in the sanctuaries of Geoksyur and Altyn-Depe is significant.

The western wall of the apartment examined by us was of double thickness and apparently was the exterior wall of the entire multi-chambered complex. Close to the wall, in a space without buildings, an oval collective tomb was found, also characteristic of the Geoksyur type of remains, as was the sanctuary with the oval hearth. In this tomb were two burials: a much earlier burial, 282, and one partly covering it, 281. The interred were positioned on their right sides, with their heads oriented to the north. Impressions of a mat were discernible on the floor of the chamber; such impressions were also found in the earth above the skeletons. Among the grave goods were two ceramic vessels, one of them a saucer with painted ornamentation of the Kara-Depe style (Plate IV, item 6), two terracotta lids, a stone bead, and a small copper triangle (perhaps an arrowhead). A part of the western wall of the chamber was disturbed by intrusive burial 283, which probably is not associated with horizon Altyn 9, but with a much higher level.

During two seasons (1970 and 1974) enough variedmaterial was obtained to characterize horizon Altyn 9, and above all its striking ceramic complex: vessels with polychrome paintings of the Geoksyur type and also vessels with ornamentation showing the developmental tradition of the style, from monochromatic to more variegated, somewhat degenerate paintings. Of particular interest was the find in this layer of imported ceramics of the Kara-Depe type, which included a fragment with a representation of snow leopards, and of local manufactures apparently imitating the painted vessels of this group.

Parts of sun-baked clay buildings were found in horizon Altyn 10. These, however, did not constitute any kind of a plan of a finished complex. An oval burial chamber positioned almost exactly under the chamber of horizon Altyn 9 was of particular interest. In it were burials at two levels. In the southwestern part of the chamber there was a compact burial of four individuals (291 to 294); the

skeletons were partly mixed and oriented in the main to the northwest by north. There were no grave goods. The major burial, 296, was located at the very edge of the chamber, on the lower level, which was separated from the upper by a 20 cm thickness of clay deposited by water. The interred was placed on his left side with his head oriented to the north. His left arm was bent at the elbow and was resting on a skeleton of a youth placed in front of his skull; his right arm was pointing to the east, to the grave goods which occupied the eastern side of the chamber. The inventory consisted of 5 ceramic vessels (Plate IV, items 3, 4, and 7), two stone vessels, one white and the other pinkish white (Plate VII, item 6), a copper, shovel-like flat pin, 10 turquoise perforated beads, and a flat, petiolate copper knife (Plate XXVII, items 7 and 10). The latter was positioned among the bones of the forepart of a young ram placed at the eastern wall of the chamber. Its jaw and several vertebrae were found with the skull of the interred.

The ceramic complex of Altyn 10 (Plate XXV) contains the same two major groups as horizon Altyn 9, although the pattern of design on polychrome vessels is much larger here, reminding one of the ceramics of the upper layers of Chong-Depe (Sarianidi 1965:pl. XIII). Together with geometric ornamentation on the vessels one also encounters stylized figures of goats. Among other finds, of note are the terracotta figures of animals, among them a very expressive small figurine of a goat, graceful statuettes of sitting women, and a fragment of a small terracotta box covered with impressed geometric ornamentation.

The next horizon, Altyn 11/12, contained remains of buildings without a clearly indicated floor plan. The painted ceramics adhere to the well-established traditions of the Geoksyur style (Fig. 3), although a fragment of a globular vessel with a painted pattern of fine netting may be regarded as a replica of its kind of the Kara-Depe painted ware (Masson 1960b:pl. XXV, item 18; pl. XXXIV, item 4; pl. XXXVI, item 7). In addition to terracotta figurines of women and various animals, a terracotta spindle-whorl of conical form was found, and also fragments of stone vessels and a button-like article of unfired clay with crosslike ornamentation on one side.

Horizon Altyn 13 yielded significant ceramics of the Geoksyur type, and among them were fragments of red-slipped vessels, also painted in beautiful red, however with an indistinct, sort of run-together pattern. This kind of vessel is probably a very early one, and represents the initial stages of the formation of the Geoksyur ceramic complex (Khlopin 1964:35, 36, 122, 123). Among the zoomorphic and anthropomorphic artifacts, there are large figures of women made of clay with a large admixture of adobe, sometimes covered with painted patterns. In the complexes of the Geoksyur type, this type of terracotta appears to be the earliest (Sarianidi 1965:32-33), and is closely tied to the sculptural traditions of the Middle Eneolithic (Masson and Sarianidi 1973:16).

Level XXXIII, containing a large number of ash pits, was separated within horizon Altyn 14. It contained unpainted, red-burnished ceramics with dark stains on the outer surface, much like the vessels of Layer III at Geoksyur 1 that separate the layer with vessels of the Geoksyur type from the lower horizons with ceramics of the Yalangach type (Sarianidi 1960:271-272). The find of the lower parts of large female statuettes with a dark-brown design on a red slip indicates for this layer terracottas of an archaic type (Plate XXVI, item 7).

The absence of building remains in horizon Altyn 14 reflects a change in the character of the cultural deposits cut through by Excavation 1. While the upper reaches of the excavation revealed a relatively densely built up part of the settlement, we came across a refuse layer at its edge, gradually sloping downward. The cut clearly shows how the refuse layer and particularly the large ash pits spread over the slope to the earlier edge of the settlement. A relatively large wall, found in arbitrary Levels XXXIV-XXXV and defined in horizon Altyn 15, acted as a sort of peripheral fence or barrier beyond which the refuse dump begins.

In horizon Altyn 15 there is much pottery with a red burnish with black stains. Vessels with a design of parallel lines below the rim are quite characteristic. There is a rim fragment with a triangle filled with netting (Fig. 3, item 102), a type of painted ceramic best expressed in Layer 5 of Geoksyur 1 (Sarianidi 1965:pl. VIII, items 14-25; Khlopin 1969:p. 21, fig. 5). This complex is completed with conical terracotta spindle whorls, fired and unfired clay figures of animals, and a large torso of a light color slipped female with a painted black necklace (Plate XXVI, item 15).

Remains of structures are absent below this level. Thus arbitrary Level XXXVI represents the wash from the mound remaining within the confines of the trench and consists of clayey sediments containing fragments of ceramics, charcoal, and pieces of adobe. Below Level XXXVI there are horizontal levels whose character indicates that we are dealing with the horizontal base of the mound; during the rainy period, streamlets deposited here various remains of the cultural ac-

tivities of man. Such layers are expressed in arbitrary Levels XXXVII to XXXIX where layered or lumpy clay was found, often of greenish color testifying to the presence of stagnant waters. Potsherds and pieces of charcoal regularly enter into the above layerings. In arbitrary Level XL the horizontal layering occurs without traces of human activity. Thus the cultural layers end at the depth of 4.5 m below the present-day surface.

It is only natural that the ceramic complex of arbitrary Levels XXXVI to XXXIX should be comparatively poor. Nevertheless, finds of thin-walled rim sherds with parallel lines below the rim (Fig. 3, items 120, 124-127), and pieces of thick-walled storage jars, with a considerable admixture of adobe in the clay and dark brown designs on a light background, point to the Middle Eneolithic ceramic complex of the Yalangach type.

Thus the stratigraphy of Excavation 1 provided fairly strong indications of cultural changes which appear to be applicable to all of Altyn-Depe. The trench, dug within the limits of the exploratory transect, did not cut through the nuclear part of the early settlement. However, even the fragmentary material obtained from the lower levels of the trench allows for the conclusion that very likely the Craftsmen's Quarters were not occupied to any great extent during the Early Eneolithic, since this period is characterized by complexes of the Namazga I type. These early layers have to be sought in the central part of Altyn-Depe where the considerably greater height of the tumulus suggests that the cultural horizons not represented in the much lower Craftsmen's Quarters will be found.

The stratigraphic trench of Excavation 11 located in a depression on the southern slope of the Tower Mound fully confirmed this supposition. The fairly deep depression gave hopes the Eneolithic layers would be encountered immediately, bypassing the Namazga IV and V chronological horizons. A trench was excavated as early as 1960, but because of heavy rains it could be deepened to only 2.5 m (Sarianidi 1965:8, 27). In 1971 a trench was planned for a new locality and was excavated to the sterile subsoil, a depth of 13.5 m from the initial surface, or 8.5 m lower than the surrounding plain. Since the maximum height of the Tower Mound is 22 m, we conclude that the greatest thickness of cultural layers at Altyn-Depe reaches at most 30 m. The first two layers of the trench were composed of dense sediment containing ceramics of the Namazga V and, in part, Namazga IV types washed down from the higher parts of the settlement. The force of the wash may be judged by the large number of pebbles and large fragments of pottery encountered in the lower half of Level II. Below it, the Eneolithic layers with remains of structures begin (Fig. 4). On the basis of painted ornamentation on ceramics, these layers may be clearly divided into three complexes: those containing pottery of the Geoksyur type (arbitrary Levels III to XI), the Yalangach type (arbitrary Levels XII to XVII), and the Namazga type (arbitrary Levels XVIII to XXVIII).

Adobe structures with thickly coated floors were characteristic of the layers of the first complex; these were represented in four horizons. Additionally, judging by the nature of the fill normally present in the structures, it is possible to project another two horizons, although the walls proper of the buildings were outside the confines of the trench. In our opinion, one of the horizons corresponds to the fill found at the end of arbitrary Levels III and IV, and the other to the fill of arbitrary Levels V and VI. All in all, then, there were six building levels within the layers containing Geoksyur ceramics, and they attained the thickness of 4.25 m. The first of these levels contained ceramics of the late Geoksyur type and also an imported vessel of Kara-Depe form which allows us to synchronize this horizon with Altyn 9. We also note the find here of a fragment of a terracotta box with cut ornamentation on its exterior. In the above-mentioned layers of our trench, as well as in arbitrary Level V of the 1960 trench, the amount of pottery fragments of the Geoksyur type with polychrome ornamentation was very limited. It is clear, though, that this assemblage can be related to the finds in Level V, among which there were also imported Kara-Depe pots, including a sherd with representations of leopards (Sarianidi 1965:pl. XVI, items 1-26). The remaining five horizons correspond to four horizons of Excavation 1 (Altyn 10, 11/12, 13, and 14), and point to a more intense occupation of Tower Mound at this time, since the cultural layers with Geoksyur ceramics are thicker here. The general evolution of painted pottery found in these horizons is about the same as seen in Excavation 1. As the trench was deepened, one encountered more polychrome vessels with larger painted designs. Occasionally, stylized depictions of goats with rectangular bodies were found on sherds. Fragments of red-slipped bowls with the same sort of spilled or trickled design as those in horizon Altyn 13 of Excavation 1 were found among the ceramics of the lowest building horizon, consisting of arbitrary Level X and the upper half of XI.

In lower levels below those just described, the character of the cultural assemblage changes abruptly. There are practically no remains of buildings or fill. These were replaced with layers of soft rubbish containing ashes and charcoal, and interspersed layers of sediments. The slightly sloping nature of these layers indicated, as it did in Excavation 1, that we had encountered the refuse which had fallen down the slope of the ancient settlement. The main part of the settlement lay outside of the confines of the trench. The lower half of arbitrary Level XI through arbitrary Level XVII contained Yalangach ceramics painted with parallel lines below the rim. Starting with arbitrary Level XIV, ceramics with a black design on a red background dominate. Of note were two sherds with polychrome designs from arbitrary Level XII, clearly imports from the region of Kara-Depe and Namazga-Depe (Masson 1962a:19-26), and from arbitrary Levels XV to XVII, torsos of large female figurines, red-slipped and decorated with black designs (Plate XXVI, item 16).

The same type of refuse and sedimentary layers, interspersed with lenses of ash and having a definite slope, are encountered in arbitrary Levels XVIII to XXIII, which contain ceramics of Namazga I type in its late, Dashlydzhi variant (Plate XXIV). Although overall there is a genetic tie with Yalangach vessels, there is a slight increase of vessels with painting on a light background, and basins with conical bases and designs on the interior surface appear. In arbitrary Level XVIII there was a fragment of a small cup with perforation in its bottom; in arbitrary Levels XXII and XXIII rims of thick-walled open cups embellished on the outside by wavy relief ornamentation were found. In arbitrary Level XXI a bone awl was found, and in arbitrary Level XIX there was a flat copper object of unclear application. Arbitrary Levels XXIV and XXVII are horizontal sedimentary layers with inclusions of charcoal and white lime. They represent the ancient base of the mound deposited by the earliest inhabitants of Altyn-Depe, whose settlement proper was far beyond the reach of our trench. The amount of potsherds found in these levels was naturally minimal, but all of them were of the Namazga I type. Sterile soil of dense clay with reddish, rustlike intercalations was reached at the bottom of the trench.

In 1974, with the goal in mind of determining the extent of the settlement during the Geoksyur period, trenches were cut in the western and southern parts of Altyn-Depe. Two of them were dug with traditional shovels, the third with a deep corer. The use of the corer was carried out with the advice and cooperation of the geologists Yu. N. Momentov and K. N. Yurgensen. The coring was

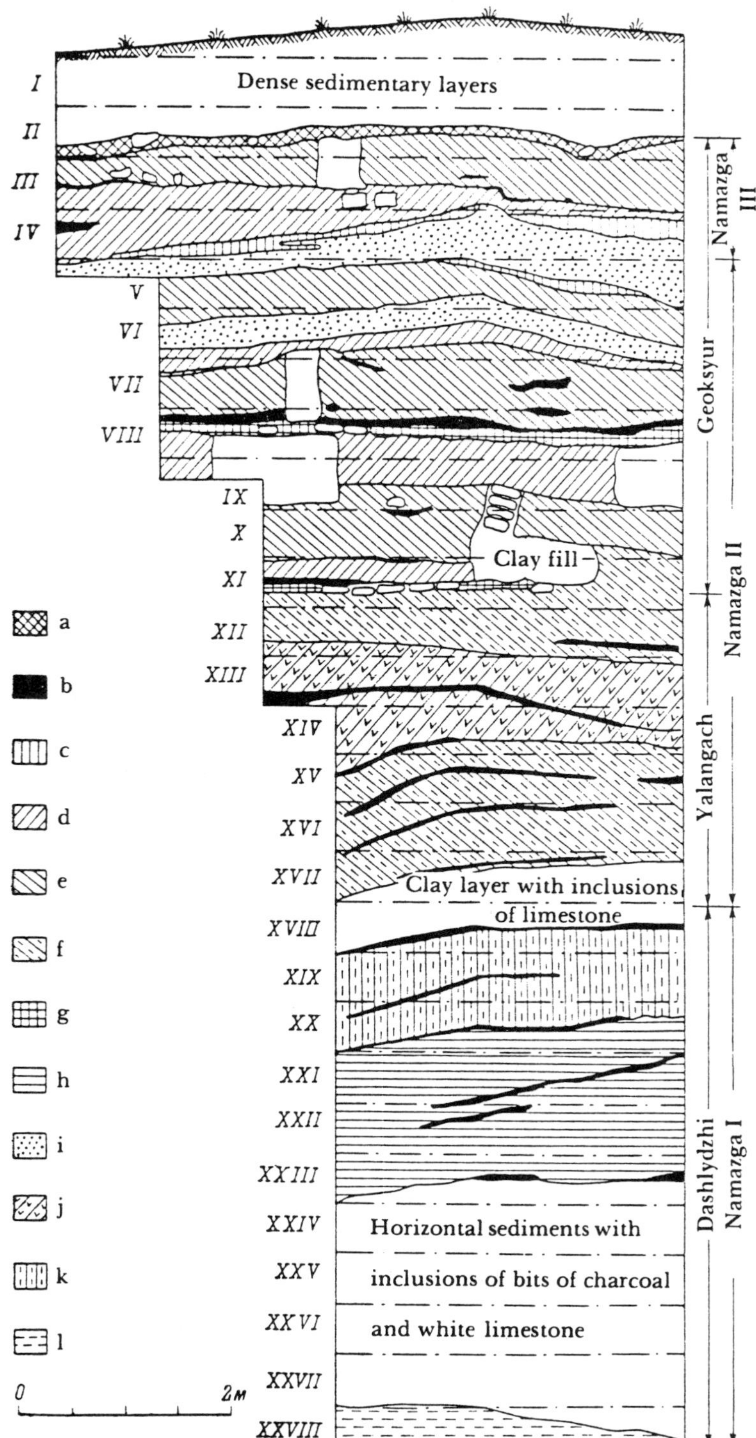

Figure 4. Excavation 11. Profile of the south wall of cut. Roman numerals here and in Figures 7, 10, and 18 indicate arbitrary 50 cm levels.

Key— a: sedimentary layer with a large collection of potsherds and large pebbles; b: ash-pits; c: greenish soil with white lime inclusions; d: sedimentary levels with bits of mud brick; e: fill of small pieces of material derived from the decomposition of mud brick and charcoal; f: loose debris layer with brownish intercalations with inclusions of white lime, charcoal, and ashes; g: levelled fill under floor; h: dense sedimentary levels with quantities of charcoal and lumps of burnt earth and greenish clay; i: sedimentary layers with pieces of mud brick and charcoal; j: loose sedimentary layer with white lime inclusions; k: loose sedimentary layer with charcoal, burnt lumps of clay, and white lime inclusions; l: dense clay with rust-colored inclusions.

65 cm in diameter, and the core was lifted every 50 cm, a thickness which corresponds well to the traditional arbitrary level employed in Central Asian archaeology. Careful analysis of the cores showed that even large sherds were seldom damaged. Also, 12 m of cultural layers could be cored in three hours. The experiment demonstrated the high efficiency and scientific profitability of preliminary trenching of cultural deposits of thickness greater than 10 m in depth.

Trench 3, excavated by such means, was located in the southern part of the Concentration of Living Quarters. Unfortunately, great quantities of ashes in the upper layers made it impossible to ascertain an accurate profile of the core, although in principle this should be possible, given an adequate diameter.

The classification of the ceramics from Trench 3 yielded the following: arbitrary Levels I to V contained ceramics of the Namazga V type, and arbitrary Levels VI to XI, Namazga IV. In arbitrary Level XII a sherd painted in the Kara-Depe style was found, allowing us to synchronize this level with horizon Altyn 9. Beginning with arbitrary Level XI, thick cultural layers with Geoksyur ceramics were encountered. Pieces of mud bricks brought up by the corer indicated the presence of structures. Vessels with polychrome designs disappear completely in arbitrary Levels XXII and XXIII; they are replaced with large numbers of ceramics with a red burnish with black stains, analogous to those of horizon Altyn 14. The base soil was a yellowish clay. Thus this area was occupied during the first period of Geoksyur ceramics.

The other trench was located at Excavation 8, at the entrance to the Central Square. Here, at the southern edge of Altyn-Depe, Eneolithic sherds were found as early as 1969 (Masson 1970a:10). Another point at which Eneolithic deposits were found was the middle part of the entrance to the town, which was excavated in 1975-1976. In 1976 an exploratory trench was dug through the lower layers, and below the level of the monumental entrance gate an encircling wall, 2.0 to 2.5 m thick, was found. Painted Geoksyur ceramics found along the wall indicate a dating to the Late Eneolithic. Excavation 8 offered the unique opportunity to study the encircling defensive wall and the entrance located within it. Among the painted ceramics are those with geometric representations of goats. The 1974 excavation revealed fairly large quantities of vessels of the Geoksyur type; they were also found in a layer with vessels of the

Namazga IV type, no doubt the result of relocation from lower horizons.

Finally, another trench (2) was dug on the sloping western edge of Altyn-Depe. Here, five building levels were encountered. The upper three contained painted vessels of the Namazga IV type, the fourth, painted ceramics like those of horizon Altyn 9, and the fifth, clear complexes of Geoksyur ceramics, including polychrome vessels. In addition to ceramics, the trench yielded a copper awl, a terracotta figurine of a goat, an elegant female statuette, and a woman's head with complex S-shaped curls—all fairly common among the Late Eneolithic sculptures of southern Turkmenistan (Masson 1962c:163; Sarianidi 1965:33).

Thus the above-described excavations allow for the construction of a comparative stratigraphy of Altyn-Depe and the early agricultural sites of southern Turkmenistan. The synchronization of the various excavations and trenches of Altyn-Depe have been mentioned, in part, above, and now they can be presented in tabular form (see Fig. 5).

The stratigraphic correspondences of the earliest layers containing ceramics of the Namazga I type are precisely determined: they relate to the lowest levels of the Geoksyur 1 settlement (Sarianidi 1965:pl. VIII) and to the Dashlydzhi-Depe complex of the Geoksyur oasis (Khlopin 1963:pl. XX). In both cases, this is the late stage of development of painted ceramics of this type. Ceramics of the Yalangach type found at Altyn-Depe also have precise eastern parallels, as do the Geoksyur 1 settlement (layers Geoksyur 4-7) and the numerous settlements of the Geoksyur oasis. Finds of sherds with polychrome Namazga II designs confirm the contemporaneity of these layers with Namazga II to Anau II complexes in the western group of sites. Materials obtained from Altyn-Depe layers with the Geoksyur type of vessels are indicators for the precise determinations of stratigraphic relationships for the Late Eneolithic of southern Turkmenistan. As is known, at Geoksyur itself this striking and elegant painted pottery was found together with the Kara 2 imported type (Masson 1962a:pl. XIX; Sarianidi 1965:pl. VII) or the final Namazga II period. At Chong-Depe, the local ceramic complex has traits that show a separate evolution and is accompanied by imported ceramics of the Namazga III type. Detailed familiarity with the relevant materials shows that the upper layers of Chong-Depe contain Kara 1B or early Namazga III ceramics (Sarianidi 1965:pl. XIV, items 1-38). Consequently, the Altyn 9 assemblage of ceramics is stylistically later than

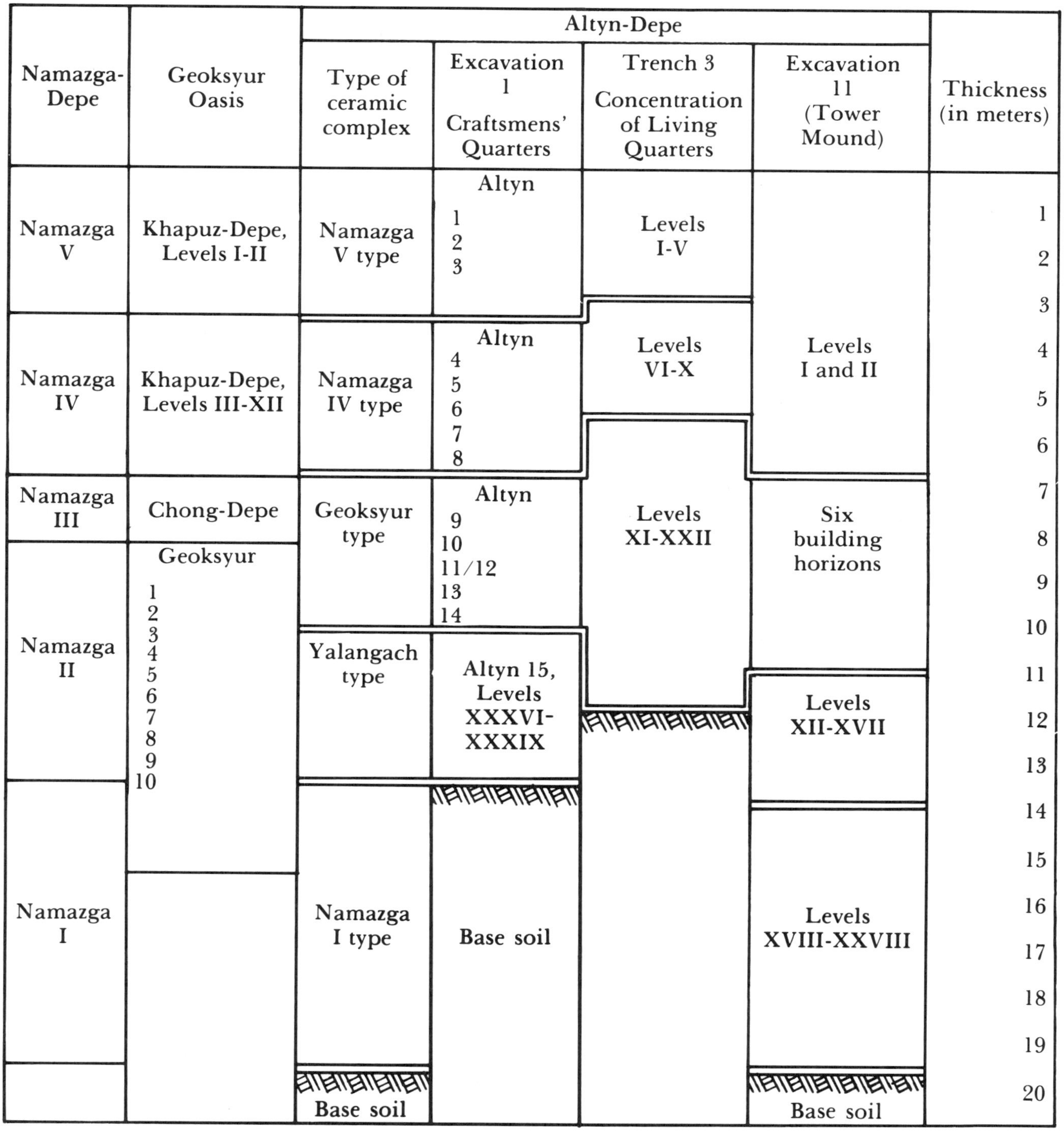

Namazga-Depe	Geoksyur Oasis	Altyn-Depe				Thickness (in meters)
		Type of ceramic complex	Excavation 1 Craftsmens' Quarters	Trench 3 Concentration of Living Quarters	Excavation 11 (Tower Mound)	
Namazga V	Khapuz-Depe, Levels I-II	Namazga V type	Altyn 1 2 3	Levels I-V		1 2 3
Namazga IV	Khapuz-Depe, Levels III-XII	Namazga IV type	Altyn 4 5 6 7 8	Levels VI-X	Levels I and II	4 5 6
Namazga III	Chong-Depe	Geoksyur type	Altyn 9 10 11/12 13 14	Levels XI-XXII	Six building horizons	7 8 9 10
Namazga II	Geoksyur 1 2 3 4 5 6 7 8 9 10	Yalangach type	Altyn 15, Levels XXXVI-XXXIX		Levels XII-XVII	11 12 13
Namazga I		Namazga I type	Base soil		Levels XVIII-XXVIII	14 15 16 17 18 19
		Base soil			Base soil	20

Figure 5.   Comparative stratigraphy of Altyn-Depe.

the Chong-Depe ceramics and accompanying finds of imported ceramics of the Kara 1A (later Namazga III) type; it represents the final stage of development of ceramics of the Geoksyur type. Apparently, one must relate to this final stage the layers of the sites of the eastern group which contain imported vessels together with diminishing quantities of polychrome painted ware of the Geoksyur type. From our point of view, the end of the Eneolithic in this region in general, and at Altyn-Depe in particular, has been determined, since a division between Namazga III (Late Eneolithic) and Namazga IV (Early Bronze) has been established. On the basis of all indications, including the results of statistical analysis (Kircho 1972), these two periods are closely linked together. Thus the stratigraphy of the Eneolithic layers at Altyn-Depe presents a picture of continuous cultural development that not only corresponds directly to that of other sites of southern Turkmenistan, but allows us to give a more precise definition to the archaeological picture which is already fairly complex and detailed.

The absolute chronology of the Eneolithic complexes of southern Turkmenistan will remain within the framework of traditional dating until more detailed studies are made, that is, from the fifth to the beginning of the third millennium B.C. Samples from Geoksyur 1 yielded two C-14 dates: 2860 ± 100 B.C. and 2490 ± 100 B.C. At Altyn-Depe the layers of Late Yalangach were dated 3160 ± 50 B.C. If one applies MASCA correction factors to these dates, a method favored by many Iranian investigators, then Early Geoksyur will date to 3410-3240 B.C. and Late Yalangach to 3810 B.C. In principle, these dates correspond to those of Shahr-i-Sokhta I, where imported ceramics of the southern Turkmenistan type were found. For other instances, we refer to finds in southeastern Iran (Tali-Iblis) of typical Kara 4 ceramics, with an uncalibrated dating of 3645 ± 59 B.C. (Caldwell 1967).

The excavation of the early layers of Altyn-Depe characterizes the development of this settlement to a considerable degree (Fig. 6). While the earliest remains may be related to the late stages of Namazga I, it is possible that somewhere in the depths of the thick cultural deposits are remains of an earlier small settlement. At Altyn-Depe itself, Late Namazga I ceramics were found in the trench of Excavation 11 and in a mixed context in Trench 3. It is possible that at this time Altyn-Depe already occupied an area of several hectares and could be regarded as a relatively large center. In any case, the Tower Mound was apparently fully

occupied, with cultural deposits many meters thick, some of which were washed down and found in the trench of Excavation 11. The painted ceramics (Plate XXIV), terracotta spindle whorls, and relatively few bone and copper artifacts make up the assemblage of sites occupied at this time. The nature of the painted ceramics incline Altyn-Depe toward the eastern group of sites, which also includes the settlements of the Geoksyur oasis. Namazga 1 layers have also been found at Ilgynly-Depe, some 10 km southeast of Altyn-Depe.

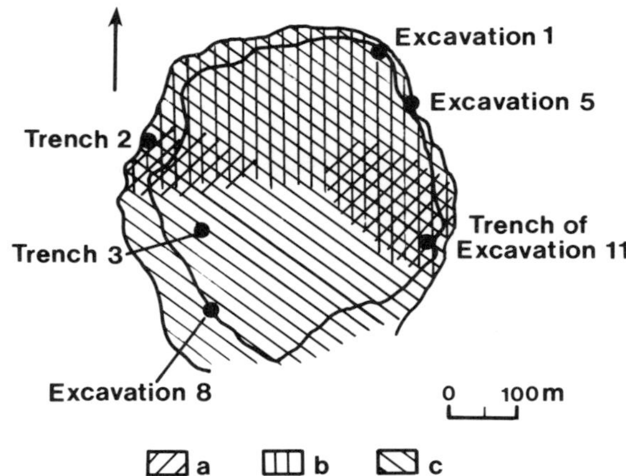

Figure 6. Schematic representation of Eneolithic layers at Altyn-Depe.
Key— a: *Early Eneolithic layers of Namazga I type*; b: *Middle Eneolithic layers of Yalangach type*; c: *Late Eneolithic layers of Geoksyur type.*

In the following period, which is characterized by the spread of Yalangach ceramics, we see an increase in the area occupied. This process is also reflected in those limited materials available to us. The Craftsmen's Quarters are occupied at this time and this occupation continued until the destruction of the fortified town. The trench of Excavation 11 yielded particularly expressive cultural materials for this period. Painted vessels with lines parallel to the rim clearly relate Altyn-Depe to the eastern group of sites, and this cultural-historical position is emphasized by finds of polychrome, imported vessels originating in the western group and strongly differing from local ware. Eastern analogies are also expressed in the large terracotta statuettes of sitting women. Covered with a light, often red, slip, they are frequently painted with black designs representing necklaces, or with hatched figures on the shoulders and thighs. At Altyn-Depe these figurines are found in layers of the Late Yalangach period, and excavations at Geoksyur 1 indicate such sculptures for the Early Geoksyur period: this underlines the genetic continuity of the two assemblages. Figurines of animals, and anthropomorphic statuettes—which are often very expressive—and conical spindle whorls complete the objects of material culture for this period. Ilgynly-Depe also yielded well-defined materials of this type, and at this time, in the Late Yalangach period, the settlement reached its maximum size of 12 hectares. Altyn-Depe, contemporary with this site, probably was not smaller.

During the Geoksyur period, Altyn-Depe reached its maximal development. The extent of the settlement increased sharply, an increase that held into the Bronze Age. Especially notable is the expansion in the southern part of the settlement, where the Geoksyur layers are directly on the base soil. This expansion is also discernible in other parts of Altyn-Depe, where Late Eneolithic layers have been uncovered. Thus in Excavations 1 and 11, the Late Eneolithic houses cover rubbish deposits accumulated there during the Yalangach period, and even here are witness to the enlargement of buildings formerly occupying the very edge of the settlement. At this time settlements are multi-chambered houses with interior shrines and nearby mortuaries-tholoi, an arrangement typical of the Geoksyur oasis. Qualitative structural changes of the settlement can scarcely be observed in the materials excavated, but quantitative growth is evident. Differences in grave inventories, characteristic of the burials of Excavation 1, indicate the complex social structure of this period. It is of note that the neighboring settlement of Ilgynly-Depe is already diminished in size in Early Geoksyur times and is completely abandoned in the Late Eneolithic. Most likely part of the site's population was absorbed by the growing Altyn-Depe, and this process of population concentration appears to be one of the important signs of the forthcoming urbanization.

During the Late Eneolithic, painted ceramics of the Geoksyur style are characteristic of the material culture of Altyn-Depe; the ceramics undergo a gradual transformation of their original motifs to the diminutive carpetlike designs so typical of local Namazga IV vessels. Also representative are stone vessels fashioned from white, marblelike limestone; terracotta boxes with the outside embellished by carved cross and half-cross ornamentation; and terracotta figurines of sitting women, sometimes with squared-off shoulders, characterized by elegant and flowing lines distinguishing them from the massive terracottas of Late Yalangach times. Quite indicative are even

the heads of such statuettes with their large, prominent noses, almond-shaped deep eyes, and S-shaped curls or pendants. This comparatively standard collection of artifacts is practically identical with the assemblages at Geoksyur 1 and Chong-Depe.

Inasmuch as there existed during Late Eneolithic times two cultural provinces in southern Turkmenistan, one must acknowledge that in basic traits Altyn-Depe belonged to the eastern one. At the same time, the differences between the two cultures in the sphere of material culture are less significant than the traits of cultural uniformity which unite the southern Turkmenistan sites of the period into a whole. The multi-chambered houses, vessels fashioned from stone, the forms of copper objects, particularly the so-called shovel pins, the style of the terracotta sculptures and the details of their finish, the tradition of collective tombs with individual burials—all of these are practically identical in west and east. Differences are expressed in the main in the painted ceramics: in the western sites there are vessels of the Kara-Depe type, and in the eastern, including Altyn-Depe, of the Geoksyur type. At the same time, it may be observed that the separate elements of the paintings—the crosses, half-crosses, stepped pyramids, *et al.*—as well as the compositional applications, are the same in both provinces and differ only in varieties of combinations and scale of depiction. For instance, at Kara-Depe the designs are smaller and more variegated, but at Geoksyur tendency toward large geometric figures not lost in a variegated ornamentation prevails. Since pottery, no matter how expressive, is only one element of a cultural complex (Masson 1974g), in this case one must speak of two variants (Kara-Depe and Geoksyur) of a single cultural community, or better, the Anau Culture.

Early Bronze Age (or Namazga IV) layers, as well as Eneolithic deposits, have been uncovered at Altyn-Depe at a number of points. In the stratigraphic plan of Excavation 1 they were discernible in detail. The encircling walls, found at the base of the Wall Mound, have been analyzed in detail. Burial chambers have been found in Excavations 3 and 4. The monumental entrance into the city was studied in Excavation 8. At least part of the buildings uncovered in Excavation 13 apparently belong to the late stages of the habitation complex of the Early Bronze Age. Finally, the deposits of this period have been extensively studied in Excavation 5, where the layers were uncovered gradually from top to bottom and the above-mentioned walls were approached from

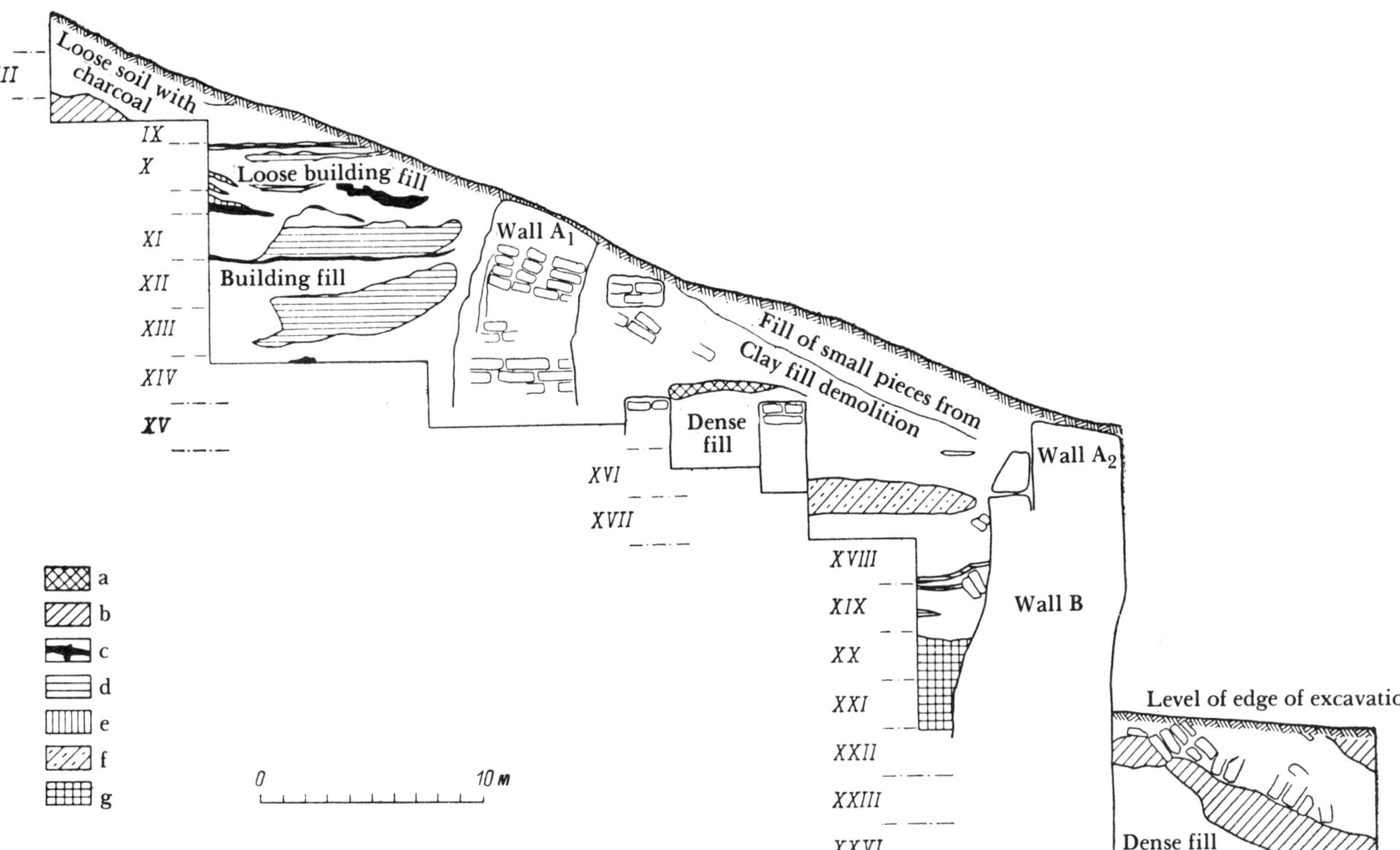

Figure 7.   Section of the eastern slope of the Wall Mound. Profile of the northern wall of transect.
Key— a: loose brown soil; b: sedimentary soils with lime inclusions; c: layers permeated with ash; d: horizontal layers of loose brown soil; e: rubbish layers of greenish color; f: loose fill with ash inclusions; g: loose fill with charcoal.

above. The general characteristics of Altyn-Depe materials have been published by L. B. Kircho (1979). Therefore, we shall survey only briefly the results of these excavations, with the exception of Excavation 8, since the structures discovered in it continued to function into the Namazga V period and they will be fully reported below (see p. 37). We shall begin with the above-mentioned encircling walls which were uncovered during 1959-1961 but were not studied in detail at the time (Ganyalin 1967). This work, however, was done during 1965, and the results yielded a complicated history of these structures which were in existence for a long time and were heightened or rebuilt more than once (Fig. 7). The earliest appears to be wall B, constructed of mud bricks with the dimensions of 46-49 x 20-22 x 15-16 cm. The thickness of the wall is 1.9 m; at places it is preserved to the height of 5 m. Topographically, it is the outer encircling wall of the settlement proper whose thick cultural layers reach next to the wall. The trench started at the outer side of wall B showed layers up to 2.5 m thick containing ceramics covered with geometric ornamentation. Analysis of these ceramics in 1965 indicated they belong to an early phase of Namazga IV. Lower were found polychrome ceramics of the Geoksyur type in its late, Chonga variant. When detailed stratigraphic studies are undertaken in the future at Altyn-Depe, it may be discovered that the layers supporting wall B belong to the Namazga III period. The outer face of the wall, although preserving a straight appearance overall, does not describe a straight line but is composed of retreating and advancing segments. In places where the wall segment "retreats" it is supported by a pilaster, rectangular in cross-section (Fig. 8). In all, wall B could be traced to a length of 60 m. The interior face of the wall slopes slightly toward the settlement. The wall existed over a long period of time. On the settlement side, there are a number of levels which fix the gradual accumulation of the cultural deposits and the heightening of

the horizon. In a number of cases, perpendicular, thin walls were added to the pilasters on the outside of the wall. It is possible that there were some dwellings attached to the outer face of the wall. Also, we cannot exclude repair work to renovate or heighten the wall proper. In one case, part of the width of the wall was filled in with ashes to the thickness of 20 cm. Partial destruction of the wall has been observed: close to the base of the outer face of the wall deposits accumulated and large blocks of the wall proper had collapsed onto them. Many burials were located at the wall; an evaluative summary of these has been published by A.F. Ganyalin (1967).

The relationship of much later walls, conditionally labeled A_1 and A_2, is less clear. The first is located in the northern part of the excavation and its foundation is formed partially by wall B and partially by the cultural layers. Like wall B, it does not describe a straight line but has recesses. It has been preserved only to the height of 1.2 m. At the place where it was possible to observe the wall, its width reached 5 m. It is possible that at this place a structure of some kind was added to the wall on the inside making it appear more massive. In length, the wall progresses for 20 m and then its northern edge turns toward the town, as if to encircle the Wall Mound at its outer perimeter.

Wall A_1, located in the southern part of the excavation, is apparently close to wall A_2 in time. This wall is also located above wall B and keeps its overall direction and in part utilizes it as a foundation. In the center of the excavation it is clearly discernible that the layers of ashes covering wall A_1 adhere also to the remains of wall A_2. This prevents us from claiming a full synchronization for the construction of the two walls, although it is possible that at some period they functioned contemporaneously. The width of wall A_2 is about 1.9 m, and it is preserved to the height of 1.5 m. Counting the separate small segments, the remains of the wall have a length of 26 m. It is of note that like

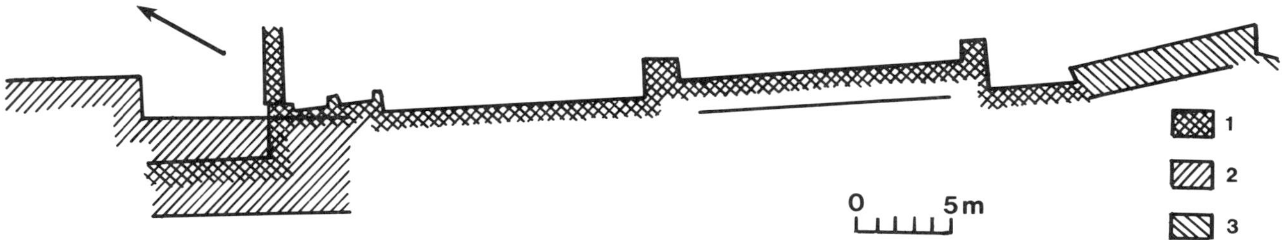

Figure 8.   Plan of structures at the base of the Wall Mound.
Key— 1: *Wall B*; 2: *Wall A₁*; 3: *Wall A₂*.

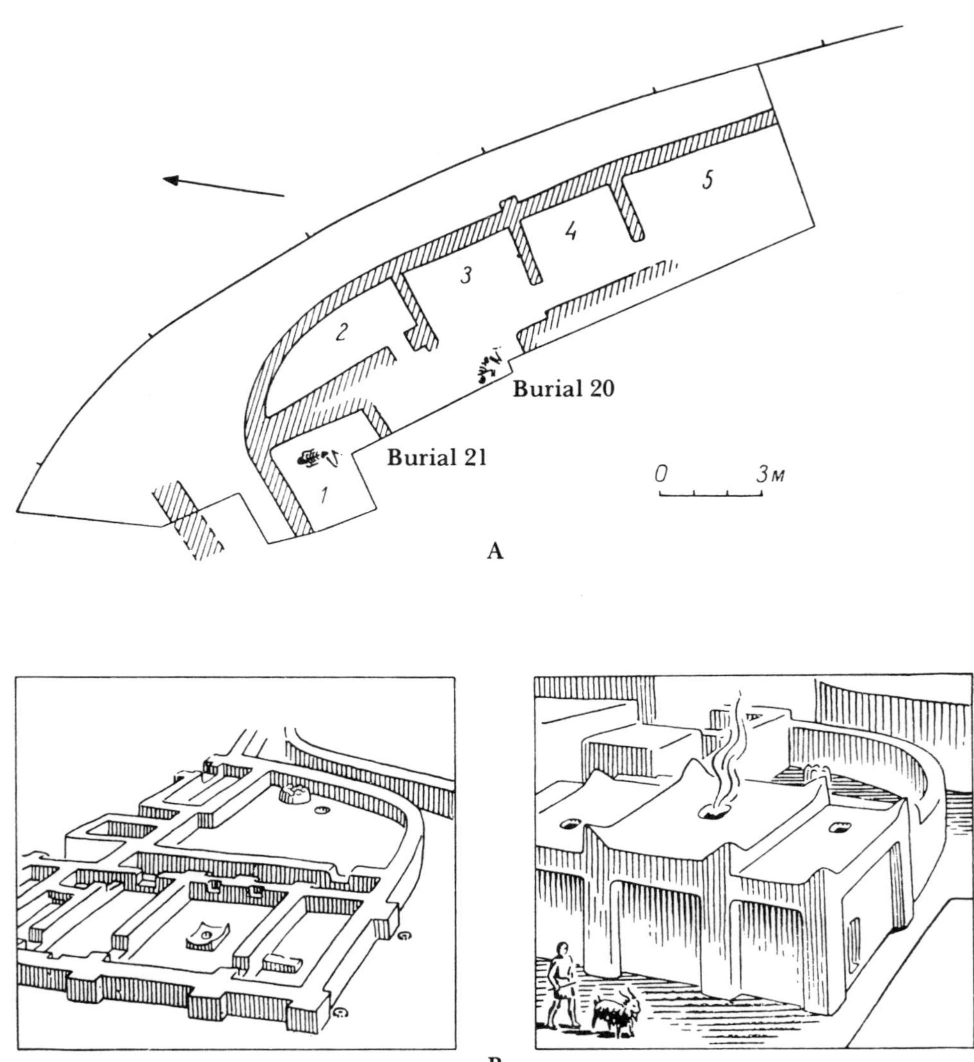

Figure 9.   Plan of structures in horizon Altyn 4 of Excavation 1 (A). V. B. Zernov's axonometric projection and reconstruction of the cult center of Layer 5 of Excavation 5 (B). The Arabic numerals here and in Figures 12, 13, 15, 17, and 19 refer to the numbering of rooms within the various dwellings.

A_1, A_2 bends toward the town at its southern end, following the outer edge of the Wall Mound.

Finally, a wall located much higher on the incline and receding into the settlement appears to be the latest. It was constructed at a time when the height of the cultural layers behind walls B and A_2 had reached the thickness of 3 m. The overall orientation of the wall is the same as that of the earlier ones, although its length cannot be traced. It is 1.9 m wide and is preserved to the height of 2 m. At the place of the excavation cut, the wall had moved and was inclined, and in the fill of the outer side lay a block of fallen mud bricks. This disturbance may be the result of some catastrophic occurrence such as an earthquake. On the outer side of the wall, a fill of mud bricks dominates, whereas on the inside there are horizontal cultural layers which include everyday refuse, such as organic remains which form greenish intercalations in the layers.

Thus there is no doubt that the outer edge of the Wall Mound had encircling walls which were restored and renovated several times. They formed the Wall Mound's outer facade as well as its side borders. Since the neighboring Craftsmen's

Quarters lacked such walls, the proposition was voiced even in the early stages of the excavation that the Early Bronze layers of the Wall Mound may contain structures with a specific function, such as a sanctuary. Indeed, in the course of stratigraphic work within the Wall Mound in 1977-1978, this proposition was in part confirmed. A Namazga IV sanctuary was uncovered there, and it is probable that the entire Wall Mound served as a cultural center during the Early Bronze Age, analogous or similar to the center of the Middle Bronze Age discovered in Excavation 7. If this is so, then a full study of the complex will take a major effort, since it is covered by several horizons which contain the living structures of Namazga V times. In this connection, the results of Excavation 7 documented the quite distinctive construction methods of early architects. They utilized the built-up mounds containing the remains of earlier structures for the erection of their monumental edifices by fashioning a steplike layering decorated with pilasters on the outer surfaces of the mound. This process will be analyzed in detail later (see p. 56). It is possible that the Early Bronze Age method of construction was similar at the Wall Mound. In such a case, the difference in the location of the cultural layers at the outer edge of the massive steplike platforms and inside the settlement may be fairly considerable. The layers of the Early Bronze Age may hardly reach the thickness of 9 m at the outer edge, as was presumed in 1965 by the comparison of the layers in the trench dug outside the edge of the wall and the trench within the settlement. That figure may be a bit exaggerated, but whether accurate or not, the outer enclosures of the Wall Mound form an important focus of construction efforts of the early population of Altyn-Depe.

The basic materials for evaluating the development of the Early Bronze Age complex at Altyn-Depe came from Excavation 1. In 1965, three horizons that contained Namazga V materials were partly dug. Also uncovered in Excavation 1 was a group of structures of late Namazga IV representing horizon Altyn 4. At this level in the excavation an edge of an early dwelling with a 0.5 m thick outer wall was encountered. At a place along the outer wall, a rectangular pilaster was constructed. On the inside, a number of walls perpendicular to the outer wall divided the space into several small, apparently household, rooms. The outer wall was traced for a distance of almost 18 m; to the north it described a smooth curve toward the town, forming one side of a street 2 m wide. Thus we have here the outer thickened wall of a

multi-chambered complex (Fig. 9A), which strongly differentiates this district from the Wall Mound with its impressively thick encircling walls. In 1967, not far from the above-mentioned buildings, a rather disturbed collection of graves was uncovered; in it were found four skulls and a number of unrelated long bones accompanied by an unpainted vessel, a flint artifact resembling an endpoint, and a few beads. To the south of the grave room there was another skull, a fill of long bones, and three painted vessels apparently removed from the graves. With the vessels was a cylindrical lamp of white stone, typical of Altyn Early Bronze Age assemblages.

In Excavation 1, much lower foundations of buildings were uncovered in a stratigraphic trench dug in 1969 and widened in 1970 in order to determine the nature of the layers more precisely. Five building horizons, with an overall thickness of 3.75 m (Altyn 4-8), related to Namazga IV times. Remains of mud- brick walls and sometimes small rooms with clay plaster floors were uncovered in these horizons. The widespread occurrences of ash, sometimes quite thickly deposited, were characteristic and indicative of the edge of the settlement to which all sorts of refuse was carried. In horizon Altyn 8 the remains of a ceramic kiln preserved as a large mass of scorified bricks were encountered. In horizons Altyn 5 and 6 two double burials were found; they were assumed to be those of twins (Shchetenko 1970b:417). The burials of Altyn 5 were accompanied by a small vessel and a cubelike terracotta box with a carved pattern (a reliquary); near the hands of the buried in horizon Altyn 6 was a single pot.

The assemblage of vessels from horizon Altyn 4-8 delineates the development of a ceramic tradition formed in the late Eneolithic in the eastern group of Anau sites. Vessels of the Geoksyur type served as the initial "take-off point," or prototype, for local ceramics during the Early Bronze Age. In the materials of Altyn-Depe one can see the gradual transformation of the ornamentation particular to vessels of this type. The major tendency is toward fractionization and reduction in size of the design. At the same time, the potter's wheel is introduced and vessels made on it begin to displace the handmade ones. Parallel with this displacement, the percentage of decorated pots diminishes. A characteristic trait of Altyn-Depe ceramics during the Early Bronze Age is the increase in red-background pottery, a reflection of the major role of Geoksyur pottery (Table 1).

The initial motifs of decorated ceramics from the above-mentioned layers are crosses of various sizes in a rhomboid frame, appliqué crosses and half-crosses. The design is in dark-brown, predominantly on a red background, rarely on a greenish-white one. Both of these motifs develop from the Geoksyur tradition of ornamentation. With this pottery, in horizons Altyn 6 and 8, there was decorated pottery in which the ornamentation clearly shows the precedence of Kara-Depe. This represents the western influence. The sun symbol in the form of two concentric circles with a dot in the center belongs to the number of western elements. The decorated ceramics of horizon Altyn 4 (Plate V, item 2), containing such fundamental elements as triangles and rhomboids with dentated edges, are closer yet to western traditions, although they do differ from the ceramics of Namazga-Depe by having a wider distribution of decorations on a red background. Of note is the preservation, in layers Altyn 5-8, of large storage vessels with polychrome decorations of crosses in dentated frames. Aside from pottery, figurines of animals, articles, and anthropomorphic figurines of unfired clay were found in horizons Altyn 4-8. Terracotta perforated beads of biconical and globular form are common. In horizons Altyn 7 and 8 conical spindle whorls were found. Other finds we should mention include a fragment of a clay reliquary, a large biconical bead of gray stone (Altyn 5), a copper hook, and a small rod (Altyn 7).

As we have already seen, in 1977 and 1978, the Bronze Age layers of Excavation 5 were extensively studied. In an area of about 500 m^2 of this stratigraphic excavation, structures were found in the fourth layer from the surface which could be synchronized with horizon Altyn 4 on the basis of its ceramic assemblage. Seven living complexes, each composed of several dwellings, were uncovered wholly or in part. Among them were large living chambers with hearths, almost rectangular in outline, elevated above the floor on a small platform and, less significant, often reconstructed auxiliary buildings. A complex in the northwestern part of the excavation has a special character: a separate rectangular house with an area of about 50 m^2, composed of a narrow corridor along the long wall of the house and five rooms connected by passages. Three of the rooms were constructed *en suite*. In the squarish main room in the center of the complex, there was an oval hearth reminiscent of the hearth-altars of Geoksyur sanctuaries and the late Eneolithic sanctuary uncovered in horizon 9 of Excavation 1. In one of the walls of this room were two rectangular niches, in another, two narrow, slitlike openings. It is probable that here we have an edifice with a specialized function—a

sanctuary or a small temple. A supplementary exit from the sanctuary led into an adjoining enclosed courtyard.

At the level of the building horizon being surveyed, 21 child burials were uncovered. All were devoid of grave goods and were located mainly under the walls of the houses in pits dug into the earth, except for one which was interred in a kitchen cauldron. In the eastern part of the excavation, closer to the ancient edge of the settlement, a collective grave with indications of reburial was excavated; at the most, remains or partial remains of 14 individuals could be discerned. In the grave proper, as well as above it along its walls, were found 14 ceramic and two stone vessels, two bronze rings, one gray stone bead, and one carnelian. During the removal of the foundations of the grave walls, a tall, rectangular lamp cut from a marblelike limestone was found. The lamp had a small depression blackened with smoke on its upper part and an oval lid with a round opening in its center.

The fifth horizon of Excavation 5 is close in ceramics to the Altyn 5 complex described earlier (Plate 1, item 2). At this level, the plan of the buildings is essentially repeated. A full succession of buildings is present, while in the upper horizons of the Middle Bronze Age (Namazga V) the plan is different. Here we also have several multi-chambered complexes and in the midst of them, in the northwestern part of the excavation, regularly adhering to the outline, the rectangular house. Initially, it was composed of four rooms *en suite*, connected with passages. In its central part was a roughly rectangular hearth, with a low retaining wall forming its perimeter and with small clay posts in the four corners. This platform hearth is in many respects close to those encountered in the sanctuaries of Eneolithic settlements in the Geoksyur oasis where, in one case, a clay post was preserved in one corner of the pit (Khlopin 1964:16). On the outside, the edifice was decorated with rectangular pilasters and, later, a long corridor was constructed along one of its walls (Fig. 9B). In outline, this edifice is identical to the small temple in layer 4, and was located directly below it. As in layer 4, there was a courtyard containing many hearths and pits attached to the temple. Here again we have a traditional cult center, encountered at least in part in Excavation 5. And in this connection we recall the impressive encircling walls of the Wall Mound uncovered by that excavation. Probably because of the special character of the sanctuary, a number of terracottas were found there. A large head with a long neck, and a female torso with arms folded across the waist and supporting a child resting on the chest stand out

became ordinary dwelling quarters during the Namazga V period. Although the complex was

TABLE 1
CHANGES IN CERAMIC ASSEMBLAGES OF THE EARLY BRONZE AGE (in %)

Horizon	Ceramic			
	Hand-modeled	Turned on Potter's Wheel	Decorated	Red Background (of the total of decorated pottery)
Altyn 4	—	100	33	71
Altyn 5	3	97	14	60
Altyn 6	31	69	67	29
Altyn 7	74	26	72	33
Altyn 8	82	18	72	25

among them; the figure of the child was made separately and attached to the torso. In the style of their execution, both of these specimens clearly follow the Eneolithic tradition and differ appreciably from the terracottas of the Middle Bronze Age so abundantly represented at Altyn-Depe.

In the eastern part of the excavation at the level of the fifth horizon, the ancient edge of the town was encountered, and below it, the massive encircling wall. Not far from the inside of the wall, two burial chambers were uncovered; they were in the form of additions to the walls of the existing buildings. In one of the chambers, two adults were buried in succession; the grave inventory was relatively abundant—five clay and two stone vessels, stone beads, and perforated beads. In time, a closet was attached to the burial chamber, and in it was interred a child accompanied by two clay vessels and two beads, one of agate and one of chalcedony. When the excavation was deepened to the sixth building level, which was partly done in 1978, evidence of the special character of this part of the settlement was readily obtained. For instance, a chamber with a wall containing a series of niches in the form of half-crosses was discovered (Plate 1, item 1). On the floor of the neighboring room there were parts of several terracotta boxes/reliquaries, among them one almost complete. We can come to the conclusion that during the Early Bronze Age there was a cult center on the Wall Mound which

traced only within the relatively limited area of the stratigraphic excavation and along the periphery of its enclosing walls, its special character now seems indisputable.

Aside from the results of Excavation 1 and 5, of vital importance was the discovery of the monumental entrance and encircling walls in Excavation 8, which will be described later (see p. 27). Of less importance were those excavations which revealed just Early Bronze Age layers rather than very detailed characteristics. Thus after the buildings in horizon 3 were removed during Excavation 7 in 1976, a number of other buildings were uncovered underneath. It should be mentioned that in the structures of horizon 3 of Excavation 7, fragments of painted pottery of the Namazga IV type were found; there was also a small painted cup among the grave goods of collective burial 32. Thus it is possible that the cult complex was built at this location during the last stage of the Early Bronze Age, contemporaneously with the massive pylons of the main entrance into town. The structures of the lower fourth horizon of Excavation 7 are definitely associated with the complex of Namazga IV times. Here characteristic painted pottery was found, including fragments of two elegant vessels with black designs on a greenish-white background, imported no doubt from the western site of Namazga-Depe. At the level of the fourth horizon, a narrow street or corridor was uncovered, which separated two complexes on the same level, perhaps two separate houses. In one of these there was a small room with excellently preserved niches.

Burial chambers of Namazga IV times were excavated in 1965 in Excavation 4 at the southeastern edge of Altyn-Depe. Four small rectangular rooms in two rows, with connecting doorways, were uncovered. Remains of seven persons were found in a corner of one of the rooms, their skeletons in chaotic disorder. Here also were 32 vessels, mostly painted, and a stone censer. Early Bronze Age layers were encountered in Trenches 1-3. In Trench 2, dug on the western incline of Altyn-Depe, three layers related to Namazga IV were uncovered and yielded, aside from painted pottery, fragments of copper awls and female terracotta statuettes of Late Eneolithic cast. In all, layers pertaining to the Early Bronze Age were uncovered in nine locations at Altyn-Depe; the character of these layers points to a lengthy occupation of the entire area of the fortified city during this period.

The Early Bronze Age (or Namazga IV) complexes of southern Turkmenistan remain relatively little studied and published. In Excavation 1 at Altyn-Depe their depth (thickness) hardly reaches 4 m, but we have to keep in mind that even here the Late Eneolithic layers are not as thick as at other points in the settlement. For instance, the results of the initial investigations at the Wall Mound revealed that the Namazga IV layers reached the thickness of nearly 9 m (Masson 1976:170). If we take into account the possible formation of the outer edge of this hill within the steplike distribution of the encircling walls, however, the cited figure of 9 m may be subject to doubt. The thickness of the three building horizons relating to the Namazga IV period uncovered on top of the hill within Excavation 5 did not reach more than 2.5 m, and they correspond to horizons 4-6 of Excavation 1. In addition, if one presumes that further down there will be found not two horizons of the Early Bronze Age corresponding to Altyn 7 and 8, but several additional ones, it is still not possible to speak of a 9 m cultural deposit. It should be mentioned that at Khapuz-Depe, the layers of Early Bronze Age deposits amounted to 5 m (Sarianidi 1964:42). At Ulug-Depe, there are six building horizons for that period (Ulug 1, 1a, 2, 2a, 3, and 4). There are several additional significant corresponding deposits in the west of the piedmont plain. At Namazga-Depe, the Namazga IV layer reaches 4 m in Trench 1, and 6.5 m in Trench 2 (Masson 1965b:302). According to A. A. Marushchenko, at Ak-Depe south of Ashkabad the Early

Bronze Age layers encompass nine building horizons and their thickness is 7 m (see Durdyev 1959:8).

At Altyn-Depe the Namazga IV complex has been inadequately investigated. On the basis of studies of the materials during the early years of excavation at the site, a division was proposed: an earlier subperiod in which designs of geometric style based on Late Eneolithic traditions (the Khapuz type of ceramics) were distributed, and a later subperiod, one with Namazga type ceramics, characterized by small latticed designs and widespread utilization of figures with small dentations along their edges (Masson 1967:172). If we use this subdivision to describe the stratigraphy of Excavation 1, then horizons Altyn 6-8 have ceramics of the Khapuz type and horizons 4-5 have pottery close to the Namazga type.

The cultural ties of Early Bronze Age Altyn-Depe are another matter. In the literature there are already discussions about the local variants of Namazga IV ceramics and it has been proposed that a division be made into a western group, where gray pottery dominates, and an eastern one, where such pottery is rare, but where the painted pottery preserves the influence of the traditions of the Geoksyur type ceramics of the Late Eneolithic. New materials confirm the presence of specific traits in the ceramic assemblages of the western group. Thus in addition to Ak-Depe, significant for a large percentage of gray ceramics (Masson 1966e:160, 162; Sarianidi 1976b), similar assemblages were found in two localities, one not far from Nova Nisa and the other in the Geok-Tepin region (Lyapin and Masimov 1974; Lyapin 1975). Here gray terracotta seals and statuettes were also found. Similar materials were found while trenching the settlement of Goch-Depe located 31 km to the east of Kizyl-Arvat; there, among other things, was found a gray-colored female terracotta statuette with rich appliqué neck ornamentations (Yusopov 1976; Yusopov, Gubayev and Durdyev 1976). Further to the south of Kizyl-Arvat, layers containing gray ceramics of Namazga IV times were found to the east of Parau, at the settlement of Chingiz-Depe. Here, the layers were topped with deposits containing vessels associated with the ancient culture of Dagestan. In this way, the region to the east of Ashkabad may be defined as a specific Early Bronze Age ceramic complex. The second ceramic province is represented by remains in the central part of the piedmont plain, principally Namazga-Depe, the third by the remains of the eastern group, beginning with Ulug-Depe. This third province is territorially identical with the area of distribution of Geoksyur ceramics. Without doubt, Altyn-Depe belongs with the sites of the eastern group, and the ceramics of the Khapuz cast, as we have seen earlier, reflect the orderly, natural development of Geoksyur traditions.

In the Early Bronze Age, Altyn-Depe existed in a framework put together during the Late Eneolithic. A division of the area of the settlement into specialized parts is noted. For instance, in the vicinity of the Wall Mound there functioned for a prolonged period of time a specific cult center surrounded by thick mud-brick walls, which gave the center a monumental cast. This contrasts with the small, rowlike constructions encountered in the neighboring Excavation 1, the Craftsmen's Quarters. The thin walls of the structures encountered in horizons Altyn 5-8 are witness to the continuance of rowlike construction throughout the period of the Early Bronze Age. The finding of the disturbed pottery kiln points to the beginnings of specialization of this part as the dwelling and working place of masters/professionals. The construction, toward the end of Namazga IV, of the monumental entrance with two towers/pylons decorated with pilasters also indicates the gradual change of Altyn-Depe into a citylike settlement. As to progress in production methods, the application of the potter's wheel is quite characteristic, leading to the complete displacement of hand-modeled pottery. At first the potter's wheel was apparently a simple revolving circular platform on which only the necks of the vessels were prepared, but toward the end of the period, judging by the traces on the ceramics, a rapidly revolving pottery wheel had been developed. Even during the times of Altyn 5, however, the kilns were of the archaic single-stage construction, as revealed in the materials of Excavation 5.

From the point of view of cultural genesis, the most characteristic traits of Altyn-Depe during the Early Bronze Age were extensions of Late Eneolithic traditions. These are expressed in the ceramics, terracottas, collective burials, and also in the forms of the platform hearths and the distribution of terracotta reliquaries. The above-mentioned initial Geoksyur cast is gradually transformed to an observable degree because of technological achievements; this transformation takes place, for instance, in the potter's work. We also find within the limits of the piedmont plain a strengthening of cultural integrations, gradually leveling the local differences which had their origins in the Eneolithic. This is visible, for instance, in the ceramics of Altyn 4 which are markedly close to the contemporary assemblages of painted pottery of Namazga-Depe. Similar expressions of cultural integration herald the major changes which took place in southern Turkmenistan during the Developed or Middle Bronze Age, when the cultural standards were uniform over considerable territory.

II

Excavations of the Fortifications

The nature and location of the fortifications of Bronze Age Altyn-Depe remained unresolved for a long time. The amorphous plan of the site, in the form of an irregular oval, cut into by many erosion gulches, suggested an absence of fortifications. True, on the eastern face of the Wall Mound a number of encircling walls were found and described above. These encircling walls, however, seemed associated with the specific function of a particular part of the settlement, more so because on the eastern face of the neighboring Craftsmen's Quarters only the thickening of outer walls of dwellings at the edge of the settlement was observed (Excavation 1). Materials from the many excavations, however, attest that the inhabitants of Altyn-Depe were attentive to the fortification of their settlement.

The very location of the Bronze Age settlement, atop a 20 m tell created by thick cultural deposits, favored its security. The excavations revealed that, in a number of cases during the Namazga V period, the steep slopes of the tell were covered with a special type of mud brick. This protected the slopes from the ravages of natural forces, and the steep inclines, reaching in places 70°, made access to the settlement more difficult for the intruder. Structures built on such a slope were defended by an encircling wall; the construction and thickness of the wall differed depending on the nature of the structures and the topography of the locality. Thus in Excavation 9, below and a short distance from the last structures built on the steep eastern slope, there was a 0.5 m thick wall reinforced on the outside by regularly placed rectangular pilasters, 50 cm in cross-section, jutting out of the wall about 30 cm. As we have seen, the reinforcement of the wall uncovered in Excavation 1, horizon Altyn 4, was analogous. Apparently all the slopes of Altyn-Depe were so treated, but the mud-brick covering and external wall have been preserved only in some localities, and in others they have been completely eroded.

A clear picture of the reconstructions and foundations associated with securing the settlement's outer edge was revealed during the 1973 season's work on the eastern face of the Wall Mound. This work was on the upper part of the slope rather than the lower where the encircling wall was studied in 1965. As the cut revealed, during the Namazga V period there were three building horizons here. At the first level, uncovered by Excavation 5 during 1966-1969, the ancient edge of the settlement was completely eroded. But already in the second horizon two multi-roomed houses with their outer walls reaching the edge of the settlement were discovered. The space between the houses, about 5 m, was reinforced by a massive foundation which, with the outer walls of the houses, formed a single line. Atop the massive foundation was a semicircular turret about 2 m in diameter. In the third horizon, the form of the outer defenses was the same, except for the turret, which was rectangular (2 x 1.4 m). The outer part of the turret was constructed with regular, neat layers of bricks, while the interior contained even fragments of bricks. Finally, at the level of the fourth building horizon, in which ceramics of the late Namazga IV period were found, the outer edge was fortified with a 2 m thick brick wall 10 m in length, but devoid of turrets or pilasters. On the outside, the wall was preserved to the height of four courses of bricks, on the settlement side only one course was preserved. Apparently, the courses were set directly onto the slope, without preliminary leveling. The turrets uncovered in Excavation 5 had a dual role. They served as a sort of massive counterbalance to the encircling wall built on the surface of a fairly steep slope and also as regular turrets protecting the defenders from the flanking arrows and sling missiles of the enemy. It is possible that it was just this architectural function of the counterbalance that provided the initial basis for the development of turrets as structures of fortification.

The open parts of the perimeter of Altyn-Depe were fortified more thoroughly. Thus the deep gullies which cut into the edge of the fortified city in antiquity, and certainly during the Bronze Age, served as additional entrances or passages. In one of the gullies where the less steep slopes indicated that the layers had not been eroded completely, investigations were made and Excavation 11 was started. Here, along a deep impression leading into the city, were accumulations 60 m in length. Excavations showed that at the outer, eastern edge of the accumulations, there was a part of an extensive, rectangular courtyard surrounded by walls 0.5 m thick. Farther to the west, toward the inner part of the city, the entire southern slope of the hill was faced with a thick, brick layer which showed signs of many reconstructions. Judging by all this evidence, this local construction flanked one of the supplementary entrances to the city. Indeed, from the direction of Excavation 13, at the level of the same depression, there was a small, short street about 2 m wide. In the plan of the above-mentioned southern slope two parts are discernible. In the first, there is a structure of the semicircular turret type with a diameter of about 1.5 m from which a direct ramp runs to the thick, brick layer. In the second part there is a clearly visible wall, about 2.3 m wide, flanked by two turrets, almost rectangular in cross-section. The wall continues for almost 12 m. There were later additions to the wall, both from the inside and the outside; in the latter case, a turret was fully incorporated into the addition and covered by it, and thus the thick layer forming the foundation reached the thickness of about 6 m. The Bronze Age traveller entering the settlement through the above-mentioned depression, would find on his right a brick wall with turrets. It is possible that the opposite side of the depression had analogous fortifications. Today, however, that part of the tell has a very steep slope from which the structures have been almost completely eroded.

The defense structures in the area of the principal entrance to the city, which is located on the southern side of Altyn-Depe and is distinctly visible in relief, were particularly complex. Preliminary excavations were started in 1969, but the main results were obtained with their extension in 1975-1976. The plan of reconstructions and changes turned out to be very complex, but it was these reconstructions in particular that enabled the detection of fortifications, fairly well preserved and adequately visible, built during the early period.

At the beginning of the excavations on the main gate, particular attention was paid to the western part where the gentle slope indicated better preservation of the structures, whereas the preliminary survey of the steep eastern slope in-

ferred substantial erosion. On the western side, enclosing structures were uncovered in 1969. They were associated with an 80 cm thick wall, parallel to the entrance, and judging by surroundings, at one time forming its center. To the south, on its outer face, the wall was supported by massive brickwork of 4 x 3.5 m, which was probably the base for a turretlike structure at the fulcrum of the gate. To the west, the gate turret was surrounded by an enclosing wall 1.8 m thick flanked by a rectangular turret with the dimensions of 2.2 x 2.8 m. Later, small rooms were built on the outside of this wall.

In 1975 when further excavations were started, these late structures, after being carefully recorded, were removed. Underneath were much earlier fortifications. Part of a mud-brick defensive wall, 6 m thick, was uncovered. Extending from this wall, toward the entrance, was a 6.2 x 3 m rectangular turret-pylon decorated with rectangular pilasters (Plate II, item 1). From the city side running toward the gate was a street which at first was 2.8 m wide and was later narrowed by surrounding structures to 1.3 m. The direction of the street, probably oriented to a major city building, deviates somewhat from the direction of the fortifying structures. To the east of the wall, which delimits the street, is the broad part of the city entrance. The entrance and the street were paved with sherds of thick-walled vessels, renovated several times, and alternated between fluvial and wind-blown layers. To the east of the angular turret were walls, many times reconstructed, which regulated the movements within the main entrance. From the city side, the enclosing wall was shaped by massive projections to which walls forming small rooms were added. Several vessels and the disturbed bones of a young male were found in one of these (room 32).

A trench cut from the city side onto the broad part of the entrance, conditionally named locality 31, and more extensive excavations beyond the outer face of the defensive wall, indicated the history of the defensive structures for this part of the city (Fig. 10). The enclosing wall, partly evident in the cut at the outer face of the wall in Levels XI-XII, belongs to the earliest period established for this locality. Its outer side is located about 1.5 m closer to the city than the major wall uncovered by the excavation. At the wall and extending from it are gently sloping cultural levels containing early Namazga IV painted ceramics (or in terms of Altyn-Depe stratigraphy, horizon Altyn 8).

During the second period, the fortification wall was enlarged and reached the thickness of 4.8 m.

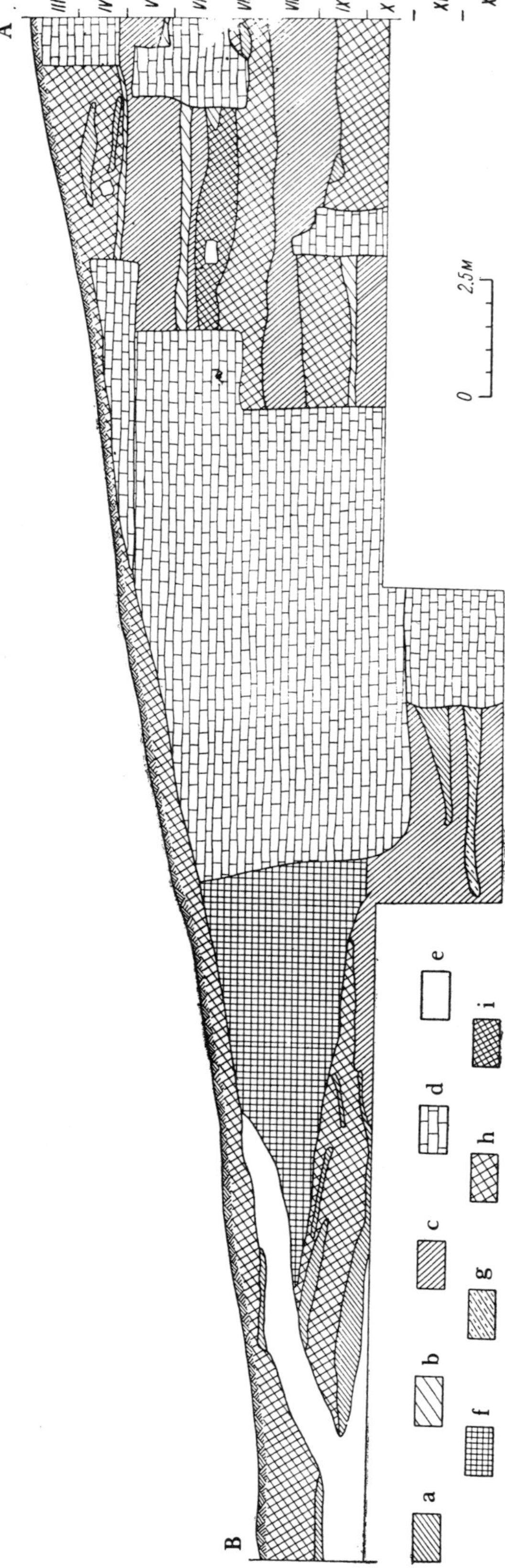

Figure 10. Excavation 8. Cross-section of enclosing walls.
Key— a: ash; b: horizontal profiles of floors; c: compact fill with pieces of raw clay; d: walls; e: compact clay sediment; f: horizontal layers of waterborne debris; g: dark-gray sedimentary layers with large inclusions of lime; h: loose fill with pieces of clay; i: fill with a large amount of charcoal.

Apparently during this period the turret-pylon decorated with pilasters was constructed at the gate. From the city side, small structures were built at the base of the wall; their remains are discernible in the second half of Level VIII to the first half of Level X. Aside from sherds, several clay balls for slings were found here. In all, the assemblage of painted ceramics resembles those of horizons Altyn 6 and 7 (middle Namazga IV).

The third period reflects the expansion of defensive structures. From the city side, the wall was once more enlarged and reached the thickness of 6 m The walls of its corresponding in-city structures form two building horizons and occupy Level V to the first half of Level VII. The ceramic assemblage found here is associated with late Namazga IV times, and on the basis of the stratigraphy of Excavation 1 corresponds to horizons Altyn 4 and 5.

Finally, the fourth period correlates with early Namazga V; throughout this segment of time the fortifications of the Early Bronze Age retained their role. The wall was probably somewhat thickened by the building of structures onto it from the city side. This type of construction is evidence of a certain amount of neglect in regard to the conditions of the fortifications. Around them are accumulations of rubbish with thick lenses of ash—the city rubbish was dumped directly at the wall. No doubt the gradual disappearance of the outer edge under rubbish was one of the reasons why in the end the old walls were abandoned and a new, less ostentatious wall was built on top of them, as was a new turret near the gate. The latter was uncovered in 1969 and, in agreement with the now established periodization, can be correlated with the last, fifth period.

In the western part of the main entrance to Altyn-Depe, the plan proved to be quite complex because the steep slope, combined with natural forces, caused substantial disruption of the clay foundations. The edge of a fairly thick foundation, trending parallel to the western wall of the entrance and into town, was uncovered here. Near the edge a single burial (359) with three painted vessels, one of which was clearly dated to late Namazga IV, was found. Painted vessels from a collective interment found here (burials 334-343) belong to the same period; the burial was substantially disturbed because of its proximity to the turf surface. Through these finds, the wall may be synchronized with the third period, as given in the scheme above. With the extension of the excavation in 1976, an outline of a second, eastern turret-pylon forming the entrance was discovered. The distance between it and the western pylon was 15 m,

which established the general width of the gates (Fig. 11). It also became apparent that this 15 m span was divided into three streets leading into the city. The width of two of these was 1.5 to 2.0 m. Judging by this width, they were designated for foot traffic. The third, middle street had the width of 4 to 5 m and was designed for wheeled vehicles pulled by one or two camels as suggested by the excavated clay models. The walls of the main street led to the outer perimeter at a somewhat slanting angle, apparently to align it with buildings inside Altyn-Depe. The end portions of the walls lining the street deviated slightly from that alignment and were oriented to the edge of the turret-pylons framing the gate. All the streets were filled with exceptionally thick clayey sediment interlayered with early pavings made from fragments of thick-walled vessels.

A summary of the results of excavations over the various years paints the following picture of the fortifications of Altyn-Depe during the Bronze Age. The amorphous plan inherited by the Bronze Age population from the Eneolithic epoch resulted in a fragmented perimeter; the encircling walls were multi-angled and comformed to the particularities of planning for the various quarters of the city. Because of the propitious location of Altyn-Depe on a high, artificial mound, here and there with very steep slopes, the early builders usually surrounded themselves with relatively limited fortifications: they faced the slopes with sun-dried bricks and as a rule built walls of limited thickness; in places they reinforced these walls with counterbalancing turrets, sometimes rectangular, sometimes semicircular. The crucial points, the various access passages leading into the city, and particularly the main entrance, were fortified more thoroughly. In the latter case the wall was rather massive, and the turret-pylons near the gate, rhythmically decorated with repeating, projecting pilasters, represent a remarkable achievement of early monumental architecture.

Thus at Altyn-Depe a number of architectural devices were worked out and combined to create a specific branch of the art of fortification. A separate fortification code was established, a code which in part is reflected in the repeated dimensions of the rectangular turrets. These turrets were massive structures of solid brickwork. In this respect they differ from the oval structures built on the outer surface of walls encircling the Eneolithic settlements of the Geoksyur oasis (Khlopin 1964:80-85). These structures, while having the role of turrets on the outer side of the walls, at the same time served as ordinary dwell-

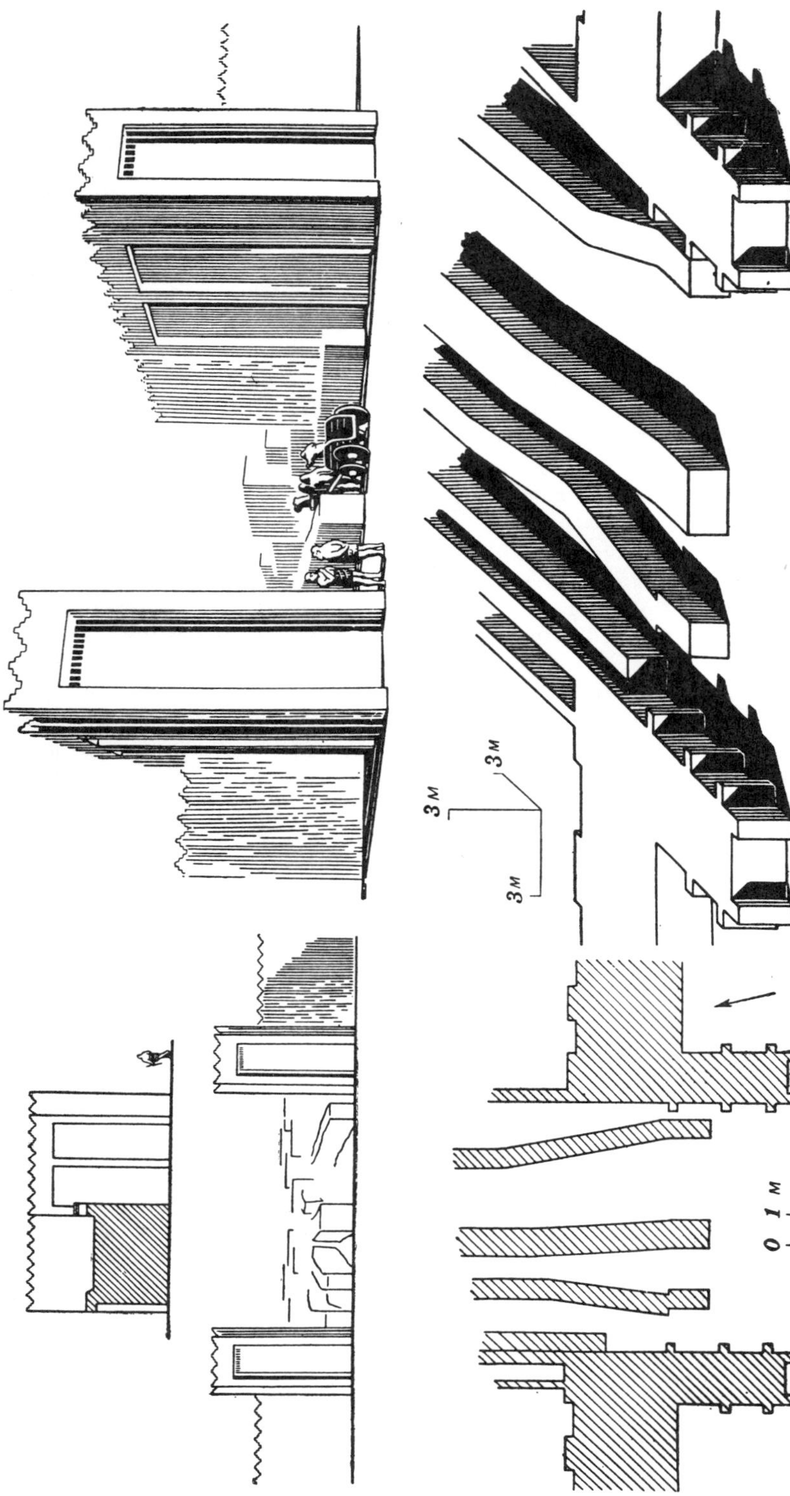

Figure 11. Excavation 8. Outer gate structures in the lower horizon. Axonometric projection and reconstruction by V. B. Zernov.

ings. This dual role is indicated by the discovery of cooking hearths in the turrets and the character of the finds in the cultural layer. Apparently, a similar functional lack of differentiation is one of the characteristic traits of primitive, initial fortifications in general (Masson 1976a:39-140). At Altyn-Depe the appearance of turrets as specialized structures, and particularly the presence of the well-designed monumental entrance, indicate the development of fortification architecture proper.

The two turret design of the city entrance (or city gate) is an early method typical of eastern fortifications (Yadin 1963:21-22, 55). At times the turret-flanked entrance was additionally embellished with orthostatic reliefs of various kinds (Frankfort 1955:171). The main entrances to monumental temple complexes in Mesopotamia were also designed with massive turret-pylons starting with the early dynastic period. In this respect the main entrance to Altyn-Depe is particularly close to such well-embellished temple entrances as the turret-flanked ones of western Asia, where military security was always paramount. At these turret-flanked entrances, the gates were very narrow and the entrance was made more inaccessible to the enemy by the erection of segments of walls across it. To the contrary, at Altyn-Depe we see the segmentation of the entrance space with elongated walls organize movement of the entering and exiting population rather than hamper it. It is possible that the three streets formed in this way were secured with gates of heavy pieces of wood held together with bronze clamps or covered overall with bronze sheeting. There is no doubt, however, that the very plan of the Altyn-Depe main entrance reflected munificent hospitality rather than watchful defense. The architecture of the gates followed the early eastern design, emphasizing the ties of Altyn-Depe with the cultural world of the Near East. The development of the Bronze Age defensive structures of Altyn-Depe appears to be one of the outward expressions of those qualitative changes which originate from within the local population.

III

Excavations of the Living Quarters

On the high mound of Altyn-Depe during the Middle Bronze Age, beyond the walls reinforced with turrets and counterbalances, there were tightly packed structures. With the goal of investigating the interior structures of the settlement, excavation was done in various localities after carefully examining their micro-relief and surface materials. In some cases, the excavations based on such examinations proved successful and informative, in others the structures were clearly outlined so that well-founded deductions could be made. In the lower parts, however, the structures quickly thinned out or proved to be disturbed by later layers of rubbish. All in all, as a result of the excavations, extensive material was gathered revealing the character of the interior buildings. The area of the excavations in which the dwelling structures were studied exceeded one hectare.

The Craftsmen's Quarters

Among the excavations, three are associated with the area of the Craftsmen's Quarters: the stratigraphic Excavation 1, carried out at the eastern edge of the hill; the large Excavation 10, which explored a considerable part of the eastern side of the quarters; and the small Excavation 12 in the lower western reaches where remains of kilns were visible.

The excavations fully confirmed the designation of this part of the mound as an area of concentration of crafts, particularly the potter's craft.

Excavation 1

In Excavation 1 all three horizons, dated to the Middle Bronze Age (Namazga V), revealed traces of the potter's art. Here the walls of the structures were built with sun-dried bricks with the dimensions 46 x 28 x 12 cm. In the first horizon (Altyn 1) within the limits of the excavation only a number of small chambers were preserved; next to them was a kiln. Of the kiln, only the lower heating chamber, about 1 m in diameter, remained. Some child burials without inventory and four adult burials were uncovered. Of the latter, three were found in a brick-lined tomb apparently meant for collective burials. The inventory was very poor: a small pot with one, and a stone bead apiece for the other two. Burial 4 was apart, and in it were found an arsenical copper dagger and a small copper cup with a long handle (Plate XXIX, items 1 and 2). The burials were found directly under the turf layer, and they probably date to the period during which this part of Altyn-Depe was abandoned and the burials in the gutted ruins were carried out by people inhabiting the western part of the settlement.

In horizon Altyn 2, the difference between the southern and northern sides was clearly defined:

on the northern were mud- brick structures, on the southern, loose rubbish layers with a considerable amount of potsherds, among them rejects. This evidence indicates the presence of a courtyard. In the courtyard was a two-tiered kiln. The structures in the northern part were thoroughly filled in with rubble prior to the erection of the buildings of the top layer. All told, nine rooms were found. They were basically small auxiliary household buildings, but there were also larger buildings, apparently living quarters, with contiguous auxiliary structures (rooms 2 and 3). The burials of Altyn 2 are principally those of children. As a rule, there is no grave inventory—only in one was there a stone bead.

In horizon Altyn 3, the division between a courtyard and a built-up area had been preserved. The courtyard was protected by a wall about 0.5 m thick, trending from west to east for almost 10 m. Remains of two ceramic kilns were uncovered. Around one of them about 100 artifacts of unfired clay were found. They were predominantly animal figurines, apparently ready for firing. The structures were packed with rubble and their floor plans were not clear. As previously, the burials, among which were three of adults, had no inventory except for one which contained a ceramic spindle whorl. There was a prevalence of small child burials under the walls, usually in a corner. For instance, four such burials were found in room 4, and two in room 3. Thus the excavation established that the traditional population of this part of Altyn-Depe consisted of master potters who lived in multi-chambered houses located next to the kilns and buried their deceased without grave goods. The above conclusion was confirmed in principle by Excavation 10 and 12, carried out in the Craftsmen's Quarters where the interior plan of the household complexes could be established in greater detail.

Excavation 10

Excavation 10 was carried out over three seasons. In 1969, the buildings of the very top layer were uncovered; on the whole they were poorly preserved (Masimov 1970a, 1970b). A considerable portion of the excavation, about 400 m², was occupied by an open courtyard surrounded by a wall. In the courtyard the lower heating chambers of two kilns, oval in cross-section, were uncovered. Three burials were also found here; they apparently date to the time of the abandonment of this part of Altyn-Depe, when activities were concentrated in the western part. One (125) was a child's burial without inventory; the other two were those of adults. Burial 124 contained an earthenware pot and decanter, and nearby a small plaque of gray stone with two drilled holes, one of them with an oval insert of white stone. The inventory of burial 109 was very rich: a pottery vessel, two seals (one stone, one bronze), and a silver pin topped with a goat's head (Plate XXIX, item 4).

Close to the courtyard were eight structures divided into two complexes by a narrow, winding street. Not far from one of them was a kiln; it is difficult to determine whether the kiln functioned contemporaneously with the living complex, or was constructed later.

In 1971 the excavation was extended to the north, where the surface markings of the first horizon were less evident and gave hopes that the better-preserved structures of the second horizon could be directly approached. Indeed, here the structures of the upper layer proved to be practically eroded, but the walls of the rooms of the second layer reached the height of 1 m in places. All structures were built of sun-dried bricks predominantly 39-47 x 20-25 x 9-13 cm in dimensions, although occasionally examples of 24 x 24 x 10 cm bricks were encountered, the latter probably representing the principal type of brick cut in half. These complexes were studied in detail by I.S. Masimov, who dedicated a number of publications to them (Masimov 1972, 1973b, 1973c, 1976b). All of the structures uncovered in an area of 1400 m² were divided into several complexes by double walls and a small street about 1.5-2.0 m wide (Fig. 12). Four artisan-household complexes can be distinguished. The living quarters are characterized by a larger area, a more careful finish on the walls (which were neatly plastered with a clay stucco), and a few potsherds. As a rule, in their center was a hearth built on a low almost rectangular platform. The characteristic traits of the uncovered houses were their systematic, planned components: a living space, usually of nearly rectangular outline, connected to the work space by a narrow passage. The area of such units was

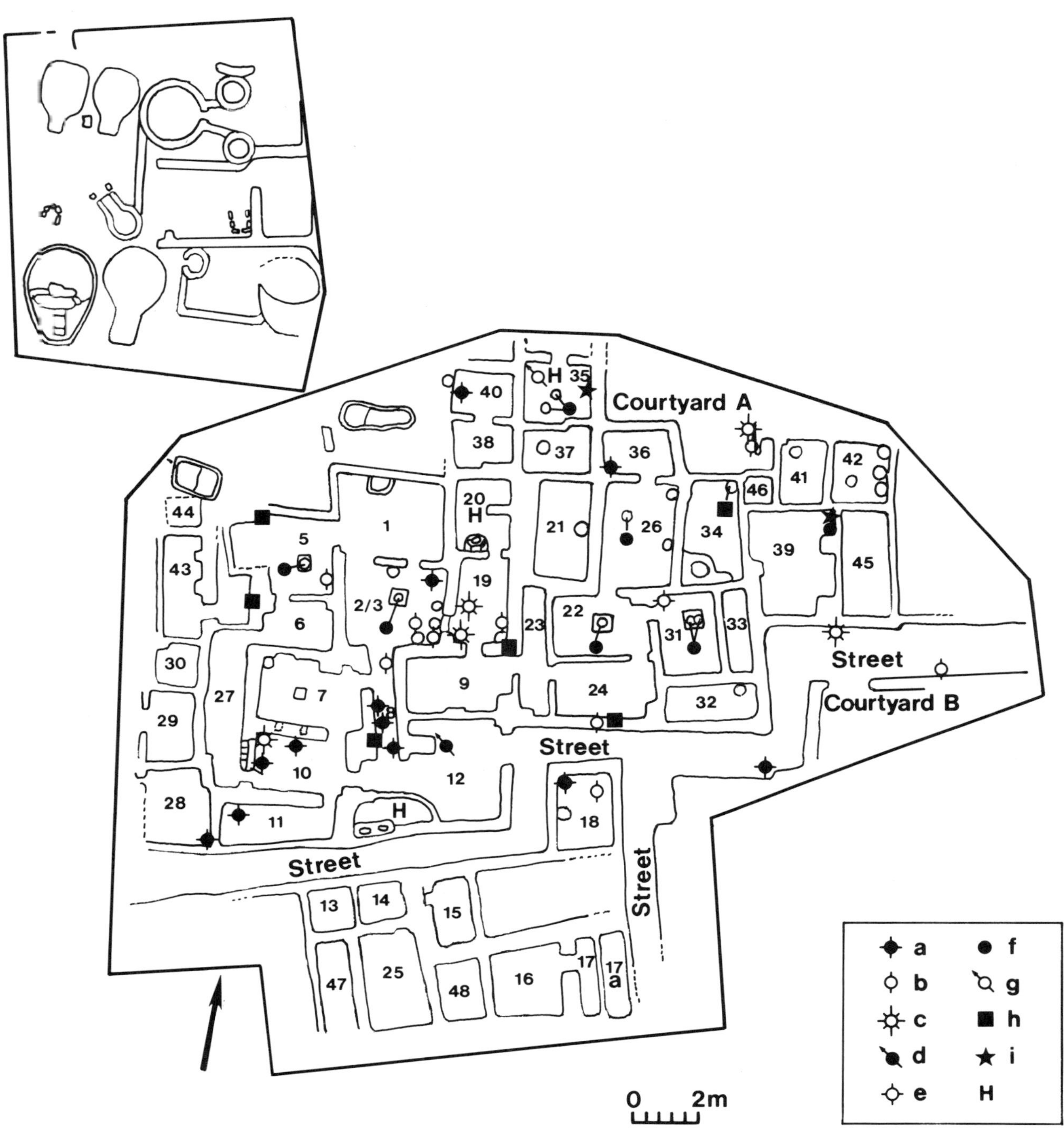

Figure 12.   Excavation 10. Plan of the uncovered structures.
Key— a: *statuette;* b: *beads;* c: *spindle whorl;* d: *arrow head;* e: *punch;* f: *stone pivot for door post;* g: *step;* h: *burial;* i: *grain grinder.* H: *hearth.*

usually between 10 m^2 and 18 m^2, although the average of an excavated unit was 16 m^2. Let me briefly characterize these complexes.

Of greatest interest is a complex, called the Central Complex, composed of 13 small enclosures and a sort of interior courtyard. The compactness of the structure was characteristic of Altyn-Depe as a whole, but for the Craftsmen's Quarters it was quite large. The courtyard had the area of about 14 m^2. At one of its walls there was a semicircular enclosure, and in the enclosure, on a low platform, were two oval cooking hearths. Outside the enclosure was yet another similar hearth. Within the courtyard fragments of three stone grain grinders, pieces of cooking cauldrons and braziers were found—this clearly points to the household functions of this part, preliminarily labeled as locality 12. During the existence of the house there were a number of reconstructions which changed the initial floor plan. The basis for this change was the above-mentioned composite planning element of a living space and an auxiliary workshop connected by a passage. In this central complex, the auxiliary buildings connect with rooms 2/3 and 19, 5 and 6, and 7 and 11. In all three cases, the rooms designated as living spaces contain a warming hearth built on a squarish platform. During the second stage in the existence of the complex, the passage from room 2/3 to room 19 was blocked and the latter room was probably added to the neighboring house. The fairly large house 1 had a hearth, built of bricks set on edge, at the wall. In the opinion of I.S. Masimov the hearth was used for manufacture: thirteen figurines of animals and anthropormorphic statuettes were found in it. Only some of them had been fired. Here three globular stones used as polishers were also found.

A structure of a decidedly specialized function, but of a different order, was locality 10. The structure had a small bench at its western wall and the wall had openings in the form of a half-cross and a quarter-cross (Plate II, item 2) identical to the ornaments on cult objects, conditionally called reliquaries. Within the chamber a considerable amount of ash, fragments of fired clay, and charcoal were found. Among the finds were two female statuettes (one had on its nape signs in the form of eight-pointed stars), six anthropomorphic statuettes, and animal figurines. All this suggests that it was a specialized household sanctuary (Masimov 1973b, 1976b:21). It is noteworthy that the sanctuary complex contained "living and auxiliary rooms" apparently closely associated with the people who serviced the cult center.

The second house unit was located close to the eastern side of the first and was preliminarily labeled the Eastern Complex. The household courtyard A was located to the north of the unit, but the house proper was connected to the central complex by a system of corridors and a corridorlike room (23). The resulting systematically planned units—a carefully stuccoed living room with a platform hearth combined with a household closet—can be traced even here with adequate clarity. Numbers 22 and 24, 31 to 33, 26 and 36, and apparently also 39 and 45, could also be traced. Various reconstructions were carried out during the time of the existence of the complex. For instance, from the large living room (31) a narrow segment was walled off (33). Two rooms with storage jars (41 and 42) were the storerooms, so common to all houses. Somewhat out of the ordinary was the hearth in room 26—an oval depression with a small central clay post preserved to the height of 7 cm. The street skirting the complex extended further to the east, to the edge of the settlement. Its direction and location is the same as that of a street that reached the edge of Altyn-Depe along the buildings of horizon Altyn 4. This correspondence indicated definite stability for the major part of the city outline, starting with the Early Bronze Age. Located to the south of the street is the large courtyard B.

The Southern Complex, separated from the first two by a small street, and similarly delimited on the eastern side, has been excavated only in part. In the initial investigation across the street, what looked like a small square was encountered, but later it turned out that most of the area was occupied by room 18, which belonged to the Southern Complex. By 1971 ten units, most of them household units, were uncovered in the Southern Complex. One of them (room 17) served as a burial chamber. Here there were seven adult burials, but the entire inventory consisted of only three ceramic vessels. In 1972, the uncovering of the Southern Complex was in part extended under the supervision of V.I. Knyshev; five additional units were excavated (47 to 49, 52, and 53). The centrally located room 48 was fairly large, contained a platform hearth, and was probably a living room. The equally large room 49 had a hearth next to a wall; in the hearth copper slag and a maul for breaking up the ore were found. Aside from these, the excavations yielded a piece of fused copper ore in a sort of clay crucible, and an unfinished stone seal. Similar assemblages of finds elsewhere indicate that this unit was a place of manufacture for various craftsmen and not of potters only. The works of the latter are particularly impressive because of the finds of the kilns. An interesting find was that of a head of a dog, apparently used as an amulet; in this respect it reminds one of the golden head of a wolf from the excavation of the cult center (see p. 68).

Finally, four small rooms (28 to 30, and 43) in keeping with the established pattern, belonged to a specific complex which was preliminarily named the Western Complex. It had not been extensively excavated. In 1972, 20 m to the west of the complex, a subrectangular building with the dimensions of 10 x 55 m was uncovered. Prior to excavation its outline could be discerned fairly well in the micro-relief. The building consisted of two small rooms (54 and 55) and a large central one (56), the excavation of which was not completed. In room 56, a statuette with an eight-pointed star on its nape was found. During the excavation, it was suggested that the separately located building could be one of the public buildings of the quarter, but because of the incompleteness of the excavation this conjecture could not be verified.

The number of burials in Excavation 10, aside from the above-mentioned collective burial, was small. In room 1 there was a storage jar burial of an adolescent male accompanied by a clay vessel, and in room 41, a burial of a 6-7 year old child without inventory. It is possible that further excavation under the walls of the Central and Eastern Complexes would yield additional child burials. Six child burials were encountered within the Southern Complex during the 1972 excavation. All were without inventory except for one of a 12-14 year old, which was accompanied by a carnelian bead.

In the northern part of Excavation 10, directly adjacent to the Central and Eastern Complexes, was a specialized manufacturing part of the city in which 15 two-tiered pottery kilns of various sizes were found. They contained an abundance of ceramic slag and rejected pottery. The kilns, which were of an elongated oval shape in horizontal section, had a deep fire-chamber usually divided in two parts. They are similar to those studied by I.S. Masimov (1976b:39-48). Thus the results of Excavation 10 fully confirmed the preliminary characteristics assigned to the Craftsmen's Quarters during Excavation 1. In this part of the settlement, densely built-up with houses comprised of small "closets," there was a concentration of various crafts. The burials of both children and adults, unlike those elsewhere, have very poor inventories. The central area of the dwellings designated as living space averaged 8.5 m^2 in Excavation 10.

Excavation 12

In at least two respects these deductions found confirmation during the course of Excavation 12 (Masimov 1974b, 1978a). Eighteen rooms apparently belonging to several household complexes were uncovered. Not one, however, was fully excavated. As a rule, the rooms were small and some of them were carefully finished. Six seals of varying types and preservation were also found within the excavation. The excavation was terminated at the western reaches of the Craftsmen's Quarters.

Excavation 8

Small structures united in large blocks were also found in Excavation 8 at a point located at the southern edge of the Copper Mound, to the east of the main gate. Here the excavation was carried out under the direction of V.I. Knyshev during 1971-1972. About 30 units were uncovered. They were situated on the slope of the contemporary mound and the abruptness of the slope disturbed the edges of the rooms. To the north of this point was a rubbish dump containing a considerable amount of ash which partly destroyed the structures. Similar dumps are characteristic of the edge of the settlement to which all sorts of rubbish was carried. In the given case, the location of the dump above the structures of the uppermost building horizon reflects one of the last stages of the existence of Altyn-Depe, during which the occupied territory had diminished severely and the abandoned houses at the edge were utilized as dumps or burial places. At times hot ashes were thrown out, which in a number of cases led to a light tempering of the mud-brick walls. Unfortunately, it was precisely this dump that did not permit a clear uncovering of the manufacturing-household complexes "locked" under this part of Excavation 8. At the most there were four such complexes, but each was represented by only a small number of structures. For instance, rooms 2-4 and 12 evidently belonged to a specific house connected by passages to a southern entrance. The careful plastering of rooms 3 and 4 indicated that they were living quarters. A second house, composed of rooms 5-11 and 13, was connected with passages oriented to the west, toward a small courtyard (14). The courtyard itself was filled with layers of loose soil which contained a large number of bones of small horned animals. The living quarters in this complex were presumably rooms 5-7. There were two hearths in the courtyard; around one of the hearths several clay figurines of animals were found. Rooms 15-19 comprised the third house. It was separated from the fourth by a double wall. Judging by the careful finish, the living quarters were rooms 15 and 18; in this third house rooms 15 and 19 represented a typical plan of a household unit of the period, with passages connecting the living quarters with the auxiliary buildings. A group of structures located in the western part of the excavation formed the fourth house (rooms 21, 22, 25, and 29). The varied orientation of the entrances is apparently related to the impossibility of including with the house the "locked" units mentioned above. In the turf layer covering location 25, a silver dagger, possibly belonging with a completely disturbed burial, and a female figure with a mark on its shoulder were found. In all, the structures were characteristically of small dimensions. They were literally closets: the area of the auxiliary rooms was 2-3 m^2, rarely 4-5 m^2, and the area of the living rooms between 7 m^2 and 8 m^2. The features of the structures in Excavation 8 were close to those of the Craftsmen's Quarters. Within Excavation 8, a piece of bronze and several bronze punches were found, but there was no trace of metal manufacture.

Within the confines of Excavation 8, four burials of boys without inventory were found. As usual these young children were interred within the confines of the house—three were found in the corners of room 19, that is, in the household's "dead-end" locality connected by a passage to living room 15. It is possible that the children, deceased at an early age, were members of the family occupying the unit.

Excavation 5

Structures of a somewhat different nature were encountered in Excavation 5 located on the Wall Mound. In Excavation 5, the larger part of the structures at the level of the upper layer was uncovered in 1966, and during 1967 through 1970 a small area was excavated by V.I. Knyshev. As a result, the structures of the upper layer were uncovered in full. Throughout the excavation, lower levels were reached to the point where buildings of the given horizons were uncovered (Fig. 13). The material obtained furnished a vivid, expressive picture, and has been published in part (Masson 1967; Knyshev 1971).

At the very beginning of the excavation a street oriented southeast-northwest, about 1.5-1.8 m wide, was uncovered. At first, it was thought to be an elongated room, and was recorded as room 3. Later another street was excavated to the west, almost parallel to the first and 1.7-2.1 m wide; it was named Broad Street. The first northwest-oriented street suddenly turns at a right angle; therefore that part of it was named Transverse Street. It cannot be traced clearly in all its parts; it seems, however, that there was open land next to it, a sort of square, to which both Broad and Transverse Streets led. Ceramic fragments used as fill were found in abundance in the streets. For instance, in a 4 m length of Transverse Street 854 sherds were found. Apparently they formed a sort of pavement which played an important role during the rainy season when the streets, sloping with the relief of the tell, became natural watercourses.

The streets surrounded on three sides a densely built-up plot of ground. On the fourth side this area was bordered by large manufacturing courtyard B. The plot, 18.5 x 12.15 m, was fully

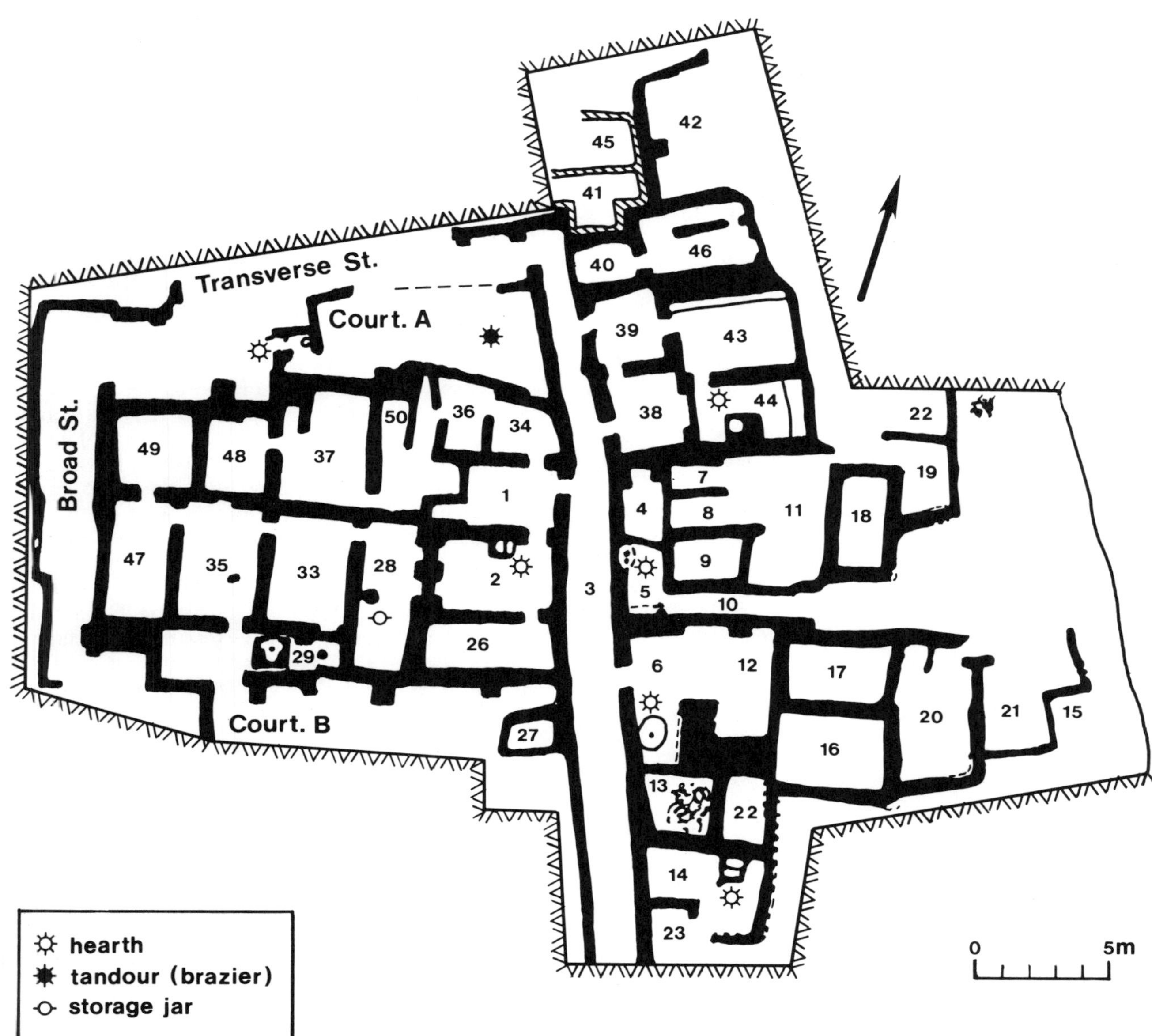

Figure 13.   *Excavation 5. Plan of uncovered structures. Hatching indicates walls of late stage.* Key— H: *hearth;* T: *tandour (brazier);* sj: *storage jar.*

uncovered and furnished a clear picture of the division into separate household-manufacturing complexes. As a rule, the excavated structures were filled with rubble, and sometimes thin walls of greenish bricks, preserved to the height of 10-20 cm, could be observed on top of the rubble. In truth, the structures observed and named the first building horizon had been covered by yet another complex of buildings, completely eroded in the course of time. Although at first the plot seemed to contain an extensive multi-chambered house, study of the system of passages revealed that there were three separate complexes—apartments, independent of each other. The first complex included six rooms (28, 29, 33, 35, 47, and 49). The central unit was clearly defined; it contained the living quarters and a storage room, namely, room 33 and the dead-end room 28 which had a passage only to the living quarters. In room 28 there was only a single layer of wall plaster. At the northwestern wall was a dug-in storage jar, surrounded by three vessels. There were also three stone lids, an arrow shaft straightener, and part of a bronze punch. Room 33 had carefully plastered walls. The plastering had been redone several times and its overall thickness had reached 7 cm. There was a small niche in the southern wall, and on the western wall there were traces of red paint on top of the last plastering. These particularities suggest the room was used as living space, but also as a reception room. In room 35 there was also a niche and three layers of plastering. On its floor was a fragment of a large grain grinder. Room 35 had three passageways: one exited through a vestibule to courtyard B, the other two to neighboring rooms. Apparently this was a walk-through passage room, which, however, does not negate the possibility that it was used as a living room. The third door from room 35 led to the west, into the narrow, longish room 47. The walls of room 47 were covered with a single rough plastering. Dead-end room 49, connected to room 47, was also carelessly finished. It is probable that the last-mentioned two rooms were household utility rooms to which interior access was possible only through living room 33. Hearths were not found in any of the rooms described. In room 29, however, there was a large hearth, nearly rectangular in outline, with a small clay pot in its center. This was probably the kitchen, placed near the courtyard and beyond the living quarters. Courtyard B proper was filled with loose alluvial and airborne layerings, and sweepings from the hearths which contained ashes and small pieces of charcoal. In contrast to the rooms, fragments

of sun-dried bricks were rarely encountered here. At the eastern wall of the courtyard, which was at the same time the street wall, there was a small closet (room 27), which was clearly a manufacturing structure. Three ceramic vessels were found in it. Unfortunately, courtyard B was only partly uncovered.

The second complex of the apartment house was at first composed of three rooms connected with passages (1, 2, and 26). Room 1 had three layers of plastering on its walls and appeared to be, like room 35 in the previously described complex, a walk-through room. One of the passages furnished with a high threshold led to street 3. The second led to the north, to courtyard A, and the third to the south, into room 2, apparently the living room. The walls of room 2 were carefully plastered three times; one wall had two niches, at another was a two-part hearth. A rather narrow passage led from this room to elongated room 26, by all appearances a utility room. A single plastering covered its walls. On the floor bones of small horned animals were found. While this complex was performing its function, its inhabitants not only renovated the finish of the main room three times, but took steps to increase their area. Part of courtyard A was partitioned off with a thin, carelessly thrown-up wall, thus separating two very small rooms (34 and 36). These rooms were filled with brick rubble containing a large number of sherds and obviously belonged to the number of auxiliary structures. Courtyard A proper contained a loose cultural layer with a mixture of ashes and kitchen refuse. Remains of an oval fireplace, reminding one of present-day tandours, were found within the courtyard. Its diameters were 57 cm and 67 cm. The wall, which separated the courtyard from the street, was put together very carelessly, mostly not with whole bricks, but with rejects. Its thickness varied, and apparently in antiquity it was not a major wall but a relatively low barrier.

The relationship of the second complex to rooms 37, 48, and 50 is not clear. Room 37 was a large living room, and the dead-end room 48 beyond it was an auxiliary household unit. Room 50 was narrow and perhaps reconstructed as a vestibule. By a system of passages, this group exited onto courtyard A, but its plan was distinctly separated from the second complex and must have been viewed as a separate apartment complex.

The complexes to the south of street 3 are not as clearly discernible, but even here we can observe different apartments. One such complex had four rooms: 38, 39, 44, and 43. Passages from street 3 led into two of them—38 and 39, which most likely were household utility rooms. On the floor of 38 were found three animal heads, a sheep, and two pigs. Room 43 was the largest. Its walls had several layers of plaster. At the base of one wall was a small, built-in bench. Room 43, then, was the living room. A terracotta animal figurine and a fragment of a stone biconical bead were found here. The door uniting room 43 with room 44 had a low, carefully plastered threshold. Adhering to the wall of room 44 was a rectangular hearth containing a small depression filled with ashes. Unlike the walls of this room, the hearth was carefully plastered. The overall area of this complex was about 32 m^2, that of room 43, 10.2 m^2. To the north of this apartment was a complex with two utility rooms (40 and 46) and living room 42, preserved only in part. In room 46 were found clay, terracotta, and stone slingshots. The presence of the latter was probably not accidental, since this could have been one of the outermost localities of the settlement.

The group of structures found to the south of these complexes was less clearly defined. The narrow, corridorlike room 10 seemed to divide them into two groups. To one group belonged rooms 4, 5, 7-9, 11, 18, 19, and 22. A wall-hearth with two small clay pots in its center was in the small room 5. The other rooms were also small. Because of the lack of careful finish, they were probably utility rooms. It was not possible to designate a living room, but then, this was an outer edge complex, part of which has been completely eroded.

Farther south, a distinct group of structures was uncovered. The combination of rooms 6 and 12 (with an exit to street 3 and two niches) was probably the living room, and the small adjacent rooms 13 and 22 were utility rooms. Room 13 doubled as a burial chamber. In room 6/12 there was an oval hearth with a central clay post. Still farther south, rooms 14 and 23 were separated by a thick major wall, with room 14 having a two-part wall-hearth.

During the excavation of the complex many burials were found. They may be divided into two groups: graves of children and tombs of adults. The child burials, principally those of 1-2 year olds, were in the corners of the houses, in pits, and in one case, in a cooking cauldron (burial 36) set in a corner of room 4. Approximately one-third of these burials had an inventory. Thus burials 29 and 38 had two ceramic vessels apiece, and at the neck of a young boy in burial 41 there were 19 gypsum beads. The disturbed child

burial, burial 105 in room 38, contained three stone beads, one of them agate, and two biconical gypsum beads covered with gold foil. During the removal process of the horizon and the deepening to the second layer, child burial 258 was encountered, in which there was a well preserved belt of paste beads near the pelvis. Adult burials were either single or collective. Room 13 is an example of the latter. The single burials were without inventory. For instance, in burial 170 in room 49, only an animal horn lay at the deceased's shoulder. Five burials without grave goods were encountered in Excavation 5 while uncovering the second layer. But there were also three adult burials accompanied by various objects: in burial 251 there were two ceramic vessels and a carnelian bead; in burial 271 a 25-30 year old woman was interred with a bead necklace and pierced gypsum bead bracelets on both wrists, as well as a silver seal; in female burial 272 there were a ceramic vessel and impressions of a woven basket.

Particularly rich was double burial 59-60 found at the edge of the tell, to the east of room 22. The major burial, 60, was that of an adult, apparently a woman, who was positioned in the customary Altyn-Depe manner: on the left side, with flexed legs. The extended left arm rested on two terracotta female statuettes (Plate XI, items 5 and 6). On the little finger were two rings of gold wire. In this burial, 96 beads of lapis lazuli, carnelian, turquoise, paste, and agate were encountered (Plate XXI, item 3). The small lapis lazuli beads found at the wrist obviously comprised a bracelet; among other beads were conical gypsum beads with gold covering and a large lapis lazuli bead in the form of a long, four-sided stick with a gold fitting at each end. The unique find in this burial was a silver seal (Plate XVII, item 12). It represented a fantastic, three-headed being, with a torso of a feline beast of prey; the three heads were that of a bird of prey and two reptiles (snakes or lizards). The other burial (59) was of a male adolescent. The complex magical symbolism (the two statuettes held in the hand, and the seal representing a fantastic being), leads to the preliminary conclusion that burial 60 is that of a priestess.

Abundant and varied grave goods accompanied burials in the tomb into which room 13 was converted. The continuation of the tradition of collective burials in chambers, particular to the Eneolithic era, is evident here. Such tombs were studied in detail by Sarianidi (1972) at Geoksyur, and as we have seen earlier, were also found at Altyn-Depe (see p. 10). The burials were sequential, and when a new burial took place the remains of those buried there in the past were unceremoniously shoved aside. In this tomb there were three layers of burials. As expected, the burials of the lowest layer were the most disturbed. The long arm and leg bones, and those of the pelvis and rib cages, were collected in a small depression where they formed a mixed heap. The skulls had been separated from the bodies, however, and judging from the number of them, 14 adults had been buried in the chamber. The inventory was quite varied. All told, 20 vessels were found, one of them of stone (Plate VII, item 2): a terracotta female statuette (Plate VIII, item 5): 86 beads, among them one of lapis lazuli and four of carnelian; a bronze ring; flint arrowheads, and two bronze zoomorphic seals—one representing a goat, the other a feline beast of prey. Specifically, the interred in burial 50 had a bronze ring on the fourth finger of its left hand and at its neck an agate bead. At the belt of the interred in burial 48 was a seal representing a feline beast of prey, and at the head of burial 56, a seal with a representation of a goat. If we divide the enumerated objects among the 14 persons buried, we see that the burials were relatively rich ones. Some particularities may be emphasized, such as the placing of a female statuette and flint arrowhead in a burial. Very likely a complete arrow was placed in the grave, but the wooden shaft and feathering had completely disintegrated. Seals were found in two burials only, and apparently they were carried on the belt.

Thus the results of Excavation 5 allow us to propose three important conclusions about the living conditions of the inhabitants of this part of Altyn-Depe. First, they lived in small, separate house-apartments containing 4 or 5 small rooms. The area of the rooms designated living rooms is between 10 m^2 and 13 m^2; the area of the household utility rooms is between 3.5 m^2 and 8.5 m^2. The houses are notable for the carefulness of finish and relative regularity of plan. Thus the first apartment complex is comprised of a group of rooms placed in line on the long axis, which shows dependence on an established architectural code. Let us recall that the Early Bronze Age structures uncovered in this excavation in the fourth and fifth horizons had an analogous plan (see p. 22). Second, the burials found at the levels of the two building horizons are characterized by a relatively rich and varied inventory in the case of adults and also in some of the subadults. The buried people had threaded bead bracelets and sometimes similarly manufactured belts; the wearing of metal rings was widespread. In its inventory the "burial of the priestess" was unique; commonplace objects, such as ceramic vessels, were absent. Third, all of the structures, aside from the distinctness of the floor plans of separate houses, were not geometrically regular in outline. This irregularity was evident in the street pattern which followed the direction of the structures only approximately. Not one of the uncovered streets was defined by walls in a straight line, but was made up of segments of walls which guided it in a general direction but at various angles. In a practical way, the streets had formed in areas left open between the massive blocks of structures, which were not built contemporaneously and account for the differences in the orientation of the walls framing the streets. A preliminary careful laying out of the streets with the help of measuring instruments was not practiced. In this respect, the pattern uncovered in Excavation 5 is close to that found in Excavation 10; it preserves the tradition of large Eneolithic settlements such as Geoksyur (Sarianidi 1965) and Kara-Depe (Masson 1960b).

Excavation 13

With the conclusion of the uncovering of houses in the upper building horizon of Excavation 5 and the poor perspective gained by the study of the much disturbed structures in Excavation 8, steps were taken to select a new locality where the excavation of the living quarters of the upper layers of Altyn-Depe could be carried out on a large scale. With this as a goal, a section on the northeastern edge of the Central Square was selected and the new Excavation 13 was started in 1974. It was worked under the leadership of V.A. Zabyalov, and extended in 1975 and 1976 (Zabyalov 1977). The structures of the excavated part (which is planned to be united with Excavation 9) were flanked on the south by a street about 1.8 m wide. This street led to a deep depression evident in the relief of the locality and the patches of wetness after rains. Below the northern face of the depression, Excavation 11 was started, and here walls with turrets were found flanking a supplementary entrance to Altyn-Depe (see p. 27). From the north the excavated part is bordered by courtyards B and C, which were filled with loose earth and rubbish. Here apartment complexes with five or six rooms united by a system of passages can be discerned.

The household interior courtyard A was located in the center of the uncovered part. At one of its walls a rectangular room had been constructed (40), which at least at some stage was utilized as a burial chamber. The first complex encountered was composed of four rooms (4 to 7). Two of these, room 4, with an area of 8.75 m^2, and room 7, with the same area, have oval heating hearths on their floors and very likely were living rooms. In the second complex, living room 11 had an oval floor hearth and an area of 9 m^2. In these and adjacent rooms a considerable number of ceramic and alabaster spindle whorls were found.

The structures uncovered in 1975 contained many painted ceramics of the Namazga IV type, among them large complete vessels located in room corners. While the artifacts from this deeper level, compared with those uncovered above it, may not belong directly to the final period of the Early Bronze Age, they do represent the first stage of assemblages of the Namazga V type, in which unbroken vessels from an earlier period could have been preserved. Three complexes, apartments comprised of four to six rooms, can be readily discerned. The first complex involves rooms 47-50. These last two have the areas of 9 m^2 and 10 m^2 respectively, and since they have oval hearths on their floors, they may be classified as living quarters. One of the walls of room 48 had a niche and below it a small, well-plastered bench. It is possible that they held cult objects and that the room had the auxiliary function of a domestic sanctuary. In neighboring room 47, three unfired animal figurines were found. The second complex is remarkable for its size. It contains rooms 35 to 37, and 44 to 46. Room 44 (9 m^2), with a rectangular heating hearth identical to the one found in Excavation 10, was the living room. The third complex contained rooms 38, 39, and 41 to 43. Because of their careful finish rooms 39 (7 m^2) and 48 (8 m^2) may be regarded as living quarters. The find of stone hide smoothers in two rooms of the complex was notable. Stone mortars and pestles were present in all three complexes. During their functional existence, the complexes

were renovated and reconstructed several times. In some rooms the clay floor was renewed four times. Of the 15 male subadult burials, only one contained a ceramic vessel. Three of the seven adult burials had such a vessel. Room 40 in courtyard A, mentioned above, contained disturbed parts of two deceased; it is possible that these remains were transferred here at some stage. Burials outside the room proved to be undisturbed. The burials next to an unfilled burial chamber are somewhat strange. For one reason or another, they were buried outside the collective "cemetery."

The part of Excavation 13 labeled as courtyards B and C is notable for the amount of ground it occupies, and perhaps it represents a sort of square between houses. Here was an interesting structure: separate room 55, with the dimensions of 2.0 x 1.4 m. Its location and dimensions are characteristic of a burial chamber, but there were no human remains in it. At the foot of two of its walls, however, were 15 large polished stones with spaces between them filled with loose earth. Forming a second row, 51 ceramic cups were lined up, mostly upside down and sometimes several to a stack. They give an impression of having been purposely placed upside down. There were also bones of animals which, according to the analysis of N. M. Ermolova, belong to cows and sheep; small fragments of all bones are present, except those of the lower parts of legs, which were not used for food. The sheep bones belong to five young sheep and to a lamb. Of interest are the remains of two sheep necks, each consisting of two articulated vertebrae. They were evidently put in place as separate slices of the neck, perhaps already picked to the bone. Ermolova concludes that the osteological evidence points to a meal followed by the collection of bone fragments which were then heaped behind the stacks of overturned cups. These findings suggest that we are dealing with a cenotaph. The remains of the deceased buried outside were represented by vertically erected fragments of flat stones. At the commemorative meal a certain amount of meat was eaten and the leftover bones were placed in the tomb, as well as the overturned cups from which a suitable drink had been imbibed. Judging by the number of cups, the ceremony was attended by 51 people. An existing structure in courtyard B, a structure which was slightly heightened, served as the commemorative complex. The ceramics found there date it to a late stage of Namazga V. At that time the eastern part of Altyn- Depe, the site of Excavation 13, was abandoned and the inhabitants who were concentrated in the western part could use the ramshackle buildings for their ceremonies.

The materials of Excavation 13 are witness to the distribution of inhabitants in individual apartment complexes, much the same as revealed by Excavation 5. The dimensions of the living rooms, however, were smaller. Not one exceeded 10 m². Rather gross carelessness was observed in the architecture; the floor plans were asymmetric, resulting in many rooms with oblique angles. A grave inventory of rather bad quality accompanied the deceased.

The Elite Quarters

Excavation 9

The greatest extent of living and utility quarters was uncovered in Excavation 9 located on the northern side of the Tower Mound. The work started in 1969. The initial point of excavation was selected on the basis of observation of the grassy vegetation which covered separate parts of the tell. A large nearly rectangular building with a carefully worked out floor plan could be traced. The grass grew in abundance on the lines of its contact with the mud-brick walls and the cultural layers deposited in the structures. This enabled one to observe the floor plan almost fully before excavation; the plan became less definite as the excavation progressed. The uncovered building, notable for its dimensions, the geometric regularity of its floor plan, and the carefulness of its finish, differed so much from all the previously excavated houses that it was called the Leader's House. In 1970 the adjacent auxiliary structures to the house were found, as was a tomb with a comparatively rich funerary inventory. The long range investigations of this segment of the excavation were intensified after the completion of the excavation associated with the cult center, when the principal effort of the expedition was transferred here. The results revealed a careful system of streets running at right angles and spacious houses accompanied by rich tombs and burials. Thus it was named the Elite Quarters.

Most likely it was at the Tower Mound, or in any case its eastern reaches, where the well-to-do of the community lived. Already during the excavations of 1959 to 1962 two caches of objects were found within the walls, which, aside from ceramics, included valuable imported items, among them items of elephant ivory (Ganyalin 1967). In 1973, farther west in the excavation, a rich burial of a 30-35 year old woman was uncovered (Fig. 14, items 2 and 3). The deceased was placed in the grave on her spine, with arms folded on her chest and flexed legs, which later were placed to one side. The deceased thus lay in a "contracted position." Judging by the impressions on the bottom of the grave and also in part atop the skeleton, the body had been wrapped in a fabric rather than in a mat, the latter being usual in other excavated burials. A small platform built of sun-dried bricks was at the head. Around the head various objects were distributed, among them two small clay vessels; a double vessel of marmorized limestone (Plate VII, item 1); an elephant ivory stick, square in cross-section and engraved with circles as ornamentation (Plate XXII, item 5); and metal artifacts—a needle, pin, a flat shovel, and a silver mirror with a short handle. The collection of personal adornments proved to be quite varied. At her temple lay bronze pendants with two twists of wire; on the skull, a band of paste beads, apparently ornamentation for an embroidered headpiece in several flattened arcs. The headpiece contained 418 small paste beads and two carnelian beads. The necklace was also unusual; it consisted of 28 beads, the majority of them agate. It also contained beads different either in material or the technique of preparation: one was bronze, another shell, and the third was composed of lapis lazuli platelets affixed to a long perforated stone base. This burial of a "prominent citizen," which was discovered in observing the surface eroded by a downpour, once again underlines the special character of the Tower Mound.

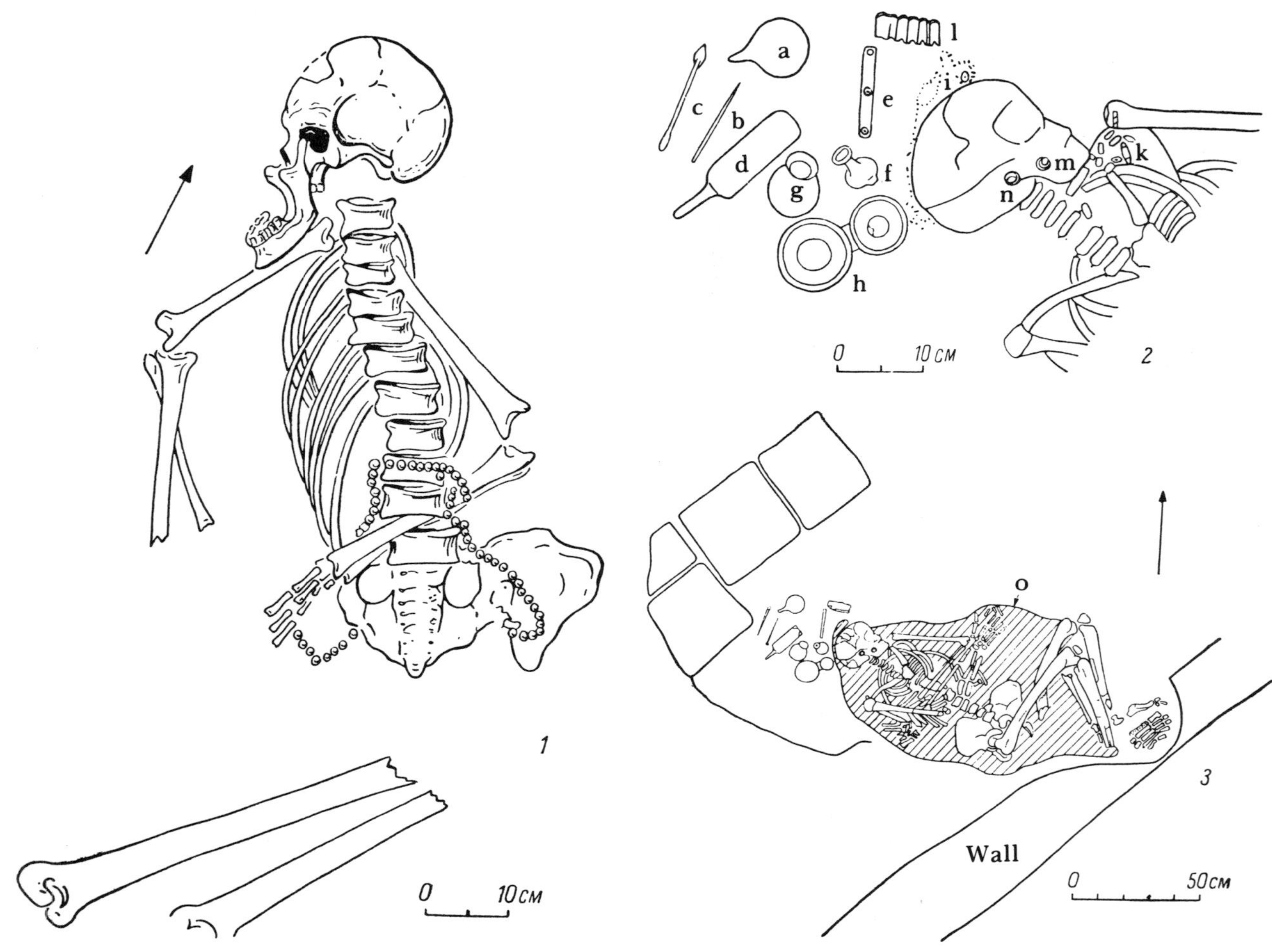

Figure 14.   Burial 198 (1) and 252 (2, 3).
Finds in burial 252.   a: mirror; b: needle; c: pin; d: shovel; e: elephant ivory stick; f and g: clay
vessels; h: double stone vessel; i: bead headband; k: necklace beads; l: animal teeth; m and n:
bronze pendants; o: traces of decayed bedding.

The excavations of 1959-1962 did not lead to a clear understanding of the lay-out. This deficiency was more than compensated for with the continuation of Excavation 9, conducted by Yu. E. Berezkin and N. N. Skakun from 1973 to 1978 (Fig. 15). In describing the structures uncovered, it is expedient to start with the Leader's House, not because it was uncovered during the first phase of the excavations, but because it serves as a standard for this particular part of Altyn-Depe.

The Leader's House was rectangular, with dimensions of 7.5 x 15 m, that is, its area exceeded 100 m^2 (Plate III, item 1). It was notable for the regularity of its floor plan: almost all its walls were straight except for the western wall which was built of segments assembled at various angles and slightly off from the vertical. The entrance to the house was from a street 1 m wide running along the eastern facade of the house. The street was paved with fragments of ceramic vessels, and the pavement had been renovated several times. The entrance led to room 2, which was squarish in plan and had a small niche and a wall-hearth. The hearth was the only one in the house and apparently its role was to hinder the flow of cold air into the other rooms which were not directly connected to the street. Room 1, in line with room 2, was of similar plan. The internal doors of both of these rooms exited to elongated room 3, which contained four wall-niches. From room 3, a door led to the central room 4, which had the dimensions of 5 x 3.5 m. There was a bench at one wall and a niche in another. All of the four rooms were carefully plastered. The two other elongated rooms, 5 and 6, were probably auxiliary utility rooms. Their walls were less carefully finished. In room 5 a small number of storage jar fragments were found. The presence in the house of small construction elements (niches, *et al.*), in addition to its dimensions and geometric regularity, points to its unusual character.

As mentioned above, the entrance to the Leader's House was from a narrow street. The street started at a right angle from a more important axial thoroughfare which was named Imdugud Street after a terracotta statuette resembling a man-bird (Plate XI, item 1) was found there. The same narrow street continued into a courtyard located immediately north of the house. In this way it formed a passageway leading specifically to the Leader's House and the household complex adjacent to it. The large courtyard A was filled with dense waterborne layers and a small amount of mud-brick fragments. There were no large amounts of ashes.

This indicates that the courtyard, as well as the Leader's House, was kept clean: ashes and other rubbish were carried to the edge of the tell and dumped on the slope, as was seen in other places in Altyn-Depe, particularly the Wall Mound (see p. 19.) Within the courtyard and contiguous with it, the small room 13 and the large room 20 were constructed. Judging by all the evidence, they were utility rooms. A discoid stone weight was found on the floor of room 13. The courtyard ended with open-walled room 102. Not far from this room was a tandour for baking bread; the preserved lower part was oval in form with a diameter of about 80 cm. In the middle of the courtyard was a separately standing building, room 11. It had been reconstructed at least twice and its interior was densely filled with mud bricks. In its early period, it was used as a burial chamber. Another burial chamber was located nearby; burial 9 was found to the west of courtyard A in the area of a separately planned complex to which there was a special passage from courtyard A. Thus the specific traits of the described complex were its large area, careful finish, and accurately planned right angles, which were not characteristic of only some rooms, but of the entire complex. Such planning implies the use of a measuring rope prior to the start of construction. These traits, to a greater or lesser degree, were typical of the basic structures uncovered by Excavation 9.

The regularity of planning was also evident in the street network of this part. Here the principal thoroughfare was Imdugud Street, 32 m long. In the east it was set against a sort of rear, perimetric complex of the Quarters of the Elite at the edge of the settlement, and in the west led to the center of an oval house. Skirting this house, Imdugud Street divided into two smaller streets. One was Mirror Street, so named because of the find of a bronze mirror there, and opposite it, Trans-Mirror Street [Zazerkalnaya; not in Fig. 15]. The latter, as additional investigation revealed, represented only a small segment of a thoroughfare which emptied onto a large lot devoid of structures—courtyard D. Perhaps it was not a courtyard, but a square. Indeed, communication with the rest of the settlement may have taken place across it. Both Mirror Street and the small street along the eastern facade of the Leader's House were dead-end streets. Mirror Street led directly to courtyard M, which was associated with large living quarters. Before Mirror Street reached courtyard M, it passed by an exit from the House with Pilasters at courtyard D. Thus these two branches of Imdugud Street were means by which the interior communication of the quarter was carried out. The structures in this quarter were only accessible from these three streets, and thus presented a closed Elite Quarter or an Imdugud mega-complex.

We shall now examine the separate household units of the mega-complex. The building methods associated with them were the same: in the great majority of cases the walls were built of sun-dried bricks, and only rarely were the utility structures of packed earth. The brick was basically of rectangular form, although sometimes with small variations: 38-46 x 20-22 x 9-11 cm. Sometimes we came across bricks with the dimensions 25 x 20 cm and 20 x 20 cm, which in fact represent one-half of the standard form. In some cases they were simply broken in half, in others they were specifically manufactured for laying at the junctures of walls.

The structures examined belonged to the second building horizon. Other buildings had been constructed on top of them during the Bronze Age, but only segments of walls 1-1.5 bricks thick remained in places. Also, the earlier rooms were partly filled with rubble. Because of the rubble, it is possible to judge that the late buildings were concentrated mostly to the east of the Leader's House. In parts to the west of this complex and courtyard A adjacent to it, the buildings of the basic, second horizon were simply filled with loose cultural layers about 40 cm thick, and in places with large dumpings of ash.

Let us first look at a group of structures to the south of the Leader's House. They are concentrated in a single massive enclosure of clearly rectangular appearance framed on the west by the street leading toward the entrance of the Leader's House and on the south by Imdugud Street. To the north, the frame was continued as a straight massive wall almost parallel to Imdugud Street. Apparently, the basic rectangle was completed by a wall in the east, but the erosional lowering of the mound there resulted in the destruction of the building remains. The main thoroughfare originally had the width of 2.15 m to 2.3 m, but because of the thickening of the house walls, it had been reduced to between 1.1 m and 1.6 m. The street was paved with flat sherds, mostly from large, thick-walled vessels. At one place it was possible to study the nature of the slope. There was a building on the surface of the slope during the Middle Bronze Age. The slope was covered with bricks which preserved the incline to a considerable degree in later times. At the edge of the slope, running parallel to the wall framing Imdugud Street, there was a

low wall about 0.5 m thick. In it was a small gate for exiting beyond the confines of the settlement.

The rectangle framed by the streets and thick walls was divided inside into a number of localities united by passages. These represented several household complexes named during the excavation after specific traits of their outlines or after finds. Such was the House with the Sanctuary, which was composed of eight rooms and occupied an area of about 90 m^2. The passage from Imdugud Street led into a narrow entryway where, in the wall opposite the entrance, there were two niches (room 32). The carefully plastered large rooms 30 and 36 in this house were living rooms. They occupied 14 m^2. Adjacent to room 30 was the narrow utility room 29. These rooms formed together the initial block outline so characteristic of Altyn-Depe. In the floor of room 36 was an oval depression for the heating hearth and at one of the short walls, a narrow bench. The auxiliary structures in room 33, centered in the house and with the dimensions of 4.1 x 2.7 m, were particularly interesting. Along two of its walls were narrow benches, and in the long walls, niches. In the center of the room was an oval hearth platform with a diameter of 70 cm; it was slightly elevated above the floor and had a small depression in its center with traces indicating prolonged use of fire. Hearth-altars, oval in section, were characteristic of the Eneolithic sanctuaries of Geoksyur, and as we have seen, also in the Eneolithic layers of Altyn-Depe (see p. 8). It can be inferred that, in this case, we are dealing with a house sanctuary. Here also was found a leg of a large terracotta statuette. Like the Leader's House, this complex was clean and free of rubbish.

The utility and courtyard parts tied in with the complex were fully separated from the living quarters. They occupied an area of 21 x 7 m, and were comprised of a courtyard (37) and three auxiliary structures (46-48). This complex had a separate entrance from Imdugud Street. In the courtyard and structures there were hearths of various types and dimensions. Thus in the courtyard, in addition to the major brick hearth with the dimensions of 1.7 x 1.3 m, a much smaller additional hearth and a tandour, oval in cross-section, were found. In addition to many fragments of cooking vessels, a large quern, a flint arrowhead, fragments of a terracotta model of a cart (a small wheel and part of the body), and a head of a camel were excavated.

To the east of the House with the Sanctuary were the remains of another closed complex which occupied an area larger than 100 m^2 and was composed, at the most, of eight rooms (21-28). In room 21, a small oval hearth was found on the floor. A massively built hearth, occupying most of the space, was found in the small, squarish room 28. It was not possible to expose the outline and finish of this corner house to the point of desirable completeness since the closely packed rubbish in all the rooms made it difficult to uncover them fully.

In the northwestern part of the above-described triangle was the third house, which was named the House of the Statuette after a unique (for Altyn-Depe) find of a large figure of a goddess crowned with a wreath of flowers (Plate VIII, item 4). Together with a number of auxiliary rooms, it contained large living rooms with square heating hearths on platforms in their centers (rooms 38, 49, and 52). The largest, room 49, had the area of 25 m^2. Altogether there were seven rooms. The exit was oriented to the north, and appeared to lead to its courtyard, which during excavation was given the conditional numbers 53 and 57. By passage through courtyard A, this house was connected to the street which led to the Leader's House.

In the above-mentioned courtyard (53 and 57), there was a separate structure, which because of the number of hearths concentrated in it was called the Baker's House. Nearly rectangular in outline, occupying slightly more than 40 m^2, the Baker's House was built at an angle to the main rectangular block previously mentioned and was differentiated by the low quality of its construction and finish. The main part of the house consisted of two rectangular rooms, 56 and 58, with the latter having in its center a heating hearth on a square platform. A five-petalled silver seal was found here. Later, on each side of the central part, narrow rooms 55 and 60 were constructed. Their outline and the character of the finds suggest that they were utility rooms. Thus in room 60 many fragments of storage jars, two stone pestles, unfired sling shots, and a ceramic disc which served as a scraper were found. The find in room 56 of a two-chambered oven which occupied almost one-fourth of its area was somewhat unusual. Within the confines of the courtyard, there were two additional circular hearths. As in the case of the Leader's House, the courtyard part stood out because of its relative cleanliness and the absence of ashes. Below the western facade of the central part of the house was long room 59, in which two ceramic spindle whorls were found. The separately standing Baker's House was unlike the basically multi-chambered houses found in Excavation 9; it was an isolated case.

Judging by the uncovered segments of walls within the confines of the rectangle, there was yet another extensive, multi-chambered house which occupied its northeastern part. Here, however, the angle of the slope is so pronounced that one could not expect to find adequately preserved remains of structures. Thus within the rectangular block, there were four large living complexes and one courtyard/utility unit included within the confines of the rectangle.

The real household utility center of the above-mentioned mega-complex proved to be the area lying to the east. Here a sort of economic support for the Quarters of the Elite was found. This part was excavated in 1974 under the supervision of A.F. Ganyalin. Three planned complexes were found; they were divided by a small street and a small square, conditionally labeled number 65. In the center of the first complex were three rooms, 62, 63, and 64. The complex was situated astride Imdugud Street as if to block the view of the unsightly farm buildings beyond it to people going back and forth to their houses. Imdugud Street turned at this house and emptied onto the square (65) where it divided into several alleys separating the complexes. The role of this "transverse house," built of bricks and packed earth, is not altogether clear. Two of its rooms had their own exits to the street. From one of them a door led to room 63, which had a wall hearth and, during the very last period, a hearth which occupied almost half of the room. The latter hearth had a base filled with pebbles. Adhering to the eastern side of the house were auxiliary structures 67 and 90. An S-shaped wall had been constructed to enclose them. Farther to the south were two courtyard structures, 68 and 69. They extended onto the slope of the tell and were filled with ashes and loose, brownish soil, the latter indicating a mixture of animal droppings. In courtyard 69 a terracotta spindle whorl and 24 globular shots for slings were found. The courtyard was located at the very edge of the settlement, but in this part the protective wall was completely eroded.

The second planned complex, which we named the Farm House, was enclosed on the west and south by straight outer walls, and consisted of rooms 70 to 76, and 89. The narrow long rooms 70 and 89 were clearly auxiliary, as was, apparently, room 74, which had two interior closets. Rooms 72 and 76, with meticulously constructed thresholds, one (76) with a wall-hearth, could be regarded as living quarters were it not for their "walk-through" character. To the east of room 76, in an area labeled 75, were layers of the courtyard type, with a large quantity of loose, brownish soil. Here also was some kind of structure oval in section, with carefully plastered walls.

The third planned complex, located to the east at the very edge of the settlement, had all the signs of the above-described mega-complex. Earlier, a drain was discovered here which led to the slope of the tell. It was constructed of narrow vessels, from which the bottoms had been removed, fitted into each other. The drainage of sewage beyond the confines of the settlement, as well as the paving of the streets, are indices of organized care for the community's well-being. The complex contained two different units, probably dating to different stages. The later unit, correlated with the basic horizon uncovered in Excavation 9, was rectangular and composed of rooms 77 to 80, 82, 83, and 92. The walls differed from those of the auxiliary structures by their massiveness. In room 80 a silver pin surmounted by a goat's head was found. To the east of this group there was a unit composed of rooms 84 to 86, and 91. It had a different axis of orientation and was characterized by thin walls. Remains of three storage jars were found in room 86. Room 86 had finely plastered walls, a small wall-bench, and a niche; it was no doubt the living room.

The second extensive part of the mega-complex described earlier was associated with economic [household and farming] functions and was located to the north and northwest of the Leader's House. Immediately to the west of the Leader's House was the small courtyard B, filled with loose, brownish soil. Judging by the soil, this courtyard was an enclosure for livestock. Close to the walls of the filled courtyard were discarded mud bricks. In one such heap, in the northern part of the courtyard, S.P. Gultov found a small cache of two elegant statuettes with their shoulders engraved with "symbols of vegetation" (Plate IX, items 3 and 7), a black-slipped cup imported from northeastern Iran, and a clasp of whitish-greenish color. Standing by itself at the center of an entire complex north of courtyard B, was a burial chamber (9). Room 115, built across from the entrance to the burial chamber, was associated with it. There was a massively built rectangular hearth on its western wall. To the east of room 115 was an area free of buildings, a courtyard labeled 99. One may propose that the structure with the hearth, as well as the courtyard, played a role in the ceremony associated with the burial cult.

Farther to the northwest was courtyard C which occupied an area of about 80 m². Unlike

courtyard B, brownish soil and cooking hearths were absent. To the north, the courtyard was enclosed by a group of small, aligned rooms, probably store rooms (106, 108, 116, and 123). Another such aligned group was uncovered to the south of the courtyard (119-121). This extensive courtyard with its structures probably served as a sort of storage complex, and because of its size, perhaps a place of public assembly. Also indicative of this role is the essential absence of finds usual in the household units: only a spindle whorl and a small wheel of a cart model were found on its entire extensive area. The exit from courtyard C did not lead to the south, to Imdugud Street, but through courtyard F to the north, where no doubt there was another street on which loads of goods could be delivered to the complex.

The mega-complex concentrated around Imdugud Street included in addition two large household units whose entrances faced Mirror Street. While one of them did not clearly present solid, geometrically regular traits, such as we have seen in the houses located to the east of the Leader's House, they did differ in their substantiality and large dimensions. In that sense they were analogues to the houses of the southern group.

The first such complex, the House with Pilasters, was located to the north of Mirror Street. The entrance was uncovered and, judging by the find of a stone door socket, was equipped with a swivel door. The pilasters framed the facade of the house. The house proper occupied an area of about 100 m² and was bordered by courtyards on the east and west. The western courtyard, labeled H, was comparatively narrow, and, during the late stage of its existence, was made smaller by narrow, rectangular, apparently utility structures (197, 198). It was through the narrow passage of courtyard H, labeled 192, that the entrance to the complex facing Mirror Street was reached. Obversely, courtyard E, to the east of the house, was a closed, dead-end courtyard. The finds in it indicate its household functions: two spindle whorls and two unfired sling shots. An anthropomorphic figurine also found here indicates the possibility of cult ceremonies, probably associated with two nearby burial chambers, the small structures 124 and 125. They were in a dead-end courtyard, not far from burial chamber 9.

The House with Pilasters proper was divided in two parts, both of them having entrances from courtyard H. The southern part consisted of three thick-walled rooms in a row (160-162), to which a fourth room (183) with a large wall-hearth was later added. This group of rooms may have been used for storage. It must be kept in mind, however, that by just walking through these rooms one arrived at dead-end courtyard E with its burial chambers. The northern part of the house was composed of five rooms—164, 168, 169, 173, and 181. Room 169, with carefully plastered walls and an oval heating hearth in the floor, probably was the living room. The other rooms were characterized by numerous finds of stone artifacts, among them six querns, nine pestles, a fragment of a paint grinder, a balance weight, three mauls for breaking up ore, a cleaver, and four abraders for sharpening metal tools. There was a high concentration of stone artifacts in room 173. A fragment of a stone staff, apparently a votive object, was of particular interest. From this group of rooms one could enter courtyard E through a doorway with a door socket at its threshold.

The next large household unit in the mega-complex was the House with Rooms in a Row, which was excavated in 1978. Its area was about 100 m^2. The small courtyard M, at which Mirror Street ends, was in a later stage diminished in size by the construction of two utility rooms. The courtyard also contained a massively built hearth of subrectangular shape and ceramic pavements at various levels. To the south of the courtyard were two rooms (226 and 230). The first was almost certainly the kitchen: here were two oval depressions within a low brick platform, similar to that found in the Craftsmen's Quarters (see p. 35). In line with these depressions was another half-oval depression, probably for the accumulation of ashes which would be later carried to the edge of the settlement. From room 226 a passage led to a row of rooms—216, 225, and 227, and to 215 and 217, partitioned off as a vestibule and corner closet. A heating hearth on a square platform was found in 225, the living room. In it a considerable number of small whole vessels and stone pestles, a balance weight, and a hide smoother were found. Ceramic vessels were also found in room 216, where there were also diverse stone implements including a quern, a weight, and a globular counterweight girdled with a groove. Parallel to this file of rooms was a block of two rooms—a living room (221) with a heating hearth on a square platform and an adjacent, narrow utility room (224). The latter was partitioned during a later period. Here a complete quern, two quern fragments, a flat discoid weight, a grooved counterweight, a pestle, a

whetstone, and two fragments of stone tools were found.

Within the confines of the surveyed mega-complex, in addition to the Baker's House, there was yet another unit, inferior in dimensions and architectural quality to the basic ones. This small house was also located on Mirror Street across from the House with Pilasters. It is possible that it was built later than the other structures, and, having been attached to the outer wall of the Semi-Oval House (described below), occupied a square which once existed there. The house occupied the area of 70 m^2 including a small courtyard labeled 146. The small rooms, which were further partitioned during the period of their existence, were clearly utility rooms (137, 138, 152, 154, 156, and 158). Room 148 was particularly finely finished and contained two niches and a small wall bench. Originally it formed a large room with 150, but it was partitioned later. The finds in this small house proved to be fairly varied. In the courtyard, a wheel of a cart model and an animal figurine were found; in 150, a spindle whorl and an animal figurine; in 148, a cart wheel and two figurines, one anthropomorphic and one of an animal. In room 152 the finds were particularly numerous. In a corner a dug-in storage jar, fragments of a reliquary, a small silver knife, a neck of a large, white marble vessel, a black-slipped cup imported from northern Iran, a camel's head, a wheel from a cart model, an animal figurine, and an anthropomorphic statuette were found. Small objects were found in 154: six spindle whorls (two alabaster and four ceramic), two anthropomorphic statuettes, and one animal figurine. The nature of the finds indicates that this was a small house sanctuary in which cult objects and other valuable items were kept. This supposition is countered, however, by the absence of a hearth-altar. Perhaps the house was occupied by someone responsible for maintaining the cult center.

The problem stated above could possibly be resolved if the function of the last component of the Imdugud mega-complex, the Semi-Oval House, could be determined. Its function as a cult center has been guardedly approached (Masson 1976b, Berezkin and Skakun 1978). From an architectural point of view, the house, with its half-oval part facing Imdugud Street, which divides into two smaller streets bending around the structure, indeed presents an unusual aspect. From the Mirror Street side there is a flight of stairs with stone steps attached to the house. This is the first instance in which this material was used at Altyn-Depe. It is difficult to judge to where the staircase led—to some stage or dais, or directly to the roof. The interior plan of the Semi-Oval House, however, is ordinary and utilitarian. A wall without openings divided the interior into two complexes. One of these, the eastern, was entered from Mirror Street and contained nine much altered rooms, part of them partitioned.

Of note is the concentration of hearths in and around room 133. A solidly built and nearly rectangular hearth was also uncovered in the much reconstructed rooms 140 and 142. Among the finds excavated were some ordinary, and some rather rare, objects. In room 131 two terracotta spindle whorls and a silver mirror were found; in room 130, a seal in the form of a pyramid; in room 133, a spindle whorl; in room 140, three anthropomorphic figurines; in room 129 (a small compartment), a spindle whorl, a model cart wheel, an anthropomorphic statuette, and an animal figurine.

The second group of structures, to the west, was entered from Mirror Street. A high threshold led into spacious room 136 with a nearly rectangular wall-hearth; in the lay-out of an ordinary house this could be regarded as the living room. Immediately behind this room, however, were found three large and nearly rectangular hearths; farther, in room 147, very close to the above, was another large and almost rectangular hearth. That such a concentration of hearths in this part was traditional is indicated by the find of a large square hearth in the very top layer. In room 136 there was a spindle whorl, an anthropomorphic statuette, and a terracotta wheel. Similar isolated objects were found in neighboring rooms. A somewhat unusual find was that of copper slag in room 147. The western complex had another exit to courtyard D through room 151. The presence of a door socket indicated a swivel door. It is difficult to interpret the western complex as a dwelling, but by the same token it cannot be regarded as a cult center. It could be that it had a specialized manufacturing role, for instance, the smelting of ore and the preparation of valuable objects such as seals, mirrors, and similar objects. This problem demands further study.

Thus the analysis of the structures which made up the Imdugud mega-complex indicates that they were different from structures elsewhere in Altyn-Depe. These differences become even more striking if we examine the burials found here. Among them, four collective burials mentioned earlier when describing the uncovered structures were of greatest interest.

Burial chamber 9, the first uncovered, was central to the entire part of the mega-complex examined. Essentially, it appeared to be the principal mausoleum in which the deceased members of the local community were interred. It is now clear that burial chamber 9 was located away from the street, among multi-chambered complexes and household units. It was in the southern part of an elongated courtyard (99). Across from the chamber was a small structure with a solidly built hearth (115), and the burial chamber itself was surrounded on three sides by walls which created a narrow space, a sort of a corridor, around the building. The southern and western segments of the corridor were narrow alleys filled with ceramics (among them whole vessels), bones of animals, and other objects (for instance, part of a basket and a large wheel from a terracotta cart model). The much wider eastern segment of the corridor, labeled 10, was clearly used to carry out the nominal rituals. Three terracotta female statuettes and three miniature ceramic vessels stood here. These small idols and vessels may have been put here at the completion of the burial ceremony of a deceased person whose status required it. All of the statuettes have an engraved symbol of a "triangle with eyelashes" (Plate VIII, item 2). Exactly the same symbol was found on a statuette in a burial chamber associated with Excavation 5.

The burial chamber proper was solidly built, with the dimensions of 2.2 x 2.2 m and walls 0.5 m thick. The entrance on the northwestern side was apparently bricked-up after each interment. At the time of excavation the interior of the chamber presented the usual picture of mixed skeletons; as a rule, the only connected parts were those of the legs and pelvis. Judging by the number of skulls, 38 adults had been buried there. In four cases the position of the spinal column, pelvis, and legs indicated the orientation of the skeletons: two to the north, two to the west. The absence of an undisturbed skeleton which would be associated with the last interment in the chamber was somewhat unusual. Thirty-four ceramic vessels dominated the burial inventory. Basically, they were pots, and biconical vessels placed in saucers. There was also a vase, five decanters, and some other unusual forms (Plate XXXIII). A few necklaces found in the chamber were represented by 210 beads, mostly gypsum and lapis lazuli. Additionally, there were two stone arrowheads, two gypsum spindle whorls, a stone plug, and a bronze cruciform seal positioned next to the pelvic bone of one of the buried (Plate XVI, item 1). In type of inventory, the chamber is close to the one uncovered in Excavation 5.

The next burial chamber uncovered in Excavation 9 was a slightly elongated structure (11) located separately in courtyard A (Fig. 16). Its dimensions were 2.2 x 2.6 m. On the basis of stratigraphy and the level of its floor, this chamber was of a somewhat earlier period than the Leader's House and burial chamber 9. All told, there were remains of 14 burials—182 to 185, 187, 188, and 191 to 198. Among the skeletons partly disturbed by subsequent burials, different orientations were discerned: a northern (185), a northwestern (198), a northeastern (195), western (196), and southwestern (197). The skeletons which were moved were found in two layers, in places in three, and were concentrated at the western wall of the chamber. The last undisturbed burial, 194, on its left side with the head oriented to the northwest by north, was also found here. Most curious was the composition of the people buried here. There was only one male, 35-40 years old. Aside from this male, there were two children 5-6 years old, three females 20-30 years old, and two about 16-17.

The burial chamber differed from the others in its rich and varied inventory: there were two statuettes with the "triangle with eyelashes" symbol located in the northeastern corner of the chamber and 28 ceramic vessels, among them three unusual vessels in the form of wineglasses. In addition, there were one silver and three bronze rings and a bronze cruciform seal. Beads dominated the personal adornments: there were 417. They were mostly paste, but also carnelian, agate, turquoise, onyx, and rock crystal. A flat carnelian bead etched white was conspicuous. The beads were placed in an interesting, regular pattern. While those of semiprecious stones were placed on the neck, those of paste were formed into special belts set around the hips. In one such case there were 77 beads in the belt (burial 195), in another 70 beads (burial 198; Fig. 14, item 1). Relevant to this, the female statuettes as a rule had belts, sometimes with several strings of beads engraved around their hips. Apparently such belts were an integral part of the dress of well-to-do women.

Such traits also characterized two other collective tombs located in courtyard E. The first was located in tomb 125 and contained seven burials, six of which were identifiable: a man 40-45 years old, a woman 20-25, three women 12-15, and a child 2-3. The predominance of female burials resembled those in chamber 11. Unlike those excavated elsewhere, including those in Excavation 5, the buried were wrapped in a thin woolen cloth. Also associated with tomb 125 was a large female statuette with the "triangle with eyelashes" symbol. There were only two ceramic vessels, but there were two seals: one cruciform, the other in the form of a bird with spread wings (Plate XVII, item 13). Seventy-four beads were also found, among them one of gold, five of agate, and one of etched carnelian.

This high level of quality was also demonstrated in tomb structure 124, which was carefully investigated by G.F. Korobkova. Five women were buried there—one about 50, two between 35 and 45, one 20-25, and one 15-16. There were also two men, a patriarch of 60-70, and a man of 30-35, as well as four children between 5 and 10 years of age. The bones of one skeleton showed traces of ochre. The child burials were usually accompanied by vessels resembling teapots. Altogether, there were 11 vessels and four baskets, the latter indicated by impressions.

A female statuette of Namazga type lay in burial 424, that of a young woman of 15-16 years. Adornments were represented by three bronze rings, one silver ring, and 213 beads. Most were paste beads, but there were some of agate and carnelian, the latter ornamented with white etching. In a number of cases, it was possible to trace the location of the beads: a bracelet on the wrist, three strings on the head. In the last case we are no doubt dealing with a sewn skull-cap. In other cases the beads lay in pairs. They were probably sewn onto the clothing or shroud. Two seals were found in the burial of an elderly woman. Of particular interest was the find of a corroded, relatively large object made of low grade silver, which can barely be identified as a bird with spread wings.

Deceased children 1-2 years old were not buried in collective tombs, but in small graves and, rarely, in vessels. The graves were usually dug under the walls of the houses, quite often in corners. In the Leader's House and the Sanctuary House, however, there were no burials; the deceased were carried to the courtyard. In the House with Pilasters, one child's burial was found in courtyard H, and two in the vestibule (room 183) added to the row of rooms. One child's burial was located in courtyard A, five in courtyard 37. To the contrary, in the House in a Row, burials were in the house proper, practically in every room. In the Baker's House, five burials were concentrated at the back wall of utility room 60. In the Semi-Oval House, four child burials were found in the small partitioned room 132. There seems to be a tendency to

Figure 16. Excavation 9. Plan of burial chamber 11. The figures in this illustration as well as in Figures 20 and 23 refer to burials and vessels described in the text.

bury the young in separate graves within the household-living complexes of their families. If this is the case, the child burials in the Farm House of the eastern part of the mega-complex may serve as a supplementary argument in favor of the presence of a large extended family. The size of this family may be judged by the presence of two rooms with a quality of finish suggesting that they were living rooms. Altogether 40 children's single burials were found in the mega-complex, all without grave goods.

The majority of adult burials were found in collective tombs, where they were often mixed with subadult burials, the youngest age 5-6. Altogether, there were 55 burials in the four tombs, not counting those in burial chamber 11, which apparently belonged to an earlier period before the full functioning of the quarter under examination. Outside the collective tomb burials, however, there were nine separate burials of adults. Two of them were located within the territory of the "household support" in the eastern part of the quarter, at the very edge of the settlement, and it is difficult to judge whether or not they were late burials dug into the abandoned ruins. One of these, an adult burial (307), lacked an inventory, the other, that of a subadult (300), contained several paste beads. Another small group of separate burials in the center of the quarter has to be viewed in different terms. Here we encountered a definite concentration of burial structures, since burial chambers 9, 124, and 125 were close to each other. Near these were seven adult burials: in courtyard 110, and in localities 10, 109, 114, and 115. The graves of some of these reach to the level of burial chamber 9, others reached somewhat higher than that level. One way or another, their presence in the area of a burial complex was obvious. Also, we have to keep in mind that even after the accumulation of cultural layers in nearby courtyards, the walls of burial chamber 9 still stood high. Three of these separate graves contained practically no objects; only a ram's jaw, hardly a sought-after edible part, was placed at the legs in burials 329, 344, and 353. Three clay vessels were in each of two others (361 and 367), and in one burial there were two agate beads at the neck of the deceased and a small turquoise bead at the pelvis. Perhaps it was sewn on a cloth belt, in this particular case taking the place of the bead belts characteristic of female burials in the collective burial chambers. One burial (362), however, was unique in the inventory (Plate XXVIII). Here four ceramic vessels and four beads (two large turquoise, one agate in the form of an elongated oval, and one elongated bronze bead) were found. There were also two large stone objects: a small "column" cut from marble, 31 cm tall, and a long staff made of gray slate, 124 cm long. It lay on top of the body of the deceased, and clearly represented his status while living. On the basis of these objects, this was a person who held a special position in the society. We called it the "priest's" burial. The placing of such a person in a grave outside a tomb in which there remained free space (and in which, perhaps, a special space had been cleared), points to the unusual status of the person. One could suppose that the "priest's" burial and those of the "priestess" and "prominent citizen" contained persons of the highest social rank whose attributes and personal objects would "crowd" the collective tombs. Those graves which contained no inventory apparently belonged to "servants" who were not members of the extended family using the tomb.

Thus the manner of house building and the burial practices are witness to the special status of the Imdugud mega-complex. In overall plan, it was tied together by a system of streets and included seven large households, each averaging about 100 m^2 in area. The area of the living rooms within these households averaged 14 to 17 m^2; they were twice the size of those encountered in Excavations 8 and 10. As a rule, each large household had its own courtyard containing traces of activities relating to agriculture and bread-baking. In addition, there were two large, general public units: the eastern supporting "rear" and the storage complex to the northwest, both apparently serving the needs of the overall population of the mega-complex. The floor plans of the houses studied differed in their irregularity. The street network and its axial walls were at right angles in a considerable portion of the quarter. The right-angled courtyard of the Leader's House and the massive rectangular unit to the east of it were characterized by a similarity of proportions. This similarity was attained by the use of rectangular mud bricks, the principal construction material. This is evidence that the constructions were subject to strict architectural norms and codes. Finally, the plentiful and varied contents of the burial chambers, which include some unique objects, also underline the special status the high standard of living, the highest within Altyn-Depe, of the extended families living here. We shall return to an analysis of these facts later (see pp. 101-103).

Aside from the mega-complex, a number of other structures were encountered during the course of Excavation 9. Among them were several multi-chambered houses connected to a different system of streets than Imdugud thoroughfare. One such house was partly uncovered to the north of courtyard A. To it belong rooms 93 to 95, 97, and 103. Room 93, with a small wall-niche, appears to be the living room. A part of another house was uncovered to the west of the House with Pilasters. It contained rooms 193 to 196 (narrow household compartments and granaries) and the large room 200, which was apparently the living room and contained a heating hearth. The five-room house located to the west of the House in a Row was oriented by a number of passages to the north and occupied an area of about 70 m^2. Here the living room (219) contained a hearth on a square platform. Next to it was the dead-end narrow utility room 218, below the walls of which five child burials were found. In line with it was a fourth house, oriented by a system of passages to the west where its household courtyard L was located. The area of the house was about 65 m^2. Incidentally, the major, eastern wall of these two houses followed the direction of the major axis of the Imdugud mega-complex, as if to separate them from the adjacent houses to the west.

The floor plan of the House of Courtyard L is fairly clear. Three large living rooms associated with four closetlike utility rooms (211 to 214) were uncovered. In one of the utility rooms was a large collection of broken storage jars. In the house and its courtyard were four child burials. Less clear was the case of the multi-chambered house adjacent to the western wall of the Semi-Oval House. It was partially disturbed by a later trench entrance, but the preserved part (rooms 157, 159, 176) indicates the importance of the structure. Courtyard G could have been the courtyard of the house. There were a number of auxiliary structures in this courtyard, as well as an oval hearth with a clay post in its center. It is possible that the courtyard and the house with its passages were oriented to the south, toward the large square preliminarily called courtyard D, onto which Trans-Mirror Street empties. In that case, the house would be associated with the Imdugud complex. It must be pointed out, however, that the direction of its floor plan was different. A unique structure, room 209, was associated with courtyard G. The floor of this room was carefully covered with alabaster and there were nine oval depressions along the walls. At the eastern wall there was a drain emptying onto an unexcavated part of the site. It is likely we are dealing here with remnants of a winery, and this activity if of considerable value in the characterization of the economy and culture of the Altyn-Depe population. Several burials were found in the area of these structures. They were clearly dug in abandoned areas partly filled with cultural deposits. Such was the group of burials in 232. Three of the burials lacked an inventory; in the fourth were three ceramic vessels and parts of a ram, the jaw and scapula. Of note was the concentration of child burials in the small utility rooms 186 and 188. Twelve were found forming an unusual children's graveyard. Judging by the stratigraphy, they also date to the time of the abandonment of the major structures of the Elite Quarters. This short account of the excavations of living quarters in Altyn-Depe presents a clear picture of the division of the society into groups with various levels of material living conditions.

IV

Investigation of the Cult Center

The size of the settlement and its general cultural traits, as portrayed by the archaeological materials, indicated the likelihood of finding a cult center at Altyn-Depe which would differ in its monumental size and complex interior structure. Indeed, the sanctuaries of the earlier agriculturalists in southern Turkmenia were present in several Eneolithic sites (Sarianidi 1962) and, as new investigations have shown, they existed already in the Neolithic (Berdyev 1970). The very first examination of the topography of Altyn-Depe, however, gave no definite indication of the location of such a complex. Only after a number of excavations were made at various points at the site, which determined more precisely its functional characteristics and specific natural conditions (all brought together in one of the seasons), was it possible to pose the question of the center's location. Later this was impressively confirmed.

The above question was specifically posed during the 1967 season, during a detailed and systematic study of the micro-relief and internal structure of Altyn-Depe, and was in part resolved by a process of elimination. Through many finds and excavations it was established that the entire northern part of the site was occupied by the extensive Craftsmen's Quarters, where many kilns for the firing of pottery were located. The existence and functioning of this extensive manufacturing center (which was briefly characterized above) over a long period of time gave little indication that a cult complex would be found there. Similar kilns were also found at the western edge of the settlement, which, at least at that time, excluded it from the areas of potential search. It had been presumed that such a complex of imposing buildings would be found in the extensive central part of the settlement, free of other buildings, which had been preliminarily called the Central Square. But there were no indications of its presence even when the relief was flooded. Heavy rains during the spring of 1967 soaked the surface of the site and the walls, rooms, and complexes became quite visible. The floor plan and dimensions of the narrow walls clearly indicated the ordinary character of unexcavated houses.

This process of elimination pointed to the eastern part of Altyn-Depe as an area to search for a monumental cult center. Excavations carried out indicated that houses and tombs of well-to-do people were indeed located here. For instance, on the Tower Mound were found two wall caches containing, among other objects, imported items of elephant ivory (Ganyalin 1967). In 1966, during work on Excavation 5, the burial of the "priestess" was uncovered; it contained a rich assortment of jewelry and a silver seal. During detailed examination of the eastern edge of Altyn-Depe an oval hillock seemed particularly promising. Some 40 x 50 m in dimensions, it was removed from other parts of the settlement and connected to them by a slightly raised topographic feature, apparently the remains of an ancient street. The surface of the hillock was fairly indicative: during rains one could see on the damp surface walls up to 1 m wide and a part of a large, rectangular hearth, quite similar to the platform hearths so characteristic of the sanctuaries of Mesopotamia and southern Turkmenistan (Sarianidi 1962). The surface of the eastern slope was quite distinctive. Almost devoid of ceramics, it looked like a loose, friable structure of natural origin rather than a cultural accumulation. Excavations proved that this area indeed formed an extensive foundation for a monumental edifice, the construction of which was conditioned by the nature of the surface.

Excavation 7, begun in May 1967, fully confirmed the indirect data which pointed to the singularity of the sloping hillock. Excavations during the first season established the existence of monumental structures at the eastern, main facade, although at first their nature could not be determined in detail (Masson 1968a, 1968b). Careful excavations in 1968 revealed a stepped, towerlike edifice clearly following the traditions of the well-known ziggurats of Mesopotamia (Masson 1969a). As for the history of the monumental structures, three periods were fairly clearly discerned. In 1969 the uncovering of structures at the level of the first building horizon of the facade was completed (Masson 1970a). In 1971 the accumulated earthen debris of the excavation was pushed aside with a bulldozer, and a separately standing building at the second building horizon was uncovered; it was named the House of the Priest (Masson 1972a). Signal results were obtained by the excavation of the third building horizon; it was begun in 1972 and completed in 1973. The excavation revealed that in addition to a number of living and household rooms beyond the main facade, there was also a complete burial complex which was the final resting place of the priestly community serving the center. The finds not only confirmed the cult nature of the center but also permitted a more precise definition of its attributes (Masson 1973d, 1974a, 1974b). In general, the uncovered architectural remains, as well as the archaeological and physical anthropological finds, present a complex of a fairly varied nature.

Let us turn first to a more detailed description, beginning with the monumental structures of the eastern facade, which indicated the three period history of the complex (Fig. 17). The periodization was established on the basis of an analysis of the sequential erection of the buildings of the complex, indicated by the seams between the brickwork of the different periods. Also, it was seen that the earlier structures were typified by bricks of a yellowish color, whereas the reconstructions of later periods often used a greenish brick with red intercalations. As a result of using such bricks, the reconstructed surfaces of the early walls sometimes took on a reddish paintlike cast. Cross-cuts to the base of the massive edifices revealed the history of the constructions, and cross-cuts of the cultural superimpositions onto the main facade allowed us to judge the history of the gradual disintegration and ruination of the complex. The numeration of the localities in the building horizons was carried out separately for each horizon, starting with 1.

On the eastern main facade, three groups of structures were determined: the monumental stepped platform tower, the House with Parapet, and the Corner House. Let us survey the history

of their functions. We begin with the first, earliest period.

Trenches dug in locality 9, the House with Parapet, and in the massive stepped tower indicated that the base of the entire complex being examined was on a small elevation dating to the Early Bronze Age, or Namazga IV times. The elevation's eastern edge was uncovered by the above-mentioned trenches. That it was indeed the edge of the elevation is shown by the inclined layering in which layers of rubbish alternate with brick fill and ash lenses. In the trench through locality 9 in these layers, burial 107 was found. There was no inventory. The skeleton was on its right side in a tightly flexed position; the head was to the south and the arms flexed in such a way that the wrists were positioned in front of the face. The painted pottery of the lower layers, mostly black-on-red, belongs to the late phase of Namazga IV, which is equivalent to Altyn 4. The find of the skeleton serves, above all, to point out the peripheral character of this part of the elevation during the Early Bronze Age, since at that time the burials in large settlements were usually carried out at its edge.

The earliest towerlike structure was erected on the cultural deposits mentioned above without any leveling of the slope created by their deposition (Fig. 18 A). It should be noted that the gradual leveling of the layers from an inclined slope to a horizontal foundation brought about a disjunction of the seams, which understandably did not render the erected structures durable and was one of the principal reasons for their relatively rapid disintegration. The earliest towerlike structure had a facade 21 m long and was oriented from north to south. At the present, the layers are preserved to the height of 6 m and contain the remains of four steps. The height of the first step, which was entirely preserved, was about 2 m, and at its base was a clay pavement (pisé) extending about 80 cm. Apparently, such a pavement protected the base of the first step from disintegration by rain and wind. The outer face of the second step was decorated with pilasters, three-stepped in cross-section. It could not be determined whether the third and fourth steps had similar decoration. At the top of the hillock, brick layering forming the massive tower was placed directly on the cultural layers of the Early Bronze Age, and the tower was adjacent to the floors and courtyards which were located in back of the main facade during the first period of the existence of the entire complex. Apparently, in external appearance, this stepped towerlike structure was three-sided and attached to the

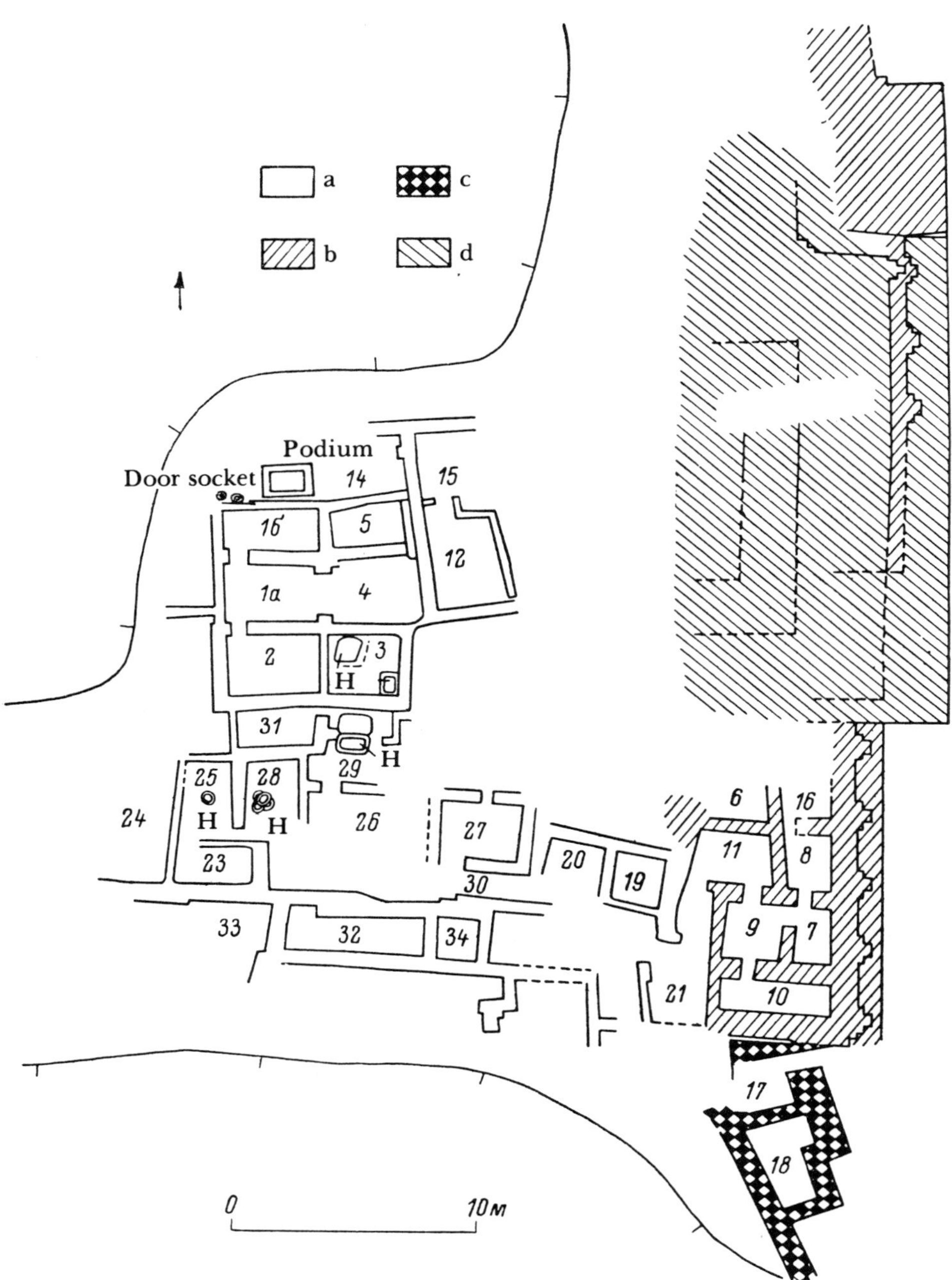

Figure 17.   Excavation 7. Plan of uncovered structures.
Key— a: *upper horizon structures;* b: *walls of the monumental structures of the Middle Bronze Age;* c: *walls of the Corner House;* d: *foundation of the monumental tower of the first period.* H: *hearth.*

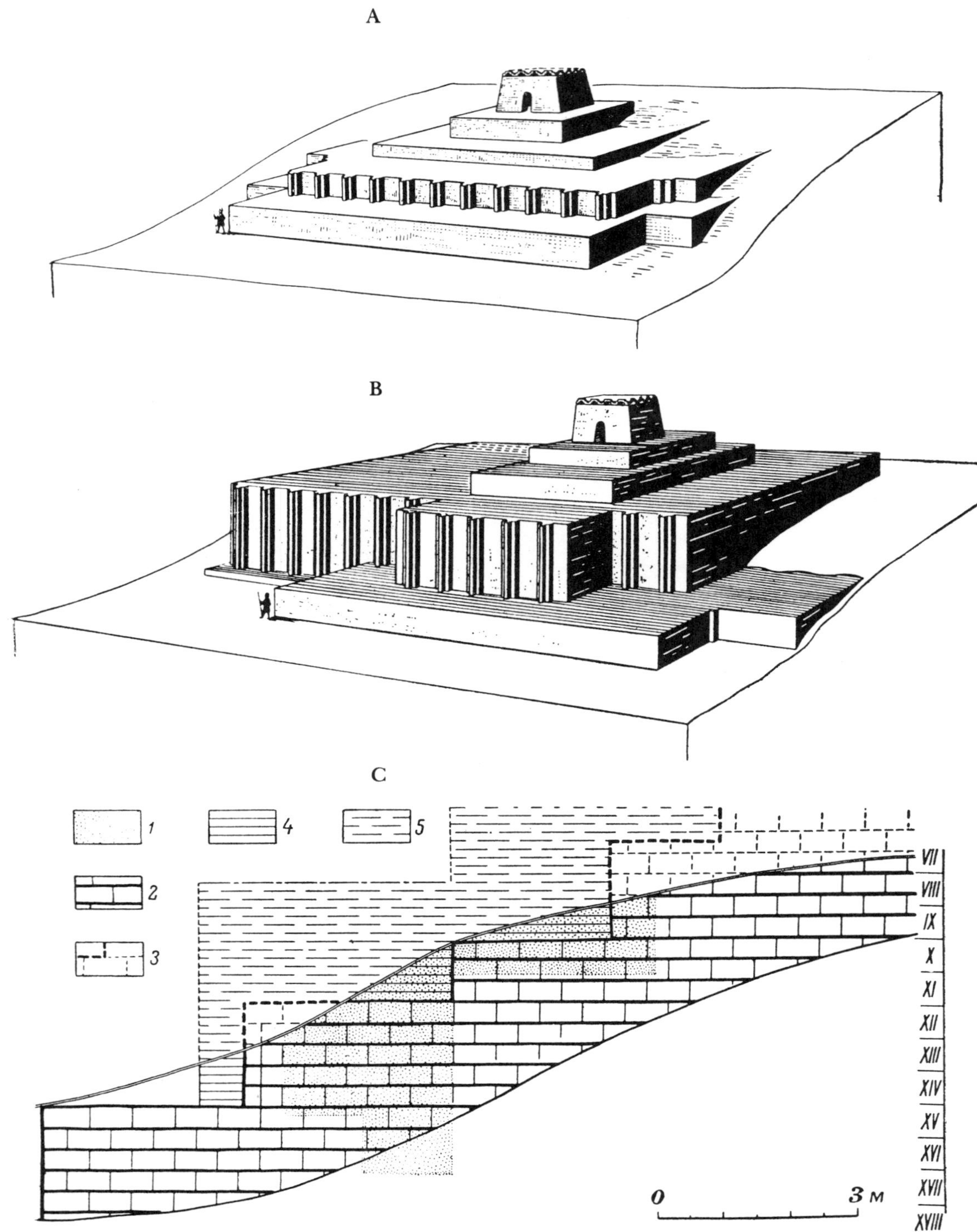

Figure 18.   Excavation 7. Structures.
A: *monumental tower of the Early Bronze Age;* B: *cult complex of the Middle Bronze Age. A and B are reconstructions of A. K. Filipov.* C: *cross-section of the towerlike structure.*
Key— 1: *contours of the trench and cross-section;* 2: *preserved layers of the Early Bronze Age;* 3: *reconstruction layers of the same period;* 4: *preserved layers of the Middle Bronze Age;* 5: *reconstructed layers of the same period.*

slope of the hillock formed by earlier cultural deposits. Neither the House with Parapet nor the Corner House existed during this period. To the south of the stepped tower was the gentle slope of the hillock on which the outer wall of the burial ensemble was built. (Of this ensemble, more detail later.)

The second period was characterized by major changes: at this time a whole new complex of monumental structures was created. To the south, the towerlike structure was preserved as before, but now it was much larger, and its interior was partly filled with the rubble of the earlier structure. The structures of the second period were made principally of greenish bricks, which visibly differentiates them from the much earlier structures. The front of this structure extends to 26 m, principally because of the addition of a cubelike mass on the northern side. The first step of the tower was fully preserved; the higher three were also enlarged (Fig. 18 C). The new outer edge of the second step was again decorated with pilasters, three-stepped in cross-section, of much larger proportions than during the first period, following the enlargement of all the proportions of the structure. The height of the second step reached 3.5-4 m; this presumes the overall height of the tower was, at the most, 12 m, provided its four-step form was preserved. Thus the second step was the same height as the Namazga IV top of the hillock, but the turret proper, even with the presence of a third and fourth step, is not perceived as larger than in the three-sided structure.

During the same period the House with Parapet was constructed as a contiguous extension of the stepped tower. The same orientation, the utilization of greenish bricks, as well as the strengthening with pilasters of identical proportions, indicates the contemporaneity of both structures. In any case, its main facade presented an architectural whole. During the construction of the House with Parapet at the edge of the Early Bronze Age hillock, a platform was erected with courses of bricks following the inclination of the slope. This construction again resulted, as mentioned above, in the disjunction of the horizontal course, which created seams of varied width. At its outer edge the height of the platform was 2.5 m. Continuous with its outer edge was the outer wall of the House with Parapet, and like one of the edges of the stepped tower, it was decorated with pilasters, three-stepped in cross-section. Immediately in front of the platform was a 3 m wide layer of lumpy greenish clay; it is not clear whether it was an artificial parapet or a natural

deposit. The rooms inside the House with Parapet were preserved to a very small degree, and judging by the uncovered bases of walls, they were small. The following points are significant: the axis of the outer wall of the House with Parapet was oriented, as was the axis of the stepped tower, from north to south, although the interior walls diverged at a slight angle from that line. The second axis of the edifice conformed to the direction of the walls of structures in the western part of the hillock and in part to the axis of the burial ensemble. The conditions cited clearly show that, particularly during the second period, an effort was made to unite the earlier, existing group of structures into a single architectural ensemble by means of a common facade (Plate III, item 2). Unfortunately, a strongly eroded gully running through the center of the hillock disturbed the northern group of rooms in the House with Parapet. Notwithstanding, two elongated rooms located in the corners of the house drew our attention because by their location they reminded us of household rooms encountered in Excavations 5 and 9. These are rooms labeled 8 and 10 in Fig. 17. In the latter, which was well preserved, a large number of fragments of thick-walled vessels were found; these discoveries would seem to confirm such a designation. A thick fill of bricks in room 10 perhaps indicates a vaulted ceiling. Additionally, fragments of cooking cauldrons were found in the rooms of the house. All this points to the utilitarian nature of the structure; it was probably for the most part a storehouse. At the same time, one cannot but note its obvious monumentality, expressed by walls of double the thickness of the usual structures of Altyn-Depe. The entrance to the house was from the west through a number of intercommunicating chambers. In part, room 21 is an exception. Its walls have the usual thickness for Altyn Depe—25-50 cm. The room itself was partly filled with rubbish, partly with a layer of clay bricks, and its walls were quite deformed. To the south of room 21 was an extensive mass of clay bricks among which no wall foundations could be found. Perhaps this was a staircase or ramp leading to the roof or second story of the House with Parapet.

The second period was the time of greatest development of the complex and was marked by the urge to achieve a united architectural whole (Fig. 18 B). Constructional inadequacies, however, and above all, courses of bricks laid directly onto the incline without preliminary leveling, caused changes demanding early repairs. As far as can be judged, the greatest danger was the leaning of the walls in the direction of the slope. Various repairs and underpinnings thus distinguish the third period of the main edifice of the eastern part of the complex. For instance, the second level of the stepped tower showed reinforcing work on some of the pilasters, which resulted in their better preservation from the point of view of the archaeologist, but clearly disturbed the overall composition. The work at the House with Parapet was particularly complex. The inclination of its walls was 20 cm at the height of 2 m. No wonder that at the place of contact of the House with Parapet and the tower, on the outside of the former, a 1 m thick wall which partially covered the decorative pilasters had to be constructed. This also delayed decay at the cost of disturbing the architectural decor. It is possible that at times separate blocks of bricks had fallen down and the subsequent leveling of the heaps raised the surface of the surrounding area, which resulted in the lowering of the overall height of the complex. Thus to the east of the first step of the tower were found huge heaps of building material, still retaining the regular courses and lying at a level corresponding to the early base of the wall. At the juncture of the tower and the House with Parapet a similar heap was covered with a parapet almost 3 m wide. Apparently there was an attempt to organize, or in any case to cover, these accumulated heaps. The surface of the parapet was covered by a layer of clay which had been eroded from the edifice during rainstorms.

Particularly revealing is the history of the Corner House located to the south of the House with Parapet. This group of structures was built during a period in which a cultural layer of 1 m had built up in front of the facade of the principal complex, that is, practically at the same time as the above-mentioned parapet of raw building materials. Two rooms were uncovered here, 17 and 18 in Fig. 17. One of these was only partly built. The plan of the Corner House reveals the following: a considerable thickness of walls, comparable to the monumental walls of the House with Parapet, and an attempt to protect or shield something to the west of this structure. Strictly speaking, this is not a house, but a wall with two interior rooms. Also of interest is the strengthened outer corner of room 18. Here was an attempt to form an architectural extension of the outer main facade of the complex, although understandably such a device fell short of the rhythmically spaced pilasters of the House with Parapet. It is interesting that no structures were found to the west of the Corner House; here we find only thick layers of ash which were dumped on the incline. It can be concluded that the structure was erected during the third period and differed from the others in its notable decay, that is, the primitiveness of architectural form. Its goal was to elongate the main facade and to cover up by its addition the accumulated heaps of rubbish, mostly ash. These were clearly signs of decay which heralded the approaching end. A number of filled trenches, perpendicular to the main facade, indicate a further decline of the complex which could not be saved by such patchwork or small repairs.

The above-mentioned trenches in the cultural layers which had accumulated to the east of the main facade illuminate the history of the destruction of the entire complex. At the same time, they indicate that during the functioning of the complex a considerable mass of ash, which was partly found in considerable quantity in front of the facade at the level of the early horizon, was generated. Above these ash deposits, starting with the first step of the tower, were sharply inclined deposits of building material, mostly clay plaster. Within the ash collections of small pieces of charcoal were often found. This warranted the conclusion that the charcoal carried to the foot of the tower by wind was generated by intensive activity in hearths of various kinds. At the same time, the ash deposits here were not nearly as large as those to the south of the complex, where a special structure was built during the third period in order to mask them.

Heaps of building material and various degrees of partial occupation were traced to the east of the above-mentioned parapet of the House with Parapet; they were tied in with the repair attempts of the third period. Layers of clay washed off the edifice covered the surface of the parapet. Afterward, pieces of plaster and bricks fell, alternating with the alluvial and wind-blown layers. A grave for burial 103 was excavated in these layers. Two ceramic vessels comprised its inventory. In one of the levels of accumulated rubbish, near the outer wall of the House with Parapet, there was a type of storage jar. Supposedly, this find demonstrated visibly the neglect of cleanliness at the monumental complex. At any rate, all of these findings point to the lack of a catastrophe leading to the decay of the center. Decaying gradually, the complex could not be saved by a few small repairs or additions of a purely cosmetic nature. And the population at large in the given period, not possessing the drive to save it, allowed the monumental complex, once so substantial and effective, to gradually deteriorate. The single, poor burial of Namazga V times, interred at the main facade, serves as a sort of symbol of the abandonment.

The major area of the hillock beyond the monumental facade can, in an analogous way, be sorted into three building horizons (or periods). Here the structures of the first period are also fully preserved. They have yielded the richest finds, allowing for a more precise analysis of the function and meaning of the assemblage of buildings. We shall now examine the characteristics of these structures and the artifacts found in them.

The four basic planned units that comprise the center can be discerned here: the early stepped tower described above, the burial ensemble which encloses the center from the south, a series of households with courtyards located between the ensemble and tower, and two dwellings at the northern edge (Fig. 19). With the goal of obtaining fuller evidence of the locational conditions of the complex of buildings being examined, the excavations were enlarged to include a small, elevated area connecting the hillock with the main part of the settlement. Here a group of household and living quarters, representing a special fifth unit, was uncovered. It is not part of the complex being examined but is merely adjacent to it. The extension of the excavation confirmed the suggestion, based on examination of the micro-relief of the area prior to excavation, that here was a small connecting street. On both sides of the street were rooms filled partly with rubble and partly with compacted refuse, making it difficult to discern the early walls and particularly the passageways. Altogether, it was possible to uncover 13 rooms, six of which formed a separate complex with its own exit to the street (rooms 17 to 19, and 21 to 23). It was possible to sort out the narrow, probably household rooms (18, 21, and 23) and the much larger living rooms (17 and 19). The combination of fairly large rooms with auxiliary household and storage rooms is quite characteristic of Altyn-Depe multichambered houses. We see such a combination in rooms 15 and 16, which clearly belong to another house. Here the living room was equipped with a wall bench and a small heating hearth in the floor.

Among the other structures in this area, a courtyard of 67 m^2, provisionally labeled 28, is of particular interest. Part of its walls are oriented on the axis of the burial complex, and the direction of the western wall is the same as that of the walls of the just-described living complex. Thus it seems that the courtyard was formed by the extension of the various architectural groups. The

courtyard itself existed over a long period of time, as manifested by three horizons of raw building material pavements alternating with compacted fill with inclusions of ash. Such floor pavements were not characteristic of household courtyards in Altyn-Depe, and perhaps this points to a special purpose for the area labeled 28.

The small street described above did not reach this part, the courtyard, but turned at right angles to the north and then zigzagged toward the main complex of structures. Apparently, in this way the street enabled an approach to the complex from the settlement. From this point it led to a group of household and auxiliary buildings which represented one of the planned units of the cult complex.

Here, bordering on the street, was household courtyard B, which over the time of its existence represented two stages. Initially, the courtyard was fairly extensive and included several rooms adjacent to the northern wall of the burial complex (44 to 46, and others). In the more spacious room (44) was a large household hearth. This hearth, as well as others within the planned unit, must have been used rather intensively, and the resulting large amounts of ash gradually filled the courtyard and some structures and stables in it. Then another plan was adopted when the level of the yard was elevated by deposits of ash and building rubble buried in it. Such a deposition of ashes in the very center of the cult complex indicates a substantially different function during the first period from that of subsequent stages, when the ashes were carried out of the complex. It should be kept in mind that not all structures distributed along the courtyard (and labeled with specific numbers) contained rooms with high walls and ceilings. Some of them could have been simply small enclosures and parts of the household. The finds of a considerable number of fragments of cooking cauldrons and storage vessels confirm the household setting of this part. In courtyard B a part of a twin-axle cart imitating an animal figure was found. This is indicated by a representation of its tail on the rear panel of the cart. Here were also found four terracotta wheels of various diameters belonging to similar models.

To the north of the area just surveyed there was the second planned unit of the complex, a group of buildings comprised principally of living quarters. A separately standing rectangular structure (6 x 8 m) contained three rooms (30 to 32). All of them had carefully and accurately plastered walls. The entry to the house was from the north, through room 30. The northeastern

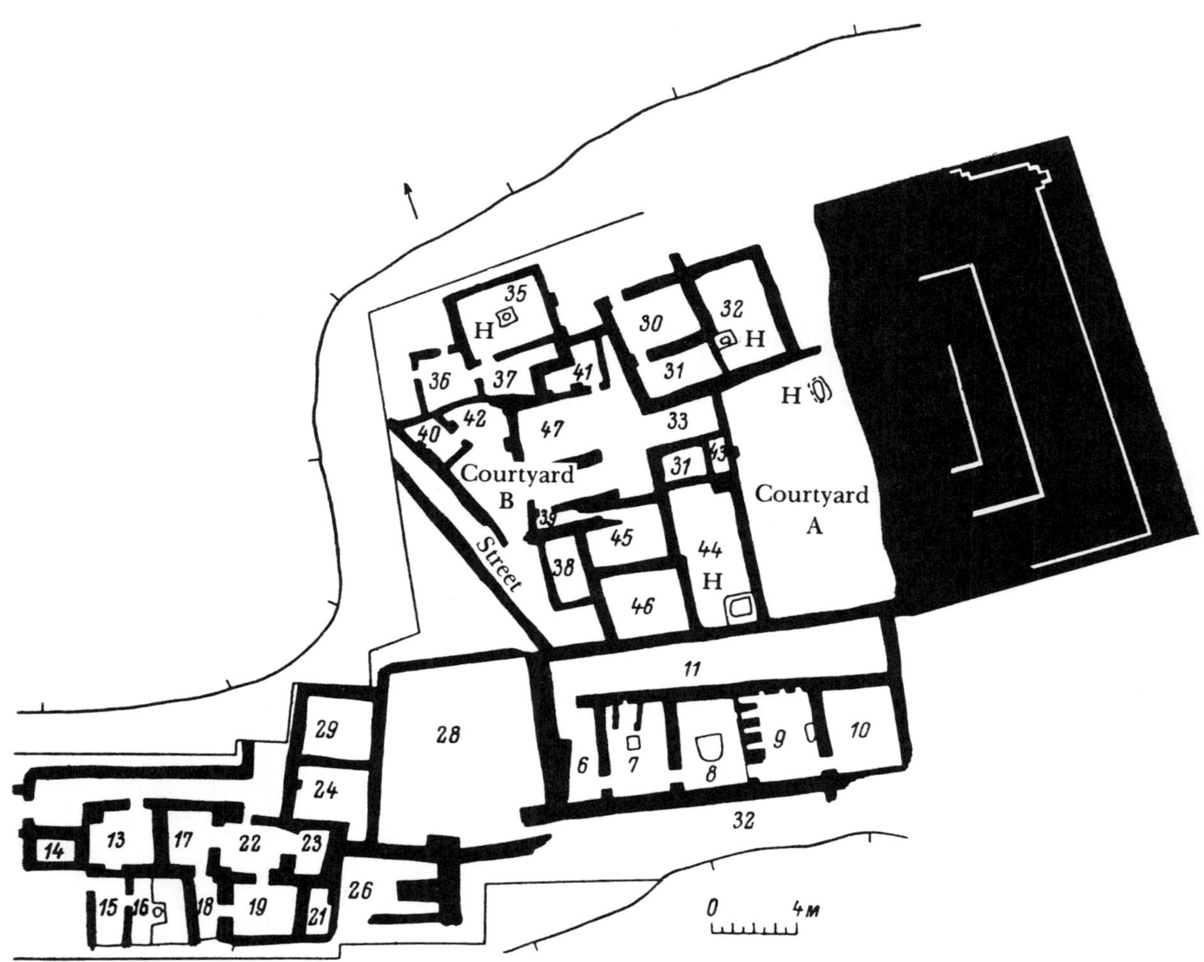

Figure 19.   *Excavation 7. Plan of uncovered buildings at the lower horizon level.* **H:** *hearth.*

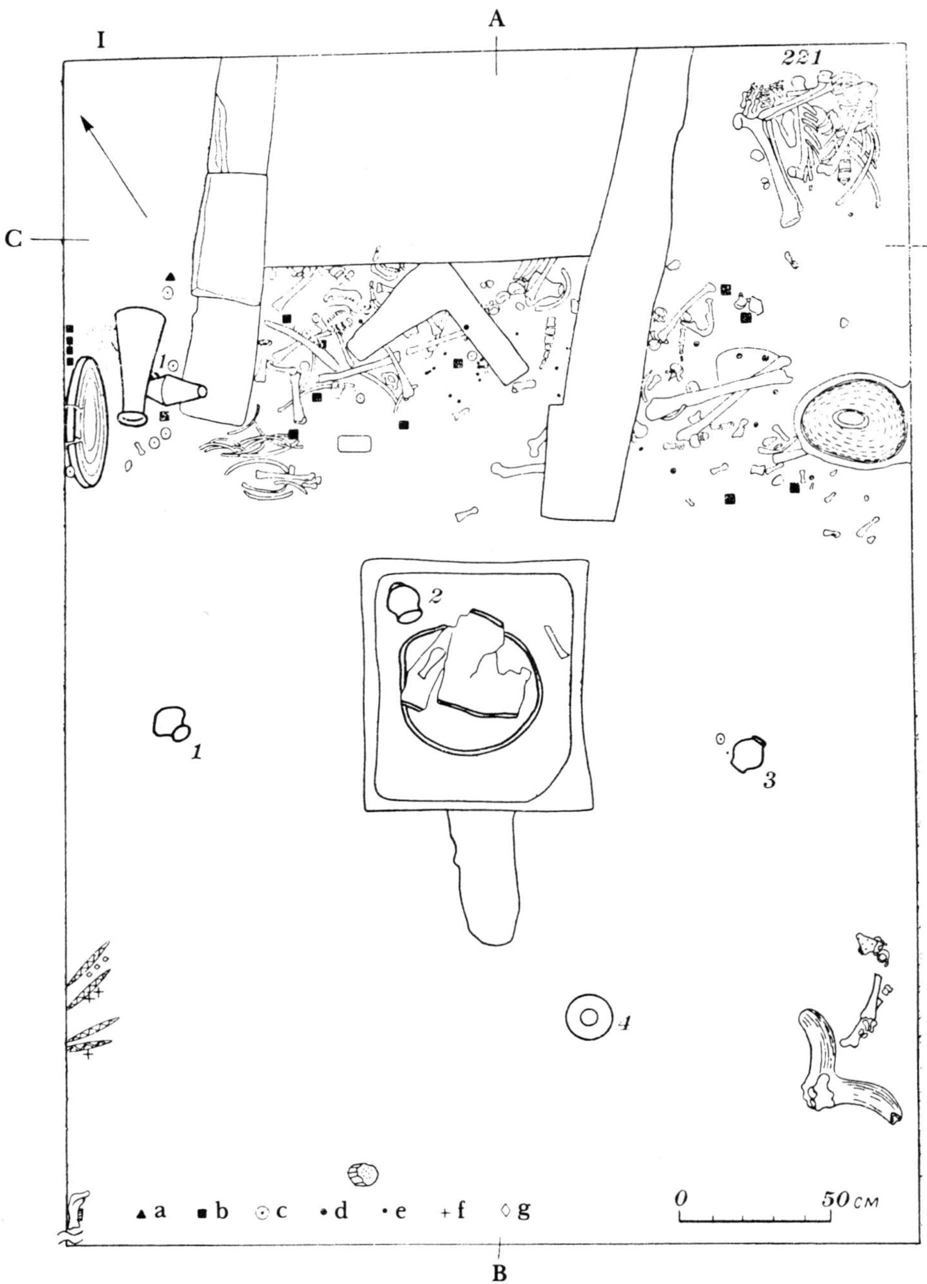

Figure 20.   Excavation 7. Burial chamber of priests. Floor plan of room 7 (I) and 10 (II).
Key— a: *carnelian;* b: *agate;* c: *metal;* d: *stone;* e: *lapis lazuli;* f: *dark stone artifacts;* g: *light stone artifacts.*

Figure 20 (Continued).   Floor plan of room 10.

corner of the house, occupied by room 32, was built on the incline of the slope and was almost completely destroyed by erosion. Five ceramic spindle whorls were found in the house and point to the common household activities, including domestic industries, of its occupants.

To the west of the above-described house was another small house which had been gradually enlarged by additional structures. Its principal part was formed by room 35, a living room (3.8 x 4.6 m) with a squarish heating hearth containing a terracotta spindle whorl in its center. In front, to the south of room 35, was a vestibule (37). Later, a somewhat irregular wall was built, thus separating 37 from courtyard B, and yet another room, also a walk-through (36), was built next to 37. It is evident that the principal axes of both these houses were aligned with the stepped tower, and it was apparently these houses that completed the assemblage of buildings in the north during the first period. The exits from the houses are oriented to the north, not to the south where courtyard B and the auxiliary buildings are found. It is possible that there was some sort of protective wall to the north, but the eroded edge of the hillock probably caused its disappearance. Thus both of the houses with adjacent buildings and exits oriented to the north were by plan separated from the household courtyard B throughout the two stages of its occupation. As a result the outer, southern wall of the three-room house took on, to the height of 0.5 m, a black cast from the ash deposits accumulated during the first period in courtyard B.

The area between the above-surveyed group of houses and the burial assemblage was occupied by extensive ground labeled courtyard A. It was 12 m long, and at most 6 m wide where it reached to the stepped tower. Rubble fill and a small squarish hearth were found in the courtyard. The courtyard also contained three clay slingshots and fragments of cart models; parts of the cart's body, a wheel, and a camel's head positioned in front of the cart were also found within its confines. In style, the dark brown ornamentation on the panels of the cart dates this object to late Namazga IV.

The burials found within the places described engender another kind of interest. First, there were seven burials of children, ranging in age from several months to 3-4 years, uncovered in courtyard B and the household structures neighboring it. In addition to these, in the three-room house at the south wall of room 41, beneath the floor of tamped clay, a double burial of children accompanied by seven ceramic vessels was found

(Plate XXXIV, items 12 and 17). The age of one of the children was between 9 and 11 years (burial 240), that of the other between 4 and 6 years (burial 241). The finding of child burials within household and living structures is not unusual. Somewhat uncommon was the find of a burial of a woman of about 60 within an ash deposit of courtyard B. This is the more strange since adults in this part were buried in a special burial complex, which represents the third planned unit of the area under survey.

The burial assemblage was a massive, rectangular edifice of very regular outline with the dimensions of 10 x 16 m. The main axis of this edifice diverges from that of the stepped tower. The thick, massive walls visibly set it off from common structures. It formed a row of five rectangular rooms (6 to 10) located south of a long corridor (11). All of the rooms were interconnected but were strongly differentiated by the nature of the finds they contained. The finds reflected the varied functions of the rooms within the overall system. Thus narrow room 6 was devoid of finds and had the role of a sort of vestibule connected with the main corridor.

Room 7 is of special interest (Fig. 20). A large number of objects covered with heaps of bricks were lying on the floor, and above them brick rubble (which appeared to be the foundations of structures of the second layer) was preserved. In antiquity the floor was covered with a woven mat, impressions of which were found throughout the room. In the center there was a clay-plastered podium-hearth, rectangular in section, with a low rim and an oval depression in the center covered with sherds of a thick-walled vessel. On the hearth was a small biconical vessel, perhaps used for libations. Two additional vessels lay directly on the floor around the podium. Near the passageway leading to room 8, the horns of a mountain sheep were found; earlier they apparently had been hung above the passageway. According to the analysis of N.M. Ermolova, they belonged to a very old mouflon. At the western wall of the room, four bone sticks ornamented with geometric carvings were found (Plate XIX, item 2). A human lower jaw and six flat, crosslike artifacts, three made of white and three of gray stone, were also found. Apparently, these formed the details of a mosaic setting around the now disturbed foundation (Plate XV, item 1).

The principal place in room 7 was occupied by a rectangular altar of mud-brick construction covered with wooden planking, traceable by the rotted remains (Fig. 21). It was located at the

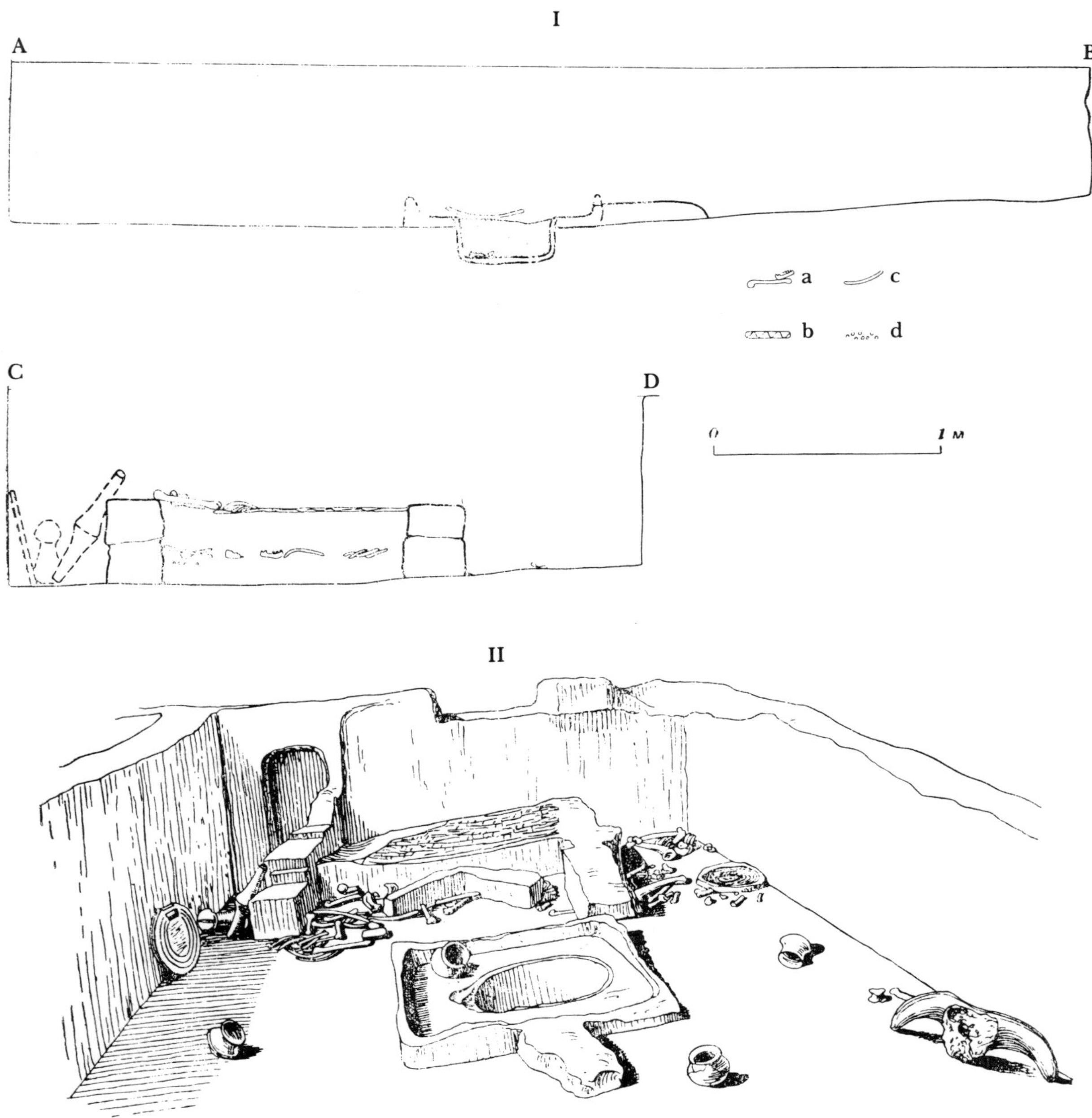

Figure 21. Excavation 7. Longitudinal section and cross-section of room 7 (I). Axonometric view (II).
Key— a:bones; b: wood; c: fragment of storage jar; d: beads and pebbles.

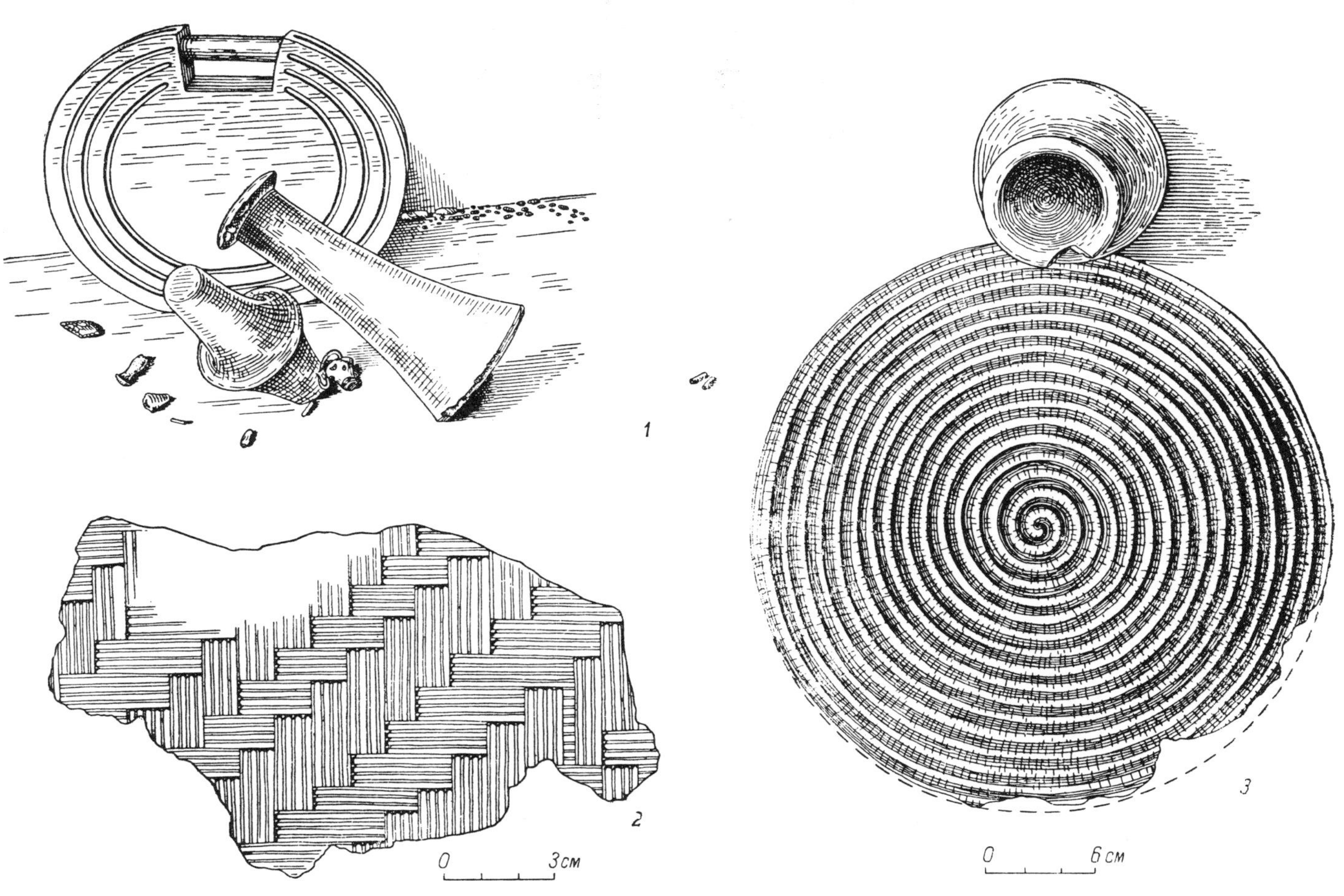

Figure 22.   Excavation 7. Room 7.1: distribution of objects near the altar; 2: mat impression; 3: ceramic vessel and impression of basket.

northern wall. Directly on the planking were the shoulder bone and ribs of an adult man. Above these remains, separated by a layer of clay, flat beads of lapis lazuli and elephant ivory were dispersed over the entire surface of the altar (Plate XX, item 1). It is probable that the altar, including the skeletal remains, was covered with cloth onto which the beads were sewn. Originally, there was a hollow space under the wooden planking, indicated by the bending of the planks. Later it was gradually filled with earth and human bones. In the fill, crumbly alluvial layers, pieces of clay plaster, and white limy inclusions were found. The mat covering the floor (Fig. 22, item 2) also covered the base of the altar, but a supplementary wooden deck, recognizable by the impression it left, had been built under the mat. On top of the mat were the disturbed bones of several people, among them two crania (burials 222 and 223) and the lower jaws of four other individuals. There were also bones of a small, horned domesticated animal. One of the crania belonged to a six year old child, and another, as concluded by T.P. Kiyatkina, to a man of 60-70.

Among the bones lay carnelian, agate, lapis lazuli, and gold beads. Some of them were arranged linearly, thus indicating the presence of necklaces.

The find of a gray and light gray stone plaque set in the floor at the very edge of the south side of the altar is of particular interest; the plaque contains representations of a crescent moon, a cross and two vertical bands (Plate XXII, item 3). A considerable number of varied objects lay to the west of the altar. Among them were three large objects of polished stone leaning against the wall and the altar: a flat, wheel-like "weight" with a small handle incorporated in it; a sort of pestle with transverse grooves at both ends; and a "mace" with a biconical widening at its center. Analogous objects are well known from Bronze Age sites in Iran, Afghanistan, and contiguous territories, and are usually interpreted as cult objects (Dales 1972a, 1977). Ornaments were also found here: gold (Plate XXII, item 2) and agate beads, and several strands of fine turquoise beads. The seals were very interesting: a lapis lazuli seal in the form of a cross (Plate XVI, item 11) and a flat white seal with a representation of a swastika (Plate XXII, item 1b). In the corner of the room to the east of the altar was a tightly flexed skeleton with its head and several cervical vertebrae missing. Here separate bones of other skeletons were also found, including a lower jaw. Next to these remains were stone and lapis lazuli beads, impressions of a woven basket, decayed remains of a flat wooden object on which lay beads of lapis lazuli, apparently ornamentation. After removal of the altar and excavation of the floor underneath, there came to light three perfectly aligned rows of beads, 18 in all: six lapis lazuli and as many each of white and gray stone.

The most interesting objects were found among those strewn on the floor to the west of the altar. Besides the already mentioned large stone objects, three oval metal clasps with openings for fastening onto some sort of object were found here, as well as a silver facing for a silver peg, a golden wolf's head 1.5 cm high, and a golden bull's head 7.5 cm high. Both were cast of solid gold with the small details done with a puncheon. Thus the wolf's eyes, eyebrows, and mouth were emphasized, the latter with two rows of dot impressions perhaps indicating the teeth (Plate XXIII, item 2). Two somewhat unusual openings on either side of its muzzle were probably made for inlays. The bull's head had horns and ears added; the horns were made of silver wire covered with gold foil (Plate XXIII,

item 1). The muzzle is roundish, suggesting a pig's snout; the mouth and the nostrils were rendered with depressions. On the forehead and in the eyes were turquoise inlays. In one of the eye-sockets a specially prepared bead with a slanting cut in it was inserted. The turquoise inlays and the ears and horns were fastened with lumps of mastic, now thoroughly dried out and shrunken, but preserving clear impressions of the details it held. As with the wolf, each side of the muzzle was furnished with openings, three to a side. Of the more durable objects found at the altar, let us recall the flint arrowhead, the large biconical bead in the form of a spindle whorl, and a large flat bead that includes in its texture the outline of a goblet with a high stem (Plate XXI, item 1). Altogether, 864 beads were found in the sanctuary, of which nine were gold, 101 lapis lazuli, 639 turquoise, and the rest other materials.

Room 8, despite its size, was practically devoid of finds. There was a large floor hearth, but no kitchen objects such as remains of cauldrons or bones were found. Room 9 was a collective burial chamber in which were found, at the most, the remains of 11 people (Fig. 23). Only eight of them were accounted for by the presence of crania, not counting the lower jaws. The distribution of the skeletons was usual for collective burials in southern Turkmenistan: the bones of those buried earlier were pushed aside, and only the last buried male lay on his side with the bones of the skeleton in anatomical order. The burial chamber differed from usual chambers by having the crania placed in niches constructed in the walls not much above the level of the floor. There were seven such niches: five deep and two shallow. In four of the deep niches crania belonging respectively to a man 35-40, a woman 25-30, a woman 16-18, and a child of 8 or 9 years were found. The inventory of room 9 was not extensive: 11 ceramic vessels, principally of the biconical type like those found in the sanctuary at the platform hearth; a woven basket (of which only the impression was preserved); four beads; and the scapulae and other bones of sheep, which in the opinion of N.M. Ermolova comprised seven or eight animals, most of them young. It is of interest that some of the crania in the niches lacked the lower jaw but sometimes were accompanied by some shoulder bones and ribs. As in room 7, fragments of lower jaws were dispersed over the floor.

Finally, room 10 also contained human remains, but in an unusual manner. In the southeastern corner was an oval heap of bones,

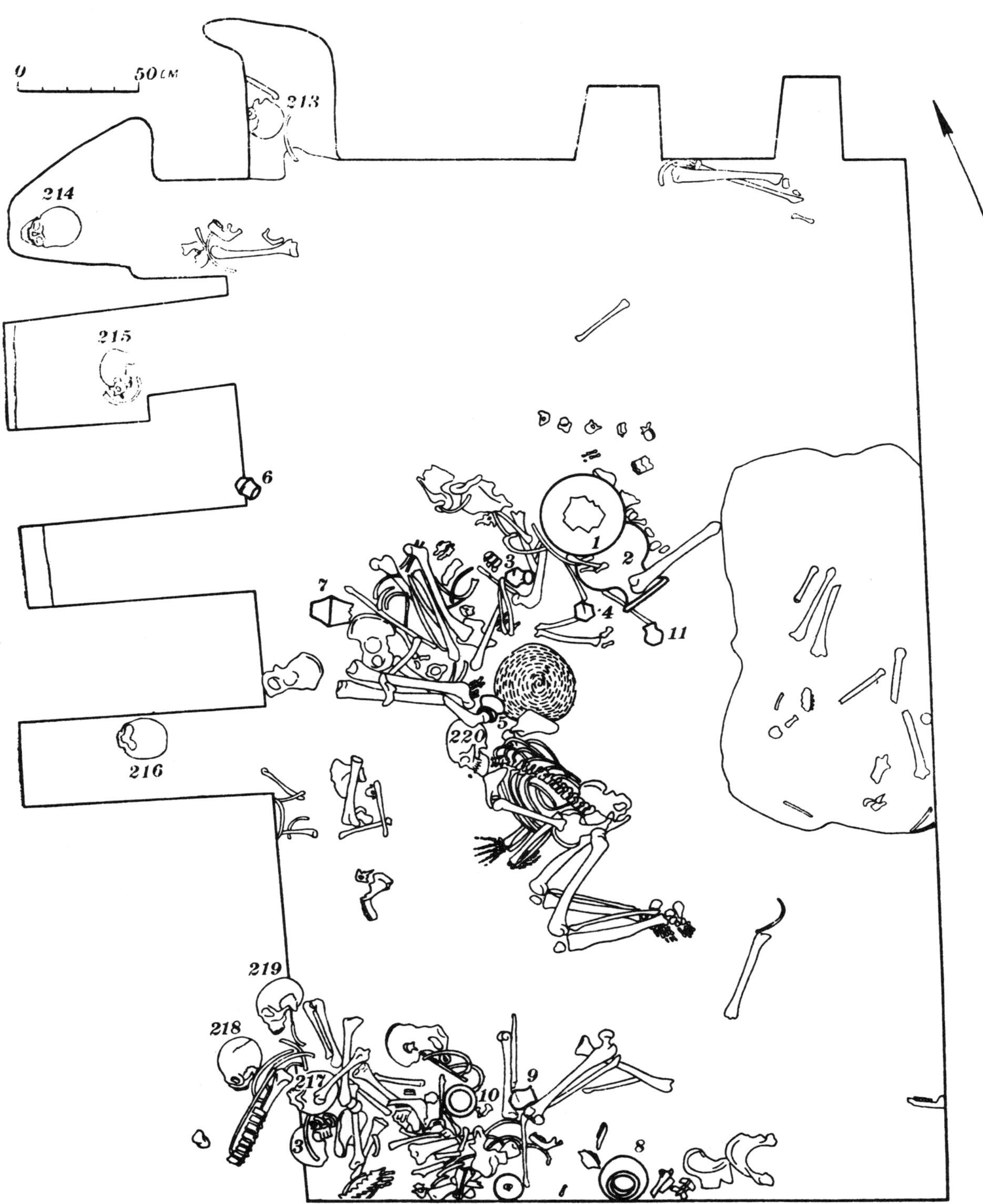

Figure 23.   Excavation 7. Floor plan of room 9.

including the long bones and crania of, at most, 13 people. Next to the heap was set a single ceramic vessel intended, it may be supposed, for the entire hecatomb. An undisturbed burial (235) oriented to the southeast, was found at the northern wall. Next to its pelvis there was a corroded bronze seal in the form of double-headed bird (Plate XVII, item 9). A small biconical vessel, placed to the south of the skeleton, apparently was part of the burial. There were two large broken vessels in the northwestern corner of the room.

The unique character of the burial complex is not problematic. Thanks to the extensive work done by T.P. Kiyatkina in analyzing the materials, it is possible to project some opinions concerning the burial ritual and ceremonies. Thus it is clear human remains were transferred from one room to another, and that the transfer took place with already substantially disturbed skeletons. As a result, the lower jaw from burial 219 in room 9 (where the cranium remained) was found in room 10. In contrast, crania from burial 227 and 232 were transferred to the general heap in room 10, but their lower jaws remained in room 9. Such transfers within the complex, with the exception of the skeleton in room 7, explain the "incompleteness" of the burials. Thus we conclude that the various rooms had specialized functions corresponding to their place in the ceremonial ritual.

The labeling of room 7 as the sanctuary is quite appropriate because of the presence of the platform hearth, a very well-known type of cult hearth in the Eneolithic sanctuaries of southern Turkmenistan, as well as in the Mesopotamian sanctuaries and temples. The nature of the finds in the room confirm such a conclusion. It may be suggested that while the next-in-turn deceased rested on the altar, the appropriate libations were performed at the platform hearth (see p. 65) and at the same time the sacred objects concentrated at the altar were demonstratively used. It is of note, for instance, that the handle of the "weight" is literally shiny from lengthy use and that the ears on the wolf's head are almost worn through. Further, the corpse, or perhaps at times only parts of it, was transferred to another room. (In burial 221, in the corner of the sanctuary, the deliberately severed head is missing.) Of interest is the find of human remains under the planking of the altar proper. It appears that they were crammed under the planking in an already disturbed state. Yet it is significant that just here the cranium of a man 60-70 years

old was found; with this exception, the average age did not exceed 35-40 years.

The empty room 8, with a very large hearth in the floor, may be looked upon as a place where the purifying fire which separated the sanctuary from the burial chamber proper was preserved. Room 9, the principal burial chamber, is a typical repository like those well known in southern Turkmenistan from the beginning of the Late Eneolithic, but in this case it was not built separately as most were, but was located within the architectural ensemble. The finding of several skulls in the wall niches engenders some thoughts. The singularity of such an occurrence suggests a special role for such individuals whose remains warranted such an honor. Because of the varied ages and sexes of the interred—a man, two women, and a child—they could have been members of one family. The remains carried to the burial chamber were accompanied by vessels for libations and, as a rule, by parts of sacrificed sheep. Finally, during the third stage of separation of the bones of the deceased, they were carried to the last, dead-end room where they were added to a neat pile. To be sure, it is not altogether clear why burial 235 was also placed here with the seal that accompanied it, underlining its special character.

Altogether, remains of more than 40 people were found in the complex described. Of these, 30 may be defined on the basis of sex and age: 15 females, 12 males, and three children older than six years. Yet the total number of those buried within the complex of the buildings of the first period was larger. Already in 1969, during the excavation of the auxiliary rooms of the upper building horizon, it was established that one of the chambers (32 on the basis of the numeration adopted for the upper building horizon) was erected on the ruins of a much earlier one, which served as a burial vault (Masson 1970a). Today it can be pointed out more definitely that the earlier room related to the lower building horizon and was added to the outer southern wall of the burial complex opposite room 9, which also served the function of a repository. Judging by the number of skulls, 14 adults were buried in the chamber (burials 110 to 123). Bones of 13 skeletons, already unceremoniously pushed aside in antiquity, were found mixed together. As a rule, only the long bones of the lower extremities were found linked together. The majority of the bones were concentrated in the central part of the room. In the western part of the room, almost devoid of bones, was the principal collection of vessels belonging to the burial inventory; the eastern part was altogether empty of grave goods. Apparently, the recently deceased were taken to the chamber from the east. At any rate, it was here where the only undisturbed burial was found on its right side, with flexed legs, hands under the body, and head oriented to the west (burial 123). The burial inventory consisted in the main of 24 ceramic vessels dominated by those with biconical form. The presence of a cup with black drawings on a red background (a late Namazga IV type) confirmed the early attributes of the burial chamber. The remainder of the inventory was represented by three beads and a flint arrowhead.

The decision to associate the above-surveyed room with the burial assemblage is well-founded. What remains unclear is the motivation for the location of room 32. Perhaps the assemblage proper was fully occupied by the remains of the deceased and it was deemed necessary to construct an addition which would join, through the wall, the sanctuaries within the assemblage. I should mention that during the 1969 excavations, the absence of seals in room 32 was cause for surprise since their presence is presumed to designate a sanctuary within the assemblage. By the same token, we cannot forget that the deceased interred in room 32 were of a different social order, and that placing them in the main burial assemblage would contradict the existing communal codes and standards. According to I.I. Gokhman, eight men and five women, between the ages of 16-17 and 40-45, were buried in room 32.

As we have seen, the entire complex of structures of the first period falls into four distinct, planned sectors differentiated by function: the stepped tower, the household structures and courtyards, dwelling houses, and the burial assemblage. Significant discoveries about the semantics of the entire complex made a more detailed interpretation of these sectors possible, and we shall return to this later.

A major reconstruction of the buildings in its center was characteristic of the next building horizon (or the second period). This reconstruction is also characteristic of the complex as a whole. All of the rooms of the earlier period were abandoned and filled in, and on their ruins, and in part utilizing the walls of the earlier structures as foundations, a separately standing house was erected in the center. Under it rooms 31 and 43 to 46 of the first period were eventually found. [cp. Figs. 17 and 19]. The house was almost rectangular in plan and consisted of four rooms. As with dwellings of the previous period, the entrance was oriented to the north. Room 1, a walk-through, was connected with room 2, on the floor of which was a rectangular platform heating hearth. Very likely, with its carefully plastered walls, it was a living room. Another room with an exit from room 1 was also in turn a walk-through to room 5, which contained a massive hearth in one corner. Appropriately, this room contained a multitude of potsherds. In room 6 there was a small stone weight. Various forms of hearths were found even beyond the confines of the house, attached to its northern wall. In addition to the hearths, various household structures were added to the outer walls; of these only structure 3 was totally preserved. It contained an unusual abundance of potsherds and also a flint arrowhead.

It is difficult to make judgments about other structures of this building horizon. To the north, the steep slope did not allow their total preservation, although the find of a platform hearth, placed almost in the center of a multi-chambered house of the lower building horizon, indicated that perhaps structures existed here. It is probable that Court A, a large open space, preserved its function into the second period. The rooms of the rubble-filled burial complex spread out to the south of the house described above. During the second period, only a few basic structures were built on top of them. Interestingly, here in the rubble fill to the south of room 5, a complete terracotta female statuette was found, the only such find in the three building horizons of the cult complex. In its iconographic type, with thick braided hair pasted to the spine, the figure fits into the usual group of terracottas found at Altyn-Depe. It lacks, however, the scratched-on marks. In the stratigraphic Excavation 1, there were finds of complete figurines under the floors of the houses. They could have been deliberately placed there because of their magical properties, as revealed in the literary sources of the ancient East (Masson and Sarianidi 1973:86). The figure found in the rubbish could be interpreted on the same basis.

Unlike the second horizon, the structures of the upper building horizon (or third period) can be traced in the central part of the complex over a considerable area. [See Fig. 17.] At this time, as in the second period, the nucleus was a large dwelling placed in the center, behind the main facade of the complex. Some of the walls of the house appear to be an elongation of those of the previous period, only slightly raised. The floor plan of the house, however, was changed by the increase in its dimensions. It was now 7.5 m wide and 8 m long. As before, the entrance was from the north, and a stone door socket was found at a low threshold. Some distance to the side, there was an oval hearth in a slight depression in the ground. Perhaps the fire in it played the role of a guardian. Unlike the four room house of the second period, this house had six rooms. The carefully plastered rooms 1a, 1b, 2, 4, and 5 indicate living or ceremonial quarters. A massive hearth occupied the major part of corner room 3. It is noteworthy that this room was located directly above room 5 of the second period, which also contained a hearth. Apparently, in this case, we have encountered an in-house kitchen of special function. It is notable that the dwelling house of the third period, even though it exceeded its forerunners in dimensions, differs in its slipshod construction and lack of straight lines; this lack is particularly noticeable in the eastern wall, which seems to have been formed step-by-step by various additions. Here we see the cohesiveness with the third period history of the main facade, when attempts were made to mask the deterioration by hasty constructions.

The six-room dwelling was surrounded by household parcels and auxiliary structures. Beyond the northern wall in a partly preserved long room (14), a large rectangular platform hearth was found, the contours of which were visible even before excavation. But the majority of the structures next to the northern facade, if they existed in antiquity, have altogether disappeared. As we have seen, only the rooms of the lower building horizon were relatively well preserved on this part of the hillock. The rooms to the east of the dwelling house (12 and 15) were only partly preserved, although traces of reconstructions and changes in ground plan were found here.

The structures located to the south of the dwelling house were in somewhat better shape. Here one can see that the early builders attempted to adhere to a straight line bordering the complex from the south. The walls of the structures forming the line are 60-90 cm thick. The relief of the locality preserved the outer edges of the structures, while to the west and north, such structures of the third period were totally eroded, and the main, eastern facade was preserved only because of its massiveness and monumentality.

Immediately to the south of the dwelling house was a sector of clearly auxiliary structures. An extensive piece of ground, it was preliminarily labeled 26; in all likelihood it was a courtyard. A row of rooms and fenced-off plots (23-25, 28,

29, and 31) were attached to this courtyard. In room 29 there was a rectangular hearth and a compartment completely filled with small sherds, approximately 800, and with stones. Rooms 25 and 28 also had oval hearths with a 0.5 m diameter. In room 28 the hearth had been rebuilt four times, each time in a different place. We concluded that this sector was concerned with intensive activities connected with the preparation of food; the finds of fragments of cauldrons also point to this function.

It is more difficult to judge the designation of the partly preserved household parts, 27 and 30, located to the east of the household sector. As was mentioned earlier, the structures on the eastern edge of the hillock were characterized by their regularity, reflecting the architectural attempt to form the southern border of the cult complex. Unlike the main, eastern facade, we do not have here a single, straight line of wall. Here are seen two parallel thick walls between which are structures, both nearly rectangular in plan (34) and very long (32 and 33). The northern wall served as a foundation for the southern wall of the burial assemblage of the lower building horizon. All of the rooms were filled with compacted rubbish or rubble, and therefore it is hard to determine their function. Perhaps they were storage rooms, even then empty and abandoned.

Such are the general characteristics of the history of the cult center during its three building horizons or three periods. Let us now turn to the interpretation of the complex as a whole, basing ourselves on the existing archaeological data and findings. The first period gives us the clearest picture. We have already mentioned the functions of the four elements comprising the complex: the stepped tower, the burial assemblage, the dwelling rooms, and the group of auxiliary household structures (courtyards, kitchens, and storage rooms). Let us examine the functions of each of these elements in greater detail.

The appearance of the stepped tower without doubt relates to the well-known ziggurats of ancient Mesopotamia. The latter are located at the temple of the principal deity and are crowned by a small temple—the house of the deity. Since, as a rule, the upper steps of the ziggurats are badly preserved, the top part is usually reconstructed on the basis of indirect sources. The foremost of these is the well-known description of the outstanding ziggurat in Babylon by Herodotus (Her., I:181). The upper terrace served as a place for the performance of various religious rituals and, apparently at the same time, as an observatory for the priests. The similarity between these architectural forms and the stepped tower at Altyn-Depe allows us to view the latter as an object of cult architecture without specifying for the present the nature of the cult or religious rites.

The second element comprising the complex, the burial assemblage, emerges as specific for the conditions at Altyn-Depe, well known for its many single and collective burials. In the burial assemblage, similar repositories were only part of a large complex which included a number of other rooms with various functions including, importantly, a sanctuary. The dimensions and floor plan of the sanctuary, as well as the find of the platform-hearth, continue the local Eneolithic traditions, as does the new phenomenon of the wall altar. V.I. Sarianidi already expressed an opinion about the relationship between the in-house sanctuaries of Geoksyur and the burial cult (Sarianidi 1965). Yet there the relationship was not entirely clear, and the sanctuary was comprised of only a small room among the living and household rooms of a multi-chambered house. Thus the burial assemblage of Excavation 7 is, in its floor plan, a unique structure. The burial vault was turned into a magnificent repository with a complex ritual. The already given circumstances underline the special place not only of the assemblage but of the group of people who served it. The collection of objects found in the sanctuary—which had a specific magical meaning and held special status because of the expensive materials of which they were made: gold, silver, semiprecious stones—support this conclusion even more strongly. The inclusion of the burial assemblage in the same complex as the zigurratlike structure confirms that this was the burial place of people who were associated with serving the cult center. The nature of the burial inventory signally underlines this conclusion. Both the number of buried (about 40 citizens, excluding those in room 32) and the sexual composition (approximately the same number of adult males and females) indicate that the tomb served several families who possibly clustered in a special closed unit, standing apart to a high degree from the system of burial centers for other inhabitants of Altyn-Depe. Such a unit was most likely a community of priests, among whom family ties could have existed. Developing further the concept of territorial unity, we suggest that the dwelling locale of the families forming the priestly community was the cluster of houses located along the street leading to the cult center from the town.

There were, however, dwelling houses directly on the territory of the cult center. First, there was the three-room house (occupying about 50 m^2). Its special location and regular floor plan clearly indicate that it belonged to a group of Altyn-Depe houses occupied by the cream of the society. Taking into account the features of the complex, this house can be labeled the Priest's House and figured as the residence of the family of the individual who headed the cult ceremonies. (Let us recall the interment of the skull of the aged man under the sanctuary's altar.) It is difficult to judge whether the one-room house with a hearth (35) was the dwelling place of another family belonging to the priestly elite, or simply a part of the same dwelling complex dislocated in the planning. The child burials found outside the confines of the burial assemblage may provide interesting materials for a similar conclusion. The finding in the burial assemblage of individuals older than 6 or 7 years agrees well with the data on other collective burials at Altyn-Depe, and also confirms the existence in the community of age groups whose representatives were buried in different places. Thus children up to six years old were usually buried within the confines of the house or adjacent household structures where their extended family lived. In the assemblage surveyed by us, remains of 37 mature people were found, and if side-room 32 is considered, the number reaches 51. Within the territory of courtyard B and its auxiliary structures, however, seven burials of children 3-4 years old were found. Such a disproportion indicates children of a special group, probably composed of one or two families whose dwellings were located in the same sector, were buried in the courtyard. It can be logically expected that the family of the chief priest, living in the center of the cult complex, fully carried out all of its functions within the same territory. In this respect, the double burials of two pairs of children of approximately the same age (4 and 6; 9 and 11) at the base of a wall in the three-room house is quite notable. The accompanying inventory, seven vessels, was comparatively large for Altyn-Depe and is witness to the special social rank of the buried. Perhaps these were children of the chief priest's family who had found their final resting place under a wall of the house where they had spent their short lives.

In the light of similar judgments, however, the burial of the aged woman in the ash layer of the courtyard is difficult to explain. It is quite clear that for some reason (a different social standing, outside the priestly community?) she could not be interred in the burial assemblage even though she spent her long life tied to this group of household and living structures. It is possible that she may have been an aged servant to the priest's family, but it would be difficult to prove such a speculative proposal.

Finally, the fourth element of the complex consists of auxiliary and household structures concentrated around courtyard B. The characteristic traits of these parts are the presence of storage rooms, kitchen utensils, and cooking hearths, and particularly traces of activities associated with them in the form of thick layers of ash, which in places are up to 1 m thick. The presence of a considerable amount of ash fill was a specific trait of the complex, confirmed archaeologically over the three periods of its existence. During the first period, such fill was concentrated in the central part, gradually filling the courtyard, which necessitated the rebuilding of auxiliary structures even on the ruins of earlier ones completely filled with layers of ash and rubble. The magnitude of activity in the hearths and firepits yielding such quantities of ash fill clearly exceeded the needs of one or two families whose dwellings were within the complex. This suggests the presence of additional cult feasts, the center of which during any period was a given object. In the cult architecture of Mesopotamia there are many examples of similar manifestations. Thus in the temple complex at Ur, next to the ziggurat of the First Dynasty (26th century B.C.), there was a group of structures with housekeeping remains and large oval and rectangular hearths. L. Woolley viewed this complex as a special temple kitchen where the meat of sacrificed animals, which ended as "food for the gods," was prepared in a practical way, by the priests and other serving personnel. An analogous kitchen was found near the gigantic ziggurat at Ur constructed during the rule of Ur-Nammu in the 22nd century B.C. (Woolley 1961:110, 144). At Altyn-Depe the extensive courtyard A, with a small hearth, could have served as the place for the solemn ceremonial feasts. The courtyard was kept clean and in order. Layers of ash and rubble were not found in it, while they had filled courtyard B. The courtyard labeled 28 (see Fig. 19) and paved with brick also could have been used for public ceremonies.

The functional analysis of the elements comprising the complex uncovered in Excavation 7 at the level of the first building horizon points to its extraordinary status. The zigguratlike tower, the burial assemblage with the interior sanctuary, and the remains of collective meals all indicate the special nature of this archaeological complex. We are convinced that we are dealing with a temple complex which included the dwellings of people who were closely associated with its functioning. Within the comparative terms of Altyn-Depe, the monumental character of the architecture confirms this analysis.

A full analysis of the layout permits us to establish the flow of the rituals associated with the body of a deceased person meriting interment in this sacred place. The procession entered courtyard B through the narrow street, and from there progressed through room 33 to courtyard A. The entryway was found blocked, and apparently, as with similar entrances in the collective burial place at Geoksyur, it was broken through as needed. It is of note that both the three-room and one-room house faced the potential route of the mourning procession with blank walls. The procession entered the corridor of the burial assemblage from the east. Here the fairly wide entrance was also blocked, duplicating in this respect the tradition of collective burial chambers. Apparently, for periods of time, the burial assemblage with its cult objects was sealed until need arose to use it.

The beautifully preserved objects found in the assemblage induce us to propose an even more specific semantic characterization of the temple complex. The absence of female statuettes in the assemblage, which is otherwise set apart by a rich collection of varied objects, is of fairly clear negative value. As a rule, in other collective burials at Altyn-Depe such figurines are present, sometimes several of them. But here the female terracottas were replaced by altogether different cult objects: the heads of a wolf and a bull, and a plaque with astral symbols. A special place was occupied by the bull's head, which is very effectively inlaid with turquoise. It is unique among Central Asian antiquities and takes its place among objects of similar nature, typical of Near Eastern archaeology, which not long ago were specifically reviewed. Without doubt, the focus of such artifacts is Mesopotamia, where bull heads were found at Ur (Woolley 1934:pls. 107, 111, 115-7, 119-21) and Khafaje (Frankfort 1936:28-29), in addition to a number of finds without precise ties to archaeological stratification (Parrot 1960:p. 157, fig. 186).

The heads of bulls found at Ur were placed on the resonators of lyres as sculptural ornamentations and were made of gold, silver, and bronze. One of the best known is the unusually expressive bull's head made of gold and embellished with lapis lazuli inlays for the eyes, a small forelock on the forehead, the tips of the large up-turned horns, and a broad beard. Lapis lazuli and gold were a favored combination of Sumerian jewelers. In this connection, it is interesting that lapis lazuli had a special significance even in Egypt. There, according to one of the variants of the Ra cycle, this sun god ruled for many thousands of years, and when he became old his bones turned to silver, his muscles to gold, and his hair to lapis lazuli (Turayev 1935:180). The Altyn-Depe and Ur heads closely agree in the method of inlaying the eyes, the placement of the ears immediately below and to the side of the horns, and the rendering of the superciliary arcs with furrows. The form of the horns, the shape of the muzzle, and the overall sculptural technique are different in principle. The more artistic and realistic renditions of the Ur bull heads, however, cover a larger area to which the Altyn-Depe find belongs. At present, according to the stratigraphic scheme for southern Mesopotamia, the royal tombs at Ur relate to stage IIIA of the Early Dynastic Period, which dates to 2600-2500 B.C.

The Khafaje bull's head was found in the brick foundation of the Sin VIII temple, and therefore can be dated to the time of the existence of the Sin VII temple, that is, to stage II of the Early Dynastic Period (Delougaz and Lloyd 1941:134), which is dated 2750-2600 B.C. The Khafaje head is made of bronze and in sculptural treatment is similar to the Ur heads and, in the same measure as the latter, also differs from the Altyn-Depe head. The eye sockets of the Khafaje head are filled with shell and lapis lazuli. There is a triangular inlay of sea shell in the forehead, also characteristic of the bronze deer head from Shuruppak (Parrot 1960:p. 155, fig. 184,B) which by its shape reminds us of the forehead inlay of the Altyn-Depe head. Other bronze bull heads are known from southern Mesopotamia that have the stylistic and sculptural traits of the Ur and Khafaje heads and inlaid lapis lazuli eyes (Parrot 1960:p. 157, fig. 186; Zervos 1935:154). All of these finds date essentially to Early Dynastic times, that is, 2900-2500 B.C. Chronologically, they pre-date the Altyn-Depe head and in stylistic respects represent a sort of realistic precursor to the somewhat schematized, conventionalized later head. The treatment of the horns and the blunt muzzle, almost like that of a pig, cannot compare to the Sumerian prototypes.

Yet the sculptural traits of the Altyn-Depe head have a fairly close analogue in the bronze bull head found, as the Altyn-Depe head, beyond the confines of the Sumerian "metropolis." We refer to the Barbar temple on the northern coast of Bahrein Island. During the excavation of Temple II, a cast bronze bull head was found with empty eye sockets indicating the lost inlays (Glob 1955, 1958). Upon detailed examination of the find, E. During-Caspers pointed out that it differed from the Sumerian heads by the frontal positioning of the eyes (in Sumer they were usually positioned to the side) and the flattening of the muzzle (reminding one of a pig's snout). There was a definite departure from the realistic style of the Sumerian prototypes, a style was closely adhered to only by Sumerian craftsmen (During-Caspers 1971). While all of these traits differentiate the Bahrein example from Sumerian sculpture, they are typical of the Altyn-Depe find. It can only be added that the character of the long, inwardly bent horns (an analogue of which During-Caspers sees in the antelope from Ur) is identical in the Bahrein and Altyn-Depe examples. It should be understood, however, that there is not complete agreement. The Barbar temple head lacks the superciliary furrows and the openings along the side of the head, and while there is general agreement in the treatment of the muzzle, the details forming the nostrils and lip are different. One must admit, however, that the Barbar example is the closest analogue to the Altyn-Depe head.

Recently, P. Mortensen devoted an article to the dating of the Barbar temples. Tentatively, he dated Temple II to the Middle of the third millennium B.C. (Mortensen 1970). He came to the conclusion that Temple III was constructed about 2200 B.C. and lasted until approximately 2000 B.C. In analyzing the Mesopotamian analogues of the Barbar bull head, During-Caspers figures that Temple II dated to stages II and IIIB of the Early Dynastic Period (During-Caspers 1971:223); this corresponds to 2750-2420 B.C. Figuring with the determined time of the erection of Temple III, however, it can be projected that Temple II continued to function until 2200 B.C., and that the objects found in it, even though they may not have been made within the 23rd or 24th centuries B.C., were in any case being used at that time. This reasoning brings the dating of the Altyn-Depe and Barbar sculptures fairly close, taking into consideration the fact that the Altyn-Depe tombs date to the very early stage of Namazga V, with Namazga IV layers found immediately below.

What is the relationship of these heads to Sumerian sculpture? During-Caspers is much inclined toward the opinion that the Barbar head is of local manufacture, yet can be traced to a definite Sumerian prototype. True, she makes the point that it is difficult to differentiate between a bad copy of a Mesopotamian model and a local product with Mesopotamian traits, either combined or adopted (During-Caspers 1971:223). I think that the Altyn-Depe bull head can serve as an example of the accuracy of such a conclusion. As we have seen, its ties with the Sumerian examples are limited, so to speak, to the general idea and analogues of separate traits: the application of inlays to the eyes and forehead, the wide spreading of the ears, and the alignment of the superciliary arcs. Possibly, the small turquoise bead found next to the head could have represented in antiquity a strand of the beard fastened by means of the two openings on either side below the line of the lip. If this is the case, the analogies with the bearded bulls of Sumer would be newly confirmed. Another material, turquoise, was used for the inlays, although lapis lazuli occurs in Turkmenia in adequate quantities, and artifacts made of it were found in plenty in the same location as the bull's head. In this connection, the known corresponding traits of the Altyn-Depe head and the Eneolithic sculpture of southern Turkmenia take on a special significance. At Kara-Depe, in Namazga III layers tentatively dated to the beginning of the third millennium B.C., a rather clumsily made bull figurine of a marblelike limestone was found. Reflecting the difficulties of the sculptor working with this fairly intractable material, this object, in general, gave the impression of being a pig, and only the horns and the long tail dispelled this impression (Masson 1960a:p. 371, fig. 24). The rendering of the muzzle as a pig's snout with a straight, depressed line for the mouth and two nostrils also represented by depressions, undoubtedly forms an analogy to the Altyn-Depe bull's muzzle. In addition, the deeply drilled eye-sockets of the Kara-Depe statuette suggest that in antiquity they were inlaid with colored stones (Masson 1960a:368). It may be concluded that the Altyn-Depe jewelers, being familiar with the results of Sumerian craftsmanship, at the same time were aware of local, perhaps even Eneolithic, traditions. The question of the formation of such a tradition is a special one, closely related to the question of the semantics of sculptures of this type. In turn, this tradition was related to the recreation of the utilitarian purpose of such objects during the time of their existence. The appearance of the Altyn-Depe head clearly indicates that even in antiquity it functioned as a separate head. In part this is shown by the

presence of golden edging which masks the view behind the head. It is noteworthy that the wolf's head also shows definite wear from long use.

The head from the Barbar temple was found with strips of copper with nail holes indicating that they may have been part of some sort of casing. P. Glob suggested that they were the remains of a wooden object crowning the bull's head (Glob 1955:191). Regrettably, a detailed drawing or photograph of the condition of the find has not been published yet. During-Caspers, basing herself on a description in the preliminary account, is of the opinion that the bull's head and the heads of other animals were fastened to wooden poles encased in copper sheathing, and in this form they were objects of worship (During-Caspers 1971:221-222). P. Barnett, basing himself on the Ur finds and some iconographic data, figured that the Barbar head, as well as the Ur heads, served as ornaments on musical instruments (Barnett 1969). Historically, at the end of the third millennium B.C., there is a known cuneiform text in which a harp ornamented with a bull's head is described, and the sound of the instrument is compared to the bellowing of a bull (Woolley 1961:78).

The conditions in which the Altyn-Depe golden bull's head was found, that is, in a relatively undisturbed layer with no traces of a decayed musical instrument which, at that, would be ornamented with one head only, compels us to give preference to the suggestion of During-Caspers. The finding of the head in the sanctuary points to it as hardly being an ordinary piece of sculpture. This idea is buttressed by the inlay in the forehead of a crescent moon, no doubt an astral symbol. The absence in the entire complex of female statuettes and the finding of the mosaic plaque, also accompanied by a crescent moon, allows the conclusion that the entire complex was associated with some astral deity, probably male (Masson 1973a:481).

The study of this problem will allow us to be more certain and definite in our statements. The Khafaje bull's head mentioned earlier was found during the excavation of the temple of Sin, the renowned Sumerian moon god. The designation of the temple can be accurately deduced from a sign on a statue of a priest found there (Delougaz and Lloyd 1971:6). The close relationship of the early Sumerian moon-god Nanna-Sin with the form of the bull is well documented in the special literature. A large sacred precinct, including in part the ziggurat, was dedicated to this deity, the patron of Ur. An inscription on the foundation frustum of the precinct announces: "For Nanna, the mighty celestial bull, the most glorious of the sons of Enlil, his sovereign, Ur-Nammu, a mighty man, king of Ur, erected this temple Etemenniguru" (Woolley 1961:134). We get the same picture in the hymn to Nanna which was preserved in an Assyrian copy in the excellent library of Assurbanibal, but without doubt originated in the Sumerian epoch. In the hymn we read: "Father Nanna, mighty youthful calf with powerful horns, a perfect body, a lapis lazuli beard, full of splendor..." (Turayev 1935:137).

In Sumerian mythology, the bull traditionally appears as a moon animal (Epos...:119), and so in the hymns, Sin himself is rendered as a young bull the color of fire (Labat 1970:280). The analogies between the texts and the archaeological materials are indubitable. This bull is also the color of Nanna, the celestial bull, very close to uncorroded bronze, and even closer to gold; here is also the lapis lazuli beard so splendidly rendered in the Ur materials. In Sumerian cosmogony Nanna is considered the son of the god of air, Enlil, and the father of the sun-god Utu and his celebrated sister Innin-Ishtar, goddess of the planet Venus. In Sumerian mythology, the planets and stars were thought to move around the moon, with the larger likened to "wild bulls" and the smaller to broadcast grains (Kramer 1965:107). The half-moon was a symbol of Nanna, as the disc was the symbol of the sun-god, and the stars were the emblem of Innin-Ishtar. The semantic connection between the moon-god, the principal of the astral dieties, with the image of the bull is a specific trait of Sumerian religion. The finding at Altyn-Depe of a golden bull's head with an inlaid crescent moon should not leave any doubt that such beliefs also existed among the Bronze Age people of southern Turkmenistan. The connection between the lunar deity and the form of the bull, however, is by no means simple or unilinear.

The cult of the bull begins with very remote sources, beginning no doubt with the traditions of hunting societies, perhaps as early as the Paleolithic. Thus the skulls of revered animals were sometimes placed in Upper Paleolithic dwellings: mammoth, cave lion, musk-ox (Efimenko 1953:409; Boriskovskiy 1958:117). As S.A. Tokarev shows, the worship of animals can be of varied forms, including direct worship of animals (zoolatry), various kinds of tabus, the bestowing of zoomorphic or anthropomorphic forms on gods, the sacrifice of animals to a god, and so on (Tokarev 1964:76). It is particularly necessary to differentiate zoomorphic deities and the animals dedicated to them, the latter often be-

coming sacrificial animals when the god and sacrifice are identified as one. The image of the bull, which was already popular among the hunters of the Stone Age, was also widely represented in the ideologies of the early agriculturalists. This is clearly illustrated in the sanctuaries of Çatal Hüyük, which date to the second half of the seventh to the first half of the sixth millennium B.C. The walls of the sanctuaries are literally covered with all sorts of representations of the bull, from colorful panels to individual horns. Of 28 sanctuaries which were extensively analyzed, only four lacked similar representations. Particularly varied are the ceramic heads of bulls, usually fastened to the wall and covered with paintings, the meanings of which J. Mellaart proposes to link somewhat directly with trophies of the hunt (Mellaart 1967:82). At any rate, there is no doubt about the very extensive role of the bull among the early agriculturalists of Anatolia. This role was preserved among the early agricultural tribes of the Balkans and central Europe who often embellished their houses or small sanctuaries with heads of bulls (Childe 1952:146; Makkay 1973), and in the Aegean world it prevailed until the Creto-Mycenaean civilization. Until a detailed analysis of the religious beliefs of the Çatal Hüyük people is carried out, it will be difficult to interpret the frescoes portraying bulls and ceramic sculptures, but in all, the serious investigators correlate them with a male deity, the partner of a female goddess whose anthropomorphic form so clearly dominates the cultural symbolism of this remarkable site (Mellaart 1967:200-201; Deshayes 1969:234). At the stage of anthropomorphization of the gods of the ancient cult, symbolism preserves its role either in a general sense only, or becomes semantically closely associated with individual gods. A classical example of this process is seen in the Egyptian materials, where the gods (patrons of individual nomes) take on specific and lasting zoomorphic traits. The place of the bull's head on a pole, the former object of worship, is taken by the bull Apis (Turayev 1935:178), who is associated with the Memphis god Ptah and officially regarded as the bearer of the godly soul. It was said that a ray of light descended from the heavens onto a cow, and from that ray she gave birth to Apis (Her., III:228).

Many iconographic materials and source data reveal that Mesopotamian deities took on an anthropomorphic form early (Tokarev 1964:504; Deshayes 1969:246). The connections between the deities and animals are preserved only in part and are reflected in the unification of the deity and its animalistic symbolism. Frankfort pointed out that in a number of cases the well-known Mesopotamian monsters appear to be purely graphic combinations of the god and his animalistic emblem, which in no measure detracts from the anthropomorphic character of the deity (Frankfort 1955:37-38).

In Mesopotamia the image of the bull has very early sources. The motif of the bull's head was exceptionally popular on the ornamental ceramics of the Halaf culture, which spread over northern Mesopotamia during the fifth millennium B.C. and possibly became a sort of symbol for tribal unification (Masson 1964b:366). The representations of edifices crowned with bull's heads, apparently small temples or sanctuaries, are known from the pictographs of Sumer at the end of the fourth millennium B.C. and from Mesopotamian and Elamite glyptics of the third millennium B.C. (Makkay 1973:3-4). In Mesopotamian glyptics of the third millennium B.C. the image of an androcephalic bull, which according to some investigators is of Elamite origin (Afanaseva 1965:6), is also widespread. In the celebrated Akkadian epic about Gilgamesh a special section is devoted to the contest of the hero with the celestial bull the gods had sent to Uruk at the pleading of Ishtar, who had been rejected by Gilgamesh. The epic relates that the horns were cast of lapis lazuli and set in gold (Epcs...:177). An analogous passage also appears in the Sumerian epos (Kramer 1965:291). Enkidu, the friend of Gilgamesh, was condemned to early death by the gods for his part in defeating the spirit of the forests, Huwawa, and the celestial bull. It is possible that the tradition of tauromachy finds a reflection in this cycle where the bull fighting preceded the slaughter of the sacrificial bull. This is well represented in Cretan iconography.

Under these conditions, it is fully plausible that the deity (the patron-protector of one of the large centers of ancient Sumer, in this case Ur) is seen to be closely tied to the image of the bull whose spread horns inferred a direct graphic association with the crescent moon. This in no way charged the anthropomorphic cast of the lunar god Nanna, although it could have been one of his hypostases. It is not surprising that the golden bull of Ur placed on the harp so strikingly duplicates this characteristic feature of the godly protector of the city described in the sacred hymn. It does not follow that representations attached to string instruments which were part of a burial inventory had a purely decorative

character and were devoid of intricate semantic associations. It is entirely possible that the temple of Nanna contained a sacred bull with special attributes such as the marks on the forehead of the Egyptian Apis, which was either dedicated to the god proper or figured as one of his embodiments. The mosaic inlay on the forehead of the Khafaje bull and the crescent moon on the Altyn-Depe head are there for a reason. The composition of the finds in the temple of Nanna-Sin in Khafaje are also of interest. In addition to the large bull head mentioned earlier, there was a golden pendant in the form of a bull and a libation cup in the form of the same animal. Also significant is the composition of the amulets probably brought to the temple as offerings (Delougaz and Lloyd 1941:29, 136-148). Amulets, portraying a bull or bull's head, were found in all of the temple's layers without exception, while figures of other animals were or were not present in a given layer. It should be understood that we are not trying to propose some kind of ritual relationship between the image of the bull and the lunar deity of Sumer only. It is well known, for instance, that in the temple of the goddess Ninhursag, not far from Ur, excellent representations of bulls were found (Hall and Woolley 1927:pl. XXVIII). The finding of the lunar symbol on the forehead of the Altyn-Depe bull and a second lunar emblem in the same complex, however, incline us toward the thought that in this case we are encountering a symbol of the celestial bull in the role of a lunar deity. Apparently, the entire cult complex of Altyn-Depe with the zigguratlike structure and burial complex was dedicated to this deity, a southern Turkmenistan variant of Nanna-Sin.

Such associations are important for the analysis of Altyn-Depe's cultural-historical position. The juxtaposition of celestial bull and lunar deity is specifically Sumerian, as opposed to the "bull-sun god" represented in Egyptian materials and even Greek sources. In the Cretan variant, the bull Zeus, who appears at the same time as the sun and, indeed, in the capacity of a sun-bull, abducts Europa (Losev 1957:121). It is not without reason that the Egyptian representations contain a sun-disc between the horns (Her., II:132). In Mycenae, a silver rhyton was found in the form of a bull's head with a golden rosette-sun on its forehead (Blavatskaya 1966:fig. 26). The finding in southern Turkmenistan of Bronze Age representations of the "celestial bull-lunar deity" is that much more important since later representations of opposite images—the sun god and the bull Mithra—spread over the same territory. It should be noted that the Avestan Mithra was associated with the sun only during a specific period, probably at the time of the beginning of a strong codification and astralization of deities (Sokolov 1963:177).

The Zoroastrian traditions preserve beliefs about the first bull and man and also about the syncretic form of man-bull, Gopat-shah (Trever 1940). Since the account of the first man has been preserved in Pahlevi texts only, the opinion has been voiced that these beliefs date to pre-Zoroastrian times. Although the bull, according to Zoroastrian mythology, died because of the intrigues of Ahriman, his family fell onto the moon and, after returning to earth, gave life to the good animals and plants. The connections between the first bull and the moon are emphasized in the early Iranian epithet for the moon, *gauchutra*, "keeper of the bull's family" (Boyce 1975:130). These beliefs unite the powerful role of the bull in the ceremonies and cults, and apparently even the mythology, of the steppe cattle-herding tribes and the ancient Eastern tradition of associating the moon god with the image of the bull (Gryaznov 1972). The astralization of deities, even though they had not yet lost their animalistic association as expressed by semantic associations, was a characteristic trait of communities practicing irrigation agriculture (Tokarev 1964:308). Southern Turkmenistan was no exception. Here the ceramic figures of bulls appear in the Late Neolithic, pointedly associated with the domestication of large horned cattle (Berdyev 1966:22). They are widely represented in Eneolithic assemblages, although in numbers they are exceeded by figurines of small, horned cattle (Khlopin 1963:p. 16, pl. XXIII, item 10; Khlopin 1969:p. 44, table XVI, item 3). Even the Kara-Depe large stone figure of a bull, probably from a complex of cult designation (Masson 1960a:347) and chronologically closest to those of Ur and Khafaje, does not bear any marks of astral symbolism. We may conclude that only at a specific stage of development, at the codification of the system of religious beliefs, did the astralization of deities became an inevitable fact (Masson and Sarianidi 1973:145). The similar iconographic traits of the Altyn-Depe bull's head and the manufactures of Sumerian craftsmen allow us to propose that the former could not have originated without the influence of the religious beliefs of Sumer and Agade.

In the first period of its existence, the temple complex of a moon god differed in its fairly complex internal structure but relatively limited monumentality. In essence, only the stepped tower, 21 m long at the base and 8-10 m in height, formed a bulky mass dominating the group of ordinary structures. During the second period, the site changed radically. The stepped tower was enlarged, and at the same time the House with Parapet was built, also set on a platform 3 m high. As a result, the main, eastern facade presented a united architectural whole, to a degree, grand and monumental. The second compositional part of the complex, the Priest's House, at this time contained four rooms and was positioned directly in the center beyond the main facade. The many hearths within the house and beyond its confines, together with the large quantities of ash on the southern slope of the hillock and in part in front of the main facade, testify to its function as a "temple kitchen." As was mentioned earlier, the House with Parapet could be regarded as an extensive storage house. At this time, however, the earlier burial assemblage was built over and we find nothing analogous to it. In essence, during the second and third periods, we have the remains of the Priest's House in the center of the hillock, the main facade in the east, and a series of auxiliary structures to the south of the Priest's House. The entire northern part of the hillock seemed to be unoccupied. Almost involuntarily the question arises: Could this be the location of the burial assemblage?

The basic functions of the temple complex were preserved even in the last, third period. The huge stepped tower, strengthened by repaired foundations and supports, rose above the surrounding houses as before. At this time the Priest's House had six rooms. One of the rooms was specially dedicated to taking care of meals, and the multiple hearths of various sizes and shapes found to the south of the house confirm the large scale continuation of the functions associated with the "temple kitchen." The large heaps of ash accumulated on the south slope necessitated the construction of the Corner House, which the early inhabitants of Altyn-Depe had hoped would mask the unsightly rubbish. The numerous storage rooms, including the House with Parapet, fully supported the temple complex in carrying out its function as protector (and distributor?) of supplementary products received by the entire community.

The uncovered architectural remains, particularly near the main facade, also furnish a separate basis for the graphic reconstruction of the outward appearance of the complex. For the first period this problem was resolved relatively simply because remains of all four steps of the massive tower were uncovered during the excavation. Under later additions a disturbed corner and one of the pilasters, three-stepped in cross-section, which ornamented the second step were preserved. In the reconstruction, it is understood that the edifice that tops the tower may not have existed. This reconstruction is based on the type of notched indentations found during the excavation of Mundigak in southern Afghanistan (Casal 1961:vol. 2, fig. 22). Realistically, we have the remains of only two steps for the second period, but we can see that the height of the second step was increased to approximately 3.5-4 m. Hence the combined height of the first and second steps reached 5.5-6 m. This figure can be confirmed in another way. The House with Parapet is positioned on a 3 m high platform, an estimate which can be determined fairly accurately. The comparatively greater thickness of the walls of this edifice allows the proposition that the height of its rooms was 2.5-3 m, which would make its outside height one decorative and architectural whole with the second step of the tower, that is, again the height of 5.5-6 m. The height of 6 m was used in the graphic reconstruction of the eastern facade during the second period by A.K. Filippov. The reconstruction of the upper parts of the tower was done mostly on a hypothetical basis but also with the assumption that the temple retained the four step construction so precisely established for the first period.

The architecture of the Altyn-Depe temple complex displays specific ties with that of Sumer. Most importantly, this similarity is seen in the walls formed by evenly spaced buttresses. Buttresses stepped in cross-section appear in southern Mesopotamia in the last third of the fourth millennium B.C. and are widely used in the architecture of the third millennium B.C., including the facade of the splendid Ur ziggurat (Woolley 1939:pls. 68-72). The idea of a stepped tower also must be included in the number of Mesopotamian influences. Mesopotamia brought its vertical architecture to southern Turkmenistan. It should be noted that the early ziggurats of Mesopotamia were not square in plan, but rectangular. Unlike Sumer, the sides of the Altyn-Depe stepped tower, rather than its corners, are oriented to the cardinal directions. There is also a difference in that only the main, eastern facade achieves the appearance of monumentality to a considerable degree.

This combination of an effective main facade and planning with the lay of the land is characteristic of the Mundigak palace, also considered a monumental structure (Casal 1961:vol. 1, pp. 49-55). Spontaneity and irregularity in planning is also seen in the very massive structures of Shahr-i-Sokhta (Lamberg-Karlovsky and Tosi 1974:23). One of these edifices is also thought to be the ruin of a palace (Tosi 1971:p. 28, fig. 10).

Investigators of the ancient Near East unanimously conclude that the ziggurats found in most large centers of Mesopotamia were structures typical of the region and, additionally, were to be found only in Elam (Lenzen 1961; Deshayes 1969:283-289). Yet the study of cultures in the broad zone to the east of Mesopotamia, cultures which were undergoing intensive urbanization, reveals that these effective architectural structures, distinct symbols of cities and filling the roles of ideological and cult centers, had spread far from the territory of their origin. In addition to Altyn-Depe, there are the ruins of the southern Baluchistan site of Edith-Shahr, where W. Fairservis observed the remains of a very large structure which he interpreted as a type of ziggurat (Fairservis 1967:fig. 7; Fairservis 1974:195-196). Unfortunately, this interesting site has not yet been excavated. Not long ago a monumental foundation was uncovered on the outer side of a hill at Tureng-Tepe, an important Bronze Age center in northeastern Iran. Deshayes postulated that a staircase led to the top of the hill framed by the foundation for the main facade, and that the finding of stone "columns" indicates that these are ruins of an ancient cult center (Deshayes 1978). On the basis of preliminary trenching at Tureng-Tepe by Americans, I projected already in 1964 that remains of monumental architecture will be found there (Masson 1964a:242). Deshayes compares the massive foundation uncovered by him at Tureng-Tepe to that of the Altyn-Depe cult complex.

Thus the temple complex of Altyn-Depe appears to be a characteristic component of the community, displaying distinct ties with the architecture of the ancient East in the broad sense of the word. Nevertheless, these ties are on the whole some of the most typical traits of the Altyn-Depe culture.

V

Altyn-Depe as an Archaeological Complex

Questions of Typology and Chronology

The results of the Altyn-Depe excavations indicated that we are dealing with the remains of a large and complicated organism which functioned several thousand years ago. At the same time, Altyn-Depe, the material expression of that organism, is a source of a special kind which can be subjected to special studies, in this case with archaeological methods. From this point of view, the level of the upper building horizon at Altyn-Depe expresses an archaeological complex with a well-defined combination of various kinds of artifacts. An analysis of such a complex and the establishment of its spatial and temporal boundaries is a specific archaeological procedure which precedes the historical interpretation of the object studied.

During the excavations of the Altyn-Depe Middle Bronze Age (or Namazga V) complexes, many archaeological objects were found, ranging from ceramic vessels to jewelry. The various manufactures comprise a collection running to tens and even hundreds of specimens. The analysis of some of the categories of artifacts has begun. Thus the preliminary questions about the typology of the seals have been raised (Masson 1970d), the classification of terracottas excavated during the early seasons was considered in detail (Masson and Sarianidi 1973), a typology of ceramic forms was presented (Masimov 1973a), and the metal artifacts were fully published in a preliminary analysis (Kircho 1980).

In this work we will naturally limit ourselves to a general characterization of the various artifacts, taking into account that many deserve a special analysis. We will start with the most numerous group, the ceramic vessels. Even during the first season, analysis in the field resulted in a four-fold classification based on color and manner of execution: (1) red or rose ware and a light surface; (2) greenish-white ware (this is the Namazga type since it is represented most fully at Namazga-Depe); (3) red or rose ware and an outer surface of the same colors; (4) cooking vessels with an admixture of gravel in the ware (Masimov 1970a). A working terminology for the forms and proportions of the vessels was also established. In the course of further work and technological investigation carried out by E.V. Sayko, it became clear that this classification could only be regarded as very preliminary, since the color of the ware was directly tied to the stability of the firing process. As analyses showed, the outer surface of the vessels was not covered with a slip, but was only smoothed with a wet rag, which rendered the effect of a pseudo-slip. With unstable firing conditions the same pot could have a differently colored body in several places.

A common characteristic of Altyn-Depe ceramics during the Middle Bronze Age was the elongated proportions of the vessels. Often the body of a vessel is supported on a high pedestal, which for better stability is not hollow but solid. The form of vessels encountered during the excavations of living quarters and other household structures differs somewhat from vessels in other areas. Thus in burials, particularly collective ones, vases and common pedestaled vessels are relatively rare, and the most frequently encountered vessels are globular and biconical. Collections of ceramic vessels in tombs are of interest because as an assemblage they chronologically limit the extent of the functioning of the tomb. The goblets are a specific form of Middle Bronze Age ceramics. They are conical, often elongated vessels with a curve near the thinned, slightly everted rim. The squat forms without the curve near the rim are regarded as cups, those with the rim slightly inverted, as small bowls. The show pieces were vases on high pedestals, often corrugated or with an encircling ridge. At times they were provided with a small spout. In all, the ceramics of the complex being surveyed are characterized by elegance of form and thinness of the body's walls. Both of these characteristics reflect the considerable success of technology in ceramic manufacture: the introduction of the potter's wheel and two-tiered kilns which provided a better opportunity to achieve stable firing conditions. Only cooking vessels were manufactured by pressing slabs of clay together. Gravel was added to the clay. The principal types were cauldrons and braziers. The cauldrons had the form of a flattened sphere with an inverted, thickened rim and were sometimes provided with a small spadelike spout below the rim. As a rule, the flat braziers had a larger diameter than the cauldrons and a low, flanged edge widening below. The thick-walled vessels for the preservation of produce were made on the potter's wheel and had the form of cylinders with bottoms raised by the addition of an anular ring. Some of the fragments of the storage jars indicate walls in excess of 1 cm thick.

The differentiation of the ornamentations of ceramics in southern Turkmenistan during the Middle Bronze Age for the purpose of achieving internal, on-site chronological divisions or expressions of local differences is a complicated subject. During the excavation of stratigraphic trench 1, where only fragmented ceramics were found, it was impossible to discern temporal changes. In this respect, the comparison of the ceramic assemblages from collective tombs was much more productive. As a result of this comparison some chronological differences among the ceramic assemblages of the Middle Bronze Age were established (Masson 1970a:12). A clear assemblage of the early period is a group of vessels from locality 32 of Excavation 7, where, on the level of the lower building horizon, the burial chamber built onto the outside wall of the priest's tomb was found (Plate XXXI, items 2-12; Plate XXXII, items 1-3, 7, 8, and 11). The antiquity of this group (even in the time frame of Namazga V) is confirmed both by the stratigraphic finds—below it are indisputable layers of Namazga IV—and by the find of a vessel with black ornamentation on a red background, a type of Late Namazga IV. Biconical vessels dominate this ceramic assemblage. They usually have a sharp carination on the lower third of the body

and a sharply vaulted bottom. There are two examples of bottles with slightly everted rims, expanded bodies outwardly curved near the base, and a ledge at the very bottom. Massive, heavy proportions are also characteristic of a large pot with a broad, bell-shaped neck and a curve near the bottom on which traces of touch-up with a metal instrument are visible. In addition, the assemblage contained a rosette, a small vase, and a cup. Synchronous with this assemblage is the collection of vessels from the double burial (240-241) found in the same building horizon of Excavation 7 (Plate XXXIV, items 12 and 17). The burial contained three potlike vessels on a base, a bowl, a rosette, and two canisters of biconical form with a short tubular spout emanating from the vessel's wall at an upward angle.

The assemblages from burials 9, 11 and 124 of Excavation 9, and burial 13 of Excavation 5 belong to the second stage of the Middle Bronze Age ceramic complex. Stratigraphically, they are located in the two building horizons above the layers of Namazga IV. Elongated biconical vessels on a high pedestal dominate burial 9; there are nine examples. There are also potlike vessels on a pedestal with a high, slightly widening neck; there are ten examples of these. A large bottle and four very small bottles of the same form, a vase, a rosette, and other single forms also belong to this assemblage. In burial 11, which is stratigraphically a little earlier than burial 9, there are also vessels of biconical form and potlike vessels with a bell-shaped neck and a pedestal, but there are more bottles with a spherical or biconical body, three and six examples respectively. The forms of a small, potlike vessel with two small handles at the rim and three wineglass-like, short vessels, two of which are covered with a red slip, are rare. In burial 124, potlike vessels of expanded form dominated, but those with elongated forms were also present. The three biconical canisters with a short spout found here are identical to those from the double burial of Excavation 7. In burial 14 the majority are potlike vessels of elongated proportions. The elongated forms are also characteristic of the relatively rare biconical vessels found there. The small bottles from burial 13 have symmetrical, spherical bodies without the ring at the bottom.

Finally, there is a third stage in the evolution of the ceramic complexes of Altyn-Depe. The ceramics from horizons 1 and 2 in the stratigraphic Excavation 1, those from the upper layers of the 2.5 m thick trench 1, and from the tomb-cenotaph 55 uncovered in Excavation 13 belong to it. Unfortunately, the materials from Excavation 1 and Trench 1 are fragmentary; whole vessels are practically absent.

Among the ceramics from horizon Altyn 1, fragments with rose or yellowish ware and a light outer surface dominate, and this tendency is clearly visible on fragments of large thick-walled vessels. There are single fragments with red ware, but not with a red burnished surface such as those encountered in the assemblages of Namazga IV at Namazga-Depe. Among the various forms of vessels there are storage jars with a cylindrical body, a ringed base, and a rolled rim. Also represented are pot-shaped vessels with a low neck widening toward the rim. On the basis of fragments we can discern the presence of vases on a hollow support with a wide spreading in the lower part and cylindrical vessels sometimes slightly widened at the bottom. There are also pot-shaped vessels on a pedestal. On the bottoms of these an image of a swirling vortex, made by the string with which the craftsman separated the bottom from the clay on the revolving potter's wheel, was clearly visible. The finds of vessels resembling an inverted, truncated cone, sometimes ornamented with drawn signs, are notable. Such pedestals, including those with drawn ornamentation or slanted incisions, were also found in horizon Altyn 2. The basic collection of forms here resembles the ceramics of the Altyn 1 horizon, although it is somewhat more diversified as a result of more numerous finds. Thus a part of a bottle with a relief band at the base of its neck and quite a few spouts, both open and tubular, with the tube pinched at the orifice, were found. There were flat braziers. Fragments of ceramic pedestals with magical signs such as crosses were found in the layers of trench 1 down to the fifth level. This evidence indicates a dating for the top 2.5 m of deposits to the late stage of Namazga V.

The ceramics of tomb-cenotaph 55 of Excavation 13 also must be dated to this stage. Fifty vessels were found. There were 13 beakers with curved walls and appliqué rims, but they were much more squat than those of the second stage. About half of the vessels were coarse bowls with a rolled rim and a detached, low conical pedestal. There is also a cup with a spout, analogous to the cup from the burial at Auchin-Depe, judged by us to be characteristic of Early Namazga VI (Masson 1959a:pl.II, item 1). The three stages surveyed here characterize the gradual development of Altyn-Depe materials pertinent to Namazga V.

Metal artifacts are extremely rare at Altyn-Depe, a fact that is explained by the absence of a nearby ore deposit in southern Turkmenistan. This circumstance made it necessary for the metallurgist to add to the melt any broken object, and the inhabitants handled metal tools carefully. As a rule, finds of metal tools come from early graves, while in the cultural levels proper finds of metal objects are singular, being in the main small fragments of punches and awls. As a result, large bronze artifacts are almost as rare as gold ones. Hacking tools are represented by large adzes with a slightly curved working edge. The only complete adze has two trunnions. The small chisels, nearly rectangular in cross-section, have an oval working edge and a flattened heel. The most numerous category is that of "household" tools—awls and needles. The awls are of three types: pointed at both ends and rectangular in section; single pointed and nearly rectangular in section, with a flat haft; and single pointed, round in section, and also with a flat haft. The last are very rare.

Cutting tools include single-edged and double-edged knives with a small haft for the handle. Knives with a narrow leaf-shaped blade, lens-shaped in section and devoid of an axial rib, are most typical. They may be very short or very long, but with all the variations they represent one typological group. Small knives with the cutting edge much worn by repeated sharpening may belong to this group. They were first interpreted as dart points and formally they resembled closely the type of knife associated with the Catacomb culture. There is also a knife with a straight haft and weakly indicated axial rib (Plate XIV, item 2). The almost triangular arrow points also have a flattened or lens-shaped cross-section and a flat haft (Plate XV, items 5 and 6). The working edge of a bronze sickle found in Excavation 13 is at almost a right angle to the long haft, which is flat in section (Plate XXIX, item 3).

Metal articles of toilet and adornment are relatively rare. They are found, and in small numbers at that, only in rich graves or collective burial chambers. Metal artifacts found in these burials include oval, slightly concave mirrors with a side handle (Plate XV, item 8); earrings made of spiraling wire; bracelets, oval in section, made from rods that overlap at the ends (Plate XIV, items 3 and 4); and beads, both flat and spherical. Finger rings are made of copper or silver wire, turned once or twice, or foil engraved with a simple stroke ornament. Long rods with one thickened end, which varies depending on the character of the representations on it, are a special group. The thickened end may be a small shovel, spirals, figures on a scythelike projection, or heads of ungulates. There are various suppositions as to the role of these artifacts, but most likely they had a double function: they were used for fastening clothing and at the same time were attributes of persons of a special social standing. In any case, of the two pins or rods with a zoomorphic representation found at Altyn-Depe, one was in a relatively rich burial (Plate XXIX, item 4), and the other, in a fragmented condition, in the Elite Quarters. Gold jewelry is also uniform: rings are made of spiraled thin wire and beads have an alabaster base covered with gold foil.

Clay figurines appear as a characteristic form of the Altyn-Depe archaeological assemblages. Among them, both in numbers and clarity of representation, first place is held by the terracotta figurines of women. The question of the typology of these Bronze Age terracottas has already been analyzed (Masson and Sarianidi 1973), and new materials have added little to the general systematics. The Middle Bronze Age female terracotta figurines of Altyn-Depe are overwhelmingly of the statue type produced as a flat female figure in a sitting position on a pointed base. The figure is bent forward with arms extended sideways. Only in rare cases are the extended arms bent downward, pointing to the genetic tie with the Eneolithic terracottas of this type. The latter type of figure was forgotten during the Bronze Age and was replaced by figures with inviting "open arms." We very rarely encounter statuettes without arms; the arms are replaced with rounded or sloping upper shoulders. Unlike the Eneolithic, this schematic aspect did not enjoy wide distribution during the Bronze Age.

The female statuettes of the Middle Bronze Age differ in a significant number of details from those of the Eneolithic. The appliqué forms and scratchings or engravings are quite different from those of the Eneolithic. The upper part of the sculpture is most thoroughly differentiated. The head, with exaggerated large rhomboid eyes and positioned on a long neck, is the first thing that strikes the observer. As a rule, the head is topped with an inverted, conelike headdress indicated on the obverse side with sometimes straight, sometimes crossing lines (Plate VIII, items 1, 3, and 5). The high headdress, basically in the form of a widening truncated cone (Plate IX, item 7), is usually provided with two openings and has, in a preliminary way, been called a crown (Masson and Sarianidi 1973:34). The large eyes were rendered by appliqué, the nose by a high pinch of the clay; a representation of the mouth is lacking in all examples. The face is framed with two pendant braids, often reaching the chest, and reminiscent of snakes (in the literature, braided snakes). On some particularly carefully made statuettes there are distinctly visible small heads of snakes on both sides of the head at the level of the eyes (Plate VIII, items 3 and 4), as if two snakes raised on their tails framed the neck and head. In the majority of the statuettes, however, the renderings of the snake heads are not discernible, and it is difficult to judge whether in these cases the semantic sense has been preserved or whether it has acquired a purely decorative meaning. On the back of many of the statuettes is a wide appliqué braid sometimes reaching below the waist. As a rule, scratched-on representations of various ornaments (apparently analogues of bead necklaces or various pendants, such as those encountered during the excavations of burials) are found on the necks of the figures. In classifying the terracottas one can discern straight, horizontally positioned necklaces (Plate X, item 4), angled necklaces (Plate IX, items 1, 3, 4, and 7), and necklaces with pendants (Plate X, item 1), the latter indicated with a few vertical strokes (Masson and Sarianidi 1973:35). Statuettes excavated later also fit this classification.

The trunks of the statuettes normally lack applied or engraved details and so are in contrast with the overloaded upper parts. Sometimes the middle front part of the trunk has a representation of a tree with the limbs pointed down (Plate IX, item 5) or up (Plate VIII, items 1 and 5) engraved on it. In the lower part of the abdomen a triangle is engraved symbolizing the female principle, similar to the triangle with a short diametrical dash which in proto-Sumerian writing signifies "female." In many of the figurines there are horizontal lines above the triangle representing a loin band or belt. Similar bead belts were found during the excavation of tomb 11 in the Elite Quarters. In other cases such belts could have been made of organic materials and, naturally, have not been preserved. Thus some details of decorations on the terracottas undoubtedly transmit ethnographic traits which were characteristic of the inhabitants of Altyn-Depe.

The symbols found engraved on a number of the figurines are of particular interest. A detailed analysis of them was given in one of the first publications on Altyn-Depe (Masson and Sarianidi 1969; Masson and Sarianidi 1973:38-40, 114-119). It should be understood, however, that their suggested characteristics are preliminary and that they should undergo special investigation. At present, 112 figurines and their fragments with engraved symbols have been found at Altyn-Depe. The symbols have definite territorial ties. Their detailed analysis is a task for the future, and here we will limit ourselves to some general observations. As a rule, the symbols are placed in pairs on the shoulders in front, and at times they are repeated on the back, predominantly below the waist. There are examples in which the same symbol is placed both on the front and back of the trunk, but such figures are a rare exception. Statuettes with varied symbols are also rare. In respect to the latter, a model figurine is one with three symbols on its back: a multi-rayed star in the center bracketed by "triangles with eyelashes" (Plate VIII, item 2).

We have divided the symbols into six groups, although further divisions would be possible. Among the symbols of the first group, the additions to the "triangle with eyelashes" change noticeably. The multi-rayed star in time is rendered with a simple cross. The symbols assigned to the third group vary most radically. In their origin, a number of symbols may be a development of signs singled out in the paintings on Eneolithic ceramics and sometimes found on female terracotta figurines. This major premise, proposed in the first publications (Masson 1967:186; Masson and Sarianidi 1969) was upheld by further investigations (Antonova 1972). Yet not all signs and the way of inscribing them find prototypes in the local traditions. Some analogues may be seen in proto-Sumerian and proto-Elamite writings (Fig. 24). Such detail as the combination of the extremities of the signs with short perpendicular strokes (Plate XI, item 5) is seen in the most carefully made examples, and may be interpreted as a quality imitation of the wedge-shaped forms of similar signs. It may be that this direct influence of eastern ancient writing, particularly proto-Elamite, which was used up to 2300 B.C. and based on a system of magical symbols, took form during the Middle Bronze Age in southern Turkmenistan societies. Three circumstances are witness to this relationship. First, identical signs were found on terracottas and rarely on other objects, not only in Altyn-Depe, but also in other sites of the Bronze Age: Namazga-Depe, Taychanak-Depe, and Khapuz-Depe. Second, given the sizeable collection of finds, the number of variants is insignificant. Third, signs of a different kind are found on figurines which, because of some details of

their iconography, belong to a separate group. This was already noted during the analyses of the first terracotta finds (Masson and Sarianidi 1973:90-97). The new materials confirm this kind of relationship between the various signs and the iconography of the terracottas. For instance, the figures of the first group, those with the "triangles with eyelashes" sign, almost without exception have the face framed with braids-snakes and a thick appliqué braid on the back covered with diverging incisions (Plate VIII). As a rule, these figures also have a high headdress. The braids-snakes are supplanted in only one case with a schematized set of touching circles (Plate XI, item 4), and in another the head has a wreath of flowers (Plate VIII, item 4). The second group of terracottas, those with the star sign (Plate IX, item 5), is also furnished with similar traits— braids-snakes in front, and so on. Other traits, however, are clearly variants: one figure does not have a high headdress but a small, triangular cap; in many the neck is provided with a multi-layered, horizontally positioned necklace with several pendants. The horizontal necklaces with three pendants may be regarded as a specific trait of the third group of statuettes, which also have their distinctive sign (Plate XI, item 5). Necklaces hanging at an angle rather than horizontally placed are one of the traits of the statuettes belonging to the fourth group. These bear on the shoulders the sign of a seed-vegetation or its derivative (Plate IX, items 3, 4, and 7). In any case, 14 of the 17 examples suitable for analysis had angled necklaces. It is possible that the design stylistically (and semantically?) duplicates one of the variants of the vegetation signs found on the shoulders of the figurines. In this group we also find figurines with a "crown," including a bell-shaped form (Plate IX, item 7). The statuettes of the fifth group, those with a zigzag sign on their shoulders, are rare, and therefore it is difficult to talk about a well-established combination of signs. The figurines of the sixth group, those with rows of vertical strokes, have fairly varied headdresses; they include a tall cone and a "crown" with perforations. This group has equal numbers of statuettes with straight and angled necklaces with pendants (Plate IX, item 6). There are quite perceptible differences among the terracottas found in different parts of the site, particularly in the various excavations. While preserving the general iconographic type, terracottas from Excavation 9 (the Elite Quarters) were more carefully made from a technical point of view. They are also more elegant sculpturally (Plate VIII, items 1-3; Plate IX,

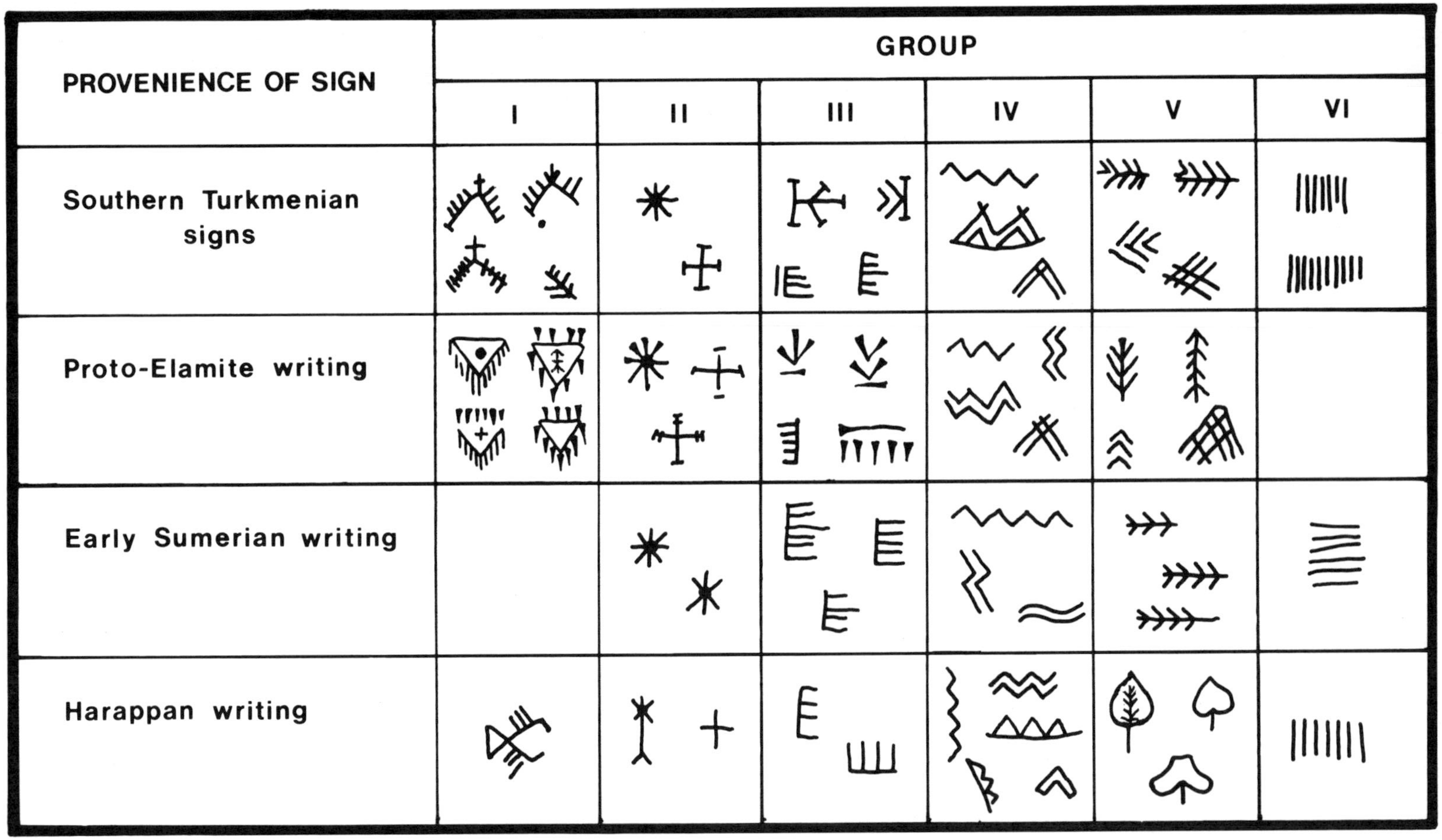

PROVENIENCE OF SIGN	GROUP					
	I	II	III	IV	V	VI
Southern Turkmenian signs						
Proto-Elamite writing						
Early Sumerian writing						
Harappan writing						

Figure 24. Comparison of signs on Altyn-Depe statuettes and early eastern writing.

items 3, 4, and 7). Figures of the same type from Excavations 5 and 10 are as a rule heavy and relatively more crude (Plate IX, item 8; Plate X, item 4).

The monograph on Bronze Age terracottas mentioned above was based to a considerable degree on materials from the excavations of the first four years and proposed two basic hypotheses regarding the interpretation of the groups of female statuettes which differed both in iconographic detail and types of signs placed on them. They could have been signs or marks of various families or communities, and in this case the figurines proper represented spirits, the protectors of the named subdivisions of Altyn-Depe society. Or, the signs could be viewed as symbols-pictograms of the various gods: the star for the goddess of heaven, Innin-Ishtar; the seed-vegetation for the gods of vegetation; the zigzag for the gods of waters (Masson and Sarianidi 1973:119-212).

New materials allow an overall evaluation of the distribution of the various types of terracottas in the different parts of Altyn-Depe (Fig. 25). Although there is a tendency for figurines with particular signs to dominate in certain excavations and divisions, it is clear that there is no exclusive relationship to specific groups of houses as proposed by the god-protector hypothesis. Thus figures and fragments with "triangles with eyelashes" are present, almost without exception, in all excavations and parts of Altyn-Depe. Their greatest concentration was in Excavation 9 where they comprised 43% of the figurines from the excavated houses and 87% from the collective tombs. The excavated houses also yielded statuettes with the seed-vegetation sign to the amount of 36%. In the Wall Mound and its Excavation 5, it is difficult to establish a predominance, since of the five figurines found in the ruins of the houses, three have the multi-rayed star, and in one sample it is repeated many times. We note, however, that with the figures found in the foundations of the houses and in tomb 13 of the same excavation (5) there was one with a "triangle with eyelashes." In the Craftsmen's Quarters, statuettes with the various signs are represented almost equally, but among the surface finds almost half carry the sign of the third group. Of course, it must be taken into account that it is very likely that all of the terracottas were manufactured here and later distributed to the various quarters. A figurine with the star sign, a surface find in the area of Excavation 1, and three such figurines from Excavation 5 were found in the foundations

of houses. On the Copper Mound and in its Excavation 8, five types of figurines were represented; the very rare zigzag type was absent. Half of the statuettes had the seed-vegetation sign. Finally, in the largest area of the settlement, the Concentration of Living Quarters, all six groups were represented, although examples with the parallel strokes dominate (45%).

The above allows us to conclude that the hypothesis tying the signs and the figurines carrying them to localities in separate parts of the community cannot be confirmed with the materials presently available. Most likely, the finds of several variants of terracottas forming the established types reflect the existence of a number of different deities or female spirits in the pantheon of Altyn-Depe. They gradually acquired more specialized functions, a process characteristic of developing civilizations. The question as to what degree this system of signs relates to the presence of a system of writing remains unresolved. Those specimens with various signs in combinations are of great importance to the resolution of this question, but as we have seen, such specimens are rare. One of these, on which a multi-rayed star (a common determinant positioned in front of the name of the diety in Mesopotamian writings) is combined with a "triangle with eyelashes" (Plate VIII, item 2), could be interpreted as meaning "the goddess (of this or that)," but this is no more than a tempting proposition. True, the most numerous sign in Altyn-Depe, the "triangle with eyelashes," suggests the personification of the female deities whose statuettes carry this sign as the guardians of the city, probably the sacred wives of the male astral deity, the god of the moon. For a more convincing solution, however, more investigations will be necessary, and above all, new finds.

Less numerous, and frankly, less significant, is the second group of anthropomorphic figurines, the male statuettes. Stylistically, they follow the flattened aspect of the female terracottas (Plate X, item 3; Plate XII, item 9). Some male figurines duplicate the outline of the female figurines by having narrow waists and wide shoulders. Judging by the available samples, the majority of the male statuettes have widely outstretched arms. A characteristic trait of the Altyn-Depe male statuettes is an appliqué belt sometimes ornamented with depressions or lines. Below the belt is placed a relief representation of the erect male sexual organ. Separate samples have three vertical lines preserved on their necks, perhaps indicating the presence of necklaces with pendants. Sometimes there are engraved representations of

Figure 25 presents a distribution table. Cell values below are the counts represented by the dot tallies printed in each cell; the "Groups of Signs" are pictographic marks shown as glyphs in the original.

GROUPS OF SIGNS	TOWER MOUND			WALL MOUND			CRAFTSMEN'S QUARTERS				COPPER MOUND		Excavation 13	Concentration of Living Quarters	TOTAL FINDS
	Surface Finds	Excavation 9; houses	Excavation 9; tombs	Surface Finds	Excavation 5; houses	Excavation 5; tombs	Surface Finds	Excavation 1	Excavation 10	Excavation 12	Surface Finds	Excavation 8			
 (sign 1)	1	13	7		1	1	1	2		1	1		1	1	30
 (sign 2)	3	3	1		3		1		2		2	1		1	17
 (sign 3)		1				1	5		2			1		1	11
 (sign 4)		11		1			1				8	1		3	25
 (sign 5)					1		1							2	4
 (sign 6)	3	4		1		1	3		1		4		1	7	25
TOTAL FINDS	7	32	8	2	5	3	12	2	5	1	15	3	2	15	112

Figure 25.   *Distribution of Altyn-Depe statuettes with signs.*

trees on the trunks. One of the statuettes has ornamentation of straight and inclined lines covering the entire area above the belt. There is even a more schematic covering of a statuette, completely devoid of arms, but with the invariable belt and rendition of sexual organs.

A special group of anthropomorphic figures is comprised of figures that are schematized to the utmost, hastily made, and apparently intended for a single use. They have a widening conical base, rarely slightly bent, and on the upper part, schematic appliqué representations of outstretched arms, and sometimes a small projection in place of the head (Plate XII, items 6 and 11). In rare cases, there is a suggestion of plaited hair and a projecting beard. As a rule, these anthropomorphic figures are poorly fired or not fired at all.

Ceramic animal figurines are also a characteristic component of the Altyn-Depe archaeological complex. Like the anthropomorphic figurines, they are basically schematic and poorly fired or not fired at all. Yet one comes across carefully made, realistic samples. In such figurines it is not difficult to guess even at the species: the powerful bull with a small hump in back of the neck and large folds about the neck, perhaps belonging to a zebulike species (Plate XIII, items 7-9); the dog with a heavy, squared-off muzzle and a cropped tail (Plate XXI, item 3); and the ram with strongly involuted horns (Plate XIII, items 4 and 5). But often it is only possible to discern that we are dealing with a complete or fragmentary specimen of a four-legged creature. Some figurines possibly portray wild animals, including the saiga. Terracotta heads of camels are often encountered (Plate XIII, items 10 and 11). These, as well as the large terracotta wheels with bilateral bushings, probably belong to cart models. The heads of the animals are sometimes attached to the model by means of a rod attached to their lower ends (Plate XXI, item 12). Fragments of the cart bodies are comparatively rare, leading to the belief that they were made partly of organic materials. Judging by the available models (Plate XIX, item 1) and their fragments, these were a type of board cart of heavy construction to which a pair of camels was rarely harnessed (Plate XXX, item 1). At times the back board, and sometimes both the back and front boards, were absent, perhaps indicating the transport of a special kind of cargo, for instance long wooden beams. Figurines of animals, largely schematic, were found in all houses in all excavations. Of particular interest was the find of a collection of unfired animal figurines in the third

horizon of Excavation 1. They lay not far from the kiln and clearly they were to be fired. The group contained 35 figurines of which the majority represented bulls of various sizes. The heads of the larger bulls were ornamented with a series of holes, and on the shoulders of one a sign (brand?) was engraved. Fifteen other figurines represented various animals, mostly rams.

An important component of the Altyn-Depe assemblages are artifacts which have been called seals. It is probable that this was their principal role, although it is possible that at the same time they were kept as amulets or other sacred objects. These artifacts have a flat surface worked with a pattern of high relief, and evidently they were meant to provide impressions since on the obverse side they are provided with a looped handle for that purpose and also for suspension. In a number of burials the seals were positioned about the hip bones; apparently they were carried on a belt. Impressions of seals are rare at Altyn-Depe and, generally speaking, they are represented only on fragments of fired clay (Plate XVI, item 13). At other sites of this period, particularly Shahr-i Sokhta, the impressions are very numerous and varied (Tosi 1969:figs. 277-292). The seals could have been used to stamp various things under the jurisdiction of a community or family. As an ethnographic parallel we mention the case of a wooden seal from Afghanistan representing a six-rayed rosette in an oval, which was used to stamp produce (Vavilov and Bukinich 1959:p. 188, fig. 89).

Technically, the seals are made in two ways. Seals of bronze mixed with low quality silver are the most widespread; they have high relief and were cast with the lost wax process. Stone seals with ornamentation made by drilling small holes close together to form lines (Plate XVI, item 17; Plate XVII, items 1 and 4) are more rare. There are rare instances of terracotta seals (Plate XVII, item 5). In form and character all seals may be divided into two large groups: zoomorphic (or representing zoomorphic motifs) and geometric. The first group is relatively small and may be divided in two subgroups. The seals of the first subgroup imitate the outline of bodies of animals although, as a rule, they are somewhat shortened so as to keep the seal in nearly rectangular proportion. From Altyn-Depe we have seals representing a goat (Plate XVII, item 14); a hooved animal, probably a ram (Plate XXIX, item 9); a feline beast of prey (Plate XVII, item 10); and a fantastic three-headed dragon with the body of a feline beast of prey, one head of a bird of prey, and two heads of a reptile, perhaps of a snake

Figure 26.   Bronze Age seals (items 1 to 3 and 7 to 9) and motifs on Eneolithic painted pottery of southern Turkmenistan (items 4 to 6 and 10 to 12).

(Plate XVII, item 12). Another syncretic form is seen on a seal representing a four-legged animal with a beak and with talons on its paws (Plate XVII, item 8). A seal representing an eagle with outspread wings was found at Namazga-Depe (Masson and Sarianidi 1972:pl. 47), and a seal with a goat was found at the small site of Shor-Depe (Masimov 1978b). At Altyn-Depe a seal with a bird with spread wings was also found, but its head was heavily corroded (Plate XVII, item 13). Examples of the second subgroup contain images in the form of a snake coiled inside a half-moon. One such seal was a terracotta seal (Plate XVII, item 3), and another was metallic and had an appendage incorporating a cross (Plate XVII, item 15).

The geometric seals may be divided into four subgroups. Those in the form of a cross are most frequent and comprise about half of the metallic seals at Altyn-Depe (Plate XVI, items 1-8, 10, and 14). There are also schematic crosses of a simplified kind and complex crosses rendered in a multi-stepped formation which appears to duplicate ornamentation on the painted ceramics. In the center of the crosslike seals we often find a supplementary figure: an oval, square, or small cross. Sawlike, dentated lines were often made at the ends of the crosses, and the addition of this detail individualizes each seal. Stone seals also are often cruciform. Square seals are very rare and often include a representation of a cross (Plate XVII, items 4 and 5). On one large oval seal four double circles surround a triangle. In two other similar seals a triangle (Plate XXIX, item 8) and a multi-rayed star respectively (Plate XXIX, item 10) were incorporated. Employing an oval as the compositional center, four-rayed and five-rayed (Plate XVI, item 9) seals were formed. A small subgroup of three seals duplicates the stepped pyramids also particular to painted ceramics. Two such seals have the form of a stepped pyramid (Plate XXIX, item 5), and the third had pyramids united at their apices (Plate XVI, item 12). As already implied, the majority of the seals are semantically linked to the symbols of the Eneolithic painted ceramics of southern Turkmenistan (Fig. 26) (Masson 1967d, 1970d). But there are a number of new examples, particularly the three-headed dragon and the snakes in the crescent moon.

At Altyn-Depe stone artifacts are fairly numerous and varied. They include flint, haft-less, and laurel leaf-shaped arrowheads which often served as drills, as shown by special microwear studies (Skakun 1972). There were also stone vessels turned from light, semi-transparent marblelike material with dark veining (Plate VII, items 2 and 4); beads of a simple profile made of semiprecious stones; and numerous large stone artifacts: grinders, pestles, mortars, spatulas for smoothing pottery, scrapers for working hides, abrading and cutting instruments for smoothing the frayed edges of metallic artifacts. Apparently the presence nearby of cobble deposits was conducive to widespread use of stone artifacts during the Bronze Age. This usage reflects the maximal technological achievements of previous epochs. In the majority of the cases, however, the stone artifacts do not form the characteristic typological groups which define the cultural specifics of the archaeological assemblages of Altyn-Depe. Some of their traits may be seen in the architecture. The rectangular clay bricks represent the traditional format in the early agricultural complexes of southern Turkmenistan. Yet such architectural particulars as the three-stepped pilasters, the rectangular edifices positioned in a row, and interior hearths on a low, almost rectangular platform with a large oval depression in the center to a certain degree make up the Altyn-Depe complex.

As for the usual combination of types of artifacts, the Altyn-Depe assemblage is characterized by unornamented thin-walled ceramics fired in two-tiered kilns. They were made with a rapidly revolving potter's wheel, and stand out because of their elegant forms. Goblets with a sharp bend in the wall near the rim; vases on high, hollow bases; and elongated biconical or pot-shaped vessels with a high, bell-shaped neck and on a high supporting base are among the most remarkable. Of the metal artifacts, the knives with a small, straight haft and a flat, leaflike blade are typical, as are the pins with a thickened end topped with a figure. The burials are either individual, flexed, and most often oriented to the northeast-by-east, or collective in rectangular tombs made of clay bricks. The predominantly cross-shaped metallic seals with internal partitions and a handle on the obverse side, in addition to the stone seals with the pattern made by a series of drilled, adjoining holes, are characteristic. Among the terracottas, the flattened, sitting female statuettes with faces framed with curling braid-snakes and signs on shoulders and back are typical, as are models of four-wheeled carts drawn by camels. Some of the surveyed artifacts have distinct local prototypes

(the seals follow a number of ceramic ornaments). Others, such as the goblets and knives, are found even outside of southern Turkmenistan, in other archaeological assemblages. It is precisely the combination of all of these types of artifacts, however, that results in the lasting Namazga V type of cultural assemblage, which, since it is the most representative collection, may be called the culture of Altyn-Depe, or the Altyn culture in the archaeological sense of the term (Masson 1974g).

The territorial extent of the Altyn-Depe archaeological assemblage within southern Turkmenistan includes the piedmont of the Kopet Dagh and, as the investigations of later years indicate, also the Murghab delta. The metal artifacts typical of Altyn-Depe, including the partitioned seals and the shapes of ceramic vessels, are found at Namazga-Depe (Kuftin 1956; Masson 1956b; Masimov 1974a). Analogous seals, ceramics, and terracotta figurines (the latter at times with engraved signs) were found in the small sites between Baba-Durmaz and Artyk (Shchetenko 1968b, 1970a; Masimov 1968). The material culture of these sites contains some specific traits, particularly notable in the ceramics, which were already noted by I.S. Masimov (1974a:44-54). Thus the corrugated high pedestals of vases and beakers are widespread at Namazga-Depe but rare at Altyn-Depe. The "teapots" of Namazga-Depe, unlike the analogous vessels at Altyn-Depe, have emphasized necks, often bell-shaped and fairly high. I might add that it is precisely at Namazga-Depe where we find a particular type of female statuettes (Masson and Sarianidi 1973:90). This type is specific enough that those that were found at Altyn-Depe (Plate IX, item 2) differed slightly because of the mode of manufacture by local craftsmen. Apparently, we have here the existence of a local Namazga variant of the Altyn culture to which Namazga-Depe, Shor-Depe, Taychanak-Depe, and Kosha-Depe belong (Fig. 27 II).

Already in the early fifties the presence of Bronze Age agricultural settlements in the Murghab delta was established. They were dated to two chronological stages of Namazga VI type: an early Auchin and a late Takhirbay (Masson 1959a). In the beginning of the 1970s the work was extended by V.I. Sarianidi, who discovered a number of sites in which even surface finds yielded significant materials, among them an interesting collection of seals (Sarianidi 1973, 1975, 1976a). But more importantly, a group of Bronze Age sites, the earliest in the new Murghab oasis

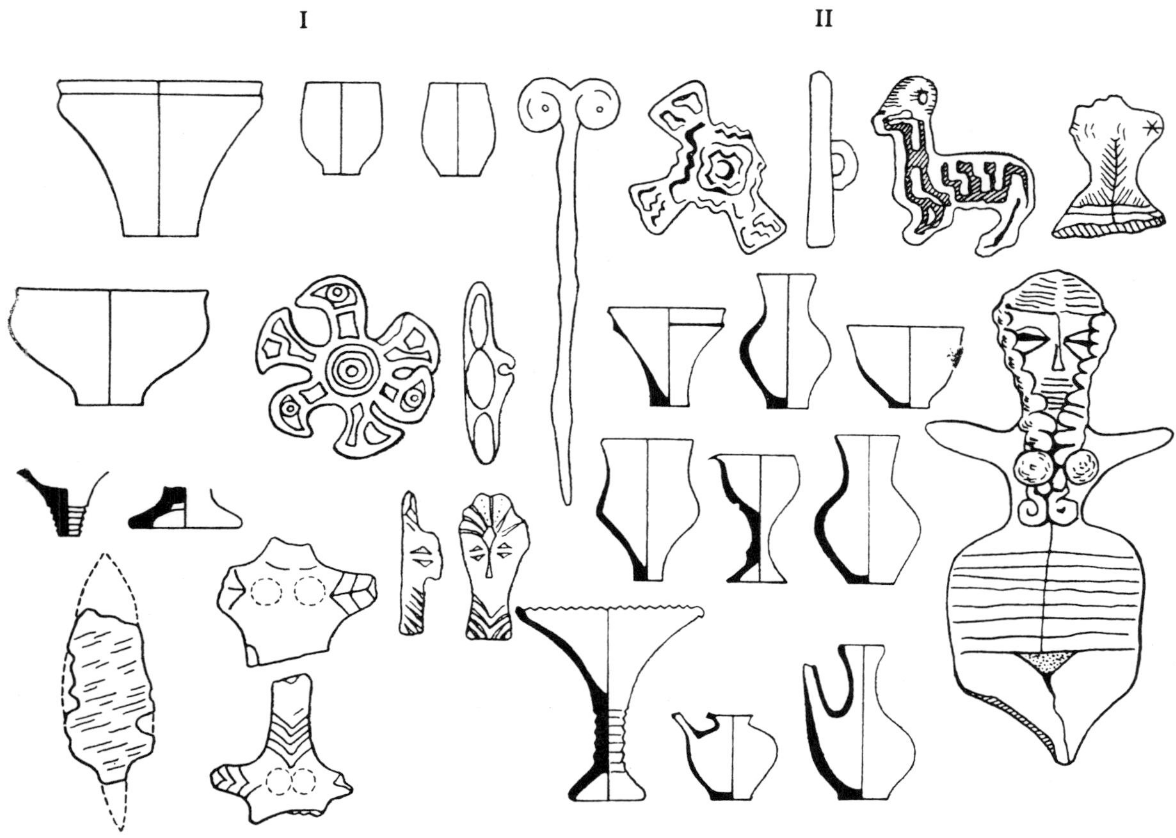

Figure 27.   The Kelleli (I) and Namazga (II) variants of Altyn-Depe culture.

area, was found. These are the Kelleli sites which were discovered and investigated by I.S. Masimov (1976a, 1979; Masimov and Lyapin 1977). His first assemblage of objects is identical to the late Namazga V of the foothill belt. The assemblage contained ceramics, partitioned bronze seals, and terracotta statuettes, including such specific statuettes as those of the Altyn-Depe fourth group [see above] (Masimov 1979:pp. 123, 128-129, fig. 7, item 6). The entire collection of materials not only points to close ties with Altyn-Depe ceramics of the second developmental stage, and in part the third, but also to its association with one archaeological culture. This conclusion allows us to propose yet another local variant of the Altyn culture, the Kelleli (Fig. 27 I). Masimov's second assemblage, which preserves specific traits of continuity, already differs in a number of indices. The composition of ceramic forms changes, and we find such new forms as goblets on a high, cylindrical base, terracottas changed in form, a new type of seals-amulets,

and also cylindrical seals. It seems that chronologically and culturally this assemblage is close to the materials which formed earlier in the Auchin stage of Namazga VI.

Having established the boundaries of the Altyn-Depe culture, let us consider the question of absolute chronology. Earlier, we already broached the subject of internal chronology and synchronization of Altyn-Depe excavations in part. Trenches cut in Excavations 9 and 10 revealed three Namazga V building horizons and, as a rule, buildings were uncovered on the level of the highest horizon. Three synchronous building horizons were also established in Excavations 5 and 7. Here the excavations were carried out over a wide area and all three horizons were fully uncovered. The ceramics found in these horizons dated to the first and second stages of the scheme devised for the classification of ceramic assemblages. All of this information allows us to synchronize the four basic excavations and to regard their uncovered structures as roughly contemporaneous within a limited period of time (possibly several decades). Significantly, the entire eastern part of Altyn-Depe where excavations were made (with the exception of the small Excavation 1 in the Craftsmen's Quarters) did not contain materials of the third stage. To the contrary, Trench 1, cut in the western part, had a 4.5 m accumulation dating to Namazga V, and on the basis of pottery, 2.5 m of this accumulation represented the late stage. This indicates the gradual abandonment of Altyn-Depe. The eastern quarters, including the Elite Quarters and the monumental cultural center, were deserted first. Gradual decay followed. This is change is clearly visible in the deterioration of the large structures in Excavation 7 and the filling of the monumental gateway uncovered in Excavation 8. The gateway was cluttered with plain structures.

We shall now turn to the problem of the absolute dating of the Altyn-Depe culture. With the first publication of a stratigraphic cross-section of Namazga-Depe, the synchronization of Namazga V and Hissar III was already established (Masson 1956b). Further analysis and new materials obtained from the early excavations of Altyn-Depe justified a similar synchronization and extended the line of comparisons to the east, establishing the contemporaneity of assemblages of the Namazga V type and the developed assemblages of Harappa (Kuzmina 1966:89; Masson 1967d:173-176). Actually, a series of analogies between the materials of the Altyn culture of the Middle Bronze Age and Hissar IIIB indicates their contemporaneous existence. This series refers to the crosslike beads (Schmidt 1937:p. 226, fig. 135) and the partitioned bronze seals, including those representing a cross. The gray vessel from the first Altyn hoard clearly belongs to a number of imports originating, if not from Hissar proper, from sites neighboring it and close to it in culture (Schmidt 1937:pl. XXXVII, H-3841).

Analogies with Harappan materials are many and varied (Masson 1967d:174-176; Shchetenko 1968a, 1970c). A Harappan origin is suggested for the Altyn potlike vessels on a base (Mackay 1938:vol. 2, pl. LII, item 10; pl. LV, item 12; Wheeler 1947:104). There are also bronze vessels of similar form (Marshall 1931:vol. 3, pl. CXLI, item 6) which were probably a resultant prototype having a high enough value, in comparison with the ceramic, to serve as a trade object. Ceramic stands, which are characteristic of the third developmental stage of Altyn-Depe, are found in the lower layers of Mohenjo-Daro, although they are very rare and nonindicatory

(Mackay 1938:vol. 2, pl. LXII, items 25, 26). They are, however, widespread in the upper layers (Mackay 1938:vol. 1, p. 206; vol. 2, pl. LVII, items 23, 24), and also in Chanaku-Daro (Mackay 1943:pl. XXVI, items 4-11) and Harappa (Wheeler 1947:p. 115, pl. XLV).

Considerable similarity also can be seen in metallic objects. Flat knives without axial ribbing are common in southern Turkmenistan during the Middle Bronze Age; they are quite unusual in Hissar metallurgy but typical for the early sites of the Indus valley (Mackay 1938:vol. 7, pl. CXXVIII, item 15). Here one can also find parallels to the metal frying pan with handle found in one of the Altyn-Depe burials (Mackay 1938:pl. XXV, items 17, 24). But it is particularly important that at Altyn-Depe objects were found which undoubtedly were carried there from the Indus valley. For instance, artifacts of elephant ivory were found at three points. In the assemblage associated with the priest's burial in Excavation 7, ring-shaped ivory beads were found. A number of elephant ivory artifacts were included in one of the hoards uncovered on the Tower Mound (Ganyalin 1967). They are square and oval flat chips and also four rectangular sticks with concentric rings on three sides (progressively, one, two, and three rings) and an ornament on the fourth. Absolutely identical objects are very common in the upper as well as the lower layers of Mohenjo-Daro (Marshall 1931:vol. 1, pp. 560-561; vol 2, pl. CXLIII, items 47, 49, 51). In 4th century A.D. Sanskrit texts, such sticks are described as having a role in fortunetelling (Brown 1964:34) in which the thrown sticks with rings representing numbers 1 to 4, that is, their various combinations, are interpreted. Both at Altyn-Depe and Mohenjo-Daro the number 4 is replaced with an ornament, but there is no doubt that they were employed to the same end, particularly since at Altyn-Depe four sticks were also found. Finally, one such stick was found in the tomb of the "prominent citizen" to the east of the Tower Mound (Plate XXII, item 5). All this points to steady and systematic contacts between the Altyn-Depe and Harappan cultures. This is emphasized by the finds of nearly rectangular seals of the Harappan type: one with a swastika in the already-mentioned priest's burial in Excavation 7, and the other with two symbols of proto-Indic writing in Excavation 9 (Plate XXII, items 1a and 1b).

Parallels with Mesopotamia have not been thoroughly studied. We can only point out that the pot-shaped vessels on a base are very close to those of the Old Babylonian period (Delougaz

1952:122, 132), and the hatched triangle and belts of line scratched on the shoulders of female terracotta figures found their analogues in the figures from Nippur dating from the end of the 3rd to the beginning of the 2nd millennium B.C. (Buren 1930:pp. 5, 16, 26-27, pl. I, item 6; pl. V, item 25; pl. VII, items 26, 38; Ziegler 1962:pl. 12, item 19b; Dales 1963:figs. 7, 33, 34). The three-stepped pilasters found in the culture center and the main gateway to Altyn-Depe were widespread in the monumental architecture of southern Mesopotamia during the last third of the 3rd millennium B.C., although they first appeared almost a thousand years earlier.

Of the other archaeological complexes which have become widely known in the scientific literature only after the initial excavations at Altyn-Depe, two should be mentioned because of their fairly clear stratigraphy and definite ties with Altyn-Depe expressed in the material culture. These are Mundigak in southern Afghanistan and Shahr-i Sokhta in southeastern Iran. The ties between the southern Turkmenistan complexes and Mundigak become evident during the Eneolithic; we shall discuss this relationship further (see p. 112). At a much later period we come across the pot-shaped vessels on a base which are close analogues in form to those of Harappa and Altyn-Depe (Casal 1961:vol. 2, fig. 73, item 232). They first occur in Mundigak layer IV, 1. In Mundigak IV, 2 a large vessel with polychrome paintings of crosses in cartouches were found (Casal 1961:fig. 91). It clearly stands out from the general mass of painted ceramics and has direct analogies in the ornamentation of large vessels of the Namazga IV period of Altyn-Depe and Namazga-Depe. In both of these southern Turkmenistan sites the paintings on such vessels are also polychrome and in reality are a coarse variant of painted ceramics formed on the basis of Geoksyur style vessels. The Mundigak seals are also of great interest. In its Complex III, stone seals with a drilled lunate ornament appear; they are widespread in Complex IV. In Complex IV, as well as earlier and later stages, there are partitioned metal seals, often cruciform, which are direct analogies of the Altyn-Depe seals (Casal 1961:pl. XLV, items 1, 3). Thus there is a basis for the partial synchronization of the complexes, in any case those of Mundigak IV and Namazga V.

Shahr-i Sokhta in Iranian Seistan, in the former delta of the Helmand River, is without doubt one of the important sites of the Middle East. Excavation started in 1967. A preliminary survey brought to view 50 early agricultural sites in the region, which are now located partly in Afghanistan and partly in Iran. On the basis of surveys carried out by A. Stein at the beginning of the century, it was possible to deduce that the most notable of these, Shahr-i Sokhta, was the regional capital during the Bronze Age (Masson 1964b:279). Since 1967 the excavation of Shahr-i Sokhta was carried out by an Italian expedition under the leadership of M. Tosi (Tosi 1968, 1969, 1971; Lamberg-Karlovsky and Tosi 1973). A detailed stratigraphy revealing four periods was established. The first included three phases (8-10), the second also three phases (5-7), the third only two (3 and 4), and the fourth again three (1, 2, and the latest, 0). At present, there are only limited publications that throw light on the materials of this stratigraphic column. Undoubtedly, period I contains materials of the southern Turkmenistan Eneolithic (see p. 112). Analogies in the later deposits are fewer, but all are present. Thus period III contained a vessel with polychrome ornamentation which is practically identical with the painting of late Namazga IV and, in part, Altyn 4 (Lamberg-Karlovsky and Tosi 1973:fig. 57). In addition, it was precisely then that ceramics made on a rapidly revolving potter's wheel became widespread at Shahr-i Sokhta. The unpainted ceramics of period IV, particularly the pot-shaped vessels on a high base, are very close to the southern Turkmenistan vessels of Namazga V (Lamberg-Karlovsky and Tosi 1973:figs. 61, 63). The Shahr-i Sokhta period II steatite seals, although they contain cruciform figures and pyramids, on the whole differ from the Namazga V Altyn examples. The partitioned bronze seals, however, are very close to those of southern Turkmenistan (Lamberg-Karlovsky and Tosi 1973:figs. 41-49). In the existing publications their stratigraphic position is not specified, and in general they are attributed to periods II and III. Possibly the first samples of such seals appeared relatively early. V.I. Sarianidi thinks that at Ulug-Depe the ceramic and stone seals with holders on the obverse side were already present during Namazga IV (Sarianidi 1977:88). A metal seal holder was found in layer IVB of Yahya-Depe. With its complex form of a multi-stepped cross, it is strikingly close to the Altyn samples (Lamberg-Karlovsky and Tosi 1973:fig. 41). We shall return to the chronology of this site, but at present we think that we have here one of the earliest examples of seals of this type. It can be proposed that Namazga V is contemporaneous with Shahr-i Sokhta IV, and at the most, partly contemporaneous with Shahr-i Sokhta III.

A similar synchronization of the Altyn-Depe materials allows us to tackle the questions of absolute chronology. In previous publications, I dated assemblages of the Namazga V type to the end of the 3rd to the first quarter of the 2nd millennium B.C., or roughly 2100-1650 B.C. (Masson 1970a:19). New efforts have been applied to correct the dating. Results obtained by the radiocarbon method suggest a somewhat earlier date for the assemblage, particularly for its early phases. Let us look at the changes made in the 1970s in the chronologies of the sites with which analogies were made earlier. Perhaps the Harappan chronology remains the most solid one. The 2500-1500 B.C. date accepted by M. Wheeler in the 1940s remained unchanged until 1962, when a series of radiocarbon dates resulted in the date being compressed to 2100-1600 B.C. (Lal 1962-1963). In the estimate of W. Fairservis (1971), the Harappan culture hardly existed longer than 500 years. D.P. Agrawal proposed the general date of 3200-1750 B.C., which in his opinion agrees with the analysis of Harappan and Harappan-like finds in Mesopotamia (Agrawal 1971:72ff.). Then, on the basis of a comparison with the stratigraphy of Tepe Yahya, the beginning of Harappa was extended to 2500 B.C. (Rao 1973b). This, of course, raised objections. Agrawal insisted on 2350-1700 B.C. for the Indus Valley Harappa and for the peripheral regions to which it later penetrated during 2200-1700 B.C. (Agrawal 1971:208). Let me add that in contrast to the stratigraphy, the absolute chronology of Yahya-Tepe does not appear to be fully resolved. Moreover, G. Dales notes that the calibrated radiocarbon dates place the beginning of Harappa at almost 2600 B.C., making it contemporaneous with the Akkadian and Third Dynasty of Ur (Dales 1973:165).

An analogous attempt to shift the dating was also undertaken in respect to Hissar. Having analyzed the analogues at hand, R. Dyson at first proposed synchronizing Hissar IIIB with the early stages of the Third Dynasty of Ur (2132-2024 B.C.) and advancing Hissar IIIC to 1900 B.C. or 1800 B.C. (Dyson 1965:241-242). Later, on the basis of calibrated radiocarbon dates, the same investigator shifted Hissar IIIB to 2800-2400 B.C., and he synchronized Hissar IIIC partly with the Akkadian, partly with the Third Dynasty of Ur, placing it in the chronological bracket of 2400-2000 B.C. (Bovington, Dyson, Mahadavi and Masoumi 1974). In this case, the earliest analogies to the splendid arms of Hissar, which D. McCown compared with the arms from the royal tombs of the First Dynasty of Ur, have

proven to be correct (McCown 1942). In addition to saying that it is preferable to utilize analogies from the latest rather than the earliest phase of this or that assemblage, it must be pointed out that not all Hissar stratigraphy is completely reliable. This inadequacy is evident in the published plans of buildings in various layers, where the indistinct outlines of the walls are in a sense concealed by superimposed hachuring indicating the walls of the lower horizons. Dyson and his co-workers undertook verifying excavations at Hissar which fully confirmed the methodological carelessness and laid foundations for a new stratigraphy of this redoubtable site.[1]

The absolute chronology of Shahr-i Sohkta is based on analogies with Mesopotamian complexes dated by radiocarbon and paleomagnetic analyses. In sum, M. Tosi and his colleagues date Period I to 3200-2800 B.C., Period II to 2800-2400 B.C., Period III to 2400-2100 B.C., and Period IV to 2100-1800 B.C. Perhaps the lower reaches of this chronological scheme need refinement. For instance, the finding of seals of the Jemdet Nasr style in the earliest layer of Shahr-i Sokhta suggests an optional date for that period, since cylinder seals were widespread in Mesopotamia even during the Early Dynastic period. A definite tendency to extend the chronology is associated with the results of the excavation of Yahya-Tepe, where the enthusiastic discoverer suddenly proposed a long chronology, placing, for instance, the lowest layer in the middle of the 6th millennium B.C. (Lamberg-Karlovsky, C.C. and Lamberg-Karlovsky, M., 1971:103). In later publications the lowest layer is more realistically dated to the second half of the 5th to the beginning of the 4th millennium B.C. (Vidali, M.L., Vidali, E. and Lamberg-Karlovsky 1976:237). I think that the dating of the most interesting complex of Yahya IV should be also corrected. It was subdivided into three phases which Lamberg-Karlovsky dated as follows: IV,C: 3400-3000 B.C.; IV,B: 3000-2500 B.C.; IV,A: 2100-1800 B.C. I visualize a much shorter and realistic chronology which would date the layer containing proto-Elamite tablets scarcely beyond the confines of the 3rd millennium B.C.; the thickness of cultural accumulations in layers IV,B and IV,C are not great enough to stretch their dating to almost a millennium. An investigation of the proto-Elamite tablets from Yahya-Tepe has shown that they date to a much earlier period than the analogous tablets from Susa proper (Vayman 1972:132).

In addition to the comparative analysis of the Altyn materials, there is at our disposal a series of radiocarbon dates done in the Leningrad and Berlin laboratories (Masson 1970c:18-19). *Without calibration,* the dates suggest the following: Namazga II complex with ceramics of the Yalangach type, 3810 ± 50 B.C.; Late Namazga IV (Altyn IV), 2620 ± 50 B.C.; Namazga V, Excavation 7, 1510 ± 60 B.C.; Namazga V, Excavation 7, 1390 ± 60 B.C.; Namazga V, Excavation 5, 3360 ± 50 B.C.; Namazga V, Excavation 7, 2650 ± 100 B.C.; Namazga V, Excavation 7, 2570 ± 100 B.C.

In addition to the above, there is a Berlin laboratory set of dates of 2646 ± 100 B.C. and 2690 ± 100 B.C. for the Late Namazga IV layers at Ulug-Depe. Taking into account that some of the dates, for reasons unknown, differ from each other as well as from the realities of the stratigraphy, and applying the MASCA correction factors to them, we conclude that the change from

Namazga IV to Namazga V occurred about 2500 B.C. This places Namazga V wholly in the second half of the 3rd millennium B.C., just as is proposed at present for the synchronous Harappa and Hissar III. Excessive lowering of the dating, however, will create a hard-to-fill lacuna in the stratigraphic column of southern Turkmenistan which so clearly illustrates the succession of cultural complexes. This hardly allows the placing of the entire Namazga V complex lower than 2000 B.C. The Mesopotamian analogies to Altyn-Depe materials, and they are certainly not insignificant, are on the whole in the same chronological bracket. More likely, and similar to D.P. Agrawal's proposition for Harappa, at present the most reasonable date for the Namazga V layers of Altyn-Depe appears to be 2300-1850 B.C.

---

[1]Professor R. Dyson kindly informed me of the results of the excavations while I was in Philadelphia in August 1979. While examining The University Museum's collection originating in the excavations of E. Schmidt, I came across a gray ornamented vessel, which in the Museum registry was dated to the Hissar IIIA complex, identical to one found in southern Turkmenistan in the upper layers of Kara-Depe in a Namazga III complex. This once again points to the necessity of re-examining all of the early material in the light of the new stratigraphy of Hissar established as a result of new and methodologically superior excavations.

VI

Altyn-Depe as an Urban Center

Structural and Functional Characteristics

The basic excavations at Altyn-Depe involved the layers of the Middle Bronze Age, that is, the Namazga V period. During this period, there were two large centers in southern Turkmenistan, Namazga-Depe and Altyn-Depe. There were also a number of much smaller settlements in the foothill belt. A still larger number were not preserved at all, having been buried by alluvial and diluvial sedimentation which reached the thickness of 10 m in the Namazga-Depe region, or they were obliterated in the expansion of fields in subsequent epochs. Of the small settlements we might mention the southern mound of Anau and three sites between Artyk and Baba-Durmaz: Shor-Depe, Kosha-Depe, and Taychanak-Depe. These formed a small agricultural oasis which culturally, and perhaps economically, gravitated towards Namazga-Depe, some 25 km away. Excavations of the upper cultural layer at Shor-Depe were carried out by A.F. Ganyalin (see Masimov 1978b) and continued by A.Ya. Shchetenko (1968b, 1970a). The latter also excavated Taychanak-Depe (Shchetenko 1968c). I.S. Masimov (1968) dug a trench at Kosha-Depe. These settlements are small and in their central parts occupy between 0.5 and 1.5 hectares. Judging by the published cross-sections of the cuts (Shchetenko 1970a:37), sometimes the materials found in trenching in the vicinity of the sites were washouts from the cultural layer of the central part. In addition to the high quality ceramics typical of Namazga V, almost all of the elements that enter into that archaeological complex were found here. These comprised the terracotta female statuettes, figures of animals, models of carts, terracotta spindle whorls, and silver and bronze seals with crosses or figures of animals. The excavated buildings were massive and multi-chambered. The plain rooms were crowded together, reminiscent of the building uncovered in Excavations 8 and 10 of Altyn-Depe. There were no craft centers, monumental structures, or carefully planned spacious houses. This lack again underlines the qualitative differences of Altyn-Depe, the large center of the Middle Bronze Age, which not only far exceeded the smaller sites in dimensions but, judging by the excavations of many years, had an entirely different internal structure.

Many forms of the internal structure were closely associated with the work of specific groups, that is, with functions carried out by the population of the Bronze Age community. The basis of the economy was agriculture and animal husbandry. At present, Altyn-Depe is in an empty steppe which comes to life only with the ephemeral green of spring. There is quite a bit of evidence, however, that during the Bronze Age the landscape was somewhat different. The analyses of charcoal from layers of different periods, starting with the Neolithic and reaching into the 2nd millennium B.C., indicate that there existed in the riverine region of the Chaacha and Meana vegetation of the tugaic type [that is, along the rivers where the water table of permanent streams was relatively high and accessible to the roots of trees], composed of poplar, maple, elm, and ash (Lisitsina 1978). Judging by this early vegetation, the region was then comparatively better watered. The small river watering it, which today is filled only during the rainy period, secured the growth of the dense tugaic vegetation. The wild boar lived in it; its bones were rarely found in Altyn-Depe excavations. It is notable that while during the 6th to 5th millennia B.C. the elm was initially prevalent on the basis of samples collected, in the 4th millennium the poplar is found more often, and at the end of the 3rd to the beginning of the 2nd millennium B.C., elm charcoal is altogether absent. Apparently, this long-lived tree was the first to be subjected to man's destructive activities. In addition, the faunal remains from Altyn-Depe indicate it was near fairly extensive areas of desert and steppe inhabited by the gazelle, wild ass, and saiga. Tugaic vegetation filled the low-lying areas along the Meana-Chaya and its tributaries, spreading widely over the depositional and detrital cones of the river and parts of the adjacent steppe. This was the natural environment of Altyn-Depe during the Bronze Age. It was in exactly this kind of environment that agriculture developed and became the basic food provider for the population. Tools for the preparation of grain were found in almost every farm dwelling in Altyn-Depe: grinders, pestles, and mortars. Experiments have shown that working a grinder could produce about 2 kg of flour in 4 hours, but such work was exceedingly heavy and tiring. No wonder that alien or external labor was usually utilized for the grinding of grain within the conditions of the domestic economy. It is interesting that even today, women using grinders produce twice as much flour as men in a given period of time (Korobkova 1974). Oval bread ovens were found in many farmyards. In southern Turkmenistan these have been present since the Neolithic. At Altyn-Depe grain was ground and bread baked practically everywhere. Apparently, only a part of the population was engaged in growing grain crops. In any case, in one of the houses in Excavation 13, a bronze scythe was found. Of course, during harvest almost the entire population could be engaged in field work.

Finds of charred grains in one of the Altyn-Depe trenches indicate that the principal agricultural product was hull-less barley, and to a lesser degree, soft club wheat. Varieties which were adapted to irrigation were cultivated; this clearly indicates the use of irrigation agriculture. The crop was pure; the absence of seeds of weeds indicates the purity which could be achieved by careful weeding by hand (Yanushevich 1977:169). Finds in other sites show that grapes and chick peas were also cultivated during the Bronze Age. The dominance of barley was typical for many countries of the ancient East. It has high nutritive value and the best yield under the conditions of irrigation agriculture. The finds of models of wheeled carts were for a long time the basis for the proposition that draft animals with some kind of primitive wooden plow were used for working the fields (Masson 1956a:246). Today, the proposition has been confirmed: a beaker

found in Afghanistan portrays a scene of bulls being harnessed to a primitive plow (Deshayes 1978). The utilization of draft animals for the difficult task of plowing rendered Bronze Age farming fairly efficient. Altyn-Depe must have consumed agricultural products from a fairly extensive region; it also preserved the produce (note the storage rooms in the cult complex and the storage courtyard in Excavation 9). Very likely Altyn-Depe was also the organizer of farm production within the boundaries of the surrounding realm.

To a considerable degree, the above also pertains to animal husbandry. The products of this activity are evident in all farm-dwelling complexes. It is interesting that, as established by N. M. Ermolova, the long bones were broken in butchering the carcass. This behavior is not characteristic of people who were quite familiar with the anatomy of animals. It seems that the knowledge of the "professional" herders was forgotten by many who used their products. Almost everywhere in the Altyn-Depe excavations, there is a strong preponderance of bones of small horned cattle, almost exclusively sheep. Among them are many large individual sheep. Bones of large horned cattle, on the other hand, are rare, and for the most part are bones of aged animals of average dimensions. Ermolova, who had studied the osteological collections in the field during the later excavations at Altyn-Depe, is of the opinion that large horned cattle were kept principally for milk and as draft animals. The cause for this was the absence in the desertic-tugaic landscape of rich pasture land appropriate for cows. Cattle herding, oriented toward the breeding of sheep, had already begun in southern Turkmenistan during the Neolithic (Masson 1976a:40). Given the natural environment, the level of productive forces, and the capability of the community, pastoralism combined with oasis, small-field irrigation crops were the most effective form of economy during the Bronze Age. The dog, which judging by bone remains was rather large with a short muzzle and powerful jaws, was at the disposal of the herders. The terracotta figurines portray a dog with a compact body, squared off trunk, short muzzle, poorly indicated ears, and a short, erect stump of a tail. Ermolova has a good base from which to conclude that this was a sheep dog with cropped ears and tail, close in appearance to those seen in present-day Turkmenistan (Ermolova 1977:32). In comparison, only a small, domesticated dog, in dimensions hardly different from a jackal, is known from the Neolithic farm communities in the Chaacha region. This indicates that over the past 3000 years the Altyn-Depe breeders developed a specialized breed capable of standing up to the wolf and being a reliable helper in herding the flock. No doubt selective breeding was also applied to domesticated cattle.

The bones of camels were seldom encountered at Altyn-Depe. Apparently the camel was not used for food. The first bones of camels were found in the Eneolithic layers of Geoksyur, Anau, and Elen-Depe. Models of four-wheeled carts with representations of camel heads are associated with the Namazga IV period. The camels are represented with their characteristic long hair on the front of the neck and are placed on the front panel. The predominant use of camels in transportation is underlined by the extreme rarity of their bones in cultural levels. The very interesting figure of a two-humped Bactrian camel from the Altyn-Depe excavations led Ermolova to propose that it was indeed in the region of southern Turkmenistan and northern Iran where this animal was first domesticated (Ermolova 1976).

It seems that the herds in the oases within the foothill belt of southern Turkmenistan were of varied composition. In the southern mound of Anau large horned cattle and the domesticated pig dominate. Perhaps this well-watered region permitted the population of the small settlement to successfully rear precisely these animals. The Namazga IV layers of Excavation 5 of Altyn-Depe yielded a somewhat greater quantity of large horned cattle bones than did the Namazga V layers. This change perhaps reflects the gradual desiccation of the region and the resulting diminution of pasturage. A similar tendency a thousand years earlier led to the gradual abandonment of the Geoksyur oasis (Masson 1976a:41).

The meat ration of Altyn-Depe inhabitants was supplemented by the hunt. The list of those wild animals which were the object of the hunt is fairly extensive. It includes the onager, wild boar, gazelle, saiga, mouflon, wild goat, and fox. The onager was preferred since it yielded the most meat. Often the onager was run down close to the settlement, and its carcass was taken there intact. This is confirmed by the rare finds of the lower leg parts, which were not consumed; if transport was from afar, the legs were usually cut off and discarded. In sum, bones of animals from the excavations at Altyn-Depe were fairly numerous and indicate the regular use of meat.

In southern Turkmenistan, agriculture, animal husbandry, and hunting had been tradi-

tional aspects of the economy since Neolithic times. Except for agriculture, in which the plow came to be used during the Eneolithic, there is no basis to project any important changes. Another development, the concentration of population at Altyn-Depe, demanded a food supply from a considerably larger area and perhaps stimulated the development of wheel transportation. But the principal progress is seen in other aspects of production.

Particularly notable advances were made in metallurgy, metalworking, and pottery making. It was in these areas that qualitative breakthroughs occurred which in many respects established a new status of production in the community system. Metalworking was studied in detail by N.N. Terekhova (1976). Metal artifacts were made of copper, silver, gold, and various alloys. Three modes of preparation were observed. First, by free, cold hammering of a cast blank. Awls, needles, punches, pins, and bracelets were made in this way. The second mode was casting in a mold with subsequent finishing. It was applied in the manufacture of flat objects such as knives, daggers, and adzes. The third mode, casting without subsequent finishing, was used for seals, pins with sculpture, and tubular objects. The method of casting was also varied: in open molds, in closed molds with the lost wax process, and in molds with an inserted plug to form hollow objects. Alloys of diverse types were available to the metalworker: a mixture of copper and silver (billon), silver and copper, copper and lead with the lead content between 7% and 12.64%, copper with lead and arsenic. In the last mixture the lead reaches 7% and the arsenic up to 8%. A mixture of copper and tin with arsenic resulting in an alloy of a kind of tin-bronze is also encountered, but it is not widely distributed, perhaps because of the difficulty in obtaining the raw materials. The alloys that are prevalent are those which in the literature are called lead or arsenical bronzes.* The most widespread alloy was lead-containing.

All of the procedures which were metallurgically analyzed reflect the high technological sophistication of the early metalworkers who knew the properties of metals and alloys well. For instance, in preparing hammered objects they avoided using alloys with high lead content. Yet at the same time the lead content of cast alloys was considerable. As a result, alloys were obtained which had excellent casting properties.

*[Though these terms are present in the literature, modern usage suggests the use of the word bronze to refer only to the alloy of copper and tin.]

These alloys were used for the manufacture of objects which would not require supplementary finishing, such as seals, which were made with the lost wax process in which the mold was artfully prepared. The superb seal portraying a fantastic three-headed being was made in this way. It is probable that the master craftsmen who made similar objects comprised a particular group of specialists. The rapid development of casting, its separation from hammering, and the growing specialization of the metalworkers appeared to be the technological precondition for metallurgy and metalworking becoming a specialized craft. The establishment of similar craft groups during Namazga V (Masson 1955a:249; Kuzmina 1966:89), a proposition presented earlier, was fully confirmed by subsequent detailed technological studies (Terekhova 1976:19).

We see similar technological development and spread of specialization in pottery making, a subject studied in detail by E.V. Sayko (1972, 1977, 1978). First, the handmade pots were already almost totally supplanted by vessels turned on the potter's wheel during Namazga V. Only cooking vessels, mainly cauldrons and braziers, were prepared by hand; the clay was admixed with gravel. All other vessels, from the small cups to the large storage jars, were turned on the rapidly rotating wheel. This was immediately expressed in their forms: the vessels took on refined traits such as thin walls, sometimes sharp-ribbed or carinated. As a result, a whole new range of varied and delicate vessel forms was introduced. The findings of Sayko have shown that the vessels were formed from one piece of clay placed on the rotating wheel. In a number of cases, it is discernible that the rotation was interrupted or jerky. In southern Turkmenistan, finds of two flat ceramic discs are known; these were likely used as the turning platforms of the potter's wheel (Masimov 1976b:87). Such finds are extremely rare, however, even though ceramic objects usually preserve well. Despite the extensive excavations in the Craftsmen's Quarters at Altyn-Depe, not even a fragment of a similar disc was found. Here the discs were most likely wooden which, by the way, would make the instrument less unwieldy. After the vessel was shaped, the excess clay was removed with a knife. The final product was then wiped with a wet rag which, after firing, gave the effect of a pseudo-slip. In the time it took to make one vessel by hand, a master craftsman could turn 10 to 20 high quality vessels on the wheel. The use of the potter's wheel clearly increased productivity and led to the standardization of the forms of ob-

jects in demand, but at the same time required greater professionalism. The potter's wheel, too, led to a highly specialized form of work.

Decisive changes also occurred in the sphere of pyrotechnology. In pottery making, kilns of a new construction were widely introduced: there were two-tiers separating the heating chamber and the firing chamber. During the deepening of Excavation 5, single-tiered kilns were found in layer 5. The introduction of the new type is tied, in the main, to Namazga V. In southern Turkmenistan kilns are quite numerous. At Altyn-Depe 25 of them were uncovered. They were studied in detail by I.S. Masimov (1973c, 1976b:37-58). The kilns differ principally in the construction of the heating chamber, which is usually dug below ground level. The most common variety is a kiln with a supporting post in the center of the heating chamber. This post supports the bottom of the firing chamber, and the chambers have a common opening. The heat enters the firing chamber through openings in the bottom. Most often the oval kilns were covered with a false arch known in southern Turkmenistan since the Late Eneolithic at the earliest. In some of the Geoksyur tombs the vault was preserved almost fully.

The clays used by Altyn-Depe potters were easily fusible and did not demand high temperatures. Results of analyses indicate that the heat reached between 700-800 and 1000 C. The principal attention of the master potter was directed toward the attainment of a steady fire and stabilization of the conditions of firing so that the required temperature would be sustained over the entire chamber. The two-tiered kiln was the answer to that requirement. The ability to sustain the fire in turn sustained the burn-off of the furnace gases for a considerable time. The unusually deep fire chamber with a large fuel-carrying capacity allowed for a much better distribution of the concentrated heat. The volume of the firing chamber was also increased in these kilns of new construction and accordingly increased their capacity. The kilns used by Altyn-Depe potters had a long fire-holding ability resulting in high, and more importantly, stable temperatures. All of this increased the production of the manufactures. In construction the kilns were of one type. Their introduction considerably increased the output of pottery and created conditions for mass production of high quality, standardized vessels. At the same time, the kilns with their complex combustion regimen made increased demands on the level of specialization of the potters. The load for a large kiln, the usual kind at Altyn-Depe, was 150 to 200 vessels of medium size. Taking into account the time necessary to prepare the kiln and manufacture the appropriate number of vessels, the procedure could be carried out once a month. Under these conditions, the kiln could produce between 1600 and 2000 vessels a year (Sayko 1973:106). Of course, this possibility was not always realized, but such calculations once again point out the highly increased potential of pottery production. The utilization of the potter's wheel and two-tiered kiln, complex and advanced instruments in their time, resulted in overall further specialization of the master potters. These innovations created technological preconditions for the separation of pottery making into a specific, specialized craft: pottery making and metalworking were finally separated from agriculture.

It is difficult to say to what degree the above applies to other crafts, the fine products of which were found during the course of excavations. In part, this refers to vessels fashioned from marblelike limestone of various hues. The findings of G.F. Korobkova, who worked also with Eneolithic materials, indicate that flint tools typologically identical to arrowheads were used in working the stone (Korobkova 1964). The investigations of N.N. Skakun (1972) confirmed that at Altyn-Depe a considerable number of arrowheads also served this purpose. Judging by the nature of the products, this involved a rotating, drilling process. Exceptional mastery was applied to the making of beads from various kinds of stones, including lapis lazuli, carnelian, turquoise, and agate. It is probable that there were specialists-jewelers who made such ornaments and who also "drilled" the stone seals.

Spindle whorls, fairly widely represented in the household complexes, as well as impressions of thin woolen cloth found in collective tombs, are witness to the development of weaving. Stone and ceramic scrapers for the initial working of hides indicate the presence of leather dressing. Additional working of the hides was probably done with much thinner metal tools. It needs to be pointed out that because of the absence of metal ores in the nearby mountains, metal artifacts were rarely encountered in the excavations. Yet metals were the basis for an industry at Altyn-Depe. Metals were also rare in burials. Regions lacking metal deposits characteristically used broken or worn out tools as scrap for new alloys.

Stone tools were used for rough work, the initial working of materials. Knapping, drilling, and abrasive techniques were used in their manufacture (Skakun 1977b). The preliminary division of stone tools carried out by Korobkova and Skakun indicates that they were principally used in agriculture (grain grinders, paint grinders, pestles), in leather dressing (scrapers), and in the making of metal tools (whetstones, platelike anvils, and rounded cobbles-hammers). Such tools were used principally for specific operations, but the burden of the manufacture lay with the metal tools. Unlike the Stone Age, stone tools of the Bronze Age did not engender a single craft. But since they were included in a manufacturing cycle with other types of tools, they played their sometimes very important role. Thus this survey of early manufacturing indicates the development of varied crafts at Altyn-Depe, with metalworking and pottery making showing the greatest advances. The community itself served as a functional center for the concentration of specialized crafts.

The various functions of Altyn-Depe gave a particular cast even to its structure. It did not simply have the most numerous collection of buildings of all kinds, but possessed a specific internal structure which comprised its qualitative difference from the small contemporaneous settlements. This different structure naturally is partially reflected even in the topography of Altyn-Depe as an archaeological site.

Earlier, we briefly characterized two such elements of the planned structure of Altyn-Depe, the fortifications and the central square. The third important element was the Craftsmen's Quarters where, as the excavations showed, the activities of the master potters and apparently other specialists were concentrated. The structural subdivisions presented earlier are an example of the planned embodiment of Altyn-Depe as a functional center of manufacture. The second important function, that of a religious center with ideological leadership, found its embodiment in the cult complex with its monumental architecture and tombs of priests with rich funerary gifts. As the analyses showed, the complex was dedicated to an astral deity, the moon god represented as a powerful bull. Presumably, this was the supreme deity of the community, and the female goddesses whose terracotta figurines were found in various places at Altyn-Depe were secondary.

Notwithstanding the above, the major part of the settlement was occupied by household complexes. The differences found in these complexes are very important for the characterization of the community. We are clearly dealing with a

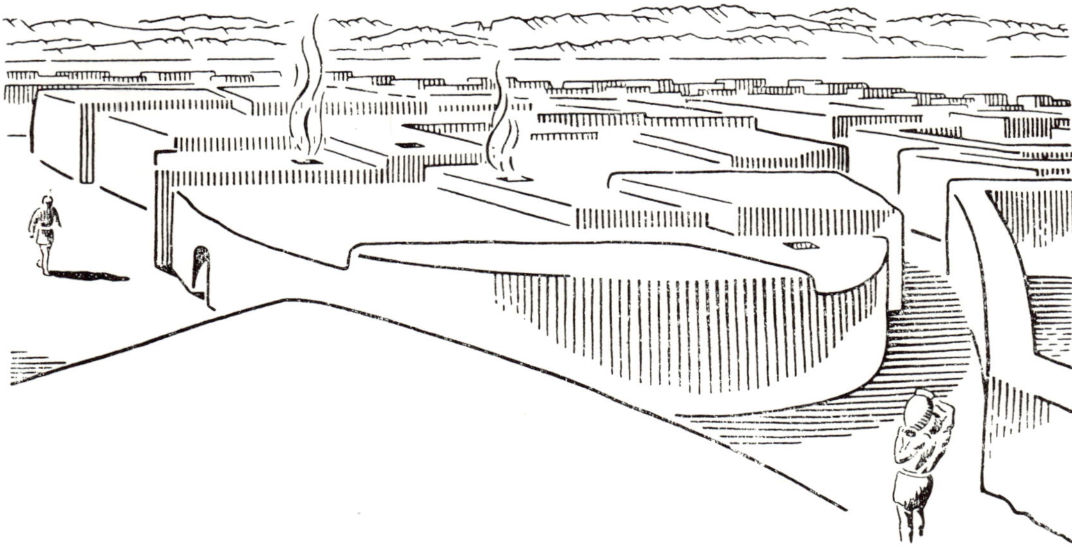

Figure 28.   General view of quarters uncovered in Excavation 9. View is from Imdugud Street. Reconstruction by V. B. Zernov.

division of the settlement's territory based on class prestige. Earlier, when describing the results of the excavations of the living quarters, a group of the uncovered buildings was outlined. The structures of Excavations 8 and 10 comprised the first group, those of 5 and 13 the second, and those of Excavation 9 the third. The megacomplex Imdugud, which presents a closed, planned unit, belongs to the third group (Fig. 28). The principal component of all three groups seems to be a household within an enclosure composed of a number of rooms united by a system of passages, usually with one major exit onto an arterial street. Each of the complexes includes living and household rooms. As far as we can judge, the latter were, in the main, storage rooms. In addition to these, as a rule each complex had a household courtyard where the cooking hearths and often the oval oven-brazier for baking bread were placed. Various finds indicate that in each complex grain was ground into flour, spinning took place, and metal tools were retouched on stone anvils or with whetstones. We conclude that these are houses of extended families living under a common roof and running a single household, as implied by the common

kitchens and the common courtyard. There are also, however, considerable differences. These differences lead us to consider a division into groups of households. Above all, the households differ in area occupied, with the largest house also having the most spacious living rooms.

In Table 2, the dimensions of the household courtyard are included in the overall area of the house. The greatest variation is found among the living rooms; the area of the auxiliary rooms varies to a lesser degree. The different groups of houses do not vary so much in the area of the housekeeping rooms as they do in the number comprising a single complex.

A detailed analysis of the plans of interiors shows that while houses in Excavations 9 and 10 have an identical area, they basically differ. During field work it was already noted that the houses in Excavation 10 were in many respects analogous to the Late Eneolithic houses at Geoksyur and Kara-Depe (Masson 1972d:527). More detailed analyses of the houses in the Craftsmen's Quarters confirmed this analogy (Masimov 1976b:91-96). A characteristic trait of the household complexes seems to be an initially planned element with a living room containing a

TABLE 2
COMPARISON OF THREE GROUPS OF HOUSES ON THE BASIS OF AREA (m^2)

House group	Excavation	Total Area of House	Living Rooms		Housekeeping Rooms	
			Range	Average	Range	Average
I	10	90	6-13	8.5	3-9	5
	8	—	5-8	6.5	2-5	3.5
II	5	40-50	9-12	10.5	—	—
	13	—	7-10	8.6	—	—
III	9	80-100	10-25	15	5-13	6.7

heating hearth and, beyond the living room, a number of housekeeping rooms. In Excavation 10, the initial block of the houses ranges between 10 m^2 and 18 m^2, the average being 15 m^2. Several such blocks form a single house with a common kitchen and courtyard. These household complexes can be viewed as extended family dwellings in which the same general economic activity was conducted. Small nuclear families occupied a living room and used the adjacent section for storage of personal property. The same distribution is seen at Kara-Depe and Geoksyur (Masson 1964b:322-325). The difference is that in the latter two, heating hearths were in the form of an oval sunk into the floor, whereas at Altyn-Depe hearths were placed on a squarish platform of mud bricks. Judging by the number of initially planned blocks in the household complexes of the Craftsmen's Quarters, each was occupied by three or four small families.

In Excavation 5 the picture is different. Here the multi-chambered complex, framed by small streets and empty spaces, is divided into several quarters comparatively small in area. Each of the quarters has a separate exit to the street and does not contain more than two living rooms. The small dimensions of such household quarters lead to the conclusion that small nuclear families lived here and each carried out its individual economic task (Masson 1968c; Knyshev 1971). In Excavation 9, we see the same picture, but here the area of the living rooms, and indeed, of the house, is substantially larger, and the quality of the structures is different. The structures are rectangular and carefully planned, indicating

purposeful, organized design. Additionally, we see the planned isolation of the large houses of Excavation 9 as the Imdugud megacomplex, and within it such an overall element as the presence of extensive storage structures in its eastern part. This implies that the families living in the well-constructed, roomy houses consolidated themselves in a high rank collective. Their economic interests were essentially of the same character, and their social standing allowed or demanded the isolation of their living quarters in a closed, planned unit.

There are some differences among the inhabitants of the three household groups even in the consumption of meat (Fig. 29). Thus in the Craftsmen's Quarters bones of wild animals clearly exceeded those of domesticated animals; it is likely that the inhabitants of this part of Altyn-Depe did not have large herds at their disposal. The engraved brand on the shoulder of a large clay figurine of a bull testifies to the existence of property claims on livestock. The small number of cattle owners among the craftsmen is indirectly confirmed by the absence of the typical brownish, loose soil layers in parts of courtyards associated with livestock keeping. On the other hand, such layers were found in Excavation 9 but in only two places: in courtyard B and in the courtyard parts of the "agricultural support" installations to the east of the dwellings, which once again underlines the separate economic community of the Imdugud megacomplex inhabitants. In addition to the clear dominance of domesticated animal bones, principally those of sheep, in Excavation 9, N. M. Ermolova noted a lesser utilization of the bones, which were seldom

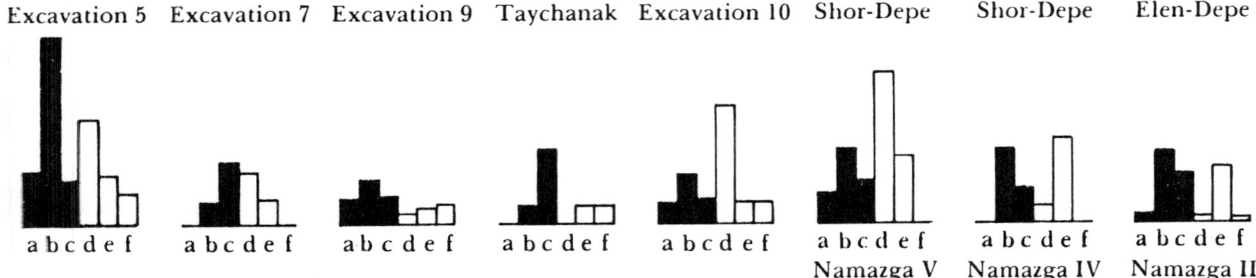

Figure 29.   Histograms of distribution of animal bones at Altyn-Depe and other southern Turkmenistan sites.
Key— a: *large horned cattle;* b: *sheep;* c: *goat;* d:*onager;* e: *gazelle;* f: *wild goat.* [Black bars indicate domesticated animals. White bars indicate wild animals.].

broken for the extraction of marrow. Together with the large living rooms, this is again witness to the relatively high level of prosperity of the inhabitants of this quarter.

Additional data for classifying the level of prosperity for the three groups of houses mentioned above are provided by the burial inventories. These are usually found in collective tombs which are an integral part of the housekeeping and living assemblages.

Let us examine the composition of the burial inventories. In the main, they are objects of two functional groups: personal ornaments and prestige symbols, most often seals. The funerary offerings were in the form of solid food (indicated by the preserved bones of animals) and liquids, some kind of libation placed in vessels. The collection of vessels could also indirectly point to the wealth of the deceased or that of the group to which he or she belonged. Because of the nature of the burial rite, the materials in the tombs were scrambled, and it was seldom possible to tell with certainty which objects belonged with a particular deceased. Therefore we have averaged the number of objects in the tombs for each deceased (Table 3). In addition to the figures in Table 3, the tombs in the houses of groups II and III also contained bronze and silver rings, seals, and female terracotta statuettes.

It should be understood that the level of prosperity is relative to the parameters of different societies. For instance, burials with a varied inventory such as those in the early agricultural sites of Tell es-Sawwan, Çatal Hüyük, and the southern Turkmenistan early agricultural sites of the Jeitun culture may be interpreted as princely. Also indicative of this standard are the gold objects with lapis lazuli. In the ancient East, objects of such materials were a standard of wealth. In the splendid royal burials of Ur, composite sculptures were made of these materials. At the northern Mesopotamian site Tepe Gawra an object made of gold and lapis lazuli is quite modest—it is a small insect (Perkins 1949:187). In the "burial of a priestess" at Altyn-Depe (see p. 40) we encountered only an elongated bead covered with gold foil. The principal approach and materials were the same, but the frame of reference differed in each case. The southern Turkmenistan Bronze Age community was not distinguished by personal wealth, which was hard to obtain in the oreless and less fertile land compared to Sumer and Egypt. The community's criteria for wealth were different than in neighboring regions.

TABLE 3
AMOUNT OF INVENTORY IN THE ALTYN-DEPE TOMBS

House Group	Excavation	Tomb	Number of Vessels*	Overall Number of Beads	Beads of Semi-precious Stone
I	10	17	0.5	—	—
II	5	13	1.5	6	0.5
III	9	9	1	5.5	0.75
	9	11	2	32	1
	9	24	1	24	0.7
	9	125	0.3	12	0.5

* In the last three columns the calculation applies to one buried.

By comparing Tables 2 and 3, one can deduce the existence at Altyn-Depe of three populations, each of a different degree of economic well-being. First, there were the craftsmen who lived in multi-family compounds and obtained half of their meat supply from the hunt. They either had no personal ornaments or did not place them in burials. For this group, the latter would be an impossible extravagance. The second group consisted of people who occupied separate houses and had varied personal ornaments, including those of semiprecious stones such as lapis lazuli, turquoise, carnelian, and agate. Sometimes they even put such ornaments in the burials of youths. This group could be called that of prosperous citizens. The third group lived, in Altyn-Depe and southern Turkmenistan terms, in spacious and well-built houses; they were not restricted in meat consumption. The women belonging to this group possessed varied jewelry: bronze and silver rings, necklaces, bracelets, and also belts of strung beads. Without doubt, they were the aristocracy, the elite, the wealthy citizens. Their tombs differ from those of the prosperous citizenry by the variety and nature of such prestigious objects as seals. This is particularly discernible in the materials of burials 124 and 125.

Additional deductions about the nature of the Altyn-Depe groups may be derived from the sexual composition of people interred in collective burials (Table 4). The age groups that once existed at Altyn-Depe are reflected in the burial ritual. Thus children of one or two years of age were in most cases buried within the limits of the household and not with adults. In a number of cases, children from four to nine were buried in tombs with adults, but their overall number was not significant. They apparently comprised a special age class, since their burial inventory differed from that of the adults. At times their burials contained vessels with spouts which may have been drinking bowls. Such vessels were not encountered in adult burials.

Unfortunately, up to the present no sex/age determinations based on physical anthropological data from tomb 13 of Excavation 5 and tomb 9 of Excavation 9 have been made. If we accept the premise that the people placed in one tomb were in life united by kinship, then the tombs of Excavations 7 and 10 may have belonged to communities with large families, although the first clearly functioned over a long period of time. The combination of the interred in the tombs of Excavation 9 is somewhat unusual. Here women and children predominate. This could be an indication of polygamy practiced in the Elite Quarters.

A large family could have been the basic unit at Altyn-Depe, even though the character of the families forming the various divisions and the levels of prosperity were different. It is significant that in a number of tombs there was a single arrowhead, that is, one to a tomb. This refers to tomb 13 in Excavation 5, tombs 9 and 11 in Excavation 9, the priestly burial chamber in Excavation 7, and the collective tomb in locality 32 of Excavation 7. In these instances, perhaps the arrowhead was one of the symbols of the col-

TABLE 4
SEX AND AGE COMBINATIONS OF PEOPLE BURIED IN TOMBS

Excavation	Tomb	Total Number of Buried	Children	Women	Men
10	17	7	—	4	3
9	11	11	2	5	1
9	124	11	4	5	2
9	125	6	1	4	1
7	Tomb of priests	40	3	16	12

lective to which the deceased belonged. Seals, worn on the belt, were found in only some of the burials. In tomb 13 there were two, and in tomb 9 there was only one among the 33 buried. Perhaps only those who occupied a special position in the large family community were entitled to seals.

One cannot be absolute in deducing the social structure of an ancient society based on the analysis of archaeological materials. Basically there are only general evaluations. It can be anticipated that future excavations at Altyn-Depe, as well as the study of materials already obtained, will lead to more specific statements and amendments. However, the overall division of the population into three groups, aside from how correct their designations may be, reflects a realistic segmentation observable in the archaeological materials. If those finds associated with the occupations of the inhabitants of Altyn-Depe point to a concentration of a considerable technical and cultural potential, then the results of analyses of the household and dwelling complexes point to a considerable concentration of people.

Excavations done in areas of different functional significance allow us to propose a differentiating evaluation of the number of inhabitants in this Bronze Age center. At present the area of the Altyn-Depe ruins, not counting the slopes, amounts to 25 hectares. It is possible that the settlement had some sort of suburbs which would be preserved in the form of small mounds in its vicinity. Investigations made in the 1970s by A.Ya. Shchetenko in the region of Namazga-Depe indicate that there were a number of complexes

beyond the reaches of the principal mound (Shchetenko 1977). This could also have been the case at Altyn-Depe, but the Bronze Age area surrounding it has been covered by an alluvial-diluvial layer almost 2 m thick.

Within the confines of the nuclear area known to us, the utilitarian structures, such as the Central Square, the monumental part of the temple complex, and the alleys (though compact and narrow), occupied approximately 2 hectares. If we accept the sociological interpretation proposed earlier, the three types of household-dwelling structures represent different population densities. Thus in Excavation 9, in an area of about 5000 m^2, seven large houses were discovered; two were small, several of their rooms apparently occupied by servants, and there were parts of at the most four or five households. Thus we can project the presence of ten families within the confines of the Imdugud megacomplex, as a rough guide, 50-60 people, and in the other houses five or six families, or 25-30 people. We can estimate that the number of people within the excavated part was between 75 and 90, and thus the density 150-180 per hectare.

In Excavation 10, with an area of 1000 m^2, parts of two multi-chambered houses were uncovered. These appear to have been occupied by large family communes, each composed of three or four families, that is, 15-20 people. This implies an exceptionally high population density— 600-700 per hectare. Excavation 8 gave evidence of exceptionally small, closetlike constructions. Presumably, at least part of the large house with living quarters were similarly constructed. Excavation 5 with its 1000 m^2 established the presence of "apartment" structures comprising four complexes occupied by small families. This configuration implies that the number of dwellers in each complex amounted to 20-24, or 200-250 people per hectare (Table 5).

There was unquestionably a concentration of several thousand people in Altyn-Depe. Analysis of the layout shows the exceptional density of the buildings and the smallness of the structures crowded on the surface of the mound. The presence of specialized functions and specific interior structures, and the projected number of inhabitants, stamps Altyn-Depe as an urban settlement qualitatively different from the contemporary small settlements of the Taychanak-Depe or Shor-Depe type.

Extensive literature has been dedicated to the problem of defining the notion of "urban" for ancient communities. I have had the opportunity to express several opinions on the subject (Masson 1975b, 1977c, 1978a), and will now briefly review the pertinent materials. The great significance of the investigations of I.M. Dyakonov and his school must be mentioned; they sought to determine the social structure of ancient towns of the

banization. In the latter case a tendency to regard the city as some sort of abstract phenomenon located outside of a concrete historical setting, in a distinct vacuum formed outside and above a specific social formation, was noted. In 1976 a conference was held in Leningrad about ancient cities and their typology (Vinogradov 1978). The papers presented at the conference were published as *Drevniye qoroda* (Ancient Cities) in 1977.

Ancient cities may be regarded as major centers, points of population concentration, instruments of production, centers of cultural potential, and as fulfilling specific regulatory, industrial, and trade functions. The role of the city as a center of specific functional concentrations is reflected morphologically in compact buildings and the development of monumental architecture.

Fortifications are one of the morphological traits of the early city. This character is closely related to the role and place of military function within social processes; this role varied in significance for different societies and for different stages of development and was directly reflected in the presence and character of defensive struc-

TABLE 5

POPULATION DENSITY IN DIFFERENT AREAS OF ALTYN-DEPE

Type of Area	Extent (in Hectares)	Number per Hectare	Total Number of Inhabitants
Utilitarian Structures	2		
Elite Quarters (Excavation 9)	6	150-180	900-1080
Quarters of Well-to-do Citizens (Excavations 5 and 13)	10	200-240	1000-1200
Craftsmen's Quarters (Excavations 1, 8 and 10)	7	600-750	4200-5250
Totals for Altyn-Depe	25	240-300	6100-7530

East on the basis of written sources (Dyakonov 1973; Kozyreva 1974). R. Adams' group carried out an interesting study of the typology of early Mesopotamian urban settlements and the dynamics of their development on the basis of archaeological maps and the area occupied by the various settlements (Adams and Nissen 1972). A number of important questions concerning early settlements were posed at a London conference (MSU) dedicated to human settlements and ur-

tures. As to monumental architecture, it is well known that depending on the class composition of early societies, special standards were worked out for prestigious buildings, palaces, and temple complexes, which as a rule were placed only in urban centers. Quantitative determination of the concentration of population apparently must take into account the actual population density necessary for different economic activities, particularly agriculture. V.G. Childe proposed that the significant distinction between city and village was a population of 5000 (Childe 1950). The usually accepted density of ancient eastern cities is 400-500 people per hectare. This density would require a minimum of 10-12 hectares. However, the area of the well-known site of Knossos, which fulfilled a number of urban functions, was only 3.5 hectares. Settlements of the urban type in ancient Asia Minor were also small. An important morphological trait of early cities was a centralized concern for the well-being of the entire population, for the major streets and system of canalization, a concern which is most clearly expressed in Harappa and Mohenjo-Daro.

Parallel to the external qualitative indices for the definition of a city are internal structural changes. Also, typological diversity cannot be disregarded. It appears early, during the first stages of development of urban-type settlements, and is reflected in the functions and in the morphological traits of these settlements. It seems that the functional typology of early urban centers is one of the ways in which specific, historical diversity can be revealed. Multi-functional centers must be based on one or two leading functions. Thus one can distinguish between cities which are centers for an agricultural region (genetically probably their earliest function) and handicraft and manufacturing cities, and military-administrative and cultural-ideological centers. The functional typology of cities cannot be regarded as some anachronistic and ahistorical operation. Early cities were not simply instruments to carry out specific functions but were complex social organisms representing a component of an entire socio-economic system and specifically embodying the system's characteristic features, as a rule in quite clear and representative forms. The study of the typology of early cities should be conducted only as an internal informational analysis and investigation of typologically related societies, with due regard for the social stratification of the city's population through which these corresponding functions are translated into reality.

Pertinent historical analysis indicates that for the different socio-econommic conditions the presence or dominance of various types of urban settlements and their corresponding fulfillment of functions is characteristic. The place of a city in a social system finds expression both in its varied composition of functions and in the very maintenance of these. For instance, the organization and social forms associated with early handicraft production are in principle different from

the forms of large machine industries which fulfill an industrial function in capitalist cities.

The materials at hand allow for a convincing characterization of the functions of Altyn-Depe as particular to early urban centers. In part these functions were outlined with the general characterization of the structures of the site. In all, Altyn-Depe emerges as an early city organism with a class conscious division of its territory, as a settlement fulfilling the functions of a regional agricultural center, and as a center of handicraft production and also of ideological leadership (Fig. 30). To a lesser degree, the development of trade may be mentioned, since objects of elephant ivory from the region of the early Indian Harappan civilization were found decorating the dwellings of the elite. As a result of regular interregional exchange, copper ore and lapis lazuli were obtained. The nature of the division of the various products among the large population of Altyn-Depe is less clear. Perhaps trading relationships based on equal value of different items begins to play an important role. The relatively widespread silver objects of various kinds found at Altyn-Depe come to mind. These include objects of purely utilitarian character, such as the large adze. In reference to equal value of different items, it has been shown that it was particularly silver that played the role of money in ancient Mesopotamia, where it was frequently kept even in the form of scrap. (Dyakonov 1973:47). In Larsa in the 20th and 19th centuries B.C., silver ornaments were part of the bride's dowry. They had a standard weight and apparently could be used as money (Kozyreva 1974). At the same time there was little silver in Larsa, and often the sum expressed in silver was paid in grain. As Kozyreva states, silver was kept by tradespeople only. The majority of economies were based on natural products. They were limited by products necessary to secure survival: flour, butter, and wool. Close cultural and very likely trade ties between the societies of southern Turkmenistan and Bronze Age Mesopotamia could be the cause for establishing here the role of silver as a form of accumulating treasure and would also explain the relatively widespread presence of silver artifacts.

The function of a fortified refuge was expressed in Altyn-Depe to an insignificant degree. We have already noted the relatively weak development of fortifications. This is in keeping with the very limited development of the military within the Altyn-Depe community, peacefully developing at the edge of the then civilized world, apart from the political contrariness and military rivalries which were ravaging Asia Minor. In fact, weapons were encountered very rarely at Altyn-Depe, and there are absolutely no traces of military trauma on the hundreds of skeletons studied by T.P. Kiyatkina.

Naturally, the question arises as to the nature of the society within which a center such as Altyn-Depe, with all the indications of an early urban organism, existed. The three types of houses and the burials associated with them, which were characterized earlier, reflect important elements of social stratification. We also, however, encountered several burials which clearly exceeded the established norms because of their "saturated" inventory. Such was the "burial of the priestess" (60) in which there were gold rings and silver seals, that is, there were qualitative differences from the traditional inventory. Of 96 beads found in the vicinity of one person, 35 were of gold and semiprecious stones (and this at a time when in the tombs the maximum was one for each buried). The burial of the priest (362) with objects of prestige such as the stone staff and baton, and that of the "distinguished lady" with a rich collection of toiletries consisting of silver and elephant ivory objects (252), were also exceptional. It was already noted that only persons of the highest social standing were buried in such tombs, since in the collective burial chambers their personal objects could be mislaid or lost (see p. 51). Their place of residence may have been the Imdugud megacomplex or another similar locality, but only members of the city's elite families were buried in tombs found in similar complexes.

Within the Imdugud megacomplex numerous adult burials lacking an inventory were placed outside the general burial vault for the quarter. Their placement, at the time when the burial vault was by no means fully occupied, points to the special social status of these persons who can be regarded as domestic slaves or servants, who in practice were the equivalent of slaves. They and their families may have occupied the small living rooms found among the household sections of Imdugud.

The complex social stratification that was found at Altyn-Depe may be viewed as a precursor of class structure. Obviously, the comparative poverty of the inhabitants of the Craftsmen's Quarters is not poverty per se, but the result of different social and economic relations and means of the distribution of products. Perhaps it is not accidental that the extensive storage courtyard was not located in the areas of craft production but within the complex of the Elite Quarters.

The organization of economic and social functioning of such a large organism as Altyn-Depe demanded a single-mindedness of action on the part of the people specifically preoccupied with these problems; they depended on the help of certain personnel. The common concerns of an urban society, generated by the entire population of Altyn-Depe, could have been discussed in meetings of elders, including patriarchs. The interment of such people of advanced age is represented by individuals both in the priest's tomb and the Elite Quarters. Their actions resulted in the erection of fortifications with a monumental main entrance and buildings, and also in the replenishment of the public storage rooms and the creation of the monumental cult complex, a prestigious symbol of unity for all of the small subdivisions of the society living in household complexes and placing their dead in collective tombs. The temple of the moon god, who appeared in the form of the mighty celestial bull, was a sort of calling card of the early urban organism in the framework of which the formation of an early class society took place. And who knows whether or not its political system was that of a theocracy.

By all appearances, the early city went through several stages of development. The materials from Altyn-Depe are characteristic of an urban organism which evolved, in a natural spontaneous way, from communal structures based on agricultural and herding societies.

In his book on the birth of civilization, C. Redman proposes the following stages of social evolution in similar societies: developed agricultural settlements, temple-town, and administrative city (Redman 1978:202). To be sure, he does not assign detailed characteristics to these stages. Altyn-Depe obviously exceeded the framework of a simple, large agricultural center; keeping the cult complex in mind, we could characterize it as a temple-town, a proto-urban or early urban organism. The next stage of development is a city with clearly expressed functions of a political-administrative center—a ruler's residence with the various attributes of a ruling authority, from palaces to tombs evincing a magnificent interment ritual. As a rule, places which have undergone the traditional development of settled agriculturalists, from that of small primitive villages to large settlements with monumental architecture, become such urban centers. In Sumer, this is well observed at Ur and Eridu where the first agricultural settlements appear in the 5th millennium B.C. The Sumerian epic tradition has it that it was in Eridu that the first ruling authority descended to earth. The society of Altyn-depe had developed in the same direction. Here also a complex organism gradually evolved from an early agricultural settlement. It is not clear, however, how far the process advanced. It is possible that the low level of militarization of the society slowed down class differentiation and the formation of a state. It is well known how important the role of a military leader and his men-at-arms is in establishing a state. A regular army subordinate to the ruler develops from the latter. The etymology of Sumerian as well as other ancient eastern terms indicates that the slave-prisoner of war was hardly the earliest, or in any case the most widespread, form of slave-holding during the early stages of class society. For the time being, we can regard Namazga-Depe and Altyn-Depe as two oasis centers, precursors of two city-states.

Materials that can be used for a comparison of an early urban center investigated in southern Turkmenistan are not very numerous. In Mesopotamia the settlements which are at a comparably developed stage have been studied only in the framework of monumental temple complexes. Their overall structure, even the type of houses, is practically unknown. The situation changes little for the periods during which city-states already existed. Thus the area of early dynastic Ur was 20 hectares, and its population within the central part delimited by that area was about 4000 (Wright 1969). The plan of one of the sections of Altyn-Depe finds an interesting parallel in Ur of 2000-1700 B.C. A sizeable area occupied by the houses of well-to-do citizens was excavated by L. Woolley (1931). I.M. Dyakonov undertook a detailed analysis of the excavation and compared the observations of the floor plan of the houses with the data contained in the cuneiform tablets, often found in the same houses. The similarity of plan in this quarter of Ur and the Imdugud megacomplex is obvious. The streets of Ur are 2-3 m wide, often only 1.5 m. Some of the side alleys branching from the main street dead-end, their principal role being to secure the approach to several houses fronting them (cp. Mirror Street in Fig. 15). The area of

the houses is between 60 m^2 and 100 m^2; some of them had a second story in addition, as indicated by preserved staircases. The houses included a main room, a small sanctuary, an interior court-yard, and auxiliary household rooms. There was a family tomb in the courtyard.

The judicial documents of Ur and Larsa demonstrate the transfer of similar structures from hand to hand: the sale of houses and individual rooms, and apparently parts of them, and also the transfer of buildings to other proprietors by right of inheritance (Dyakonov 1968, 1973; Kozyreva 1974). According to Kozyreva, at the beginning of the 2nd millennium B.C., a house of a family in Larsa had an area of between 46 m^2 and 93 m^2, and the salable or inheritable rooms, between 11 m^2 and 30 m^2. In Ur there was a record of a sale of a 2 m area. The Ur documents mention a small internal courtyard with an area of 9 m^2. The documents also specify the materials necessary to build a house: 4320 sun-baked bricks and 10 beams for the roof. The costs of buildings are also known. Thus according to the laws of Hammurabi, a builder of a house on an area of 35 m^2 was to receive two shekels of silver (about 16 g). The value of a house or a built-up area of the same size, however, fluctuated in Larsa and sometimes reached 1 mina and 56 shekels of silver (977 g). Kozyreva is of the opinion that such great fluctuations were conditioned, in part, by complex credit and promissory note relations between buyer and seller.

Of course, there is no basis to directly transfer what was said above to Altyn-Depe, even though it dates to the same period of time. What is significant is the agreement in the architectural planning tradition. One may propose that the plan reflects the communality of needs (which had to be satisfied by the construction works) and functions (they were implemented in sections of inner city houses), and, most importantly, agreement on the direction of development. The last, in conditions existing in ancient eastern cultures, led to the formation of suitable canons and conventions.

VII

Altyn-Depe in the Cultural System of the Ancient East

The archaeological culture of Altyn-Depe may be sociologically characterized as a reflection of a formative process of early urbanization amidst settled agrarian and livestock-raising communities. The process, however, did not take place in a blank space. We can trace all the stages of cultural development in the site, from a primitive settlement of early agriculturalists to a community of an early urban type with a complex internal structure. The local genesis of the civilizations of Altyn-Depe can be distinctly traced. Starting at least with the Late Eneolithic, which is represented by the Geoksyur variant of the Anau culture, a clear succession of a number of cultural phenomena can be established. For instance, the oval hearth of the Late Eneolithic sanctuary is analogous to a hearth in one of the houses in the Elite Quarters. Analogies regarding funerary rites are also remarkable. During the Bronze Age, both individual tombs and collective burials were found, although they were not rounded but rectangular. The old, Late Eneolithic practice of orienting the bodies generally toward the north is most common in the burials. During the Middle Bronze Age as well as during the Late Eneolithic, terracotta boxes were made with their walls covered with cutout geometric ornamentation developing into the motifs of crosses and half-crosses. Thus there is a basis to speak of the preservation of some traditions of the Eneolithic in the culture of Altyn-Depe. The reworking of these traditions, both by natural cultural evolution and technical innovation, took place during the Early Bronze Age and is characteristic of the Namazga IV type of assemblage. Using materials from Altyn-Depe, L.B. Kircho convincingly demonstrated that the Early Bronze Age painted ceramics are a direct continuation of development from the Geoksyur tradition (Kircho 1972, 1976). This development can be traced even more graphically in the ter-

racotta sculpture; in limited cases this occurs even earlier (Masson and Sarianidi 1973:20-21). The deduction stated above found full confirmation when terracotta figurines with an Eneolithic cast were uncovered in Namazga IV assemblages at Altyn-Depe. As materials from stratified Excavation 1 and particularly Excavation 5 show, the transition from Early Bronze Age culture to the Namazga V type of assemblage occurred without any extensive alterations. Although Namazga V ceramics are differentiated in design, they show close ties to ceramic forms of Early Bronze Age assemblages in the early stage. Finally, the continuity in the composition of the population which created the material culture we had studied is of great importance. Skeletal materials from the upper layers of Altyn-Depe indicate the continuation of the eastern Mediterranean physical type of earlier times, and in separate cases even greater gracility is observable (Ginzberg and Trofimova 1972:68-69; Masson and Kiyatkina 1976).

Moreover, the formation of the culture of Altyn-Depe is not just a local, southern Turkmenistan phenomenon which would illustrate a single case of the development of an early agrarian community into an urban civilization. Altyn-Depe belongs with a number of other, developmentally similar sites spread over the extensive zone between Mesopotamia and India. While earlier this zone was looked upon as part of a belt of sedentary agricultural societies, now new discoveries lead us to perceive internal developments among the peoples inhabiting the zone. Decisive changes took place here during the 3rd millennium. These discoveries confirmed that during this time there existed, between Mesopotamia and India, not simple aboriginal tribes but developing civilizations undergoing early urbanization (Masson 1970f). Thus archeological excavations opened a new page in the history of the ancient Middle East.

Altyn-Depe and southern Turkmenistan sites of the same type occupied a definite place in the system of ancient cultures of the Middle East. The chronological and typological comparisons introduced earlier (see p. 93ff.) are by no means fortuitous. The community of Altyn-Depe and the populations that built the sites, surveyed earlier, in Iran, Afghanistan, and India had close ties and reciprocal interests. True, the ties were diverse in substance, significance, and mechanics of implementation. For instance, we can say with certitude that the Altyn-Depe culture was linked with the Harappan civilization through trade. Cultural parallels between southern Turkmenistan and Harappa became evident even during the first excavations at Altyn-Depe. The point was made that beside the southern coastal trade, which resulted in ties between Harappa and Sumer, there also existed an overland trade route reaching from the Indus Valley to the northeast and to the settled oases on the southern edge of the Kara-Kum (Masson 1966b:70; 1967d:188-189; Shchetenko 1970c). New investigations not only enlarged the collections of artifacts which reflected the international (in the terms of the times) exchanges, but also resulted in the discovery of a Harappan settlement in the middle reaches of the Amu-darya, far from the confines of the Harappan ecumene proper. We refer to the settlement of Shortugay which contained in its lower layers clear-cut Harappan ceramics, thus leaving no doubt about its cultural relationship (Frankfort and Pottier 1978). Apparently, these are remains of one of the trading stations situated on the trade routes uniting early cultures and civilizations.

A relationship between Altyn-Depe and the Mesopotamian centers of early civilization may be established through an analysis of works of art. Two lines of connections are clearly traceable. One leads to local traditions of the Eneolithic, with a special role played by the ornamentation derived from the vessels of Geoksyur style. At the same time, the community experiencing urbanization made use of the achievements and cultural standards of the highly developed centers of Mesopotamia. In the sphere of architecture it was the idea of a multiplatformed tower, the ziggurat, that found local realization in the cult center of Altyn-Depe; the same influence is also evident in the design of the city gates with two massive pylons, as well as the mode of embellishing and strengthening the plain vertical walls of monumental buildings with stepped pilasters. Individual details of the new style terracottas, which were widely distributed in Altyn-Depe during the Early Bronze Age, have Mesopotamian parallels such as large appliqué eyes, multi-stranded necklaces, and belts and triangles filled with slanting incisions at the lower abdomen. But the style of the new sculpture, as well as the overall cast of the terracottas, is peculiarly local. The modeling differs from the Mesopotamian samples and corresponds to them only in separate details organically incorporated in the examples of local gods. This difference is also characteristic of such Altyn-Depe products as the golden head of a bull. The manner of drawing the superciliary arches, the spreading ears fashioned from gold blades inserted in the matrix of the head, and the incrusted semiprecious stones all point to the Sumerian world of jewelry making, leading off with the remarkable heads of bulls on the lyre resonators from the royal tombs at Ur. But unlike in Sumer, turquoise rather than lapis lazuli is used. Furthermore, the sculptural treatment of the head with its large, piglike snout is also an extension of local traditions clearly represented by the marble figure of a bull from the Namazga III strata of Kara-Depe (Masson 1960b:p. 372, fig. 24). This combination of Mesopotamian traditional traits and their local reworking in the form of the Altyn-Depe bull is similar to a bull from one of the Bahrein temples, which is also outside the realm of the Sumerian metropolis (During-Caspars 1971).

The interaction of the culture of Altyn-Depe with other 3rd millennium B.C. urban centers between Mesopotamia and India has another aspect. In the historical development of the zone and in the process of cultural genesis associated with manifestations of urbanization, we encounter now two major periods. The first belongs to the end of the 4th to the first half of the 3rd millennium B.C. Settlements of peoples with a culture of the Geoksyur type accompanied by the standards and patterns of southern Turkmenistan and the strong influence of the proto-Elamite culture are characteristic of this period. The dynamic processes of the proto-Elamite culture are a subject of diverse discussions.

The earliest contacts of the southern Turkmenistan peoples are evident in the assemblages of Quetta in northern Baluchistan (Masson 1960a:437) and later in Mundigak (Sarianidi 1965:49-50). Today, a number of corresponding sites have increased in importance. In this regard, Shahr-i Sokhta, in which the earliest materials lay directly on virgin soil and were consolidated in the complex Shahr-i Sokhta I, which is subdivided into three horizons, is of exceptional interest (Tosi 1969:287-288; Lamberg-Karlovsky and Tosi 1973:25-26). From the very beginning of the excavation, the Italian investigators noted considerable similarity between the painted ceramics found there and those of the southern Turkmenistan samples, and in a number of cases they were identical (Biscione 1973). In some cases the similarity is with the ceramics of Kara-Depe, in others with vessels of the Geoksyur type. According to the refined data of M. Tosi, the painted ceramics of the Shahr-i Sokhta I assemblage can be assessed as follows: Local type—48.1%, Geoksyur type—27%, Kechi-Bergs type (one of the northern Baluchistan kinds of pottery)—24.7%. The distribution of ceramics of the Geoksyur type in the various layers is as follows: Horizon 8—24.3%, Horizon 9—31.9%, Horizon 10—21%. Among the published specimens there is a painted fragment which extends the traditions of Late Namazga II represented by the Kara level 2; part of the material reveals a direct analogy to vessels of the Kara 1A type of Early Namazga III (Masson 1962c:pl. XII, item 12; fig. 8, items 7 and 8; Tosi 1969:fig. 37, items d, n). A separate group of painted ceramics from Shahr-i Sokhta I, including those ornamented with appliqué figures, may be compared with the ceramics of horizons Altyn 9 and 10. These ceramics represent the late stages of development of vessels of the Geoksyur culture which are absent in the Geoksyur site proper (Tosi 1969:fig. 37, item k). A more detailed and layer-by-layer examination of the Shahr-i Sokhta ceramics may establish the provenience of the various stratigraphic horizons. In this way the ceramics of the southern Turkmenistan sphere in the lower layers of Shahr-i Sokhta may be compared with both the western and eastern provinces of Namazga III. Clay female figurines found in the more recently formed layers of Shahr-i Sokhta clearly follow the Geoksyur/Kara-Depe traditions of modeling (Tosi 1969:p. 360, fig. 37), and in this sense are close to the terracottas of Namazga IV. These examples let us conclude that the corresponding cultural parallelism is no longer based on only one painted vessel.

The ceramic assemblage of Quetta with its geometric ornamentation bears distinct traces of Namazga III and IV ceramics of southern Turkmenistan. This has already been noted in the literature and today is widely accepted by the specialists. Tentatively, such analogies may be present in almost 25% of the ceramic types or ornamentations, and the parallels in the female terracottas and seals underline the strong, not fortuitous southern Turkmenistan ties. Thus Shahr-i Sokhta and the group of sites in the Quetta region display their most significant ties with the cultures of southern Turkmenistan (Fig. 31).

Less varied but also fairly distinct parallels are revealed in the materials of southern Afghanistan sites, namely, Mundigak, Deh-Morasi-Gunday, and Said-Q'ala. The painted ceramics of the Mundigak III assemblage have designs with clear ties to Kara Ia ceramics (Masson 1960a:pls. XXII, XXX, item 1; Casal 1961:vol. 2, figs. 54, 65, 69) and also with the traditions of Altyn 8 and 9 which correspond chronologically to the assemblages of Namazga III and in part Namazga IV. From the Mundigak IV,1 period there is a fragment with a representation of a spotted leopard (which is a typical motif of the ceramics of Late Namazga III in its Kara-Depe variant). With it are vessels of the Quetta style which have clear analogies in the southern Turkmenistan ceramics of Early Namazga IV (Casal 1961:vol. 2, p. 269, fig. 77). In general, the relief stone vessels of the Mundigak IV period show the same ornamentation tradition. The collective burials of Mundigak III period are also of note. Unlike the Late Eneolithic tombs of Geoksyur and Altyn-Depe, however, they are not oval but rectangular and in this respect are closer to those of Kara-Depe.

Also, judging by the preliminary information on the excavations at Said-Q'ala, the painted ceramics described have direct analogies with two types of ceramics in the Altyn 8 and 9 assemblages: the Morasi, which can be regarded as local, and the Quetta, which can be interpreted as imported. According to the text of the report, the Quetta type is represented throughout the cultural deposits which reach the thickness of 7.5 m. The large number of female statuettes is significant. They were found in the lower layers and, according to J.G. Shaffer, have direct Central Asian parallels (Shaffer 1971:93, 102). The abundance of female terracottas immediately differentiates the early southern Turkmenistan settlements from synchronous sites in Iran, and the large numbers of terracottas in the lower layers indicates the considerable influence of Central Asian traditions specifically in the early stages, since later they occur relatively rarely at Said-Q'ala.

Terracottas representing seated women and modeled in the Central Asian (Geoksyur) style have been found in a number of early agricultural sites which precede the Harappan culture

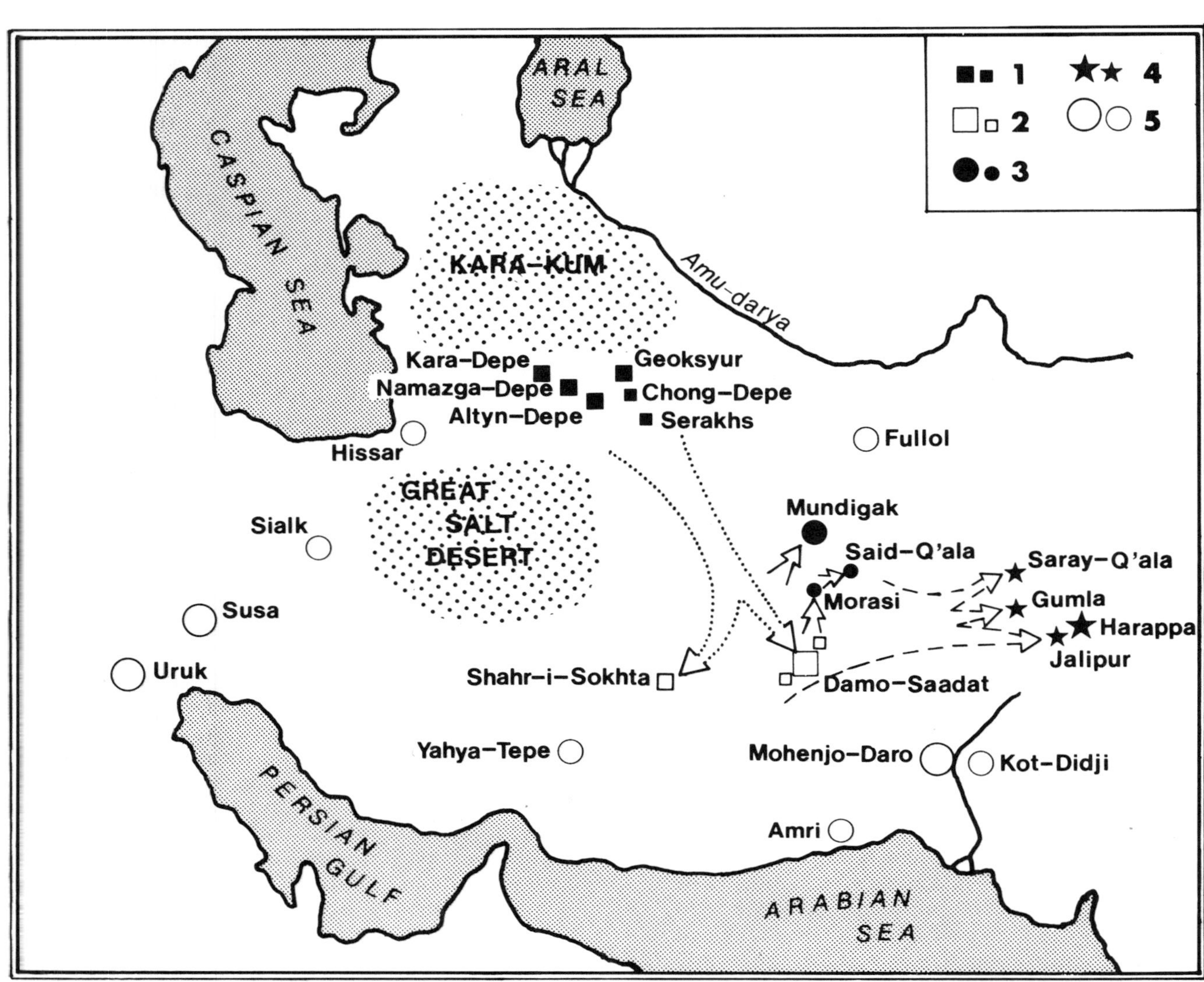

Figure 31.   Cultural influences in the Middle East during the Eneolithic.
Key— 1: *large and small settlements of the Anau culture;* 2: *settlements with significant Anau cultural elements;* 3: *settlements with rare Anau cultural elements;* 4: *settlements with single Anau cultural elements;* 5: *other archaeological sites.*

in the Indus Valley (Dani 1970-1971; Dales 1972b:p. 174, fig. 83). The location of such sites, particularly in the northern zone (that is, in territorial proximity to the southern Afghanistan assemblages) is evidence that behind these analogies are realistic, historical contacts. Quite noteworthy is the stratigraphy of Jalipur, about 50 km from Harappa. Here the lower layers produced coarse pasted vessels which are gradually replaced with ceramics made on a potter's wheel. According to M. Mughal, some of the sherds have their nearest analogies in Mundigak III (Mughal 1974:111-112). In the same layers, terracottas of the Geoksyur type were found.

A detailed analysis of the analogies and parallels mentioned above is somewhat difficult because of the preliminary nature of many of the reports and publications. Yet they may indicate the directions of the ties. In his time, J.M. Casal vigorously supported the hypothesis that northern Baluchistan ceramics of the Quetta style were based on the Susa traditions and distributed from there to southern Turkmenistan (Casal 1961:vol. 1, pp. 100, 105). It is easy to see, however, that vessels with appropriate comparable paintings comprise only a limited percentage in the fairly diverse local assemblages of sites in the Middle East, and that the percentage diminishes with the distance from southern Turkmenistan. The same can be said about the terracottas of southern Turkmenistan. In the Quetta and Said Q'ala regions, together with statuettes of the Geoksyur and Kara-Depe types, there occur statuettes of the so-called Zhob style with an iconographic resolution in principle strongly different from the southern Turkmenistan statuettes. It is exactly the southern Turkmenistan ceramics with geometric designs that have acquired the name "Quetta style" in northern Baluchistan and that with local terracottas comprise the basic assemblage. Even with the findings of cultural ties with Mesopotamia and Iran (Masson 1964b:423, 433; Sarianidi 1965:48-50), the local populations of Kara-Depe, Geoksyur, and Altyn-Depe modified a large number of traits of the preceding traditions. Both the Geoksyur and Kara-Depe types of ceramics, as a ceramic assemblage, represent a single, final manifestation in which only separate elements or motifs (and never the entire style) can be associated with non-Turkmenistan traditions.

Southern Turkmenistan may be regarded as one of the centers of active cultural influence (Fig. 31), above all directly associated with the native peoples occupying the Middle East at the end of the 4th to the beginning of the 3rd millennium B.C. Today, a number of investigators lean toward this point of view (Biscione 1973; Dales 1973; Lamberg-Karlovsky and Tosi 1973). Since these influences are particularly strong in Shahr-i Sokhta and the Quetta group, it may be proposed that this was precisely the basic direction of the influence. This strong stream reaches, to a somewhat lesser degree, Mundigak III, where a corresponding tradition is prolonged even in the times of Mundigak IV, partly because of the stimulating contacts with the Quetta group of early agricultural peoples. Only separate impulses are observable in the northern Indus Valley, as revealed by the types of terracottas. Thus the Late Eneolithic culture of Turkmenistan played an important role in forming the substratum on which the early urban cultures of Central Asia and the Middle East were formed. Also, in the northern reaches of the Indus Valley, where during the first half of the 3rd millennium B.C. there was an intensive development of early agrarian cultures which formed the incipient horizon for the Harappan civilization, we find clear traces of southern Turkmenistan influence. The Geoksyur horizon was one of the more important components in the cultural geneses flowing through that part of the ecumene of the Ancient East.

The second important factor in the process mentioned above is tied in with a cluster of manifestations definable as a proto-Elamite type of assemblage. Its characteristic index is the presence of clay tablets with proto-Elamite texts, cylinder seals, and ceramics obviously developing into the tradition which is most clearly represented in the Mesopotamian assemblage of Jemdet-Nasr. The first time this assemblage was discovered beyond the Elam realm was at Sialk, where it was named Sialk IV. Here it covered the local culture Sialk III, in this way underlining the obvious break with tradition (Ghirshman 1939). Today, the number of such assemblages has grown, as is clearly evident in the summary of C. Lamberg-Karlovsky (1978). In northwestern Iran it was uncovered in the settlement of Godin V. Not of lesser interest are the excavations at Tal-e Malyan in the vicinity of Shiraz. Investigators are inclined to identify the latter with the ancient Anshan of the Elamite texts. Also, a single proto-Elamite tablet was found in the lower layers of Shahr-i Sokhta. The excavations of Lamberg-Karlovsky at Yahya-Tepe in southeastern Iran provided widely known results. Yahya-Tepe is located in the southern part of Kerman province [*ostan*] in the valley of one of the small rivers northeast of the town of Dolatabad. The water-surrounded mound is high but small in area, about 1.5 hectares. Its lower layers, Yahya V and VI, contained remains typical of an early agricultural settlement of this region, with painted ceramics and beginnings of arsenical copper production stimulated by the presence of ore deposits. Distinct traits of a proto-Elamite assemblage were present in layer IV-C together with some preserved local types of ceramics. On the floors of excavated buildings clay tablets were found with proto-Elamite texts, cylinder seals and their impressions, and also ceramics obviously developed from the Jemdet-Nasr tradition. The striking brilliance of the materials leaves no doubt about their archaeological provenience.

Naturally, so widespread an occurrence of proto-Elamite assemblages begs for an explanation. On the basis of the Sialk materials, Childe expressed the opinion (which became the traditional one) that "the Elamites occupied a key position on the trade routes and because of that controlled the trade in lapis lazuli" (Childe 1956:295). An analogous hypothesis of a merchant colony is proposed by the discoverers of Godin V (Weiss and Young 1973). Lamberg-Karlovsky took a new overall approach to the problem. He holds that the distribution of proto-Elamite assemblages reflects a process of integration achieved through economic and political interaction among societies located considerable distances from each other. Further, he proposes that these interactions were coordinated by the Elamite city-state established in southwestern Iran in Khuzistan (Lamberg-Karlovsky 1978:118). Aside from striving for broad historical generalizations, Lamberg-Karlovsky tends to consider particularly the processes of cultural genesis which, unlike many other historical manifestations, are directly reflected in archaeological materials. The concept of cultural integration for highly developed societies can be employed at least for the hypothesized interpretation and the more traditional one of diffusion and migration. This sociological straightfowardness, however, unwarrantedly captivates the author. The exploitation of cultural resources developed in a metropolis by societies which have reached an appropriate level of socio-economic development is adequately known. The mechanism of distribution of these resources may be quite different, including itinerant merchants, frequently combined in the ancient East in half merchant-half military

caravans. Besides, there is a basic difference between the appearance of proto-Elamite assemblages in, say, Sialk and Tepe Yahya. In the first, there is an interruption of cultural traditions, an influx of a population with another culture. In the second, we find a distribution of cultural resources which were formed in the same culture and perhaps the same ethnic context because of the gravitation of southern Iranian assemblages of painted ceramics, as is well known, toward the Susiana traditions. It should be understood that we cannot talk about some kind of personal role of the Elamite state in this process. This would undoubtedly be a modernization, since for a long time Elam was a collection of small, mutually hostile city-states which, notwithstanding considerable cultural unity, could not form a solid, political unit until the 22nd century B.C. There is no reason to modernize the actions of these first islets of class societies which grew up from the depths of the primordial epoch.

At the same time, the widespread influence of the proto-Elamite culture on societies of the Iranian upland is evident, and this influence undoubtedly provided the preconditions for cultural integration. In dimensions and meaning it reminds me of the influence of the Ubaid culture which in the 4th millennium B.C. involved northern Mesopotamia and spread further to the northwest and to some degree to the northeast (Masson 1964b:410-415). Apparently, the nature of these phenomena were similar in the initial hearths of civilization: Sumer and Elam. In part, in the process of Sumer-Elam interactions, cultural resources were developed and became models and examples for societies undergoing, albeit at a slow tempo, the same mode of socio-economic development. The mechanism of the spread of developed resources could have been, and in reality apparently was, quite diverse. It included direct settlement of the Elamites, perhaps by merchants-traders, as well as imitation and conformation to the ruling fashions of the epoch. The proto-Elamite tablet in the lower horizons of Shahr-i Sokhta is in a demonstrably different cultural context than similar tablets in Yahya IV-C. The basic mass of clay vessels at Shahr-i Sokhta is a product of the traditions of Baluchistan societies with the added ceramic tradition brought in by southern Turkmenistan immigrants.

Under the influence of two powerful cultural impulses, the proto-Elamite and Geoksyur traditions, tendencies toward urbanization developed in the Middle East during the first half of the 3rd millennium B.C. To a considerable degree these developments were preconditions to urbanization. A concentration of population was reflected in the appearance of large populated points, centers of oases and separate regions, and specialization of activities, clearly reflected in the specialization of production. In southern Turkmenistan, particularly at the time of the Late Eneolithic, the formative process which resulted in the development of Namazga-Depe and Altyn-Depe as large population centers was completed. As we have seen, layers in the southern part of Altyn-Depe containing Geoksyur ceramics lay directly on virgin soil, thus reflecting the rapid growth of the settlement. On its northern edge a ceramic kiln of the same age was uncovered, but it was difficult to say to what degree a specific quarter of master potters formed here. At Shahr-i Sokhta in Seistan there is also a steady enlargement of the housing area. In Period I, the investigators estimate its area at 15.5 hectares, in Period II (2800-2500 B.C.) at 45 hectares, and in Period III (2400-2100 B.C.) at 80 hectares. At Rud-i-Biyaban, some 29 km from Shahr-i Sokhta, a concentration of about 50 ceramic kilns was found. The rapidly revolving potter's wheel makes its appearance at Shahr-i Sokhta only during the second half of the 3rd millennium B.C., about the same time as in northern Turkmenistan. The working of lapis lazuli and turquoise becomes an important specialization (Tosi and Piperno 1973). A sociological interpretation of the small site of Tepe Yahya is more complex, although traces of specialized activities such as mass production of artistically cut soapstone vessels were found (Lamberg-Karlovsky and Tosi 1971:106-111; Kohl 1975). Because of its small dimensions, however, Tepe Yahya can hardly be called a point of population concentration, unlike Tal-i Iblis to the north, which at the time apparently was the center for the entire Kerman region. It is of interest that in the vicinity of Tepe Yahya, particularly during period IV-C, the time of the appearance of the proto-Elamite assemblage, the agricultural settlements existing there were abandoned (Vidali, M.L., Vidali M. and Lamberg-Karlovsky 1976:250).

It remains to dwell briefly on the question of motivation for the projected processes of urbanization. The American investigators are inclined to ascribe special meaning to early trade. For instance, Lamberg-Karlovsky initially writes in general terms that trade was one of the principal stimulants of urbanization, and later specifically that it was trade between resource-poor Mesopotamia and the population of the remote parts of Iran that appeared to be the principal economic basis for the urban development of Tepe Yahya (Lamberg-Karlovsky, C.C. and Lamberg-Karlovsky, M. 1971:111). From our point of view such a "trade model" (at the time rather a popular one among Western investigators) becomes a modernization and exaggeration when applied to early societies.

The so-called trading was conducted without the participation of the entire society and affected only a limited sphere of the then existing production directed to the satisfaction of the needs of the upper crust of the society. Sometimes trade was limited to the transportation of raw materials. For the lands of the Middle East the principal precondition for the development of urban cultures in the 3rd millennium was the presence of a balanced economy able to provide a considerable and steady surplus of food products under the conditions of the various forms of field agriculture. It was exactly this type of economy that, in regulating cycles of production in a unified, single irrigation system, provided the preconditions for the concentration of populations and the formation of large centers, the distinct early agrarian capitals. In its turn, the concentration of population led to additional needs for products of specialized manufacture. And it was the same agricultural-animal husbandry economy that created the conditions for technological progress in the emerging specialized activities. Undoubtedly, the development of systematic barter which matured into regular trading played its own role, particularly in the dispersal of cultural resources, but its purely economic impact was not as yet great in the early agricultural societies of the Iranian plateau, unlike the situation in Asia Minor during the 2nd millennium B.C.

In the second period of development of urban centers in the Middle East during the second half of the 3rd millennium B.C., the situation substantially changes. The gradual decay of Tepe Yahya at this time reflects the diminished role of the Elamite impulse in the processes of cultural genesis. This may have been caused to no small degree by the weakening of the Elamite metropolis itself, which had fallen into direct political and cultural dependence on Agade. The majority of inscriptions emanating from Elam during 2400-2300 B.C. are in Akkadian. Some development is found in Seistan, but toward the end of the period. Shahr-i Sokhta as a large population center falls into neglect. There is, however, intensive development in northeastern

Iran and in southern Turkmenistan, as shown by the results of investigations at Tureng-Tepe, Hissar, and Altyn-Depe. Everywhere there is an intensive development of handicrafts, particularly of metallurgy and pottery making, there is an ongoing process of social differentiation, and the structure of large population centers becomes complicated with the appearance of monumental edifices. As far as cultural genesis is concerned, the urban culture of Altyn-Depe represents a natural development of Late Eneolithic Geoksyur traditions with changes that reflect technological progress. The preservation of Iranian ties and the utilization of specific cultural resources of the Mesopotamian-Elamite world were traditional for southern Turkmenistan. Ties with the Harappan civilization were a new trait, but overall they did not play an important role. The distinctive cast of the Altyn-Depe culture appears as an archaeological reflection of the polycentric process of the formation of early urban societies amidst the settled agricultural peoples of the Middle East.

The materials obtained during the excavations at Altyn-Depe also introduce questions about the ethnic affinity of the creators of its highly developed culture. In this regard, the finds of two proto-Indian seals play a special role. One of the seals depicts a swastika, and the other depicts two signs. These depictions leave no doubt that they belong the group of analogous objects of the proto-Indian type. Thus the seal with the swastika which fills the entire frame appears among the finds at Mohenjo-Daro. The signs carved into the second seal are typical of proto-Indian writing and are entered in the catalogue of signs compiled on the basis of materials from Mohenjo-Daro as numbers 15 and 96 (Marshall 1931:vol. 3, pp. 374, 434-439, pl. CXIV, and pp. 500-515). While it is true that an inscription composed of just these two signs has not been found in the materials of India, two sign inscriptions appear there fairly often. If we follow the variant of decipherment proposed by N.V. Gurov (1971), the signs in the Altyn-Depe seal may be classified as a sacrificial inscription, where Y may be interpreted as "hand," "handful," or "sacrificial tribute," and ⱉ as a name of a god. A personal communication from Gurov suggests that the Altyn-Depe signs may be read as "Great God." Since there is no overall acceptance of a decipherment of proto-Indian texts, the latter is only one of the possible interpretations (Krishnarao 1973; Rao 1973a). The form of the Altyn seals, with an ear handle on the obverse side, and their size are characteristic of Harappan

glyptics. The size varies between 15-25 mm. The absence of an accompanying image on seals with signs is somewhat unusual for Harappan glyptics, but seals, including those of rectangular form with only one sign, are also known from Indian materials, although they are relatively rare (Marshall 1931:vol. 3, pp. 471-477, 479-482, pl. CXIV).

In one of the latest compendiums, 2,469 objects were accounted for, most of them seals (Mahadevan and Visvanathan 1973:292). Their distribution is very significant. Most came from the two early capitals: 1,390 from Mohenjo-Daro and 891 from Harappa. They are followed by towns of secondary rank, centers of ancient provinces: 67 from Chanhu-Daro, 54 from Lothal, 37 from Kalibangan. Finally, one to three were found in six small sites in India and Pakistan, and 12 in various Mesopotamian centers such as Ur, Kish, and Tell-Ashmar (Eshnunna). In this regard Altyn-Depe, as a new locality where inscriptions of proto-Indian types were found, is of particular interest.

The presence of proto-Indian seals at Altyn-Depe confirms more than just the steady ties between India and southern Turkmenistan during the Bronze Age. Thanks to the finding of a seal with a pictographic text, attention can be directed to another aspect of the problem.

A seal of the proto-Indian type with a striking representation of an animal, accompanied by a pictographic text, could have played a cult role in regions neighboring India merely because of the presence of the representation. But in the case of a find of a seal with one inscription only, the question arises as to whether or not the information contained on it can be used, that is, can be read. Seals with handles on the obverse side and various representations on the face are fairly common in the Namazga V cultures of southern Turkmenistan. These include seals of rectangular form, but none of the latter have inscriptions. The finds of proto-Indian seals at Altyn-Depe, including those with proto-Indian texts, compel us to turn to the question of the ethnic affinity of the local population during the Eneolithic and Bronze Ages.

Although at present there is no generally accepted system of deciphering proto-Indian texts, the view that the language they contain is proto-Dravidian seems most credible. This view was expressed comparatively long ago and has now been confirmed by the study of the texts through various methods, including positional-statistical analysis (Preliminary report 1965; Proto-Indian reports 1972, 1973; Parpalo, Koshenniemi *et al.*

1969). The historical-linguistic materials also support this point of view. They have established with certainty the role of the Dravidian substratum in the Indo-Aryan languages. This role can be traced in the vocabulary, as well as phonetics, morphology, and syntax (Vorobev-Desyatovskiy 1956a). Extensive data allow the conclusion that earlier Dravidian languages were distributed over a relatively large area. The presence in northern Baluchistan of the Brahui (or Braui) tribe speaking a language of the Dravidian group is evidence of this. The large part of the Brahui live in Pakistan, but they are also found in Afghanistan, Iran, and among the Baluchi of Turkmenia (Andronov 1971:9-11). The Brahui of most ancient origin inhabit northern Baluchistan in the region of Kelat, and their ethnonym is semantically best rendered as "northern mountaineers" or "people of the northern mountains." At present, the Brahui live intermixed with the Baluchi. The culture and daily activities of both groups are very similar, and overall the Brahui may be regarded as a kind of ethno-linguistic relict, disappearing as they assimilate the influence of the Iranian and Indic speaking populations. There is evidence that just a few centuries ago a part of the Seistan population spoke a Dravidian language related to that of the Brahui, but that later the language was lost (Vorobev-Desyatovskiy 1956a:101).

For identification of the territory over which the ancient Dravidian languages spread, their ties with the Finno-Ugrian groups are important and were established long ago. It was thought that the ties were based on genetic kinship, but the majority of investigators lean toward the conclusion that the evidence suggests more distant connections (Andronov 1969:312-320). In any case, it was S.P. Tolstov who quite justifiably proposed that during the pre-Indo-Iranian epoch, at least during the 4th to 3rd millennium B.C., Dravidian or Dravidian-related tribes existed in contiguity with Central Asia under conditions of broad possibilities for cultural contact with peoples of the Aral Sea basin (Tolstov 1948:350). The Neolithic Kelteminar culture that spread over Khoremia at that time had strong ties with the cultures of the Urals and Western Siberia. The literature even suggests the possibiltiy that during the 4th to 3rd millennium B.C. there existed an extensive cultural community which included the area west of the Aral Sea, the Urals, and the southern part of Western Siberia that was composed of groups of related tribes that were most likely the ancestors of the Ugrians. The analysis of Dravidian glottochronology by

M.S. Andronov (1964, 1965) is particularly interesting. Lexico-statistical analysis led him to conclude that the division in the proto-Dravidian language took place in the beginning of the 4th millennium B.C. when the Brahui language split off in northwestern India; the differentiation of other linguistic groups took place with subsequent movements into the depths of the subcontinent. The Finno-Ugrian ties with the Dravidian languages imply that the latter spread to India from north to south, which was the basis for the map drawn by Andronov (see Fig. 32).

Certain coincidences between the above model and the stages of development in India of early agrarian cultures using painted ceramics demand our attention (Masson 1964b:246ff; Fairservis 1971:111ff). Settlements of farmers were quite extensive during the 4th millennium B.C. in the mountain areas of northern Baluchistan. (Could it be that the ethnonym of the Brahui, "people of the northern mountains," dates to this time?) In the first half of the 3rd millennium, early agricultural tribes were already occupying the Indus Valley fairly extensively, and the Harappan civilization developed there during the second half of the 3rd millennium. Together with local elements and the formation of clearly distinctive Indian cultures (a process which Fairservis calls "Indianization"), the Iranian-Central Asian relationships are indisputable in the archaeological assemblages. Their appearance was most probably associated with tribal movements from the Sialk-Hissar regions in central and northern Iran and Kara-Depe and Geoksyur in southern Turkmenia, particularly noticeable at the end of the 4th to the beginning of the 3rd millennium B.C. In the middle of the 2nd millennium B.C., several groups of settled farmers with painted ceramics were formed in central India. In their cultures we see a combination of the local stratum of Neolithic hunters and gatherers and such innovations as field tilling, metallurgy, and painted ceramics made on the wheel—all clearly associated with the Harappan civilization (Shchetenko 1968a). The mechanisms of these movements have been insufficiently studied, but they certainly were associated with migrations of ethnic groups. In turn, these sedentary farmers in central India influenced the formation of the so-called Megalithic culture in southern India during the 1st millennium B.C. Even with some chronological discrepancies, the coincidence of the general tendency of settled farming to spread from north to south, as established by archaeological data, in the same pattern as the distribution of Dravidic-speaking tribes, as

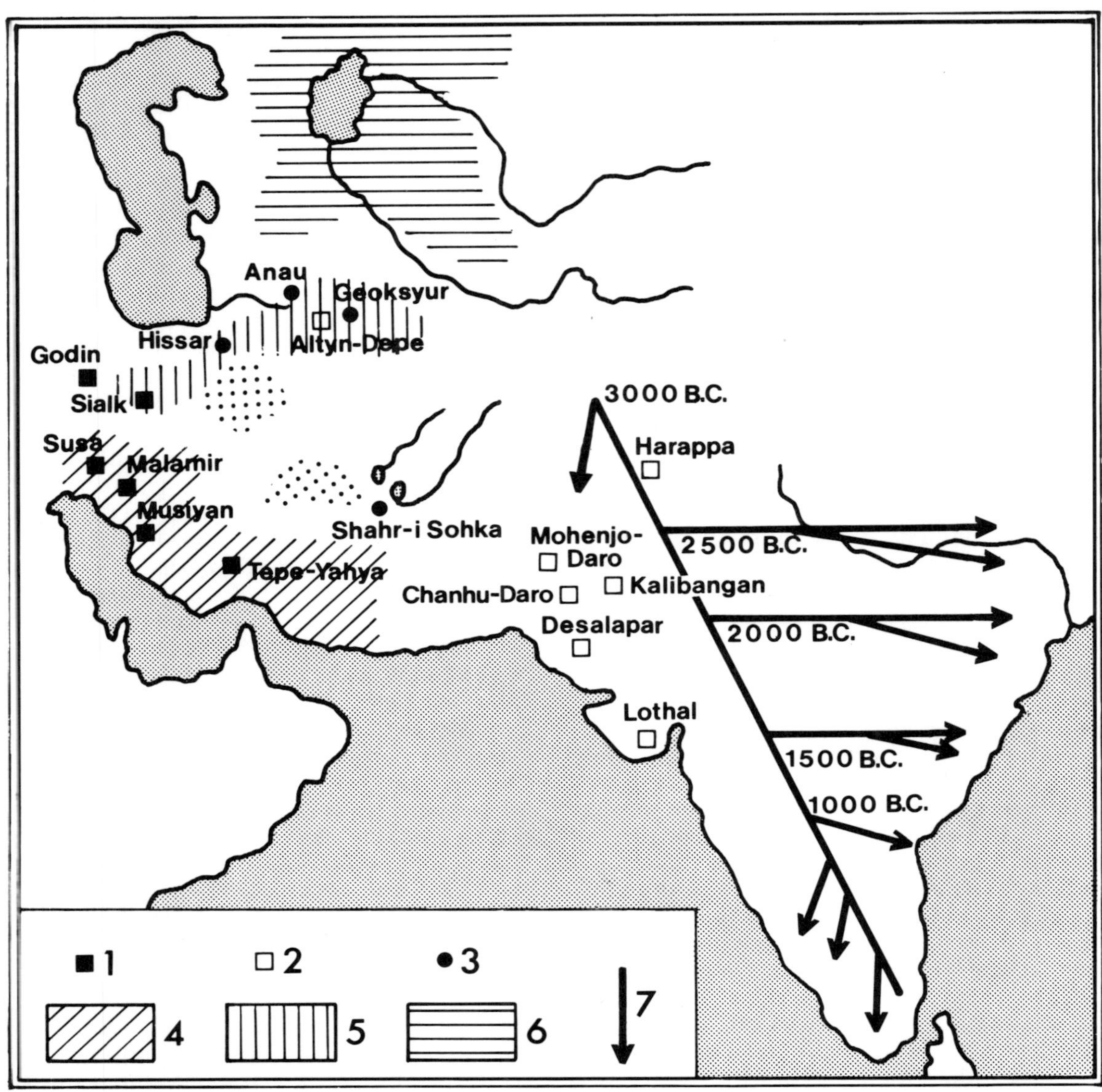

Figure 32.   Cultural zones and distribution of sites in the Middle East with evidence of early writing.
Key— 1: *sites with proto-Elamite writing; 2: sites with proto-Indic writing; 3: other archaeological sites; 4: southern cultural zone of early farmers; 5: northern cultural zone of early farmers; 6: Kelteminar cultural community; 7: resettlement of Dravidic-speaking tribes according to M. S. Andronov.*

established by lexico-statistical analysis, must be noted.

A number of attempts have been made to compare this or that archaeological assemblage or culture with Dravidic-speaking populations of an ancient period. The point of view prevails, however, that the inhabitants of Harappa were proto-Dravidians (Gankovskiy 1964:28-32; Bongard-Levin and Ilin 1969:297), as presumably were some of the Eneolithic tribes of more southerly regions. At other times, attempts were made to identify more precisely the position of the proto-Dravidians in the extensive population of northwestern India during the Bronze Age (Zvelchil 1965).

The complicated problem of studying ancient ethnic processes requires particular care in the use of methods and a clear-cut initial methodological concept. In this field Soviet ethnographers have carried out major and fruitful work, summarized in the book of Yu.V. Bromley (1973:175). He points out that the principal bearers of ethnic qualities are ordinary consciousness, everyday language, and traditional everyday culture. As a rule, archaeological materials make it possible to identify the traditional everyday culture, with its characteristic stable set of objects and individual elements of ordinary consciousness, on the basis of artifact types associated in some way with the ideological sphere. The parameters of the physical anthropology of a population that has left archaeological assemblages do not carry ethnic information as such; the parameters should be used only as indirect evidence that may, in part, resolve a question of ethnicity. For instance, in the case that is of interest to us, concepts like Dravidian languages or Dravidian physical types become homonymous concepts for various disciplines, and do not have the strong connections that are often assigned to them, at least not in ancient times. In addition, it must be kept in mind that with the present level of knowledge, questions concerning the reconstruction of the ethnic history of the Middle East during the paleo-metallic epoch can be resolved only on the level of generalized comparisons. Thus apparently there existed a number of tribal groups, and perhaps even nations, of the proto-Dravidian or early Dravidian linguistic family that today have completely disappeared in the process of assimilation. A similar process occurred with one of the Dravidian groups in medieval Seistan. On the level of general comparisons, however, the considerable closeness and connections between the Dravidian and Elamite languages, already

noted by V.S. Vorobev-Desyatovskiy, are particularly important (1956a:100-101; 1956b:76). This relationship, according to the conclusions of I.M. Dyakonov, permits the proposal that "tribes related in language to the Elamites and Dravidians in the 4th and 3rd millennium B.C., and perhaps even later, were widespread throughout Iran, at least in its southern part" (Dyakonov 1967:87). The evidence of Finno-Ugrian contacts with the Dravidian languages permit even broader variants of Dyakonov's formulation.

In such a case, the broad zone of early farming tribes who made painted ceramics and during the 4th to 3rd millennium B.C. lived in groups between the Zagros Mountains and the Indus Valley, may be looked upon as the territory of tribes who spoke a language close to Elamite and Dravidian. On the basis of extensive archaeological materials which revealed a stable everyday culture, D. McCown as early as 1942 identified two types of assemblages on the Iranian Plateau: the northern, occupying Sialk, Hissar, and Anau, which he tentatively named "the red ware region," and the southern, manifested most clearly in Susa and Tal-i Bakun where yellow and cream-colored ceramics prevailed (McCown 1942:48-50). Today, as a result of the discovery within this territory of a very large number of new sites, the division retains its significance only at the most general level and does not characterize archaeological cultures or cultural communities, but most likely an even larger unit approximating the concept of a territorial or cultural zone.

It can be shown that it was precisely within the boundaries of the southern zone that the Elamite language prevailed to the degree we know from the earliest sites with written materials (Fig. 32). Significant differences between the northern and southern cultural zones emerge quite clearly in the materials from Shahr-i Sokhta in Seistan, which is in the region of contact between the two zones. Here in the lower layers we see a unification of the two traditions: the southern, emerging in the style of the ceramics of Tal-i Bakun, and the northern, which is tied in with ceramics of the Geoksyur type, that is, with Central Asia. When tablets with proto-Elamite pictographs appear at Sialk V in the depths of the northern cultural zone, the entire assemblage of the traditional culture is sharply differentiated from the local one, as represented in Sialk I-III, and may be regarded as essentially foreign, that is, Elamite-Mesopotamian, if not purely Elamite. Therefore it seems quite legitimate to compare the southern cultural zone, whose distinctive features as a unified zone formed at least in the 4th millennium B.C., with the region of dissemination of the Elamite language or, to put it differently, with the Elamite ethnic community.

In such a case the question naturally arises as to whether or not the northern cultural zone, inhabited by farmers using painted ceramics, had any ties with the proto-Dravidic-speaking tribes, whose gradual migration from the north through Afghanistan and Baluchistan is shown on the map illustrating the spread of Dravidic languages established by lexico-statistical analysis. Let me mention that a similar case nicely clarifies the Ugro-Dravidic linguistic parallels, which have their archaeological parallel in cultural ties between the Keltiminar Neolithic in the area north of the Aral Sea and the painted ware culture of southern Turkmenistan (Vinogradov 1957, 1968:82-83; Masson 1964b:177-178). If we take this stand, the seal with a proto-Indian inscription found at Altyn-Depe may be viewed as evidence that a local community, which had achieved the level of civilization, used an already existing system of writing adapted from a language related to that of the local population. In other words, one could see the creators of the Altyn-Depe civilization, as well as the contemporary Harappans, as tribes of the proto-Dravidian ethnic group.

It should be understood that such a hypothesis can be offered only in the most general terms, but in my opinion the find at Altyn-Depe of a specific epigraphic seal without an image, whose cult magic may have been valued by illiterate peoples peripheral to Harap-

pa, is evidence in favor of this hypothesis. It may be that further study of questions pertaining to the paleo-ethnic situation in the Middle East during the time of the early farmers with painted ceramics will be connected in many ways with the identification of stable cultural groupings, that is, cultural variants and cultures, of people who once lived there. This can be done through the detailed analysis of archaeological materials. In his excellent analysis of Dravidian-Elamite correspondence, I.M. Dyakonov notes that "one may acknowledge as plausible the hypothesis that the Elamite language is a very early and rather remote branch of a common Dravidian language base, or that the common Dravidian language base and Elamite belong to a single common prototype" (Dyakonov 1967:112). From the point of view of cultural genesis, the Zagros cultural community of the 7th to the 6th millennia B.C., represented by such sites as Jarmo and Guran, was of great importance for the earliest settled farming tribes of the northern and, to a considerable degree, the southern zone. The spread of the Zagros farmers in two streams, northern and southern, bypassing the formidable deserts of the Dashti-Lut and the Dashti-Kevir, has already appeared in the literature (Masson 1964b:202). Linguistic affinity made assimilation easier for the migrating tribal groups so often observed in the 5th to the 3rd millennia B.C. within the great mass of early farming tribes to the east of Mesopotamia.

In whatever way these questions will be resolved, it is quite clear that the archaeological culture of Altyn-Depe will play an important role in the resolution of paleo-ethnographic problems in the Near and Middle East.

VIII

Early Urban Centers and Ancient Civilizations

The excavations at Altyn-Depe and the sociological interpretations of the materials obtained induce us to turn to the general questions pertaining to the history of ancient urban centers. In answering these questions, particularly those pertaining to origins, we will see that Altyn-Depe played a considerable role because it was a center formed from an early agricultural base. In this respect, specific analyses of urban or proto-urban communities by archaeologists are of paramount significance. It is demonstrable that the ancient Babylonian city, relatively well-studied by Soviet orientalists, does not represent a city organism which was formed in a natural way, but "the development of a specific type of city formed as a result of the destruction of an almost fully despotic monopoly of a royal economy which was characteristic in the preceding period in general and in the city specifically" (Dyakonov 1973:36). Written sources hardly touch upon the early Sumerian settlements of the city type dated to the end of the 4th through the beginning of the 3rd millennium B.C., but archaeological materials reveal their general dimensions and cult centers. Beyond these limits, however, in the quarters of the city proper, excavations as a rule were carried out on a restricted scale. Yet, the significance of early cities in the history of society was major and, moreover, within the past decade has attracted the attention of investigators (Adams and Nissen 1972; MSU 1972). In the appropriate definition of Dyakonov, the city occupies a leading position as a center of economic, social, and political life (Dyakonov 1973:30). Social contradictions and the cultural achievements of the epoch became discernible in the city in the clearest and most representative forms.

Sources on the development of settlements of the city type take us to the depths of the primitive communal system which formed within the early settled agricultural societies. Engels aptly underlined the particularity of the city as an institution conceived within the framework of a primitive social formation: "Not put up in vain are the formidable walls around the new fortified cities: In its depths yawns the grave of kin-based social formations, but its towers already reach civilization" (K. Marks and F. Engels 1936:vol. 21, p. 164). The conditions were also noted by Marx: "The greatest differences between material and spiritual works are seen in the separation of city and village. The contradiction between city and village begins with the transition from barbarism to civilization, from a kin-based on structure to the state" (1936:vol. 3, p. 49).

The study of the preconditions which led to the formation of the city is of utmost significance. The first of these preconditions was the ability to obtain food products which would support the high population density and which, first of all, offered the possibility of a concentrated population. The sharp increase of population in settled agricultural societies is well known; compared to the epoch of hunter-gatherers, it increased almost a hundredfold (Braidwood and Reed 1957:24-25; Masson 1976a:102-104). It is no wonder then that even in the early stages of development of societies there appear relatively large populated centers. For instance, such is Çatal Hüyük in Asia Minor which dates to the second half of the 7th to the first half of the 6th millennium B.C., occupied an area of about 12 hectares, and, according to the different methods of estimation, had a population of 2000-5000 people (Masson 1971b:147-148). Çatal Hüyük, located on the Konya Plain with 22 additional small settlements, no doubt functioned as a center for the agricultural vicinity and the political center for a group of tribes. In southern Turkmenistan settled agricultural communities with a population of 1000-2000 and a hierarchical structure started forming in the 4th through the beginning of the 3rd millennium B.C. (Masson

1976a:142-143). Ethnographically, large populated points are well known for the settled Pueblo Indians, Papuans of New Guinea, and a number of other peoples. It follows that it was particularly in agricultural communities where the major precondition, the ability to gather adequate foodstuffs, formed and, under certain conditions, led to the development of cities and in many respects defined the role of such communities in the world's history.

The next major precondition for the formation of early urban centers appears to be the separation of craftsmanship from agriculture, the second major social division of labor securing for a town a position as a point of concentration of specialized productive functions. The process of technological production proceeded in many respects simultaneously with the formation of cities. Often the question is posed: Did the volume of craft production in the early cities result in a striking dominance over agriculture? However, here volume by itself is not as important as the fact of the presence of a specialization, the more so since with the development of the city new requirements arise in its population, stimulating the expansion of the traditional industries and the creation of new ones. The city and crafts exist in a complex interaction of direct and indirect ties. In settled agricultural communities of the Old World, including southern Turkmenistan, the bearers of technical progress during the period of formation of the cities were the metallurgists and pottery makers with their considerable achievements in the sphere of pyrotechnology.

The third group of preconditions is associated with social developments: the social differentiation of the community, including all the more complex developments and isolation of the organs of administration, particularly in connection with the necessity to organize the seasonal agricultural work. Large population nodes become the natural centers for the concentration of such activities once they became feasible within the framework of a primitive social structure.

An important precondition in the formation of cities was the development of communication in its various aspects, including the technological development of progressive forms of transportation. The study of the topography of early settlements in Mesopotamia shows the existence of spatial boundaries separating the city and its farming environs (Adams and Nissen 1972:31-32). This implies, among other things, the ability to transport various kinds of cargo within a limited period of time. In southern Turkmenistan at the end of the 4th through the beginning of the 3rd millennium B.C. there already appear the first clay models of four-wheeled carts with camels harnessed to them, and in one case, a bull (Lisitsina 1972:pp. 14-15, fig. 1; Lisitsina 1978: p. 56, fig. 6, item 5). In Mesopotamia the development of wheeled transport is tied to the time of the formation of cities (Piggott 1969), although there dry land communication was successfully augmented by water arteries. The development of transportation promoted the regional functions of the city and above all its function as a center of an agricultural region, a place for the concentration and redistribution of both necessary and surplus products. In this regard, the role of wheeled transport was particularly important. In the absence of good roads, the heavy and cumbersome four-wheeled carts served principally for the transport of cargoes for short distances, while porters or beasts of burden were used for export trade.

To the number of factors which promoted the formation of cities, we can add the establishment of a hierarchal structure of religious ideas, with a principal deity or pair of deities to whom, accordingly, the most significant and effective cult edifice was dedicated. Under these conditions, the phenomenon of ideological leadership became crystallized and, as a rule, its support came from the first urban centers.

Finally, the military-political situation must be regarded as a factor spontaneously influencing the concentration of population in specific nodes viewed as areas of refuge. In regions with a high density, polyethnic population, the frequency of armed conflict increased with the accumulation of various kinds of riches and surpluses in the developing early agricultural communities, resulting in forcible redistribution. This is particularly noticeable in the improvement of armaments and fortification structures. Thus in the Aegean Bronze Age world, a characteristic attribute of a grown man was a dagger (Renfrew 1972:363) which was even placed in its owner's grave (Blavatskaya 1973:16). The military-political situation in 3rd millennium B.C. Asia Minor, in pre-Dynastic Egypt, and in earliest Mesopotamia was also under such strains. We must keep in mind that all these factors and preconditions did not act in isolation but in relationship to each other, and were modified by specific historical situations.

The rising cities also became centers of the earliest state systems and were accordingly called city-states. As a rule these were relatively small areas encompassing an early agricultural oases and containing one or rarely several small settlements of the city type. In ancient Egypt such a socio-political organism was called a nome [*nomos*] and, as Dyakonov concluded (1973:31), represented a sort of territorial limit of community-state integration. A corresponding pattern for southern Turkmenistan, where this socio-political transformation took place, includes a group of sites comprised of Taychanak-Depe, Shor-Depe, and Kosha-Depe, as well as the area of Altyn-Depe. They are located on the piedmont plain and gravitate toward Namazga-Depe. In the Altyn-Depe area, small centers thus far have not been found. This may be due to the magnitude of man-made irrigation deposits which, at the base of the cult center, reached the thickness of almost 2 m since Namazga V times. The oasis pattern, with a strongly expressed central settlement, is also seen in the Bronze Age sites in the Murghab delta. Here natural conditions allowed the preservation of several small mounds (Masimov 1979). Moreover, the capitals with the initial cells of early class societies, the so-called city-states, in principle had a different character than the large settlements of the primitive epoch, and we have endeavored to describe that transitional stage on the basis of the specific materials from Altyn-Depe.

First, there were qualitative changes in those parts of the settlement that at one time gave it its specific character. The concentration of handicrafts as specialized kinds of activities took on a greater significance, and the apportionment of these activities (called by Engels the second major social division of labor) changed the very character of production. Urban type settlements with their concentration of handicrafts, and in a number of cases, trading activities, became at the same time places of concentration of cult and secular monumental edifices, and also organs of governing. In addition, qualitative changes in the socio-economic structure of the community appeared. This aspect is often neglected by investigators. The investigation of early cities allows us to observe the typology of the various modes of life created by the intensification of differentiation within the society. The initial stages of this differentiation are also clearly evident in Altyn-Depe materials. It is exactly in an urban setting where the crystallization of classes as historical communities of people possessing, aside from other peculiarities, quantitative, demographic parameters takes place. The mass character of an urban population converted some individuals and their families, who occupied a special position in the society, into a cohesive group which

was in contrast to groups occupying other social positions. Without taking this circumstance into account, the nature of early cities and their role in the formation of a class society cannot be correctly appreciated.

The decipherment of proto-Sumerian writing throws light on the earliest stages of development of a class society in Mesopotamia. In the archives of such urban centers as Uruk and Jemdet Nasr, the inequality of property holdings and social status is fairly clearly characterized. In this respect, the canonical list of positions and professions, containing from 80 to 130 designations, is adequately indicative of the inequality (Nissen 1969; Vayman 1976:583). In one of the documents information is recorded about the division of fields with an overall area of 9000 hectares, of which two-thirds go to the "chief priest" or "ruler" and the rest is divided among five other functionaries including "trade agent," "priest-soothsayer," and "chief priestess" (Vayman 1966). At this point we are not concerned about the origin of this land area (which perhaps was initially temple land, a form of collective property of the community), but we nevertheless note its exceedingly large area. There were also slaves in the society. Terms for identifying them clearly reveal their origin: "man of foreign country" or "woman of foreign country," that is, non-tribal members, most likely prisoners of war. In the early documents, 30 male slaves and 27 female slaves were listed, and in much later ones, 602 male and 300 female slaves (Vayman 1974). In part, the work of the female slaves was done in the foundries where they apparently worked the bellows. Deaths of slaves are also mentioned in the documents (Vayman 1979).

All investigators assign great significance to the processes of administration and the isolation of authority in early class societies. Chang (1974) is also inclined to emphasize above all the socio-political aspect of the "urban revolution" while underestimating the role of economic preconditions. Again, the urban type of settlement became the place where administrative organs were concentrated. While analyzing this process, Gulyaev wrote that the political-administrative function of early cities is often undervalued. At the same time, he also traces morphological traits in archaeological materials relating to the functional aspects of early cities: the palace as the residence of the ruler, the royal burials, the art motifs, the ties between the ruler and the ruled (Gulyaev 1979:11). It should be kept in mind that as a rule the political authority in the initial early class societies was not based in a remote place, but in a natural center of an area in a major settlement in which the framework of social differentiation to a considerable degree stipulated the isolation of the political authority.

This problem demands special consideration. Of serious methodological importance are the studies of Perfilev's experiment with the systematization of social relationships. He distinguishes three kinds of social relationships: economic, social, and political. In the political, Perfilev differentiates between relations in the management of production and the management of personal contact (1974:135, 197-202). The necessity of management of production is conditioned by the very work process, by the importance of coordinating individual activities in a system of cooperative work. This traditional function of any human society reached a particularly significant scale in urban settlements, since as a rule the first cities were centers in an agricultural setting. The complex system of managing agriculture, the stock-taking and division of the acquired products, led to the appearance of a qualitatively new system for the preservation and transmission of information—writing. The complexity of early writing systems, which took considerable time to master, stimulated the formation of a specific stratum of professional scribes who were then incorporated into the developing administration. This was not, however, a simple quantitative growth of relationships in the management of production. The society of early cities was already split into classes, and the economically ruling class endeavored to keep other classes from governing the society. In a class-divided society the governing apparatus does not simply grow, but also qualitatively changes its function as compared with the primitive epoch. This change is particularly clearly manifested in the management of personal relationships. In primitive societies, this kind of activity was directed toward the preservation of traditional norms and morals, while in early class societies the organs of management aimed to maintain the class structure and, by all means available, to support the interests of the ruling class. The apparatus for managing the first cities became the administrative machine representing itself as the state. In times to follow, the managing organs of an urban community were established in many regions. They included (at least theoretically) a peoples' assembly, a council of elders, and various types of magistrates, with the latter in almost all spheres of activity. Similar structures were found in the eastern Mediterranean (Shifman 1977) and even in southern Arabia where the formation of an early class society took place independently (Lundin 1977). In many of the countries of the ancient Middle East, royal power gradually appropriated these organs, but even in the early stages they were aimed to serve the interests of the society's elite. The state apparatus of early class societies was derived from the base of urban societies with their organs of administration.

The formation and subsequent development of the first urban centers is inseparable from the formation and development of the first civilizations. If we view the organization of a city as a kind of a system, then the city in turn becomes a composite part in the macrosystem of civilizations. Early civilizations are a complex of cultural manifestations achieved by a society at a specific level of development, and this level, as Engels has shown, is closely tied to the development of class relationships and the establishment of the state (Marx and Engels 1936:vol. 21, pp. 165-169). A similar approach to the understanding of civilizations has been recognized in recent years by investigators in the West who experienced the progressive influence of Marxist historical science or were led to objective deductions by the logic of scientific investigations. Thus Adams in his works successively associates civilization with class society, a system of political and social hierarchy supplemented by an administration and territorial division, with the organization of a state, and also with the division of labor which leads to the apportionment of craft production (Adams 1966). In a book dedicated to the Aegean civilization, while defining the very concept of civilization, Renfrew also assigns special significance to social stratification and division of labor (Renfrew 1972:7). In this respect, Flannery expresses himself even more definitely. In his formulation, civilization is an assemblage of cultural phenomena associated with a form of a sociopolitical organization, such as a state (Flannery 1972:400).

In the formation and development of civilizations, the role of the city was a leading one. It is known that in general during its early history, the city played a leading role in the economic, social, and political spheres (Dyakonov 1970:1). At the time of the emergence of civilizations, the city was a point of concentration of those qualitatively new elements which determined the entire process of development in general and was the carrier of new ideas, standards, and models. The accumulation of riches and the social differentiation that took place in the city were particularly significant. The city as a special economic organism regulated economic activity in a regional framework, while its temples and palaces were the material embodiment of the ideological functions of the leadership. Therefore, we can say that the formulation of the economic and cultural bases of civilization and class society was, as a rule, accompanied by the appearance and intensive growth of urban type settlements, often definable by the concept of "urban revolution" (Masson 1968a).

In the literature, particularly in the works of archaeologists, the term "civilization" is often used as a sort of a synonym for "developed culture." Thus, now and then, the expressions "civilization of herdsmen" or "Neolithic civilization" appear. Given the clearly woven net of history, this is hardly justifiable. It is another matter when we examine the cultures and archaeological sites which reflect the intensive process of composing those phenomena (the division of crafts, the social differentiation, and the state system) with which early civilizations are most closely bound. In such a case we may discern an initial or formative period of civilizations, when their separate traits have already formed. Apparently, it is only in this aspect that we may view the Chavin civilization of South America (Berezkin 1977) which in developmental terms, as well as chronologically, is close to the Mesoamerican assemblages of the Olmec type. The latter is characterized, according to Gulyaev (1972:105), as " a transitional period from archaic to civilization."

The earliest civilizations are associated with that level of community development which in recent years most often is defined as early class society. This was the epoch during which social inequality and government arose in primitive forms, but at the same time there was no clear separation of the classes which were then defined only by their different relations to the means of production (Danilova 1968:30). Butinov (1968:148) characterizes this condition as "the period of combination of class and community tendencies." Indeed, in this case we find a continuously developing society at a stage at which the transformation of primitive structures, both social and political, is far from complete. But at the same time in this development, there is a tendency toward slave-holding based on the exploitation of dependent or involuntary laborers of the slave type (Masson 1979b). The typology of early civilizations may play an important role in studying the general and particular aspects of

this complex developmental process. In general, it may be viewed as an internally forming type of early class society, or, with other internal developments, an early slave-holding society. As philosophers analyzing the problems of historical materialism note, "within the framework of socio-economic formations, differences are generated which are tied to the different conditions and influences of the geographic environment [and] the particularities of cultural development in a given human society" (Boroday, Kelle and Plimak 1972:71). These differences are most noticeably manifested in a weak development of means of communication and bonds with other communities. Zhukov especially emphasizes the importance of favorable conditions in the natural environment for these early developments. Such conditions create advantages in the development of the productive forces (Zhukov 1973:93). Indeed, when early civilizations are viewed as definite historical manifestations, we see that a process takes place, particularly during the formative stage, which in classificatory studies is usually called the "process of optimization," that is, the adjustment of the system to the natural environment. The result of the adjustment secures the best functioning of the system in desired directions. Correspondingly, a given natural environment will encourage the rise of those economic subsystems which can become most effective. One must remember that this is never an automatic process but a complex phenomenon in which the role of the regulatory body is determined by the social structure. The most favorable natural environment could never produce a single civilization by itself.

From my point of view, the system-forming ability which allows for a self-generating type of early civilization lies in the sphere of agriculture acting as a subsystem within the frame of all the systems of the society. Intensification of early agriculture led to a quantitative increase, a surplus product. As a component system, agriculture enters into the economic base of a society and its development determines all subsequent changes. It should be understood that the system-forming role of agriculture must never be viewed as straightforward and mechanical. Thus the presence of a surplus product by itself did not result in the spontaneous formation of classes. For the realization of that process a social differentiation of the society was necessary which was brought about by the alienation of ownership of the very product.

Ethnic and ethno-psychological factors played an important role in the formation of some aspects of early civilizations. These factors are expressed in works of art and literature in the particular style of the epoch. In many respects these factors defined the real and unique aspects of early civilizations. The grouping of separate types of civilizations will result in a better appreciation of some aspects of the regular character of the historical process (Fig. 33).

The above proposed approach permits the division of early civilizations into three types: (1) civilizations based on irrigation agriculture producing a huge surplus; they have quite a wide distribution and are represented by Sumer, Egypt, Harappa, and Yin [Shang] China; (2) civilizations with an economy based on tropical rainforest slash-and-burn agriculture such as those of Mesoamerica, most particularly the Maya; (3) civilizations with an agriculture of the Mediterranean type in which the basic effort was to preserve ground moisture by frequent tillage to loosen the soil; the earliest example here is the Creto-Mycenaean society. An important index for the analysis of civilizations, aside from the reconstruction of the agricultural subsystem, are the demographic parameters of the early societies (Masson 1971d).

Civilizations of the first type may be divided into two subtypes (Dyakonov 1963): centralized irrigation agriculture in the basins of large rivers (the Sumerian development) and irrigation agriculture under the conditions of limited water resources, including stream watering (the Anatolian development). The first subtype is associated with agriculture of particularly high productivity, although the specific type of irrigation could differ depending on local conditions (cp. China, where a particularly important role was given to the protection of crops from the catastrophic floodings of the Huang-Ho, with Sumer). Yet, with all its variants, it was really irrigation agriculture in a favorable natural setting (one which provided two harvests a year) that led to the development of productive forces. Correspondingly, here we find the rapid growth of production and the accumulation of riches which in the end determined the rapid pace of historical development. For instance, in southern Mesopotamia about 2500 years separates the first agriculturalists and the first civilization. Thus subtype 1 is characteristic of very early, spontaneous development of great civilizations. This subtype is also characterized by high population density; in Mesopotamia the population density was $68/\mathrm{km}^2$ (Adams 1966:24).

The independent origin of systems of writing is significant. Writing was stimulated by the necessity of recording the complicated economic organizations and calendric arrangements associated with the regulation of agrarian cycles. The famous temple complexes of Sumer, grandiose architectural edifices and structurally complex organisms, appear to be the entities in which the economic and ideological leadership were unified. Moreover, under the conditions of irrigation agriculture, economic leadership led to the development of a complex administrative apparatus and the prosperity of numerous bureaucracies. High population densities and the early and vigorous development of crafts and trade led to the appearance of large urban centers. The sources of their formation go back at the most to the beginning of the 4th millennium B.C., when, during the time of Late Ubaid period, inhabited centers occupying an area of about 10 hectares arose in southern Mesopotamia. They contained monumental temple complexes. As investigations in the Uruk region have shown, at the end of the 4th to the beginning of the 3rd millennium B.C., a three-part hierarchical structure of the settlements was revealed; it was headed by the large urban centers, not unlike Uruk itself which by the middle of the 3rd millennium B.C. absorbed almost all of the rural environment (Adams and Nissen 1972:18). During this period Uruk became a sort of super-center, reminiscent of the Mesoamerican Teotihuacan. In the Nippur region a similar concentration of settlements occurred several centuries earlier. Apparently, it was in the 4th millennium B.C. that the "urban revolution" took place in southern Mesopotamia, at the same time early class society formed. Judging by initial investigations (Gribov 1973; Dyakonov 1973; Kozyreva 1974), the internal structure of early Mesopotamian cities was very complex. For instance, in documents on financial transactions of various sorts in Larsa, one can count representatives of almost 25 professions. This clearly testifies to the great number of functions performed by a given city organization.

Civilizations of subtype 2 experience a much longer formative period. In Asia Minor 5000 years elapse between the first farmers and the first civilization. In the Near East they arise under the influence of the already existing great civilizations and usually acquire a number of already formed standards in the realm of art, architecture, and writing, and sometimes in ideological, administrative, and social spheres. This development is typical of Syria, Palestine, Hittite Asia Minor, and northern Mesopotamia.

In Asia Minor, the building of civilizations takes place in the 3rd millennium B.C. (Mellaart

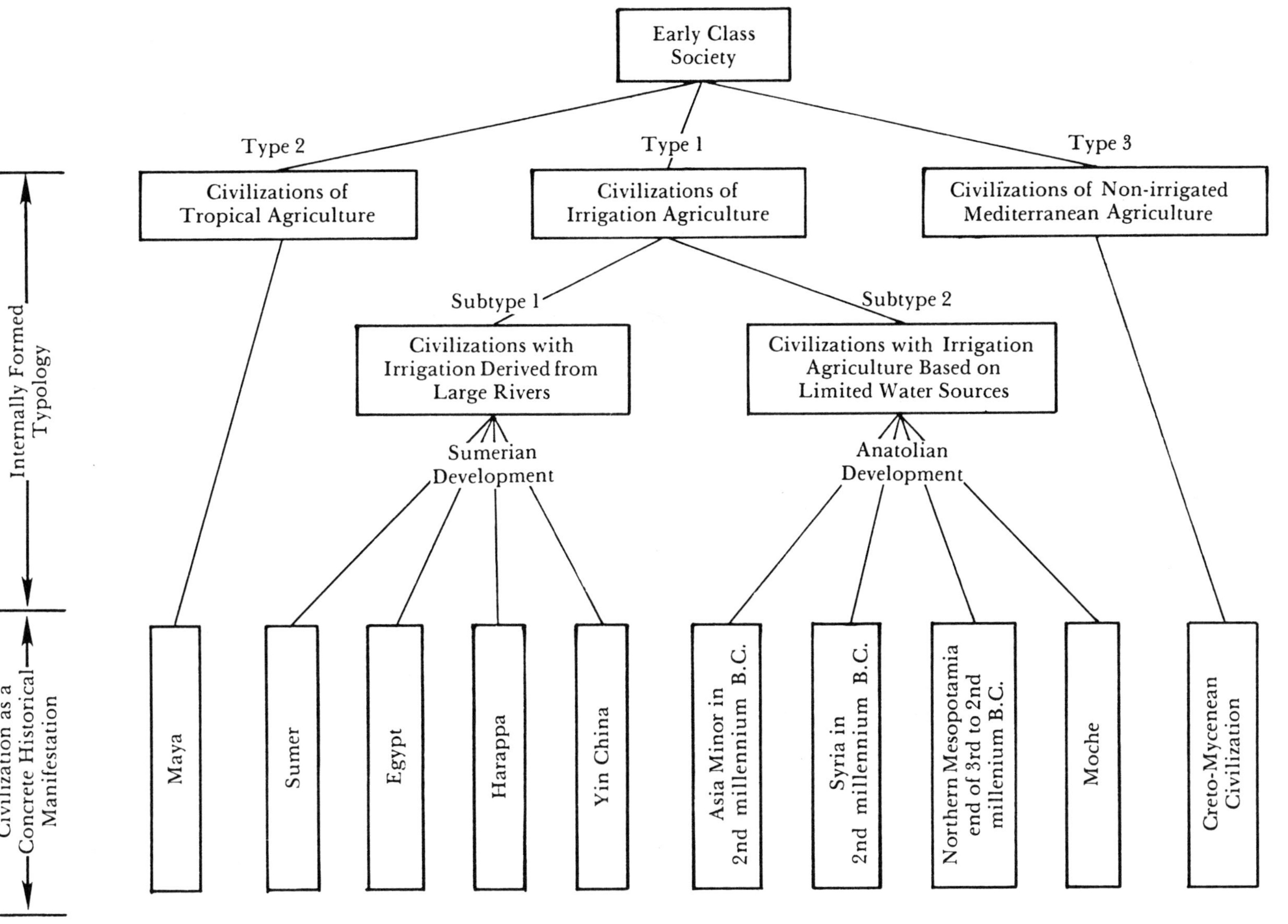

Figure 33.   Typology of Early Civilizations.

1964, 1965). There is no reason to assume that at this time any principal changes had occurred in the agrarian subsystem since the time of the Neolithic agriculturalists. An exception is perhaps the use of metal artifacts. Detailed paleodemographic analyses have not been done here, but contemporary materials have assigned to the basic regions of early cultures a population density of 11-17/km^2 (Allan 1972:215). In handicraft production, the progress of metallurgy is particularly notable. It was based on the rich ore reserves of Asia Minor. The increase in the number of hoards in which we do not find copper axes as formerly, but gold vessels and ornaments, as well as examples of the development of the jeweler's craft, documents the intensive process of accumulating riches. Numerous data point to the intensification of military attitudes, and the 25th to 23rd centuries B.C. may be characterized with full justification as the "times of swords and fortresses." The making of armaments, distinguished as an independent craft, supplied battle axes, daggers, swords, and helmets. Even small centers strove to protect themselves from the outside world with fortification walls. To be sure, their dimensions are not large, within one or two hectares, and only Beycesultan, surrounded by a stone wall 5 m thick, occupied the area of 24 hectares. The cult edifices were also small. The sanctuary of Beycesultan had a length of 15-17 m and cannot at all be compared with the 4th millennium B.C. temples of Sumer.

The accumulation of riches and the function of the military leadership resulted in the isolation of a community elite which we can evaluate on the basis of the Alaca Hüyük burials and some others which, without special reasons, are sometimes designated as royal tombs. With the conditions of tribal overlapping and discord so characteristic of Asia Minor, the function of the military leadership became particularly significant. To a degree, the specific process of forming an early class society was held back but never interrupted by any of the events that took place at the end of the 3rd millennium B.C. At the beginning of the 2nd millennium B.C., Beycesultan became a city with a separately fortified citadel, and a seal with hieroglyphic signs found in it points to the development of writing. At Alisar there is also a citadel with a wall surrounding it. The military aristocracy, members of which were no longer interred in the cemeteries of Dorak and Alaca Hüyük, found a genetic extension as princelings who ruled different regions. Written sources indicate that the head of Kanesh (Kultepe) was a princeling and that the

administrative apparatus was located in the citadel (Yankovskaya 1965, 1968). The structural and terminological dependence of this local Kanesh civilization on a number of Mesopotamian canons is manifested quite boldly and definitely.

In Palestine and Syria corresponding processes of development of crafts and formation of urban centers took place during nearly the same chronological interval. In northern Syria, the codes and norms of the Mesopotamian civilization were adopted (as seen in the cuneiform seals and tablets of the end of the 3rd through the beginning of the 2nd millennium B.C. at Alalakh and the recently discovered Ebla archive), while in coastal Syria and particularly in Palestine, Egyptian ties and contacts are evident.

The archaeological materials of past years indicate a significant zone of civilizations formed between Sumer and India which clearly belong to subtype 2 (Masson 1970f). Here a number of local centers, or local civilizations, arose: Altyn-Depe in southern Turkmenistan, Mundigak in southern Afghanistan, Shahr-i Sokhta in Seistan. Handicraft production and irrigation agriculture with limited water resources comprised the basis for the growth of the Altyn-Depe civilization during a formative period approaching the 3rd millennium B.C. The slight development of fortifications, limited to small wall-fences with abutments, and the paucity of weapons indicate that the functions of the economic and ideological leadership, together with property differences, played a major role in the composition of the socially polarized groupings. Located on the edge of the contemporary cultural world and separated from the primitive cultures of the North by the formidable barrier of the Kara Kum, the civilization gave small heed to the development of the military, which may be one of the reasons for its fall. Moreover, the demographic displacement and the composition of the hierarchal system of the community are quite distinct. At the beginning of the 2nd millennium B.C. two of the principal centers, Altyn-Depe and Namazga-Depe, absorbed, to a certain extent, the neighboring agricultural regions. In its character, but never its scale, this process is reminiscent of the hyper-urbanization of the Uruk region in the middle of the 3rd millennium B.C. As was shown (see p. 108), in dimensions and functions Altyn-Depe at the beginning of the 3rd millennium B.C. could be definitely regarded as an early city. Its monumental cult complex and objects from the priestly tomb show traits obviously influenced by Mesopotamia. The process of social differentiation conditioned by modes of life is also found here. True, thus far no royal tombs or palatial edifices have been found. Most likely we are dealing with a civilization just about to complete its formative period.

The earliest civilization of the Peruvian plain, represented by the Moche culture, belongs to the subtype of civilizations based on irrigation agriculture of limited dimensions (Bashilov 1972:117-123; Berezkin 1975). It is little known in the general historical literature, but for the civilizations of South America, including the Inca, it played the same role of a basic cultural substratum as did Sumer, in many respects, for the Near East. The material culture of Chavin, and above all the monumental cult complexes, suggest that the formation of civilization and an early class society began in the mountainous region of northern Peru in the 2nd millennium B.C. (Bashilov 1972:22; Berezkin 1977:103). The economy of Chavin was based on the cultivation of such a high-yielding crop as corn. The zone occupied and influenced by Chavin included mountainous regions with subtropical valleys and coastal oases, but there are no data on the nature of the agriculture itself. Perhaps the instability of the economic base was one of the reasons for the decline of Chavin, although it was just then that a number of cultural precepts were established which gained noticeable influence in subsequent Peruvian civilizations.

The earliest of these appears to be the Moche civilization dated to A.D. 100-600. It is a fairly clear example of a basically independent development which began with primitive farmers and fishermen. Significant irrigation systems were created in the valleys occupied by the Moche peoples, and the progress in agriculture, in the first place, made for the growth of handicraft production. Significant development of handicrafts is seen in metallurgy (casting was widely used) and ceramics. In the latter, mass production was achieved, although probably not to the degree as with the potter's wheel of the Old World, by molding the vessels in forms. Various kinds of weapons and battle scenes pictured on the vessels testify to the development of a military cadre, and an iconographic analysis points to a special caste of soldiers and military leaders who combined military function with other kinds of activities (Berezkin 1975). Regrettably, our knowledge about the types of Moche settlements is very limited, although Lanning writes in rather vigorous terms about early Peruvian urbanization and the presence of settlements with a focal center in the form of a monumental architectural complex and a population of up to ten thousand (Lanning 1967).

The largest center of the Moche peoples, probably their capital, is located in the valley of the Moche River. Enormous architectural complexes were built there: the Pyramid of the Sun, with an area of 228 x 136 m and a height of 18 m, and the Pyramid of the Moon, which is somewhat smaller. It may be suggested that similar grandiose structures were the symbol of at least the functions of the ideological leadership existing in this center of the Moche peoples. It is noteworthy that in the Viru River valley there are also stone or clay pyramids but of considerably smaller dimensions, 2.0-6.5 m high. They probably represent the foci of much smaller settlements. The detail of the regulation and, in its way, the pedantry of the Moche culture may be fully observed in the subject matter portrayed on the ceramic vessels. There are clear-cut relationships between the personages portrayed and their attributes and activities are observable, which to some degree enabled the researchers to extract information to resolve problems of social stratification. Within the specific conditions of South America, where at that time no other civilizations existed, the majority of Moche achievements had an original cast but were limited in their potential, as were subtype 2 civilizations in the Near East, by a comparatively slow tempo of development: almost 4000 years transpired between the appearance of the first agriculturalists and the first civilization.

Those subtype 2 civilizations whose economic base has been studied in adequate detail over the past decades (Drucker and Heizer 1960; Cowgill 1962) are of undoubted interest. The slash-and-burn system of agriculture was perfected in these civilizations. This type of agriculture apparently was formed in the Olmec period, during which the principal traits of the civilization were molded. These traits became the basis for the celebrated Maya civilization. Great success in the selection and careful working of the calendrically regulated agricultural system led to a stable surplus resulting in a high demographic index— from $20/km^2$ in the Yucatan to $60/km^2$ in the lowlands. Other systems of agriculture were also practiced. Crafts production reached a high level, very likely attaining the greatest efficiency possible in a pre-metallurgical stage. Artistic crafts were mastered and professionalized and produced at great expense. The extent of monumental cult architecture engendered the widespread notion of the theocratic character of the communal system in early Mesoamerica.

However, Gulyaev, who studied the representations of the rulers in the monumental art of Mesoamerica, correctly emphasizes the presence of a secular government as well (Gulyaev 1972:206-214). Remains of writing and monumental architecture are the most expressive traits of Mayan civilization. Problems pertaining to the existence of cities are considerably more complex. The dispersed population, which was characteristic for the basic regions of the Maya, generated the belief that there were no cities at all. It seems to me, however, that in regard to discharging functions, the temple complex of the Maya must be regarded as a center of both ideological and economic leadership. A population of approximately ten thousand, the same number occupying Ur in the first half of the third millennium B.C., is indicated for the 6.6 km^2 of Tikal by paleodemographic evaluations. Looked upon as cities from a functional point of view, the morphology of the Maya centers is characterized by vertical architecture and a dispersed layout, reflecting, just as the congested layout of Altyn-Depe does, all the traits of a socially differentiated society, as is so well shown by Gulyaev (1972:182; 1979). Civilizations of this type, with autochthonous basic cultural achievements, including writing, are a most interesting historical phenomenon.

Civilizations of subtype 3 are well represented by the Cretan (Minoan) and Mycenaean cultures of the 20th to 12th centuries B.C. A fundamental attempt to investigate their origin from the point of view of the "new archaeology" was recently undertaken by Renfrew (1972). While he did not consistently pursue the hierarchical principle (characteristic of a systematic approach), he limited himself to the isolation of five basic subsystems of the same level within the culture—from my point of view, within the society—of the time (Masson 1974e). Somewhat earlier, though in a more traditional manner and terminology, the formation of the earliest civilizations on mainland and insular Greece (with the exception of Crete) was fairly clearly described by Blavatskaya (1966). On the basis of the sources indicated, the Creto-Mycenaean society took shape in the 3rd millennium B.C., the formative period of civilizations.

In the development of productive forces a central role was played by the "Mediterranean triad" of polycultural agriculture and progress in crafts. (For a definition of the "Mediterranean triad" see Myres 1943.) The work of Renfrew, based on extensive materials, confirmed the importance of the mixed system of agriculture to Creto-Mycenaean society. The system was based on the cultivation of cereals, olive trees and vineyards, the latter two possessing a high degree of commodity potential. The mapping of 3rd millennium B.C. sites clearly showed that the settlements of the formative period were concentrated in a zone potentially most favorable to the development of polycultures. A large population increase just in these given areas testifies to the intensive development of productivity in the 3rd millennium B.C. Another mainstay of early Aegean economy is seen in the crafts which, during the 3rd millennium B.C., surged forward in such leading branches as metallurgy. Hoards and the development of the jeweler's art clearly reflect the process of accumulating riches. Corresponding to these manifestations if the importation into Crete of elephant ivory both in the form of finished artifacts and raw material for local costume jewelry. One of the specific developments for this region was the spread of armed conflict in the form of naval warfare or piracy. Even the epic poems about the Trojan War and the celebrated expansion of the "sea nations" which shook the eastern Mediterranean to its foundations at the end of the 2nd millennium B.C. reflect these tendencies. Warlike shepherds and nomads, the usual neighbors of Near Eastern civilizations, were replaced by armed daredevils on fast-moving ships. The development of fortifications and warfare in the 3rd millennium B.C. reflects this process. And as Renfrew remarks, the distribution of these fortified points on the coast or in the immediate vicinity of that invariable source of peril and anxiety is significant (Renfrew 1972).

Despite the intensive development of agriculture and crafts and the dangers of war, all of which should have led to the concentration of the population, the very small size of settlements in the Aegean is remarkable. As a rule, they are 1-1.5 hectares, and even Minoan Knossos was hardly larger than 3-4 hectares. Confused by the small size of these settlements, investigators have called them proto-cities (Blavatskaya 1966:116) or proto-urban settlements (Renfrew 1972:242). Very likely, this small size was bound to the specific nature of the agriculture, which was spread over the mountain valleys but even so yielded comparatively high density populations. For Crete it was 26.1/km^2. Differences in Aegean grave inventories are witness to the ongoing parallel process of social stratification. In the centers of the small cities large houses stand out—the residences of the elite, the sociological forerunners of the palaces of later periods. The royal burials at Mycenae (and I am not inclined to include those of Grave Circle A among them), writing, and palatial complexes serving as centers of economic and ideological leadership complete the process of the formation of civilization in Crete by the beginning of the 2nd millennium B.C. and on the mainland by the 14th century B.C.

The specialized nature of Aegean agriculture and many traits of the ancient world associated with it were well expressed in one of the works of Blavatskiy (1970). In the region described, the very nature of the agricultural work did not require, as an indispensable condition, the organization of the collective forces of the entire community or the alliance of the community. The role of personal initiative in an agriculture, which was decentralized in those parts of the valleys favorable for cultivation, was relatively large. Correspondingly, the role of the priesthood and cult architecture turned out to be less significant in Creto-Mycenaean Greece than in the regions of irrigation agriculture. Palaces rather than temples are the obvious remains of monumental architecture. Creative work and individual initiative are well expressed in the remains of art, both applied and monumental. Moreover, development was rather slow; more than 5000 years elapsed between the first agriculturalists and the first civilization.

Surely, it does not follow that absolute values have to be assigned to the relationship of the types of agriculture and fairly complex and numerous subsystems of developed civilization. It seems to me, however, that a typological classification of civilizations based on the characteristics of agricultural economies is sufficiently conducive to the understanding of a number of phenomena, particularly the tempo of historical development and productive potential of different civilizations. The society which left the Altyn-Depe cultural remains (to which this book is dedicated) also occupies its own place in this system.

Conclusion

The analysis of archaeological materials leads to the conclusion that during the Middle Bronze Age (or the time of Namazga V) Altyn-Depe developed into an urban type settlement with a complex interior structure which reflected the social differentiation of the society and the functions of handicrafts and ideological leadership. The process of developing the early urban organism progressed far enough; therefore, taking into consideration the relationship of the first cities and early civilizations, we may postulate that in southern Turkmenistan at the end of the 3rd to the beginning of the 2nd millennium B.C. (in terms of the traditional chronology, which may have to be revised downward) we are observing a local civilization of the Ancient East in at least its formative stage. The Altyn-Depe civilization was a natural, component part of the early eastern cultural area. The utilization of Mesopotamian cultural standards and the close ties with the early Indus civilization of Harappa are significant. Located between these two important cultural hearths, Altyn-Depe became a sort of focus of the complex processes of interaction and mutual influence which united the countries and peoples of the Ancient East into a single system forming a zone of Old World civilizations.

From the standpoint of early Soviet history, the Altyn-Depe civilization, from the end of the 3rd to the beginning of the 2nd millennium B.C., signifies a transformation from the Central Asian agricultural and livestock-herding cultures with primitive social attitudes to societies with complex social stratifications within which classes and the first class antagonisms form. An analogous process took place at the end of the 2nd to the beginning of the 1st millennium B.C. in the agricultural and livestock-herding cultures of the Caucasus and was completed in 900-800 B.C. with the Urartu civilization and state. The lands north of the Black Sea contained the third agricultural and livestock-herding hearth. With the fall and disintegration of the Tripolye cultural community during the Bronze Age, primarily livestock-herding and agricultural cultures developed, which in the end led to the formation of the Scythian society (600-400 B.C.) with its distinctive traits of an early class structure.

In the light of archaeological work, the downfall of the Bronze Age early urban center, which now bears the name Altyn-Depe [Golden Hill], does not appear to be a catastrophic occurrence but one of gradual decay and abandonment. Toward the end of the Middle Bronze Age, the entire eastern part of the settlement, including the Elite Quarters and the monumental cult center, was abandoned. Life continued only in the crowded western half. There are no signs of demolition or cataclysm; the inhabitants simply left their houses, taking with them movable property and only rarely gladdening the archaeologists with forgotten pottery. The Kelleli complex of sites in the Murghab delta discovered by Masimov and dated to Namazga V leaves no doubt that at least part of the population of the foothill zone moved there from the west. I have already mentioned that the movement of settled agricultural tribes during the Late Bronze Age from the foothills to the Murghab delta could be explained by the growth of population, a population disaffected with the limited possibilities of irrigation agriculture (Masson 1959a:110). New materials from Altyn-Depe indicate that during the Middle Bronze Age, compared to the Early Bronze Age (Namazga IV), changes occurred in the composition of herds, testifying to slowly increasing aridity. The number of cattle steadily decreased and sheep decisively dominated in the make-up of herds. Vinogradov and Mamedov actively promote the thesis that within the 3rd and 2nd millennia B.C. climatic desiccation took place in Central Asia and there was possibly also dislocation of landscape zones (Vinogradov and Mamedov 1972:95-97; 1975:234-255). Of late, Lisitsina, while adhering to a previous position of relatively stable climate in Central Asia throughout the Holocene, does not exclude smaller cyclic or individual fluctuations within a generally arid climate (Lisitsina 1978:191-193).

Such an individual fluctuation could have been one of the provocations which shook the unstable economic system of a formative civilization. Also, we cannot dismiss the possibility of secondary, man-caused salinization of tilled soils as a side effect of irrigation agriculture. Salinization played a considerable role in the reshuffling of Mesopotamian cultural centers. In the region of the Meana and Chaacha rivers, extensive tilling of large areas started at least in the second half of the 5th millennium B.C. when two large centers of settled agriculture arose here: Altyn-Depe and Ilgynly-Depe. After 2500 years of intensive exploitation of soils with the then existing agricultural techniques, irreversible environmental damage could arise, leading to additional reasons for the fall and abandonment of a once flourishing early urban center. However that may have been, only in the Parthian epoch did any sizable inhabited centers exist in this region. The complete fall of Altyn-Depe and the contemporaneous partial abandonment of an analogous center of the foothill zone, Namazga-Depe, may have regional relevance, since at the same time some of the Iranian and Indian centers were abandoned. They include Hissar, Tureng-Tepe, Shahr-i Sokhta and both capitals of the early Indus valley civilization, Harappa and Mohenjo-Daro.

The Altyn-Depe civilization, a notable achievement of the ancient tribes and peoples of Central Asia, was the base for the subsequent development of settled cultures in the region, reaching a particularly rapid pace in the ancient epochs of Parthia, Bactria, Soghdia, and Khorezmia. The source of many facets of these early urbanized cultures—building works, monumental architecture, pottery-making and fine glyptics—is the Bronze Age and the traditions of the Altyn-Depe archaeological culture. Even the specific routes that the culture-building process took in transmitting and transforming these traditions are observable. We have in mind the settled agricultural complexes of the Sapalli and Dashly type, which in recent years were discovered along the middle reaches of the Amu-darya (Askarov 1973, 1977; Sarianidi 1976c, 1977). It is generally acknowledged that these highly developed complexes apparently represent variants of a single archaeological culture (which Askarov proposes to call the Sapalli culture) and did not have local roots either in southern Uzbekistan or in northern Afghanistan. Yet their striking analogies with Namazga V materials of southern Turkmenistan are indisputable, and today these are most clearly expressed at Altyn-Depe. We

may deduce that what we are encountering here is a clear-cut example of expansion of an urbanized culture (Masson 1973c:4, 1974d:7). Some investigators, however, evaluate the original center of this interesting cultural manifestation differently. In his last works, Askarov proposes that such a center must have been among the early agricultural communities of [Soviet] Central Asia (Askarov 1976:27, 1977:110). Sarianidi, recognizing the importance of the southern Turkmenistan analogies for the mass of northern Afghanistan materials, prefers to describe southern Turkmenistan and northeastern Iran in a common mold, not abandoning the thought of finding a single major source for Late Bronze Age tribal resettlement from there to both northern Afghanistan and southern Turkmenistan (Sarianidi 1977:77, 100, 105-106).

The new hearth of highly developed cultures of an ancient eastern cast, discovered by Askarov and Sarianidi on the middle reaches of the Amu-darya, is genetically more closely tied to the southern Turkmenistan complex of Namazga V. We see before us a clear result of the resettlement of organized masses of a population with a highly developed culture of an urbanized type (Fig. 34). To carry out such resettlement, a level of communal organization with an adequate system of administration regulating the economic and political activities of united communities was assuredly needed. It is precisely in southern Turkmenistan, as a result of the Altyn-Depe excavations, that we see a gradual formation of this highly developed culture from local resources founded on local complexes of the Late Eneolithic.

Among the cultural components found in the Murghab and middle Amu-darya complexes of the Late Bronze Age, the glyptics and metal articles stand out particularly clearly, together with the prevalent traditions and various kinds of innovations. As for the origin of glyptics, it seems to me that while finding a single center has not been convincingly successful, a search for it is not really necessary. In conditions of intensive cultural ties, all additional widespread developments take on the appearance of cultural integration. The new kinds of seals belong to this group, which most likely developed on a local basis, although individual motifs and examples from western regions, principally Mesopotamia, were also utilized. Western analogies are also clearly observable in metal objects. All of this allows us to conclude that in the Middle East and in southern Central Asia, in the middle and later part of the 2nd millennium B.C., there was an in-

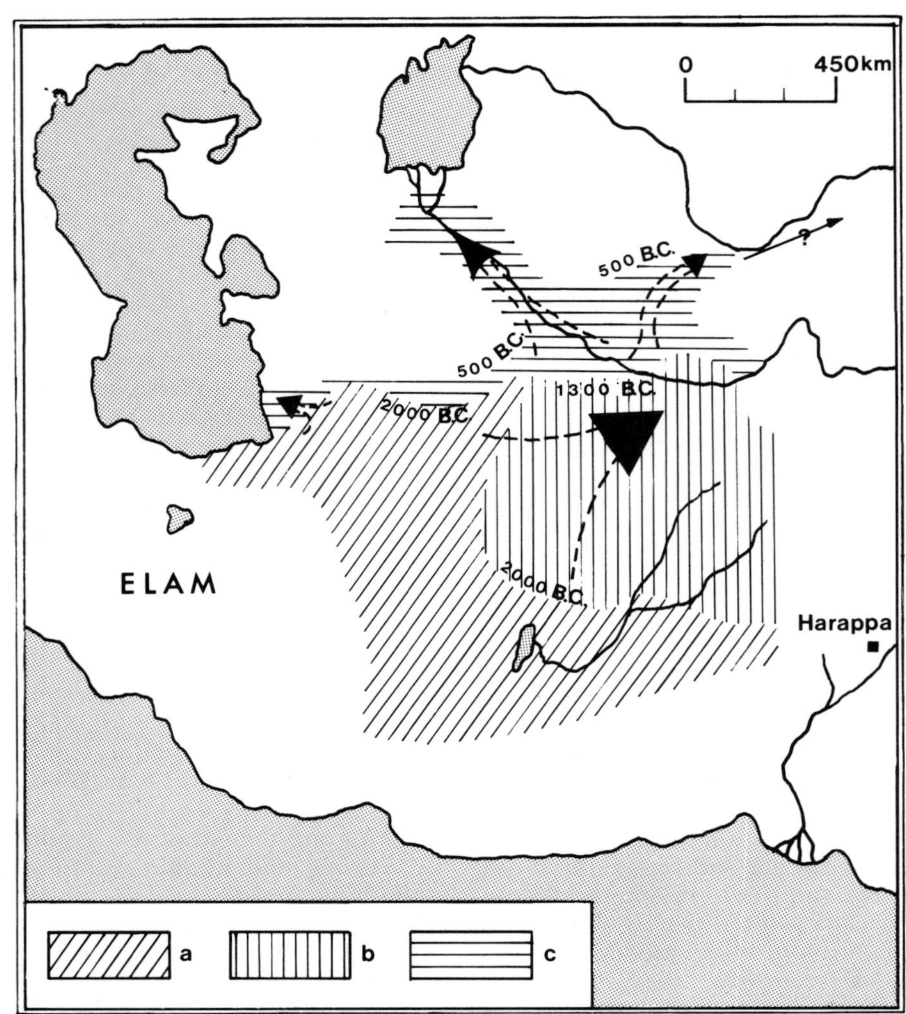

Figure 34. Schematic distribution of urban cultures in Central Asia.
Key— a: 2300-1850 B.C. b: 1850-650 B.C. c: 650-350 B.C.

tensification of western, Mesopotamian-Luristan ties and influences. To what degree this phenomenon is associated with resettlement of tribes of the Indo-Iranian speaking group is yet to be investigated. But it is perfectly clear that these western elements were integrated into the local culture which was genetically associated with the Altyn Depe culture. Thus new archaeological investigations most clearly elucidate the complex developmental processees of early cultures in their concrete historical distinctiveness and variety. Synthesis and mutual influence were the most characteristic traits of cultural genesis in ancient Central Asia and neighboring regions.

Bibliography
Russian-Language Sources

Alekshin, V.A.

1973   Kamennye giri s drevnezemledelcheskikh poseleniy Yuzhnoy Turkmenii (Stone Weights from Early Agricultural Settlements in Southern Turkmenia). *SA*, no. 4.

1977   Sotsialnyy stroy rannezemledelcheskikh obshchestv po pogrebalnym pamyatnikam kultur Sredney Azii i Blizhnevo Vostoka (The Social Structure of Early Agricultural Communities on the Basis of Burial Remains of the Cultures of Central Asia and the Near East). *Aftoreferat kand. dis.*, Moscow. [Doctoral dissertation.]

Andronov, M.S.

1964   Leksiko-statisticheskiy analiz i fakty istorii o khronologii raspada protodravidskogo yazyka (A Lexical-Statistical Analysis and the Historical Facts about the Chronology of Decay of the Proto-Dravidian Language). In: *Indiyskaya i iranskaya filologiya*. Moscow.

1965   *Dravidskiye yazyki* (Dravidian Languages). Moscow.

1969   O kharaktere dekano-uralskikh analogiy (On the Nature of Deccan-Uralic Analogies). In: *Yazykovye universalii i lingvisticheskaya tipologiya*. Moscow.

1971   *Yazyk Braui* (The Brahui Language). Moscow.

Antonova, E.V.

1972   K voprosu o proiskhozhdenii i smyslovoy nagruzke znakov na statuetkakh anauskoy kultury (On the Origin and Semantic Meaning of Signs on Statuettes of the Anau Culture). *SA*, no. 4.

Askarov, A.

1973   *Sapallitepa*. Tashkent.

1976   Bronzoviy vek Yuzhnogo Uzbekistana (The Bronze Age of Southern Uzbekistan). *Aftoreferat dokt. dis.* Moscow. [Doctoral dissertation.]

1977   *Drevnezemledelcheskaya kultura epokhi bronzy yuga Uzbekistana* (An Early Bronze Age Farming Culture in Southern Uzbekistan). Tashkent.

Afanaseva, V.K.

1965   Mifologiya i epos v shumero-akkadskoy gliptike (Mythology and Epos in Sumerian-Akkadian Glyptics). *Aftoreferat kand. dis.* Leningrad. [Doctoral dissertation.]

Bashilov, V.A.

1972   *Drevniye tsivilizatsii Peru i Bolivii* (The Ancient Civilizations of Peru and Bolivia). Moscow.

Berdyev, O.K.

1964   Chagylly-Depe. *IAN TSSR SON*, no. 1. Ashkabad.

1966   Chagylly-Depe—novyy pamyatnik neoliticheskoy dzheytunskoy kultury (Chagylly-Depe—A New Site of the Jeitun Neolithic Culture). In: *Materialnaya kultura Sredney Azii i Kazakhstana*. Moscow.

1970   Nekotorye rezultaty izucheniya drevnezemledelcheskikh poseleniy (Some Results of the Study of Early Agricultural Settlements). *KD*, no. 3.

1971   Nekotorye rezultaty arkheologicheskikh rabot Instituta istorii imeni Sh. Batyrova AN TSSR—1959-1966 gg. (Some Results of the Archaeological Works of the Sh. Batyrov Institute of History of the Academy of Sciences of the Turkmen Soviet Socialist Republic in 1959-1966). In: *Materialnaya kultura Turkmenistana*. Ashkabad.

Berezkin, Yu. E.

1975   Mochika—Peru. Opyt istoriko-etnograficheskoy rekonstruktsii (Mochica—Peru. An Experimental Historical-Ethnographic Reconstruction). *Aftoreferat kand. dis.*, Leningrad. [Doctoral dissertation.]

1977   Drevneyshaya tsivilizatsiya Yuzhnoy Ameriki (The Earliest Civilization of South America). *Priroda*, no. 11.

Berezkin, Yu. E. and N.N. Skakun

1978   Gorodskomu kvartalu 4000 let (The City Quarters are 4000 Years Old). *PT*, no. 1 (25).

Blavatskaya, T.V.

1966   *Akheyskaya Gretsiya* (Achaean Greece). Moscow.

1973   Cherty voennoy demokratii v doriyskom obshchestve (Features of Military Democracy in Dorian Society). In: *Konferentsiya "Voznikoveniye klasovogo obshchestva." Tez. dokl.* Moscow.

Blavatskiy, B.D.

1970   *Antichnyy mir i Drevniy Vostok* (The Ancient World and the Near East). Moscow.

Bongard-Levin, G.M. and G.F. Ilvin

1969   *Drevnaya Indiya* (Ancient India). Moscow.

Boriskovskiy, P.I.

1958 Izucheniye paleoliticheskikh zhilishch v SSSR (The Study of Paleolithic Sites in the U.S.S.R.). *SA*, no. 1.

Boroday, Yu. M., V. Zh. Kelle, and E.G. Plimak

1972 *Naslediye Karla Marksa i nekotoriye metodologicheskiye problemy issledovaniya dokapitalicheskikh obshchestv i genezitsa kapitalizma* (The Legacy of Karl Marx and Some Methodological Problems in the Investigation of Pre-capitalistic Societies and the Rise of Capitalism). Moscow.

Bromley, Yu. V.

1973 *Etnos i etnografiya* (Ethnos and Ethnography). Moscow.

Butinov, N.A.

1968 Pervobytnoobshchinyy stroy—osnovnye etapy i lokalnye varianty (Primitive Social Structure—Principal Stages and Local Variants). In: *Problemy istorii dokapitalicheskikh obshchestv.* Moscow.

Childe, G.

1952 *U istokov evropeyskoy tsivilizatsii* (At the Sources of European Civilization). Moscow.

1956 *Drevneyshiy Vostok v svete novykh raskopok* (The Most Ancient East in the Light of New Excavations). Moscow.

Danilova, L.V.

1968 Diskussionnye problemy teorii dokapitalicheskikh formatsiy (Debatable Problems in the Theory of Precapitalistic Formations [Social Structures]). In: *Problemy istorii dokapitalicheskikh obshchestv.* Moscow.

1977 *Drevniye goroda* (Early Cities). *Proceedings of the All-Union Conference: Kultura Sredney Azii i Kazakhstana v epokhu rannego srednevekovya* (The Culture of Central Asia and Kazakhstan during Early Medieval Times). Leningrad.

Durdyev, D.

1959 Itogi polevikh rabot Sektora arkheologii Instituta istorii, arkheologii i etnografii Akademii nauk Turkmenskoy SSR 1954-1957 gg. (Results of Field Investigations of the Sector of Archaeology of the Institute of History, Archaeology and Ethnography, Academy of Sciences of the Turkmenistan Soviet Socialist Republic). *TIIAE*, vol. 5.

Dyakonov, I.M.

1963 Obshchina na Drevnem Vostoke v rabotakh sovetskikh issledovateley (The Ancient Middle Eastern Community in the Works of Soviet Investigators). *VDI*, no. 1.

1967 *Yazyki drevney Peredney Azii* (Languages of the Ancient Near East). Moscow.

1968 Gorod Ur pri Rim Sine I i Khamurapi (Ur in the Times of Rim-Sin I and Hammurabi). In: *IV sessiya po Drevnemu Vostoku. Tez. dokl.* Moscow.

1970 *Economy of the Ancient Oriental City.* Moscow.

1973 Problemy vavilovskogo goroda II tys. do n.e. (The Problems of Babylon City in the 2nd millennium B.C.). In: *Drevniy Vostok. Goroda i torgovlya.* Erevan.

Efimenko, P.P.

1953 *Pervobytnoye obshchestvo* (Primitive Society). Kiev.

Epos o Gilgameshe

1961 (The Epos of Gilgamesh). Translated by I.M. Dyakonov. Moscow-Leningrad.

Ermolova, N.M.

1970 Novye materialy po izucheniyu ostatkov mlekopitayushchikh iz drevnykh poseleniy Turkmenii (New Materials for the Study of Mammalian Remains from Ancient Settlements in Turkmenia). *KD*, no. 3.

1972 Ostatki mlekopitayushchikh iz drevnikh pamyatnikov Yuzhnoy Turkmenii po raskopkam 1970 g. (Mammalian Remains from the 1970 Excavations of Early Sites in Southern Turkmenia). *KD*, no. 4.

1976 Gde zhe odomashnili dvugorbogo verblyuda? (Where was the Two-humped [Bactrian] Camel Domesticated?) *Priroda*, no. 10.

1977 Zhivotnye v skulpture i v zhizni drevnego naseleniya Turkmenistana (Animals in Sculpture and Everyday Life of the Ancient Population of Turkmenistan). *PT*, no. 2 (24).

1979 K kharateristike mlekopitayushchikh Turkmenii bronzovogo veka po osteologicheskomu materialu iz raskopok Altyn-Depe v 1975 g. (On the Characteristics of Mammals of Bronze Age Turkmenia Based on Osteological Materials from the 1975 Excavations at Altyn-Depe). *KD*, no. 8.

Gankovskiy, Yu. V.

1964 *Narody Pakistana* (The Peoples of Pakistan). Moscow.

Ganyalin, A.F.

1959 Altyn-Depe po materialam rabot 1953 g. (Altyn-Depe Based on Materials from the 1953 Excavations). *TIIAE*, vol. 5.

1967 Raskopki v 1959-1961 gg. na Altyn-Depe (The 1959-1961 Excavations at Altyn-Depe). *SA*, no. 4.

Ginzburg, V.V. and T.A. Trofimova

1972 *Paleoantropologiya Sredney Azii* (The Paleoanthropology of Central Asia). Moscow.

Gribov, R.A.

1973 Severomesopotamskiy gorod v kontse XIX—pervoy polovine XVIII v. do n.e. po tekstam Mari (A Northern Mesopotamian City at the End of the 19th—First Half of the 18th century B.C. Based on Mari [Archival] Texts). In: *Drevniy Vostok, Goroda i torgovlya.* Erevan.

Gryaznov, M.P.

1972 Byk v obryadakh i kultakh drevnikh skotovodov (The Bull in the Rituals and Cults of Early Cattle-herders). In: *Tez. dokl. na sessii i plenume posvyashch. itogam polevykh issled. v 1971 g.* Moscow.

Gulmuradov, D.

1975 Novye dannye o torgovykh svyazyakh Turkmenii i Indostana v bronzovom veke (New Data on Trade between Turkmenia and Hindustan During the Bronze Age). *USA*, no. 3.

Gulyaev, V.I.

1972 *Drevneyshiye tsivilizatsii Mezoameriki* (The Oldest Civilizations of Meso-America). Moscow.

1978 Goroda drevnikh mayya (Ancient Maya Cities). *Avtoref. dokt. dis.* Moscow. [Doctoral Dissertation.]

1979 *Goroda-gosudarstva mayya* (The City-States of the Maya). Moscow.

Gurov, N.V.

1971 Nekotorye problemy lingvisticheskoy interpretatsii protoindiyskikh tekstov (Some Questions Concerning the Linguistic Interpretation of Proto-Indic Texts). *Avtoref. kand. dis.* Leningrad. [Doctoral Dissertation.]

Herodotus

1885- *Herodoti historiarum libri IX.* H.R. Dietsch, ed.
1887   Ed. 2 curavit H. Kallenberg. Lipsiae, Teubner.

Kircho, L.B.

1972 Stratigrafiya Altyn-Depe i kolichestvennyy metod opredeleniya otnostelnoy khronologii (The Stratigraphy of Altyn-Depe and a Quantitative Method of Establishing a Relative Chronology). *KD*, no. 4.

1976 Problema proiskhozhdeniya kultury ranney bronzy Yuzhnoy Turkmenii (Problems Associated with the Early Bronze Culture of Southern Turkmenia). *IAN TSSR. SON*, no. 6.

1979 Altyn-Depe v epokhu ranney bronzy (Altyn-Depe During the Early Bronze Age). *IAN TSSR. SON*, no. 4.

1980 Metallicheskiye izdeliya epokhi eneolita i bronzy iz Altyn-Depe (Eneolithic and Bronze Age Metal Artifacts from Altyn-Depe). *SA*, no. 1.

Khlobistina, M.D.

1977 "Malenkiye bogini" turkmenskogo eneolita (The "Small Goddesses" of the Eneolithic of Turkmenia). *KD*, no. 6.

Khlopin, I.N.

1963 Eneolit yuzhnykh oblastey Sredney Azii (The Eneolithic of the Southern Regions of Central Asia). *SAI*, part B3-8, no. 1.

1964 *Geoksyurskaya gruppa poseleniy epokhi eneolita* (The Geoksyur Group of Eneolithic Settlements). Moscow-Leningrad.

1969 Pamyatniki razvitogo eneolita Yugo-Vostochnoy Turkmenii (Remains of the Developed Eneolithic in Southeastern Turkmenia). *SAI*, part B3-8, no. 3.

Kiyatkina, T.P.

1977a Kraniologicheskiy material iz Altyn-Depe, 1971 g. (The 1971 Craniological Material from Altyn-Depe). *KD*, no. 5.

1977b Kraniologicheskiy material iz Altyn-Depe, 1972 g. (The 1972 Craniological Material from Altyn-Depe). *KD*, no. 6.

Kler, M.M.

1979 Khimicheskiy sostav nekotorykh bronzovykh izdeliy iz poseleniya Altyn-Depe, Yuzhnyy Turkmenistan (The Chemical Composition of Some Bronze Age Tools from the Settlement of Altyn-Depe in Southern Turkmenistan). *KD*, no. 8.

Knyshev, V.I.

1971 Raskopki zhilykh kompleksov epokhi bronzy na Altyn-Depe (The Excavation of Bronze Age Living Quarters in Altyn-Depe). *KSIA*, no. 127.

Kozyreva, N.V.

1974 Starovavilonskiy gorod Larsa (The Ancient Babylonian City of Larsa). *Aftoref. kand. dis.* Leningrad. [Doctoral Dissertation.]

Korobkova, G.F.

1964 Kamennye i kostyanye orudiya iz eneoliticheskikh poseleniy Yuzhnoy Turkmenii (Stone and Bone Artifacts from Eneolithic Settlements in Southern Turkmenia). *IAN TSSR. SON*, no. 3.

1969 Orudiya truda i khozyaystvo neoliticheskikh plemen Sredney Azii (Work Tools and the Economy of Neolithic Tribes in Central Asia). *MIA*, no. 158.

1974 Trudnyy khleb pervykh gorozhan (The Difficult Daily Bread of the First City Dwellers). *PT*, no. 2 (18).

1977 Skornyaki kamennogo veka (Stone Age Fur-dressers) *PT*, no. 2 (24).

Korobkova, G.F. and V.T. Volovik

1972 Gadymi-Depe—novyy pamyatnik dzheytunskoy kultury (Gadymi-Depe—a New Jeitun Site). *USA*, no. 2.

Kramer, S.N.

1965 *Istoriya nachinayetsya v Shumere* (History Begins in Sumer). Moscow.

Kuzmina, E.E.

1966 Metallicheskiye izdeliya epokhi eneolita i bronzovogo veka Sredney Azii (Eneolithic and Bronze Age Metal Artifacts in Central Asia). *SAI*, part V4-9.

Kurbansakhatov, K.

1976 Novyy tip zhenskoy terrakotovoy statuetki s Altyn-Depe (A New Type of Female Terracotta Statuette from Altyn-Depe). *SA*, no. 3.

Kurochkin, G.N.

1970 "Bogatstvo" usopshikh (The "Riches" of the Deceased). *PT*, no. 1 (9).

Kuftin, B.A.

1954 Raboty YuTAKE v 1952 g. po izucheniyu "kultur Anau" (The 1952 Excavations of the Institute of History, Archaeology and Ethnography in Connection with the Study of "Anau Cultures"). *IAN TSSS. SON*, no. 1.

1956   *Polevoy otchet o rabote XIV otryada TYuTAKE*
        (Field Report on the Excavations of Section XIV of
        the Southern Turkmenistan Inter-Disciplinary
        Archaeological Expedition). TYuTAKE, vol. 7.

Lisitsina, G.N.

1968   Rastitelnost Yuzhnoy Turkmenii v VI-I tys. do n.e.
        po dannym opredeleniya ugley (The Vegetation of
        Southern Turkmenia in the 6th to 1st Millennia
        B.C. Based on Carbon Determinations). *KD*, no. 2.

1972   Istoriya oroshaemogo zemledeliya Yuzhnoy Turk-
        menii (The History of Irrigation Agriculture in
        Southern Turkmenia). *USA*, no. 1.

1978   *Stanovleniye i razvitiye oroshaemogo zemledeliya v
        Yuzhnoy Turkmenii* (The Formation and Develop-
        ment of Irrigation Agriculture in Southern Turk-
        menia). Moscow.

1979   Istoriya drevnego oroshaemogo zemledeliya (The
        History of Early Irrigation Agriculture). *Avtoref.
        dokt. dis.* Moscow. [Doctoral Dissertation.]

Lollekova, O.

1978   Drevniye zemledeltsy v gorakh Kopetdaga (Early
        Farmers in the Kopet-Dagh). *Priroda*, no. 6.

1979   Khozyaystvo neoliticheskikh plemen yuga Turk-
        menii v svete eksperimentalno-trasologicheskikh
        dannykh (The Economy of Neolithic Tribes in the
        South of Turkmenia Based on Experimental Trasso-
        logical Data). *Aftoref. kand. dis.* Leningrad.
        [Doctoral Dissertation.]

Lovev, A.F.

1977   *Antichnaya mifologiya v ee istoricheskom razvitii*
        (Ancient Mythology in its Historical Develop-
        ment). Moscow.

Lundin, A.G.

1977   Gorod v drevney Yuzhnoy Aravii (The City in
        Ancient Southern Arabia). In: *Drevniye goroda.*
        Leningrad.

Lyapin, A.A.

1975   Novye pamyatniki epokhi bronzy Yuzhnogo Turk-
        menistana (New Bronze Age Remains of Southern
        Turkmenistan). *USA*, no. 3

Lyapin, A.A. and I.S. Masimov

1974   Obsledovaniye pamyatnikov ranney bronzy (In-
        vestigation of Early Bronze Age Remains). *AO 1973
        g.* Moscow.

Marks [Marx], K. and F. Engels

1936   *Sochineniye* (...Collected Works). Moscow.

Masimov, I.S.

1968   Izucheniye pamyatnikov epokhi bronzy i rannego
        zheleza v rayone stantsii Baba-Durmaz (The Study
        of Bronze and Early Iron Age Remains in the
        Region of Baba-Durmaz Station). *KD*, no. 2.

1970a   Raskopki remeslennogo kvartala epokhi bronzy na
        poselenii Altyn-Depe (Excavation of the Bronze
        Age Craftsmen's Quarters at Altyn Depe). *KD*,
        no. 3.

1970b   Remeslennyy kvartal gorodishcha Altyn-Depe (The
        Craftsmen's Quarters in the Fortified City of Altyn-
        Depe). *AO 1969 g.* Moscow.

1972   Raskopki na remeslennom kvartale Altyn-Depe
        (Excavations of the Craftsmen's Quarters in Altyn-
        Depe). *AO 1971 g.* Moscow.

1973a   Keramicheskoye proizvodstvo Yuzhnogo Turkmen-
        istana epokhi bronzy (Bronze Age Manufacture of
        Ceramics in Southern Turkmenistan). *Avtoref.
        kand. dis.* Leningrad. [Doctoral Dissertation.]

1973b   Raskopki svyatilishcha epokhi bronzy na Altyn-
        Depe (The Excavation of a Bronze Age Sanctuary in
        Altyn-Depe). *SA*, no. 2.

1973c   Raskopki keramicheskikh pechey epokhi bronzy
        na poselenii Altyn-Depe (Excavations of Bronze
        Age Ceramic Kilns in Altyn-Depe). *AO 1972 g.*
        Moscow.

1974a   Kompleks keramiki iz raskopa A-1 poseleniya Na-
        mazga-Depe (The Assemblage of Ceramics from
        Excavation A-1 of the Settlement Namazga-Depe).
        In: *Materialnaya kultura Turkmenistana.* Ash-
        kabad.

1974b   Novyy raskop na Altyn-Depe (A New Excavation in
        Altyn-Depe). *AO 1973 g.* Moscow.

1976a   Novyy oazis bronzy v nizovyakh r. Murgab (A New
        Bronze Age Oasis in the Lower Reaches of the
        Murghab River). *AO 1975 g.* Moscow.

1976b   *Keramicheskoye proizvodstvo epokhi bronzy v Yuzh-
        nom Turkmenistane* (Bronze Age Ceramic Manu-
        facture in Southern Turkmenistan). Ashkabad.

1978a   Raskopki zhilykh kompleksov na Altyn-Depe (Ex-
        cavations of Living Quarters in Altyn-Depe). *KD*,
        no. 7.

1978b   Nakhodki s Shor-Depe (Finds from Shor-Depe).
        PT, no. 1(25).

1979   Izucheniye pamyatnikov epokhi bronzy nizovev
        Murgaba (The Study of Bronze Age Remains from
        the Lower Reaches of the Murghab River). *SA*,
        no. 1.

Masimov, I.S. and A.A. Lyapin

1977   Arkheologo-topograficheskiye raboty v nizovyakh
        drevnego Murgaba (Archaeological and Topo-
        graphical Surveys in the Lower Reaches of the
        Ancient Murghab.) *AO 1976 g.* Moscow.

Masson, V.M.

1956a   Pervobytnoobshchinnyy stroy na territorii Turk-
        menii (Primitive Social Structure in Turkmenia).
        TYuTAKE, vol. 7.

1956b   Raspisnaya keramika Yuzhnogo Turkmenistana
        po raskopkam B.A. Kuftina (Painted Ceramics of
        Southern Turkmenistan from the Excavations of
        B.A. Kuftin). *TYuTAKE*, no. 7.

1957   Drevnezemledelcheskiye plemena Yuzhnogo Turk-
        menistana i ikh svyazi s Iranom i Indiey (The
        Ancient Agricultural Tribes of Southern Turk-
        menistan and Their Ties with Iran and India).
        VDI, no. 1.

1959a   Drevnezemledelcheskaya kultura Margiany (Early
        Agriculture in Margiana). *MIA*, no. 73.

1959b O kulte zhenskogo bozhestva u anauskikh plemen (The Cult of Goddesses among the Anau Tribes). *KSIIMK*, no. 73.

1960a Yuzhnoturkmenistanskiy tsentr rannezemledelcheskikh kultur (The Southern Turkmenistan Center of Early Agriculture). *TYuTAKE*, vol. 10.

1960b Kara-Depe u Artyka (Kara-Depe near Artyk [in Turkmenia]). *TYuTAKE*, vol. 10.

1962a Eneolit yuzhnykh oblastey Sredney Azii (The Eneolithic of the Southern Regions of Central Asia). *SAI*, part B-3-8, no. 2

1962b Drevneysheye proshloye Sredney Azii ot voznikoveniya zemledeliya do pokhoda Aleksandra Makedonskogo (The Remote Past of Central Asia from the Beginnings of Agriculture to the Invasion of Alexander of Macedonia). *Aftoref. dokt. dis.* Leningrad. [Doctoral Dissertation.]

1962c Novye raskopki na Dzheytune i Kara-Tepe (New Excavations at Jeitun and Kara-Tepe). *SA*, no. 3.

1963 Srednaya Aziya i Iran v III tys. do n.e. (Central Asia and Iran in the Third Millennium B.C.). *KSIA*, no. 93.

1964a Istoricheskoye mesto sredneaziatskoy tsivilizatsii (The Historical Place of Central Asian Civilization). *SA*, no. 1.

1964b *Srednaya Azia i Drevniy Vostok* (Central Asia and the Ancient East). Moscow-Leningrad.

1966a K evolyutsii oboronitelnykh sten osedlykh poseleniy (On the Development of Defensive Walls in Inhabited Places). *KSIA*, no. 108.

1966b Raskopki na Altyn-Depe (Excavations in Altyn-Depe) *AO 1965 g.* Moscow.

1966c *Strana tysyachi gorodov* (The Country of a Thousand Cities). Moscow.

1966d Ot vozniknoveniya zemledeliya do slozheniya ranneklassovogo obshchestva—etapy kulturnogo i khozyaystvennogo razvitiya po materialam Aziatskogo materika (From the Beginnings of Agriculture to the Formation of Early Societies—Stages of Culture and Economic Development Based on Asian Sources). In: *VII Mezhdunar. kongr. doist. i protoist. Doklady i soobshch. arkheol. SSSR.* Moscow.

1966e Rastsvet i upadok kultury zemledeltsev Yugo-Zapada (The Flowering and Decline of Agriculture in the Southwest). In: *Srednyaya Aziya v epokhu kamnya i bronzy.* Moscow-Leningrad.

1967a Drevnosti Meana (The Antiquities of Meana). *PT*, no. 3

1967b Stanovleniye ranneklassovogo obshchestva na Drevnem Vostoke (The Formation of an Early Class Society in the Ancient East). *VI*, no. 5.

1967c Protogorodskaya kultura Altyn-Depe (The Proto-urban Culture of Altyn-Depe). *AO 1966 g.* Moscow.

1967d Protogorodskaya tsivilizatsiya yuga Sredney Azii (Proto-urban Civilization in the South of Central Asia). *SA*, no. 3.

1968a K voprosu o "gorodskoy revolyutsii" (To the Question of "Urban Revolution"). In: *IV sessiya po Drevnomu Vostoku. Tez. dokl.* Leningrad.

1968b Otkrytiye monumentalnoy arkhitektury epokhi bronzy v Yuzhnom Turkmenistane (The Discovery of Bronze Age Monumental Architecture in Southern Turkmenistan). *SA*, no. 2.

1968c Monumentalnaya arkhitektura Altyn-Depe (The Monumental Architecture of Altyn-Depe). *AO 1967 g.* Moscow.

1968d Urban Revolution in South Turkmenia. *Antiquity*, no. 167.

1969a Priroda i proiskhozhdeniye tsivilizatsii (Natural Environment and the Origin of Civilization). *Priroda*, no. 3.

1969b Chetvertyy sezon raskopok na Altyn-Depe (The Fourth Season of Excavations at Altyn-Depe). *AO 1968 g.* Moscow.

1969c *Arkheologicheskiye izyskaniya i izucheniye drevney i srednevekovoy istorii Turkmenii* (Archaeological Investigations and the Study of the Ancient and Medieval History of Turkmenia). Ashkabad.

1970a Raskopki na Altyn-Depe v 1969 g. (The 1969 Excavations at Altyn-Depe). *MYuTAKE*, no. 3.

1970b Stanovleniye remesel v svete dannykh arkheologii (The Formation of Crafts Based on Archaeological Data). In: *Domashniye promysly i remesla. Tez. dokl.* Leningrad.

1970c Raskopki na Altyn-Depe (Excavations at Altyn-Depe). *AO 1969 g.* Moscow.

1970d K semantike znakov sobstvennosti epokhi bronzy (The Semantics of Bronze Age Property Signs). In: *Sibir i ee sosedi v drevnosti.* Novosibirsk.

1970e Ekonomicheskiye predposylki slozheniya ranneklassovogo obshchestva (Economic Prerequisites for the Formation of Early Class Societies). In: *Leninskiye idei v izuchenii istorii pervobytnogo obshchestva, rabovladeniya i feodalizma.* Moscow.

1970f Zona rannegorodskikh tsivilizatsiy mezhdu Shumerom i Indiey (The Zone of Early Urban Civilizations between Sumer and India). In: *Tez. dokl. na zased. posvyashch. itogam arkheol. issled. 1969 g.* Moscow.

1971a Izucheniye stratigrafii i topografii Altyn-Depe (The Study of the Stratigraphy and Topography of Altyn-Depe). *AO 1971 g.* Moscow.

1971b Poseleniye Dzheytun—problema stanovleniya proizvodyashchey ekonomiki (The Jeitun Settlement—Problems of Establishing a Productive Economy). *MIA*, no. 180.

1971c Sredneaziatsko-kavkazskiy sotsiologicheskiy parallelizm (The Central Asia-Caucasus Sociological Parallelism). In: *Vsesoyuz. sessiya posv. itogam arkheol. issled. v 1970 g. Tez. dokl.* Tbilisi.

1971d *Early Agriculture and the Ancient Civilization Types.* Moscow.

1972a Shestoy sezon rabot na Altyn-Depe (The Sixth Season of Excavations at Altyn-Depe). *USA*, part 1.

1972b Review of G. Daniel's, The First Civilization. In: *Narody Azii i Afriki*, no. 3.

1972c Ponyatiye kultury v arkeologicheskoy sistematike (The Concept of Culture in Archaeological Systematics). In: *Kamennyy vek Sredney Azii i Kazakhstana. Tez. dokl. soveshch.* Tashkent.

1972d Izucheniye obshchestvenoy struktury rannegorodskogo poseleniya Altyn-Depe (The Study of Social Structure in the Early City Center of Altyn-Depe). *AO 1971 g.* Moscow.

1972e Evolutsiya pervobytnykh poseleniy Sredney Azii (The Evolution of Primitive Settlements in Central Asia). *USA*, part 1.

1972f Remeselnoye proizvodstvo v epokhu pervobytnogo stroya (Handicraft Production in Primitive Society). *VI*, no. 3.

1972g Prehistoric Settlement Patterns in Soviet Central Asia. *Man, Settlement and Urbanism*. London.

1973a Obmen i torgovlya v pervobytnuyu epokhu (Barter and Trade in the Primitive Epoch). *VI*, no. 1.

1973b Paskopki zhecheskoy grobnitsy v Turkmenii (The Excavation of a Priest's Tomb in Turkmenia). *Priroda*, no. 3.

1973c Protsess urbanizatsii v drevney istorii Sredney Azii (The Process of Urbanization in the Early History of Central Asia). In: *Tez. dokl. sessii posv. itogam. arkheol. issled. 1972 g.* Tashkent.

1973d Raskopki pogrebalnogo khramogo kompleksa na Altyn-Depe (Excavations of the Temple Burial Complex at Altyn-Depe). *AO 1972 g.* Moscow.

1973e Izucheniye obshchestvennoy struktury Altyn-Depe (A Study of the Social Structure of Altyn-Depe). In: *Tez. dokl. na sektsii plenuma 1971 g.* Moscow.

1973f Razvitiye obmena i torgovli v drevnikh obshchestvakh (The Development of Barter and Trade in Ancient Societies). *KSIA*, no. 138.

1973g Sotsialnye i ekologicheskiye faktory v formirovanii ranneklassovogo obshchetva (Social and Ecological Factors in the Formation of Early Class Societies). In: *Voznikoveniye ranneklassovogo obshchestva. Tez. dokl.* Moscow.

1974a Novye raskopki na Altyn-Depe (New Excavations at Altyn-Depe). *AO 1973 g.* Moscow.

1974b Raskopki pogrebalnogo kompleksa epokhi bronzy na Altyn-Depe (Excavations of a Bronze Age Burial Complex at Altyn-Depe). *SA*, no. 4.

1974c Review of Adams, R. and Nissen, H., Uruk Countryside. *VDI*, no. 3.

1974d Problema drevnego goroda i arkheologicheskiye pamyatniki Severnoy Baktrii (The Problems of Early Cities and the Archaeological Sites of Northern Bactria). In: *Drevnaya Baktriya*. Moscow.

1974e Review of Renfrew, C., Emergence of Civilization. *VI*, no. 7

1974f Tsivilizatsiya Altyn-Depe (The Altyn-Depe Civilization). *PT*, no. 2(18).

1974g Kamennyy vek Sredney Azii i ponyatiye arkheologicheskoy kultury (The Stone Age of Central Asia and the Concept of an Archaeological Culture). In: *Istoriya materialnoy kultury Uzbekistana*, no. 1. Tashkent.

1975a Altyn-Depe: raskopki 1974 g. (Altyn-Depe: The 1974 Excavations). *Priroda*, no. 3.

1975b Pervye goroda: k probleme formirovaniya gorodov v srede rannezemledelcheskikh kultur (Early Cities: On the Problem of Establishing Cities in an Early Agricultural Environment). In: *Noveyshiye otkrytiya sovetskikh arkheologov*, part 1. Kiev.

1975c Izucheniye sloyev eneolita i bronzy na Altyn-Depe (The Study of Eneolithic and Bronze Age Stratification at Altyn-Depe). *AO 1974 g.* Moscow.

1975d Obraz nebesnogo byka v epokhu bronzy (The Image of the Celestial Bull in the Bronze Age). *PT*, no. 2(20).

1975e Novaya tsivilizatsiya drevnevostochnogo tipa na yuge Sredney Azii (A New Civilization of the Ancient Near Eastern Type in Central Asia). In: *Pamyatniki kultury. Novye otkrytiya*. Moscow.

1975f The Art of Altyn-Depe. In: *To Illustrate the Monuments*. London.

1976a *Ekonomika i sotsialnyy stroy drevnikh obshchestv* (The Economy and Social Structure of Ancient Communities). Leningrad.

1976b Chelovek i pustynya: istoricheskiye aspekty vzaimdeystva (Man and Desert: Historical Aspects of Interaction). In: *Konf. po izucheniyu pustyn SSSR. Tez. dokl.* Ashkabad.

1976c Raskopki zhilykh kvartalov oboronitelnykh sooruzheniy Altyn-Depe (Excavations of the Living Quarters and Fortification Structures at Altyn-Depe). *AO 1975 g.* Moscow.

1976d Svit urbanizacii (The Dawn of Urbanization. *Problemy*, no. 10.

1976e Altyn-Depe and the Bull Cult. *Antiquity*, vol. 50, no. 1.

1977a Altyn-Depe v epokhu eneolita (Eneolithic Altyn-Depe). *SA*, no. 3.

1977b Raskopki zhilykh kvartalov i pogrebalnykh kompleksov Altyn-Depe (The Excavation of the Living Quarters and Burial Complexes at Altyn-Depe). *AO 1976 g.* Moscow.

1977c Tipologiya drevnikh gorodov i istoricheskiy protsess (The Typology of Early Cities and the Historical Process). In: *Drevniye goroda*. Leningrad.

1977d Pustynya i obshchestvo. Dinamika vzaimodeystva v istoricheskom aspekte (Desert and Society. The Dynamics of Interaction from a Historical Aspect). In: *Pustyni Sredney Azii i Kazakhstana*, no. 6. Ashkabad.

1977e Pechati protoindiyskogo tipa iz Altyn-Depe (Proto-Indic Types of Seals from Altyn-Depe). *VDI*, no. 4.

1978a Gorodskiye tsentry ranneklassovykh obshchestv (Urban Centers of Early Class Societies). In: *Istoriya i arkheologiya Sredney Azii*. Ashkabad.

1978b Izucheniye osedlozemledelcheskikh poseleniy v Yuzhnom Turkmenistane (An Investigation of Permanent Agricultural Settlements in Southern Turkmenistan). *AO 1977 g.* Moscow.

1978c Altin-Depe—die Stadt des heiligen Stiers. *Das Altertum,* Heft 2. Berlin.

1979a V.V. Struve i izucheniye drevney istorii Sredney Azii (V.V. Struve and Studies of the Early History of Central Asia). In: *VIII Vsesoyuznaya konferentsiya po Drevnemu Vostoku. Tez. dokl.* Moscow.

1979b O kharaktere drevneyshikh klassovykh obshchestv na Vostoke (On the Character of the Earliest Class Societies in the East). *IAN TSSR. SON,* no. 5.

Masson, V.M. and A.F. Ganyalin

1969 K izucheniyu religioznykh predstavleniy Yuzhnogo Turkmenistana epokhi bronzy (To the Study of Bronze Age Religious Ideas in Southern Turkmenistan). *IAN TSSR. SON,* no. 5.

Masson, V.M. and T.P. Kiyatkina

1976 Chelovek na zare urbanizatsii (Man at the Dawn of Urbanization). *Priroda,* no. 4.

Masson, V.M. and V.I. Sarianidi

1969 O znakakh na sredneaziatskikh statuetkakh epokhi bronzy (Signs on Central Asiatic Bronze Age Statuettes). *VDI,* no. 1.

1972 *Central Asia. Turkmenia before the Achaemenids.* London.

1973 *Sredneaziatskaya terrakota epokhi bronzy* (Central Asian Bronze Age Terracottas). Moscow.

Naumov, V.D.

1970 Khimicheskiy sostav nekotorykh bronzovykh predmetov Yuzhnogo Turkmenistana (The Chemical Composition of Some Bronze Objects from Southern Turkmenistan). *KD,* issue 3.

Perfilev, M.N.

1974 *Obshchestvennye otnosheniya* (Social Relations). Moscow.

1965 *Predvaritelnoye soobshchenie ob issledovanii protoindiyskikh tekstov* (Preliminary Report on the Investigation of Proto-Indic Texts). Moscow.

Sayko, E.V.

1972 Tekhnologicheskaya kharakteristika keramiki razvitoy bronzy iz Altyn-Depe (The Technological Characteristics of Developed Bronze Age Ceramics from Altyn-Depe). *KD,* issue 4.

1973 *Stanovleniye goroda kak proizvodstvennogo tsentra* (The Establishment of the City as a Production Center). Dushanbe.

1977 O teplotekhnike keramiki drevnezemledelcheskikh poseleniy—Altyn-Depe. (Ceramic Heat Technology in Early Agricultural Settlements—Altyn-Depe). *KD,* issue 5.

1978 K izuchenyu teplotekhniki keramicheskogo proizvodstva epokhi bronzy v Yuzhnom Turkmenistane (To the Study of Ceramic Heat Technology in Bronze Age Products from Southern Turkmenistan). *KD,* issue 7.

Sarianidi, V.I.

1960 Eneoliticheskoye poseleniye Geoksyur (The Eneolithic Site of Geoksyur). *TYuTAKE,* vol. 10.

1962 Kultovye zdaniya poseleniy anauskoy kultury (Cult Edifices in Sites of the Anau Culture). *SA,* no. 1.

1964 Khapuz-Depe kak pamyatnik epokhi bronzy (Khapuz-Depe as a Bronze Age Monument). *KSIA,* issue 98.

1965 Pamyatniki pozdnego eneolita Yugo-Vostochnoy Turkmenii (Late Eneolithic Sites in Southeastern Turkmenia). *SAI,* issue B3-8, no. 4.

1966 Raskopki mogilnikov na Geoksyure i Altyn-Depe (The Excavation of Burial Grounds at Geoksyur and Altyn-Depe). *AO 1965 g.* Moscow.

1967 Raskopki na Altyn-Depe i Khapuz-Depe (Excavations at Altyn-Depe and Khapuz-Depe). *AO 1966 g.* Moscow.

1969 Prodolzheniye rabot na Ulug-Depe (The Extension of Archaeological Works at Ulug-Depe). *AO 1968 g.* Moscow.

1972 Kollektivnye pogrebeniya i izucheniye obshchestvennogo stroya rannezemedelcheskikh plemen (Collective Burials and An Investigation of the Social Structure of Early Agricultural Tribes). *USA,* issue 1.

1973 Drevnosti nizoviy Murgaba (Ancient Remains on the Murghab Plain). *AO 1972 g.* Moscow.

1975 Novye otkrytiya v nizovyakh Murgaba (New Discoveries on the Murghab Plain). *AO 1974 g.* Moscow.

1976a Pechati-amulety murgabskogo stilya (Seals-Amulets of the Murghab Style). *SA,* no. 1.

1976b Yuzhnyy Turkmenistan v epokhu bronzy (Southern Turkmenistan in the Bronze Age). In: *Pervobytnyy Turkmenistan.* Ashkhabad.

1976c Issledovaniye pamyatnikov Dashlinskogo oazisa (Investigation of the Remains in the Dashlin Oasis). In: *Drevnyaya Baktriya.* Moscow.

1977 *Drevniye zemledeltsy Afganistana* (The Early Agriculturalists of Afghanistan). Moscow.

Sarianidi, V.I. and K.A. Kachuris

1968 Raskopki na Ulug-Depe (Excavations at Ulug-Depe). *AO 1967 g.* Moscow.

Semenov, A.A.

1946 Razvaliny gg. Meykhene i Chekhche v drevnem Khaverane (Ruins of the Cities Meana and Chaacha in Ancient Khaveran). *Isv. Tadzh. fil. AN SSSR,* no. 12.

Shifman, I. Sh.

1977 Razvitiye gorodskoy organizatsii v drevnem Peredneaziatskom Sredizemnomorye (The Development of Urban Organization in the Ancient Mediterranean Near East). In: *Drevniye goroda.* Moscow.

Shchetenko, A. Ya.

1968a Raskopki na Altyn-Depe v Yuzhnoy Turkmenii (Excavations at Altyn-Depe in Southern Turkmenia). *KSIA,* no. 114.

1968b Raskopki poseleniya epokhi bronzy Taychanak-Depe (Excavation of the Bronze Age Site Taychanak-Depe). *KD*, no. 2.

1968c *Drevneyshiye zemledelcheskiye kultury Dekana* (The Earliest Agricultural Civilizations of the Deccan). Moscow.

1970a Raskopki melkikh poseleniy epokhi bronzy (The Excavations of Small Bronze Age Sites). *KD*, no. 3.

1970b Raboty artykskogo otryada Karakumskoy ekspeditsii (Works of the Artyk Detachment of the Karakum Expedition). *AO 1969 g.* Moscow.

1970c O torgovykh putyakh epokhi bronzy po materialam turkmenistano-kharrapskikh paralleley (Bronze Age Trade Routes on the Bases of Turkmenistan-Harappa Parallels), *KSIA*, issue 122.

1977 Raboty Kaakhkinskoy ekspeditsii (Works of the Kaakhka Expedition). *AO 1976 g.* Moscow.

Skakun, N.N.

1972 Funktsionalnoye issledovaniye kamennhykh nakonechnikov strel epokhi bronzy (Functional Investigation of Bronze Age Stone Arrowheads). *KD*, issue 4.

1977a Eksperimentalno-trasologicheskiye issledovaniya keramicheskikh orudiy truda epokhi paleometalla (po materialam Altyn-Depe i Tekkem-Depe) (Experimental-trassological Investigations of Ceramic Artifacts from the Paleometallic Epoch Based on Materials from Altyn-Depe and Tekkem-Depe). *SA*, no. 1.

1977b Kamennye orudiya epokhi bronzy po materialam Altyn-Depe 1970-1972 gg. (Bronze Age Stone Artifacts Based on the 1970-1972 Materials from Altyn-Depe). *KD*, no. 6.

Sokolov, S.N.

1963 Religioznaya sistema zoroastrizma (The Religious System of Zoroastrianism). In: *Istoriya tadzhikskogo naroda*, vol. 1.

1972 Soobshcheniye ob issledovanii protoindiyskikh tekstov (Report on the Investigations of Proto-Indic Texts). *Proto-Indica: 1972.* Moscow.

1973 Soobshcheniye ob issledovanii protoindiyskikh tekstov (Report on the Investigations of Proto-Indic Texts). *Proto-Indica: 1973.* Moscow.

Terekhova, N. N.

1976 Istoriya metalloobrabatyvayushchevo proizvodstva u drevnikh zemedeltsev Yuzhnoy Turkmenii (The History of Metalworking Among the Early Farmers of Southern Turkmenia). *Avtoref. kand. dis.* Moscow. [Doctoral dissertation.]

Tokarev, S.A.

1964 Ranniye formy religii (Early Forms of Religions). Moscow.

Tolstov, S.P.

1948 *Drevniy Khorezm* (Ancient Khorezm). Moscow.

Tosi, M.

1971 Seistan v bronzovom veke (Seistan During the Early Bronze Age). *SA*, no. 3.

Trever, K.V.

1940 Gopat-Shakh—tsar-pastukh (Gopat-Shah—The Herdsman-Czar). In: *Trudy otdela Vostoka Ermitazha*, vol. 2. Leningrad.

Turayev, B.A.

1935 *Istoriya Drevnego Vostoka* (The History of the Ancient East), vol. 1. Leningrad.

Vavilov, N.I. and D.D. Bukinich

1959 Zemedelcheskiy Afganistan (Agricultural Afghanistan). In: Vavilov, N.I., *Izbr. trudy*, vol. 1. Moscow-Leningrad.

Vayman, A.A.

1966 K rasshifrovke protoshumerskoy pismennosti (Toward the Deciphering of Proto-Sumerian Writing). In: *Peredneaziatskiy sbornik.* Moscow.

1972 O svyazi protoelamskoy pismennosti s protoshumerskoy (On the Relationship of Proto-Elamite and Proto-Sumerian Writings). *VDI*, no. 3.

1974 Oboznacheniye rabov i rabyn v protoshumerskoy pismennosti (The Designation of Male and Female Slaves in Proto-Sumerian Writing). *VDI*, no. 2.

1976 O protoshumerskoy pismennosti (On Proto-Sumerian Writing). In: *Tayny drevnikh pismen. Problemy deshifrovki.* Moscow.

1979 Istolkovaniye nekotorykh znakov v protoshumerskikh spiskakh rabyn (An Interpretation of Some Symbols in Proto-Sumerian Rosters of Female Slaves). In: *VIII Vsesoyuz konf. po Drevnemu Vostoku. Tez. dokl.* Moscow.

Vinogradov, A.V.

1957 K voprosu o yuzhnykh svyazyakh kelteminarskoy kultury (To the Question of Southern Ties of the Kelteminar Culture). *SE*, no. 1.

1968 *Neoliticheskiye pamyatniki Khorezma* (Neolithic Remains in the Khorezm). Moscow.

Vinogradov, A.V. and E.D. Mamedov

1972 Landshaftno-klimaticheskiye usloviya pustynykh ravnin Sredney Azii v golotsene (Landscape and Climatic Conditions of Desert Plains in Central Asia During the Holocene). In: *Kamennyy vek Sredney Azii i Kazakhstana. Tez. dokl. soveshch.* Tashkent.

1975 *Pervobytnyy Lyavyakan* (Primitive Lyavyakan). Moscow.

Vinogradov, Yu. A.

1978 Konferentsiya "Tipologiya i sotsialnaya struktura drevnego goroda." (The Conference on "Typology and Social Structure of Early Cities"). *VDI*, issue 4.

Vorobev-Desyatovskiy, V.S.

1956a K voprosu o roli substrata v razvitii indoariyskikh yazykov (On the Role of the Substratum in the Development of Indo-Aryan Languages). *SV*, no. 1.

1956b Drevnyaya Indiya (Ancient India). In: *Ocherki istorii Drevnego Vostoka.* Leningrad.

Vulli [Woolley], L.

1961 *Ur khaldeyev* (Ur of the Chaldaeans). Moscow.

Yankoyevskaya, N.B.

1965   Mezhdunarodnoye torgovoye obedineniye Kanisha (The International Trading Society of Kanish). *VDI*, no. 3.

1968   *Klinopisnye teksty iz Kyul-Tepe* (Cuneiform texts from Kyul-Tepe). Moscow.

Yanushevich, Z.V.

1977   O nakhodke yachmenya na poselenii Altyn-Depe (The Find of Barley at Altyn-Depe). *KD*, issue 5.

Yusunov, Kh.

1976   Terrakota iz Goch-Depe (Terracottas from Goch-Depe). *PT*, no. 1(20).

Yusunov, Kh., A. Gubayev, and M. Durdyev

1976   Vtoroy sezon rabot na Goch-Depe (The Second Field Season at Goch-Depe). *AO 1975 g.* Moscow.

Zavyalov, V.A.

1974   Raskopki zhilogo kvartala (Excavations of the Living Quarters). *PT*, no. 2(18).

1977   Memorialnyy kompleks epokhi bronzy iz raskopok Altyn-Depe (A Bronze Age Memorial Complex at Altyn-Depe). *PT*, no. 1(23).

Zhukov, E.M.

1973   Nekotorye voprosy teorii sotsialno-ekonomicheskikh formatsiy (Some Queries About the Theory of Social-Economic Formations). *Komunist*, no. 11.

Other Sources

Adams, R. Mc. C.
1966　*Land Behind Baghdad*. Chicago-London.

Adams, R. Mc. C. and H.J. Nissen
1972　*The Uruk Countryside. The Natural Setting of Urban Societies*. Chicago-London.

Agrawal, D.P.
1971　*The Copper Age in India*. New Delhi.

Allan, W.
1972　Ecology, Techniques and Settlement Patterns. *MSU*.

Barnett, R.D.
1969　About Musical Instruments from Ur. *Iraq*, vol. 31:2.

Biscione, R.
1973　Dynamics of An Early South Asian Urbanisation: The First Period of Shahr-i Sokhta and Its Connections with Southern Turkmenia. *SAA*.

Bovington, C.H., R.H. Dyson, A. Mahadavi, and R. Masoumi
1974　The Radiocarbon Evidence for the Terminal Date of the Hissar IIIC Culture. *Iran*, vol. 12.

Boyce, M.
1975　*History of Zoroastrism*, vol. 1. Leiden-Köln.

Braidwood, K.J. and Ch. E. Reed
1957　The Achievement and Early Consequences of Food Production. *Cold Spring Harbor Symposia on Quantitative Biology*, vol. 22. New York.

Brown, W.
1964　The Indian Games of Pachisi, Chauper and Chausar. *Expedition*, no. 3.

Buren, E.D. van
1930　*Clay Figurines of Babylonia and Assyria*. New Haven.

Caldwell, J.R. (ed.)
1967　*Investigations at Tal-i-Iblis*. Illinois State Museum Preliminary Reports, no. 5. Springfield, Illinois.

Casal, J.M.
1961　*Fouilles de Mundigak*, vols. 1, 2. Paris.

Chang, K.C.
1974　Urbanism and the King in Ancient China. *World Archaeology*, no. 1.

Childe, G.
1950　The Urban Revolution. *City Planning Review*, vol. 21.

Contenau, G.
1931　*Manuel d'archeologie oriental*, vol 2. Paris.

Cowgill, U.
1962　An Agriculture Study of the Southern Maya Lowlands. *American Anthropologist*, vol. 64, no. 2.

Dales, G.F.
1963　Necklaces, Bands and Belts on Mesopotamian Figurines. *Revue d'assyriologie et archeologie oriental*, vol. 57, no. 1. Paris.
1972a　Prehistoric Research in Southern Afghan Seistan. *Afghanistan*, no. 4.
1972b　Turkmenistan, Afghanistan and Pakistan. *Propyläen Kunstgeschichte*. Berlin.
1973　Archaeology and Radiocarbon Chronologies for Protohistoric South Asia. *SAA*.
1977　Hissar III Stone Objects in Afghan Seistan. *Bibl. Mesopotamica*, vol. 7.
1977a　Shifting Trade Patterns Between the Iranian Plateau and the Indus Valley in the Third Millennium B.C. *PI*.

Dani, A.H.
1970-　Excavations in Gomal Valley. *Ancient Pakistan*,
1971　vol. 5.

Delougaz, P.
1952　Pottery from the Diyala Region. *OIP*, vol. 63.

Delougaz, P. and S. Lloyd
1941　Pre-Sargonid Temples in the Diyala Region. *OIP*, vol. 58

Deshayès, J.
1960　Les outiles de bronze de l'Indus au Danube. *Bibl. archeol. et hist.*, vol. 71:1. Paris.
1969　*Les civilisations de l'orient ancien*. Paris.
1978　A propos des terrasses hautes de la fin du III millenaire en Iran et en Asie Centrale. *PI*.

Drucker, P. and R.F. Heizer
1960　A Study of the Milpa System of La Venta Island and its Archaeological Implications. *Southwestern Journal of Anthropology*, vol. 16, no. 1, pp. 36-45. Albuquerque.

Dupre, L., Ph. Gouin, and N. Omer
1971　The Khosh-Tapa Hoard from North Afghanistan. *Archaeology*, no. 1.

During-Caspers, E.C.L.
1971　The Bull's Head from Barbar Temple II, Bahrain. A contact with Early Dynastic Sumer. *EW*, vol. 21, nos. 3-4.

Dyson, R.H.

1965   Problems in the Relative Chronology of Iran 6000-2000 B.C. In: *Chronologies in Old World Archaeology*. Chicago-London.

Fairservis, W.A.

1967   The Origin, Character and Decline of an Early Civilization. *Am. Museum Novitates*, no. 2302.

1971   *The Roots of Ancient India. The Archaeology of Indian Civilization.* New York.

Flannery, K.V.

1972   The Cultural Evolution of Civilization. *Annual Review of Ecological Systematics*, vol. 3.

Frankfort, H.P.

1936   Progress of the Work of the Oriental Institute in Iraq, 1934-1935. *Oriental Institute Communications*, no. 20.

1955   *The Art and Architecture of the Ancient Orient.* Baltimore.

Frankfort, H.P. and M.H. Pottier

1978   Sondage préliminaire sur établissement protohistorique harappéen et postharappéen de Shortugai. *Arts asiat.*, vol. 34.

Ghirshman, R.

1939   *Fouilles de Sialk*, vol. 1. Paris.

Glob, P.V.

1955   Udgrauninger pa Bahrein. *Kuml.*

1958   Bahrein Five Thousand Years Ago: The Temples of Barbar. *ILN*, no. 4.

Hall, H.R. and L. Woolley

1927   *Al-Ubaid.* London.

Kohl, P.S.

1975   Carved Chlorite Vessels: A Trade in Finished Commodities in Mid-Third Millennium. *Expedition*, no. 3.

Krishnarao, M.V. N.

1973   Foreign Rulers in Indus Seals. *RIA.*

Labat, R.

1970   *Les religions du Proche Orient asiatique.* Paris

Lal, B.B.

1962-   A Picture Emerges on Assessment of the Carbon-14
1963   Datings of the Proto-historic Cultures of the Indo-Pakistan Subcontinent. *Ancient India*, vols. 18-19.

Lamberg-Karlovsky, C.C.

1970   *Excavations at Tepe Yahya, Iran, 1967-1969.* Cambridge, Mass.

1971   The Proto-Elamite Settlement at Tepe-Yahya. *Iran*, vol. 9.

1972   Trade Mechanisms in Indus-Mesopotamia Interrelations. *Journal of the Oriental Society*, no. 2.

1978   The Proto-Elamites on the Iranian Plateau. *Antiquity*, vol. 52.

Lamberg-Karlovsky, C.C. and M. Lamberg-Karlovsky

1971   An Early City in Iran. *Scientific American*, vol. 224, no. 6.

Lamberg-Karlovsky, C.C. and M. Tosi

1973   Shahr-i Sokhta and Tepe-Yahya: Tracks on the Earliest History of the Iranian Plateau. *EW*, vols. 1, 2.

Lanning, E.P.

1967   *Peru Before the Incas.* Englewood Cliffs, New Jersey.

Lenzen, H.L.

1961   *Die Entwicklungen der Zikkurat.* Leipzig.

Mackay, E.

1938   *Further Excavations of Mohenjo-Daro*, vols. 1, 2. New Delhi.

1943   *Chanhu-Daro Excavations.* New Delhi.

Mahadevan, J. and K. Visvanathan

1973   Computer Concordance of Proto-Indian Signs. *RIA.*

Makkay, J.

1973   Shrine with Bucranium. A Tentative Interpretation of the Tataria Sign 3,5. *Kadmos*, Bd. 12, Heft 1.

Marshall, J.

1931   *Mohenjo-Daro and the Indus Civilisation*, vols. 1-3. London.

McCown, D.E.

1942   The Comparative Stratigraphy of Early Iran. *Studies in Ancient Oriental Civilizations*, no 23. Chicago.

Mellaart, J.

1964   *Anatolia before c. 4000 B.C. and c. 2300-1750 B.C.* Cambridge.

1965   *Anatolia c. 4000-2300 B.C.* Cambridge.

1967   *Çatal-Hüyük. A Neolithic Town in Anatolia.* New York.

Mortensen, P.

1970   On barbartemples datering. *Kuml.*

Mughal, M.R.

1974   New Evidence of the Early Harappan Culture from Jalipur. *Archaeology*, no. 52.

Myres, J.

1944   *Mediterranean Culture.* The Frazer Lecture 1943. Cambridge.

Nissen, H.J.

1969   *Materials for the Sumerian Lexicon.* vol. 12. Roma.

Parpalo, A., S. Koshenniemi, S. Parpalo, and P. Aalto

1969   *Decipherment of the Proto-Dravidian Inscriptions of the Indus Civilization.* Copenhagen.

Parrot, A.

1960   *Sumer.* Paris.

Perkins, A.L.

1949   The Comparative Archaeology of Early Mesopotamia. *Studies in Ancient Oriental Civilizations,* no. 25. Chicago.

Piggott, S.

1969   The Earliest Wheeled Vehicles and the Caucasian Evidence. *Proceedings of the Prehistoric Society for 1968,* vol. 34. London.

Rao, S.R.

1973a   The Indus Script—Methodology and Language. *RIA.*

1973b   C^{14} Dates as Applicable to Harappan Sites. *RIA.*

Redman, Ch. L.

1978   *The Rise of Civilization.* San Francisco.

Renfrew, C.

1972   *The Emergence of Civilization.* London.

Shaffer, J.G.

1971   Preliminary Report of Excavations at Said-Cala-Tepe. *Afghanistan,* nos. 2,3.

Schmidt, E.

1937   *Excavations at Tepe-Hissar.* Philadelphia.

Tosi, M.

1968   Excavations at Shahr-i Sokhta, a Chalcolithic Settlement in the Iranian Sistan. Preliminary Report on the First Campaign. *EW,* vol. 18.

1969   Excavations at Shahr-i Sokhta. Preliminary Report on the Second Campaign, 1968. *EW.* nos. 3,4.

1974   The Problem of Turquoise in Proto-Historic Trade on the Iranian Plateau. *Studi di Paleoetnologia, Paleoantropologia, Paleontologia a Geologia del Quaternario,* vol. 2.

Tosi, M. and M. Piperno

1973   Lithic Technology Behind the Ancient Lapis-lazuli Trade. *Expedition,* no. 1.

Tosi, M. and R. Wardak

1972   The Fullol Hoard. *EW,* nos. 1, 2.

Weiss, H. and T.C. Young

1975   The Merchants of Susa Godin V and Plateau-Lowland Relations in Late Fourth Millennium B.C. *Iran,* vol. 13.

Wheeler, M.

1947   Harappa 1946. The Defences and Cemetery R-37. *Ancient India,* vol. 3.

Woolley, L.

1931   Excavations at Ur, 1930-1931. *Antiquaries Journal,* vol. 11, no. 4.

1934   *Ur Excavations,* vol. 2. London.

1939   *The Ziggurat and Its Surroundings. Ur Excavations,* vol. 5. Oxford.

Wright, H.T.

1969   The Administration of Rural Production in An Early Mesopotamian Town. *Anthropological Papers of the Museum of Anthropology, University of Michigan, Ann Arbor,* no. 38.

Yadin, Y.

1963   *The Art of Warfare in Biblical Lands.* London.

Vidali, M.L., E. Vidali, and C.C. Lamberg-Karlovsky

1976   Prehistoric Settlement Patterns Around Tepe-Yahya: A Quantitative Analysis. *Journal of Near Eastern Studies,* no. 4.

Zervos, C.

1935   *L'Art de la Mesopotamie.* Paris.

Ziegler, C.

1962   *Die Terrakoten von Warka.* Berlin.

Zvelchil, K.

1965   Harappa and the Dravidians—An Old Mystery in A New Light. *New Orient,* no. 3.

List of Abbreviations

AO	*Arkheologicheskiye otkrytiya.* Moscow.
EW	*East and West.* Rome.
IAN TSSR. SON	*Izvestiya Akademii nauk Turkmenskoy SSR. Seriya obshchestvennykh nauk.* Ashkabad.
ILN	*Illustrated London News.*
KD	*Karakumskiye drevnosti.* Ashkabad.
KSIA	*Kratkiye soobshcheniya Instituta arkheologii AN SSSR.* Moscow.
KSIIMK	*Kratskiye soobshcheniya Instituta istorii materialnoy kultury AN SSSR.* Moscow-Leningrad.
LOIA	Leningradskoye otdeleniye Instituta arkheologii AN SSSR.
MIA	*Materialy i issledovaniya po arkheologii SSSR.* Moscow-Leningrad.
MSU	*Man, Settlement and Urbanism.* London, 1972.
MYuTAKE	*Materialy Yuzhno-Turkmenistanskoy arkheologicheskoy kompleksnoy ekspeditsii.* Leningrad.
OIP	Oriental Institute Publications. Chicago.
PI	*Le Plateau Iranien et l'Asie Centrale des origines a la conquete islamique.* Paris, 1977.
PT	*Pamyatniki Turkmenistana.* Ashkabad.
RIA	*Radiocarbon and Indian Archaeology.* Bombay, 1971.
SAA	*South Asian Archaeology.* London, 1973.
SA	*Sovetskaya arkheologiya.* Moscow.
SAI	*Svod arkheologicheskikh istochnikov.* Moscow-Leningrad.
SE	*Sovetskaya etnografiya.* Moscow.
SV	*Sovetskoye vostokovedeniye.* Moscow.
TIIAE	*Trudy Instituta istorii, arkheologii i etnografii AN TSSR.* Ashkabad.
TYuTAKE	*Trudy Yuzhno-Turkmenistanskoy arkheologicheskoy kompleksnoy ekspeditsii.* Ashkabad.
USA	*Uspekhi sredneaziatskoy arkheologii.* Leningrad.
VDI	*Vestnik drevney istorii.* Moscow.
VI	*Voprosy istorii.* Moscow.

Plates

Excavation 5, room with figure niches in Layer 6.

Excavation 5, Sanctuary, Layer 5.

Excavation 8, uncovered encircling wall with the gate tower-pylon.

Excavation 10, wall with niches in House 10.

Excavation 9, Leader's House.

Excavation 7, general view of the eastern facade of the monumental complex.

Items 1, 2: *Excavation 5, 4th horizon, burial chamber 47.* Items 3, 4, and 7: *Excavation 1, horizon Altyn 10, burial 296.* Item 5: *Excavation 5, 5th horizon, room 15.* Item 6: *Excavation 1, horizon Altyn 9, burial 282.*

Item 1: *Excavation 5, 5th horizon, room 1.*

Item 2: *Excavation 1, horizon Altyn 4.*

The vessels from Excavation 5 in this plate are from the 1st horizon. Item 1: *Excavation 5*. Item 2: *Excavation 5, room 23*. Item 3: *Excavation 5, room 24*. Items 4, 6, 8, 10, 11, and 12: *Excavation 5, burial chamber 13*. Items 5 and 7: *burial 252*. Items 9 and 15: *Excavation 5, burial 39*. Items 13 and 14: *Excavation 1, upper horizon*.

Item 1: *burial 252*. Item 2: *Excavation 5, 1st horizon, burial chamber 13*. Item 3: *Excavation 5, 4th horizon, room 47*. Item 4: *Excavation 9, room 136*. Item 5: *Excavation 1, horizon Altyn 9, hearth*. Item 6: *Excavation 1, horizon Altyn 10, burial 296*.

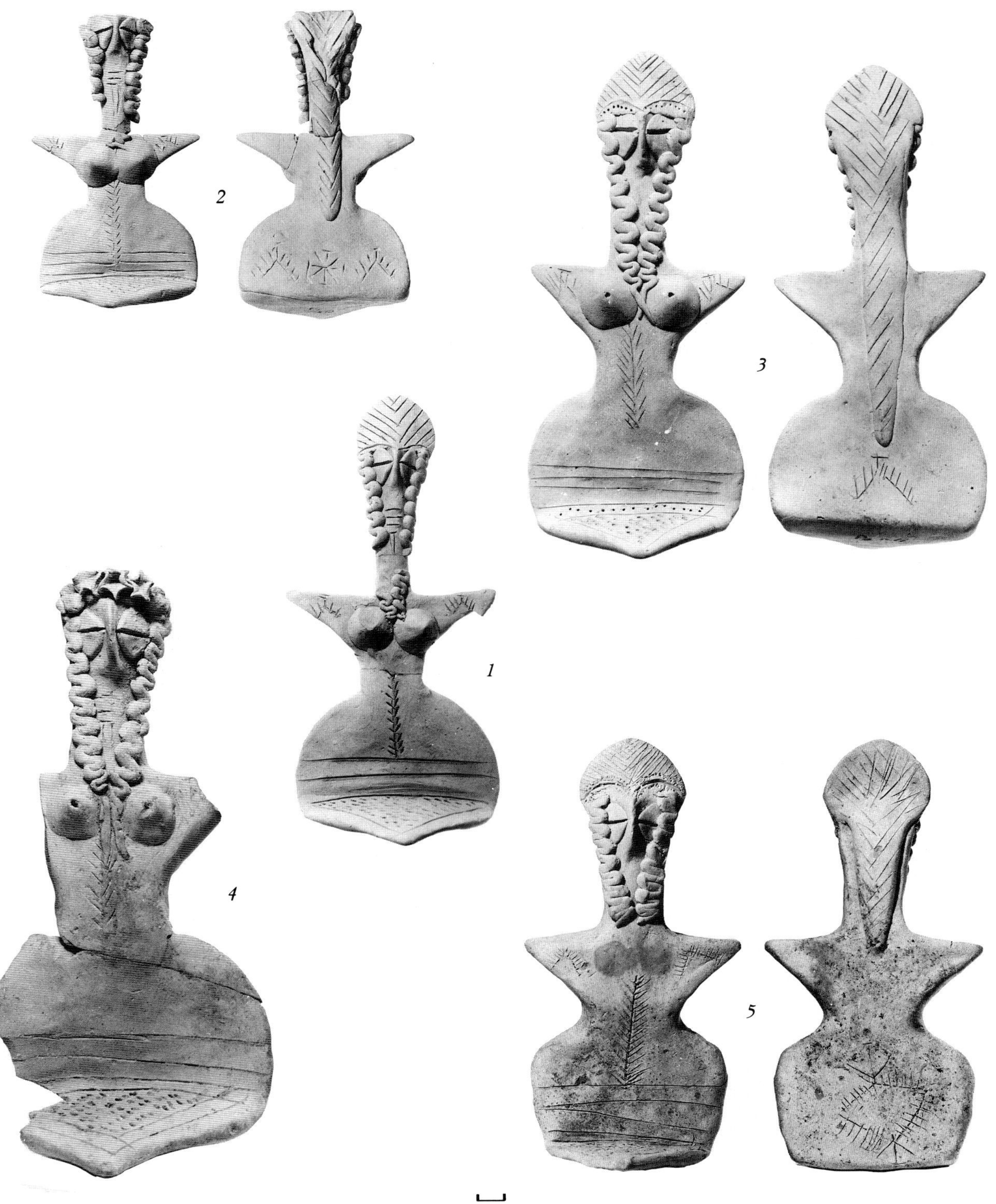

Item 1: *Excavation 9, room 10.* Item 2: *Excavation 9, corridor of burial chamber 9.* Item 3: *Excavation 9, burial chamber 11.* Item 4: *Excavation 9, room 44.* Item 5: *Excavation 5, 1st horizon, burial chamber 13.*

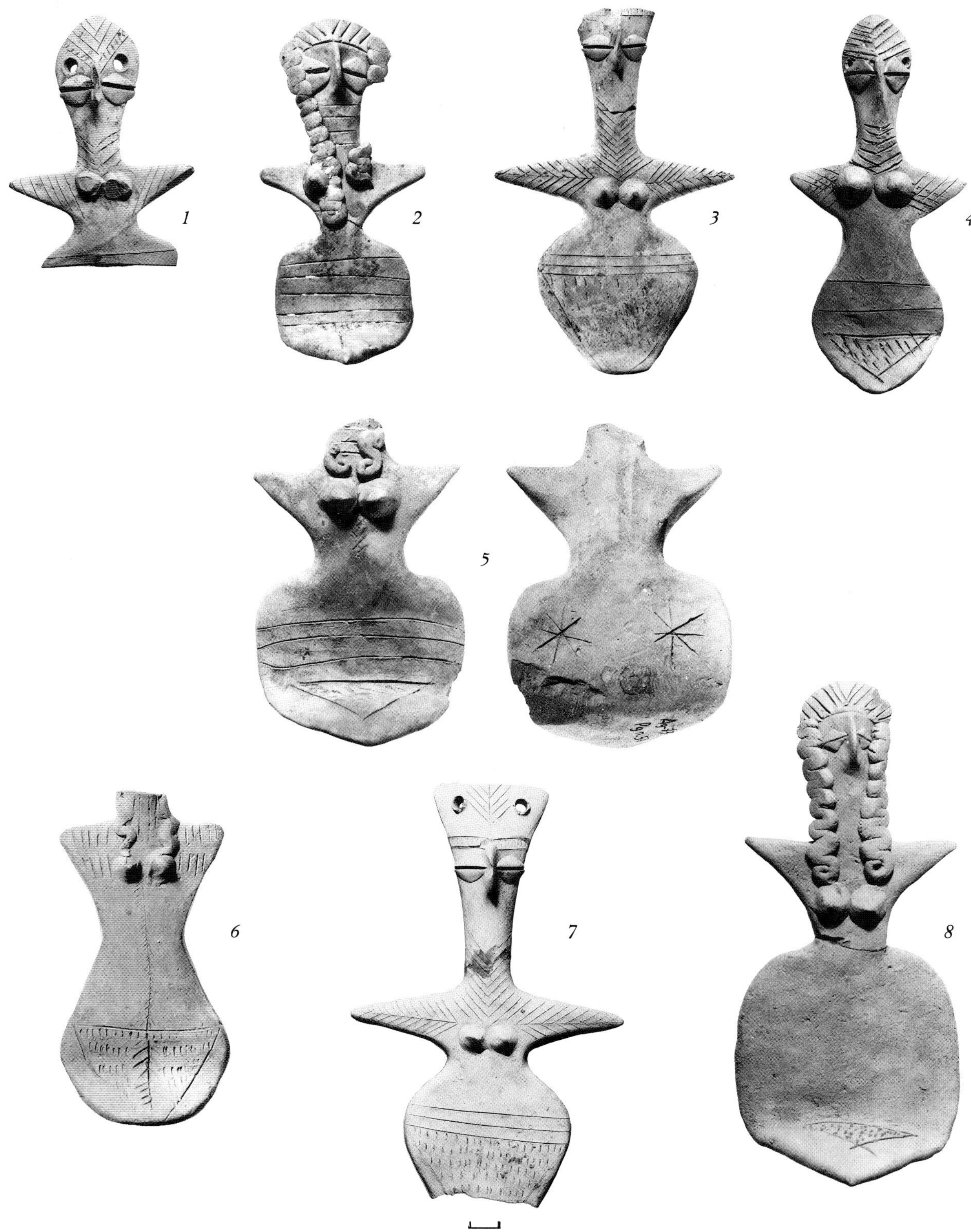

Item 1: *Excavation 9*. Item 2: *Excavation 9, room 124*. Items 3 and 7: *Excavation 9, courtyard B*. Item 4: *Excavation 9, turf layer*. Item 5: *Excavation 9, room 51*. Item 6: *Excavation 9, room 210*. Item 8: *Excavation 10*.

Items 1 and 4: *Excavation 5, 2nd horizon.* Item 2: *Excavation 9, room 125.* Item 3: *Excavation 9, turf layer.*

Item 1: *Excavation 9, Imdugud Street.* Item 2: *Excavation 9, turf layer.* Item 3: *Excavation 9, room 72.* Item 4: *Excavation 9, room 62.* Items 5 and 6: *Excavation 5, 1st horizon, burial 60.*

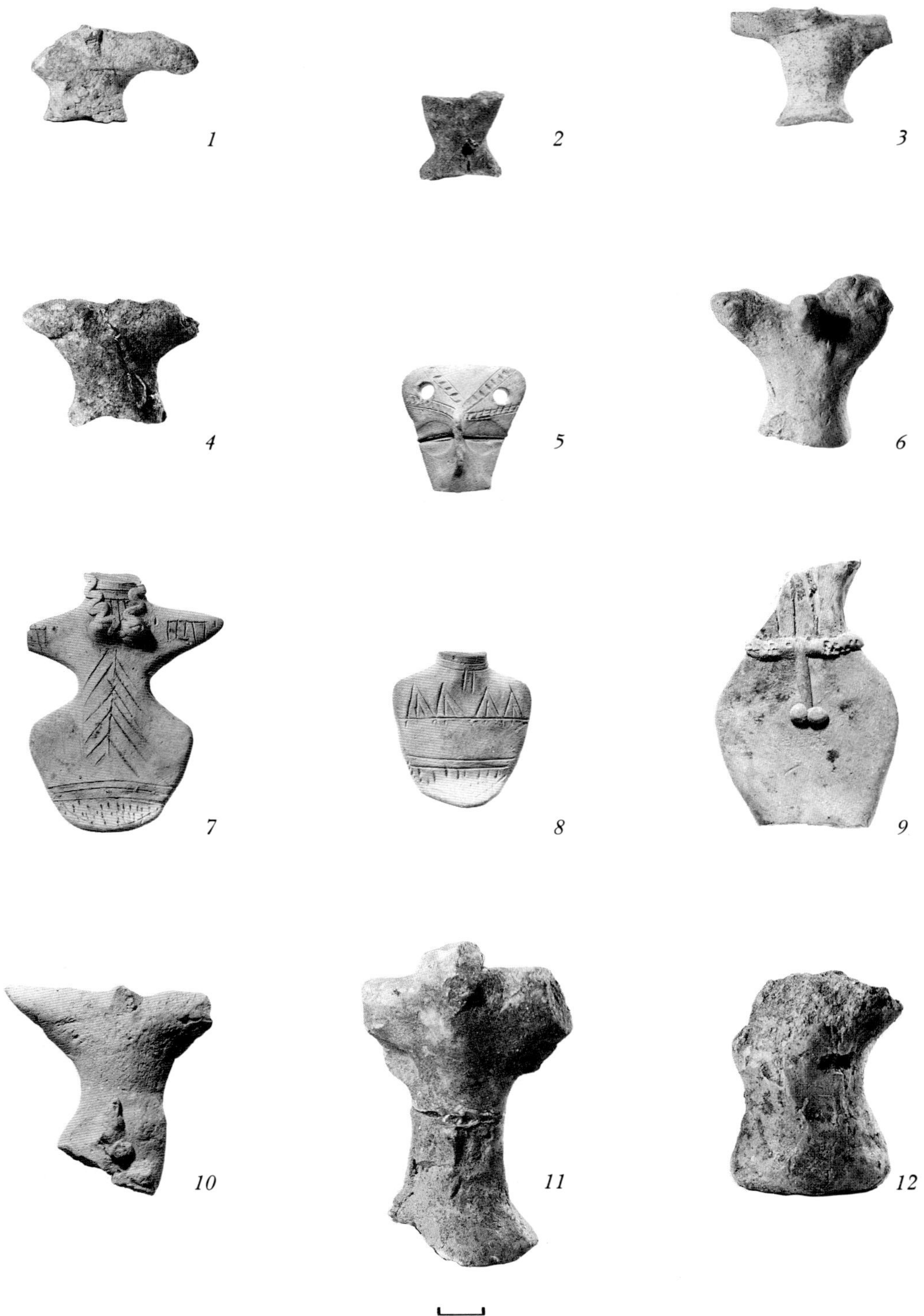

Items 1 to 6 and 10 to 12: *Excavation 1, horizon Altyn 3*. Item 7: *Excavation 8, room 25*. Item 8: *surface material*. Item 9: *Excavation 5, turf layer*.

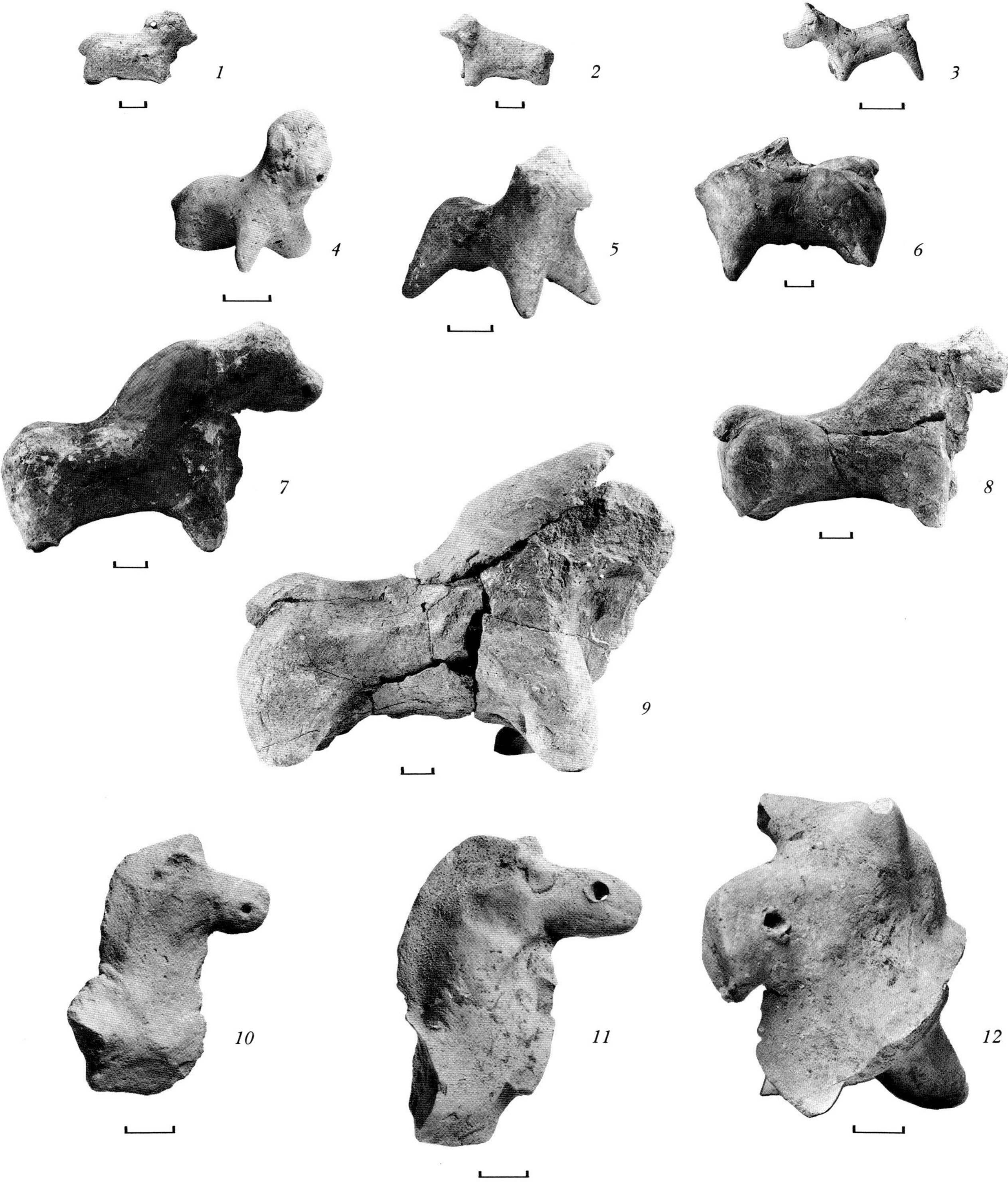

Items 1 to 3 and 6 to 9: *Excavation 1, horizon Altyn 3*. Item 4: *Excavation 9, room 110/114*. Item 5: *Excavation 9, room 115*. Item 10: *Excavation 7, lower horizon*. Item 11: *Excavation 8, room 32*. Item 12: *Excavation 9, room 152*.

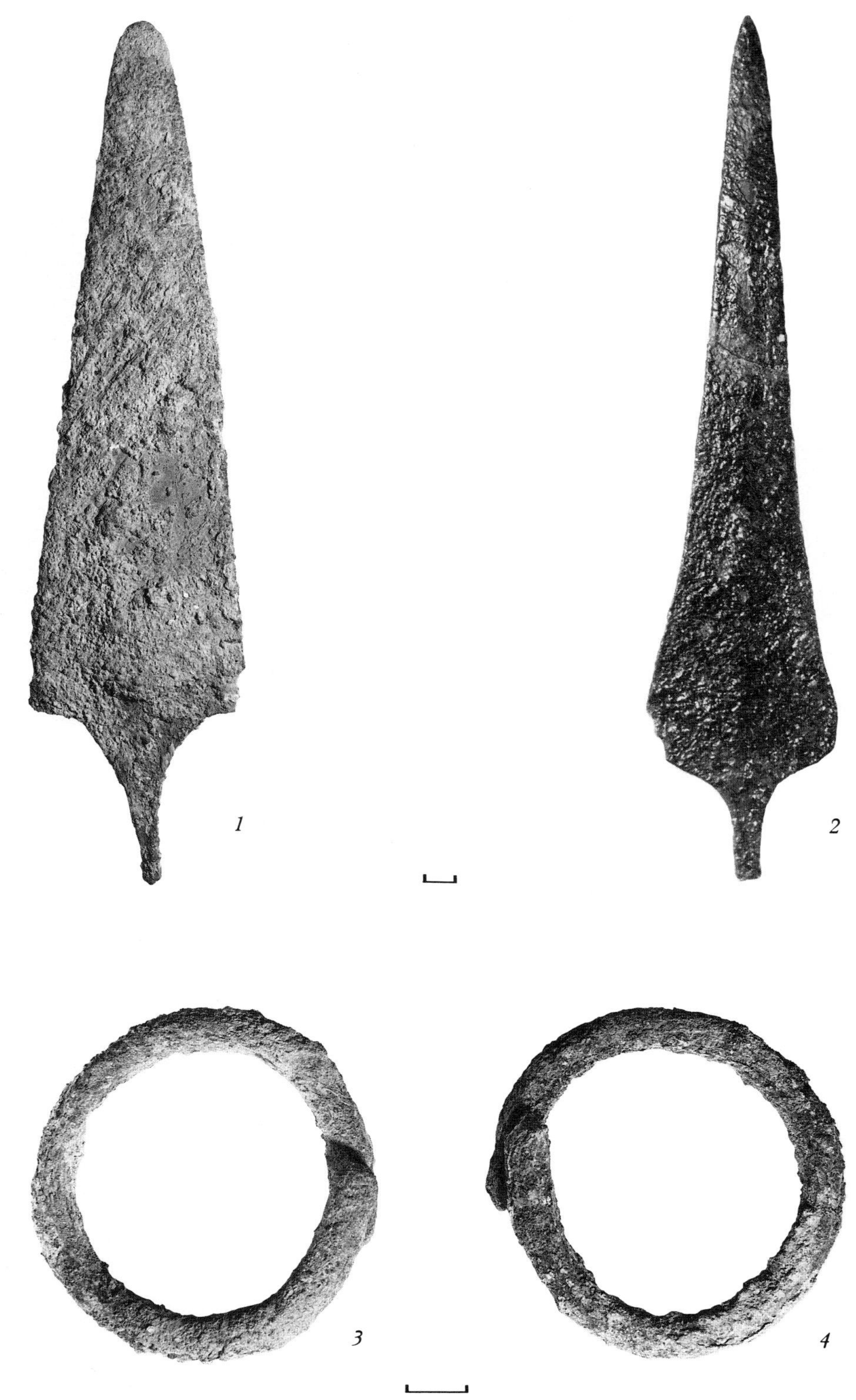

Item 1: *Excavation 1, burial 4*. Item 2: *Excavation 8, room 25*. Items 3 and 4: *surface material*.

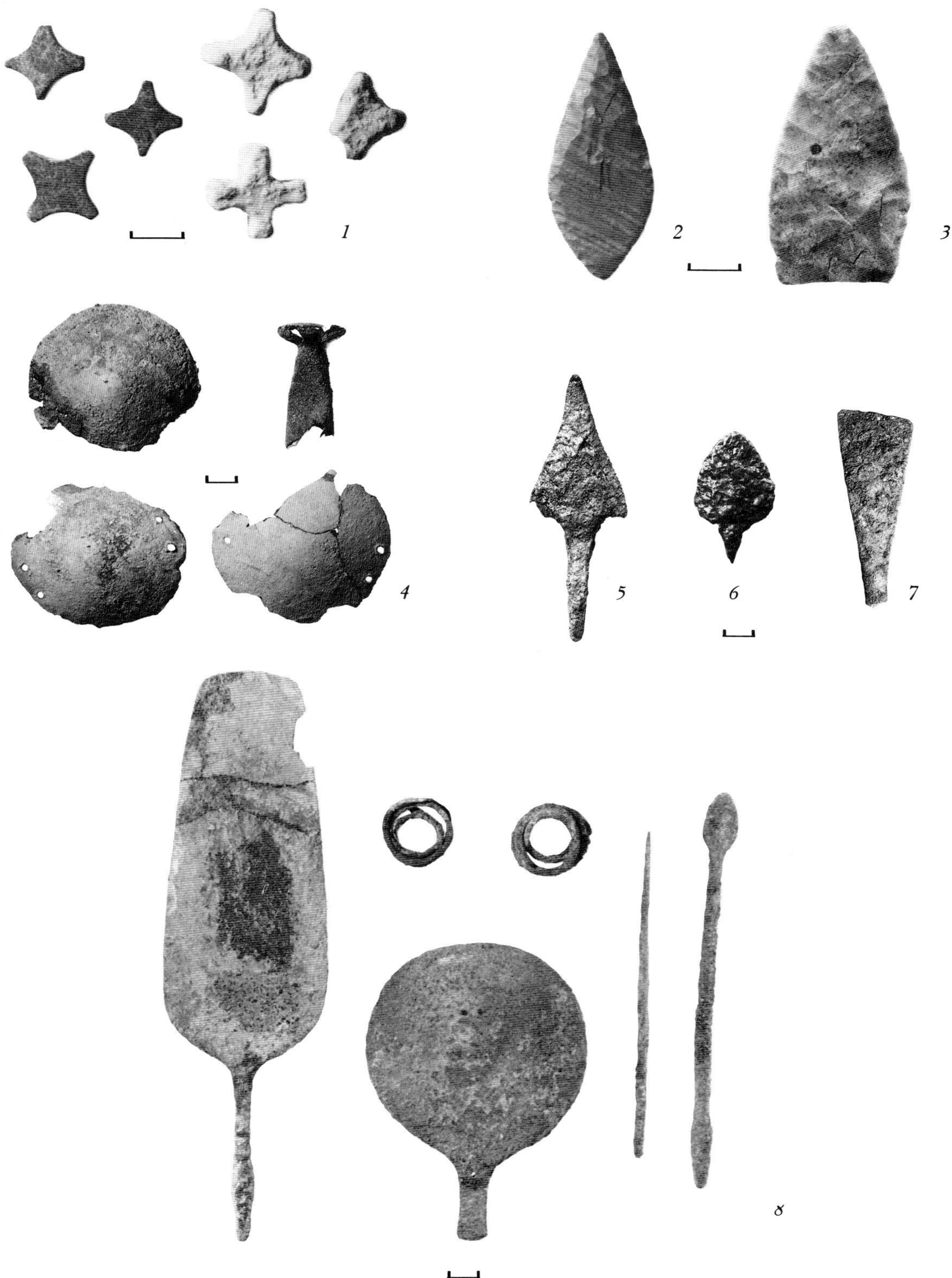

Items 1, 2, and 4: *Excavation 7, priest's tomb, room 7.* Item 3: *Excavation 9, turf layer.* Item 5: *Excavation 5, 3rd horizon.* Item 6: *Excavation 10, turf layer.* Item 7: *Excavation 11, Level XIX.* Item 8: *burial 252.*

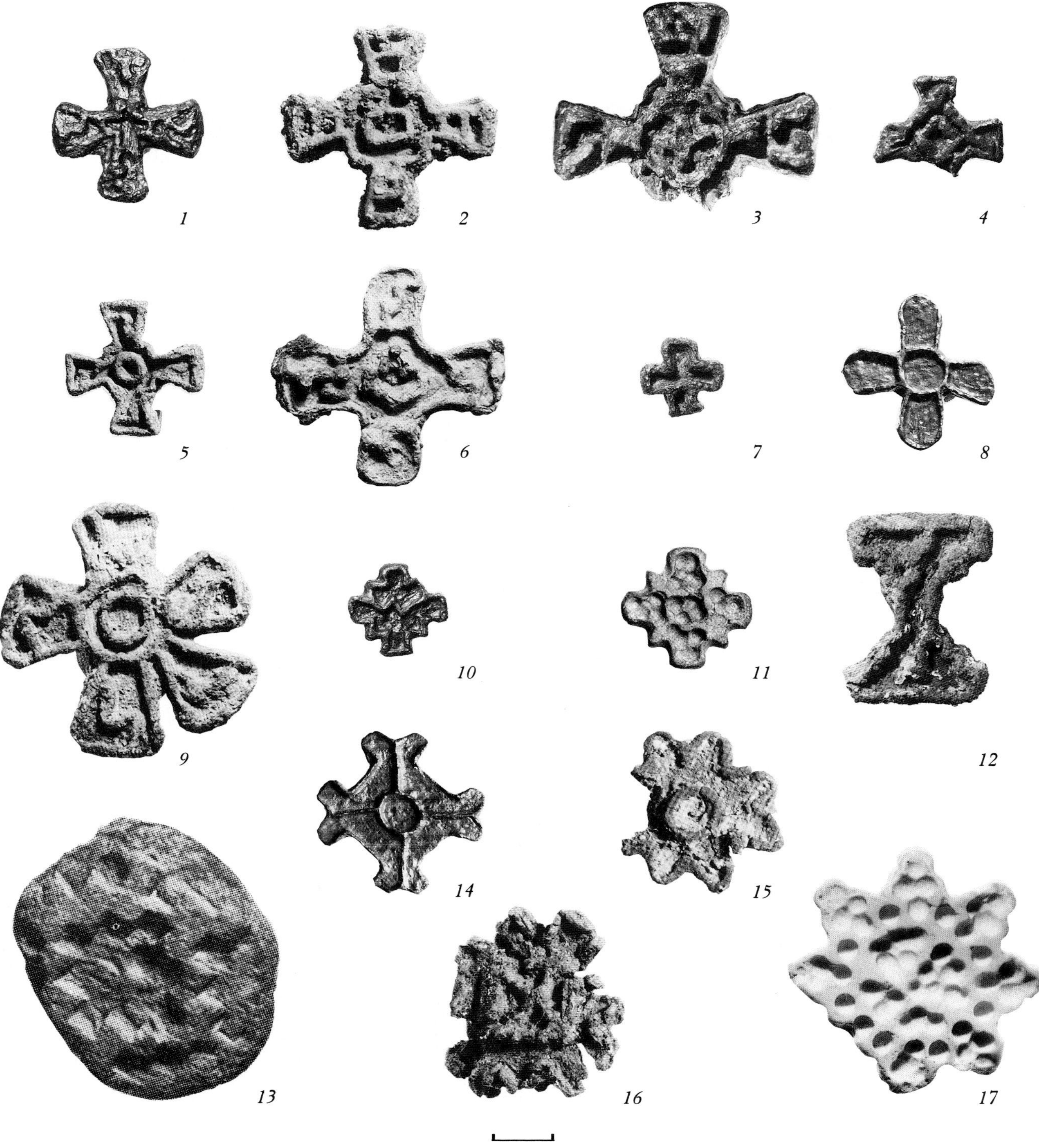

Items 1 to 10, 12, and 14 to 16 are metal; 11 and 17 are stone; 13 is terracotta. Item 1: *Excavation 9, burial chamber 9.* Items 2 to 4, 8, and 13 to 17: *surface material.* Item 5: *Excavation 9, burial chamber 125.* Item 6: *Excavation 9, burial chamber 124.* Item 7: surface material, Central Square. Item 9: *Excavation 9, room 58.* Item 10: *surface material, Craftmen's Quarters.* Item 11: *Excavation 7, priest's tomb, room 7.* Item 12: *Excavation 5, 2nd horizon, burial 271.*

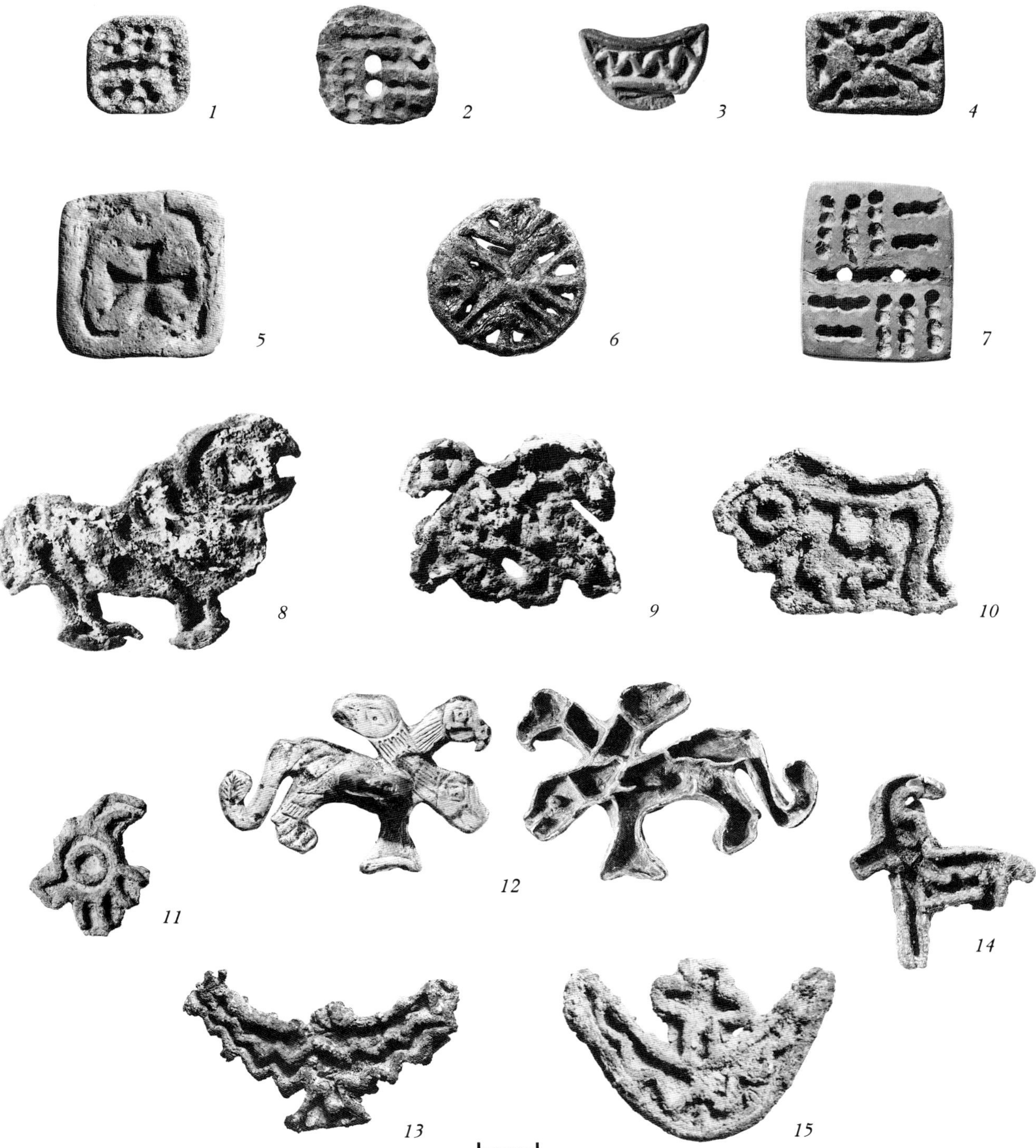

Items 1, 2, 4, and 7 are stone; 3 and 5 are terracotta; the others are metal. Items 1, 2, 4, and 6: *surface finds*. Item 3: *Excavation 9, eastern part of courtyard A*. Item 5: *Excavation 11*. Item 7: *Excavation 8*. Item 8: *Excavation 9, room 60*. Item 9: *Excavation 7, priest's tomb, room 10, burial 235*. Items 10 and 14: *Excavation 5, 1st horizon, burial chamber 13*. Item 11: *surface material, Concentration of Living Quarters*. Item 12: *Excavation 5, 1st horizon, burial 60*. Item 13: *Excavation 9, burial chamber 125*. Item 15: *Excavation 9, burial chamber 124*.

Item 1: *Excavation 1, horizon Altyn 6.*

Item 2: *Excavation 9, room 118.*

Item 1: *terracotta model of a vehicle, Excavation 5.*

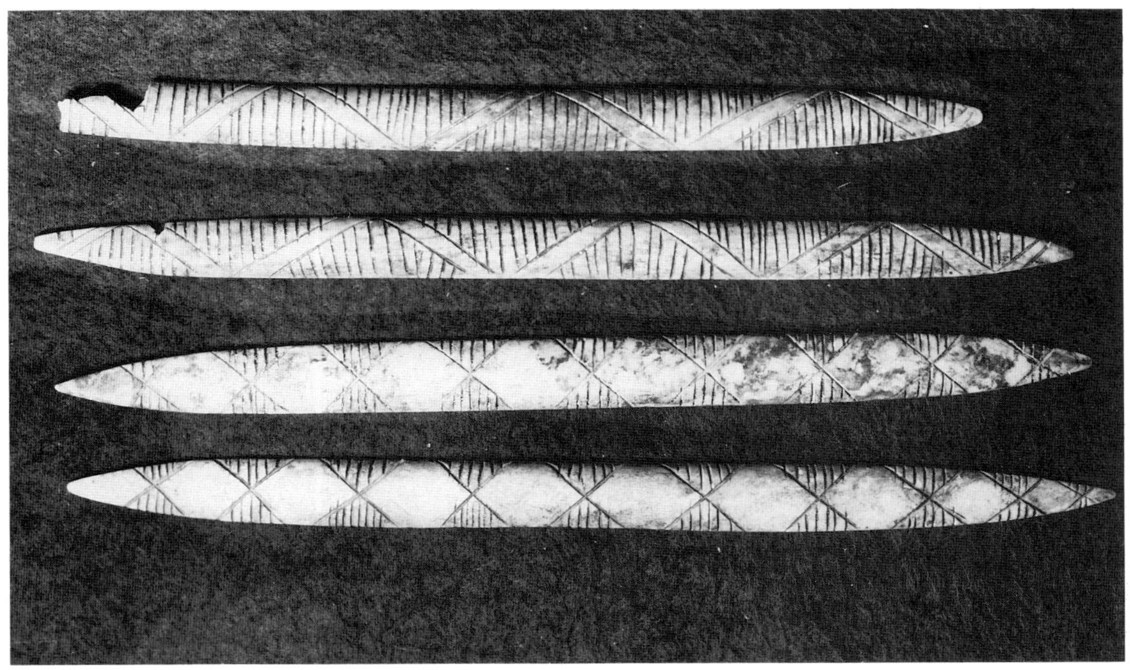

Item 2: *bone sticks, Excavation 7, priest's tomb, room 7.*

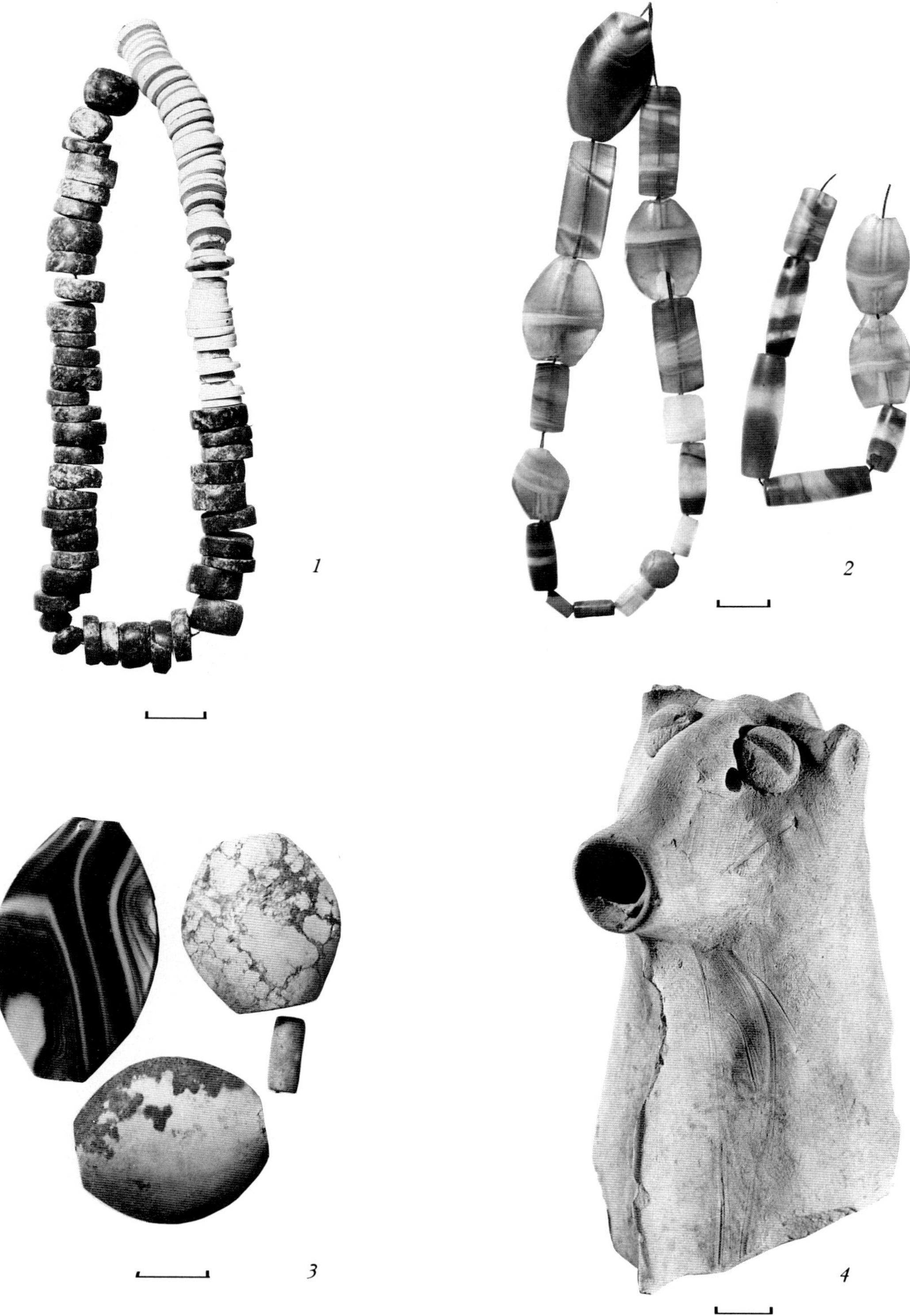

Items 1 to 3 are stone and elephant ivory beads. Items 1 and 2: *Excavation 7, priest's tomb, room 7.* Item 3: *burial 362.* Item 4: *zoomorphic pourer, Excavation 5, street.*

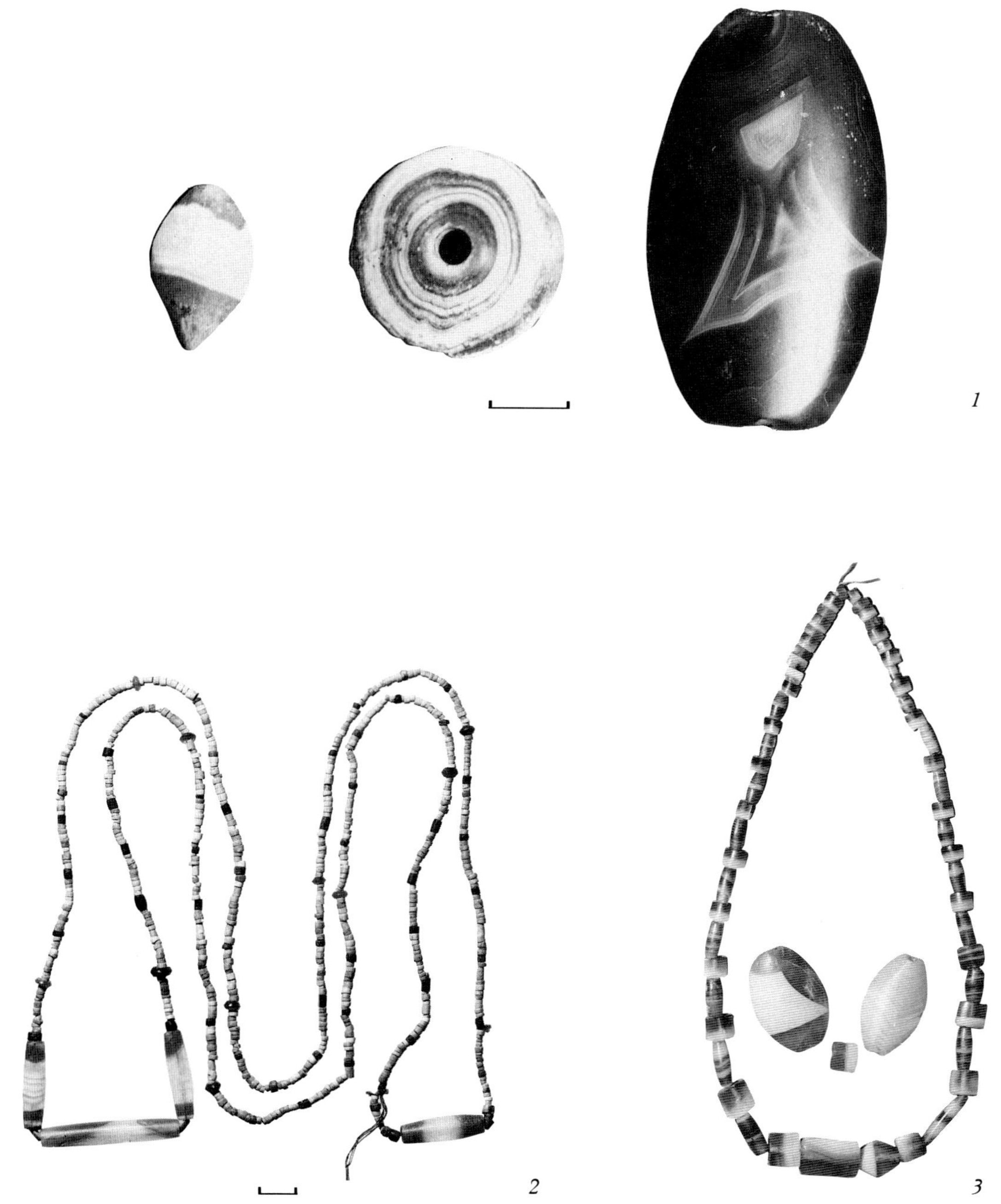

Items 1 and 2; *Excavation 7, priest's tomb, room 7*. Item 3: *Excavation 5, 1st horizon, burial 60.*

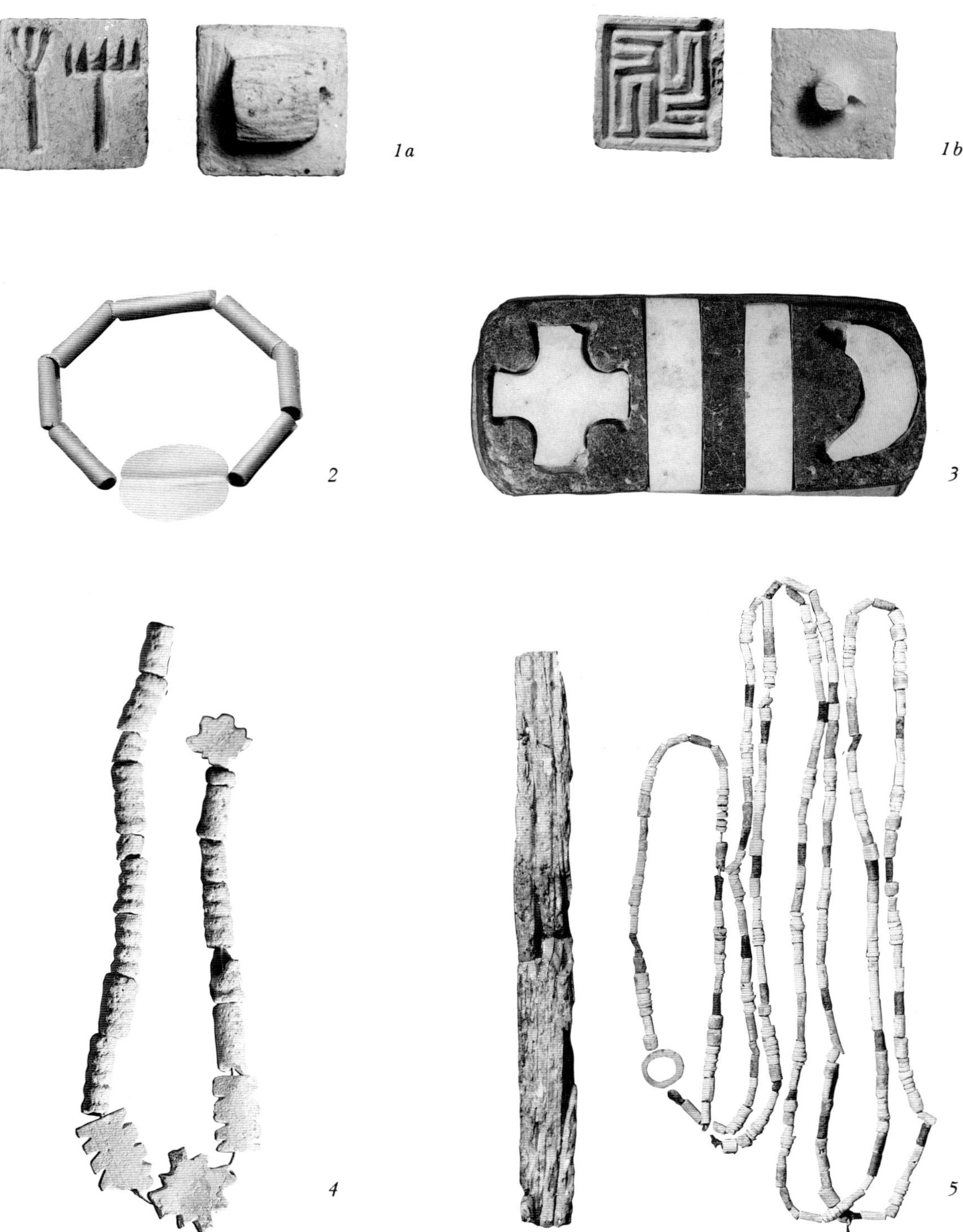

Item 1a: *seal of proto-Indian type, Excavation 9.* Item 1b: *seal of proto-Indian type, Excavation 7, priest's tomb, room 7.* Item 2: *gold beads, Excavation 7, priest's tomb, room 7.* Item 3: *stone plaque, Excavation 7, priest's tomb, room 7.* Item 4: *elephant ivory beads, Excavation 5, 1st horizon, burial 41.* Item 5: *elephant ivory beads and stick, burial 252.*

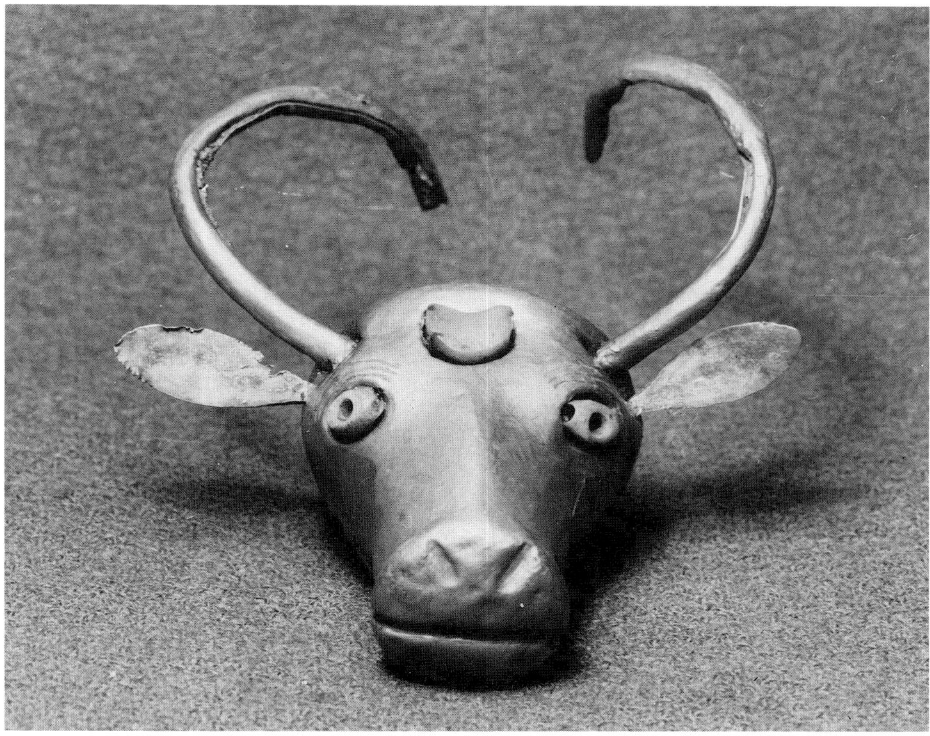

Item 1: *gold head of a bull, Excavation 7, priest's tomb, room 7.*

Item 2: *gold head of a wolf, Excavation 7, priest's tomb, room 7.*

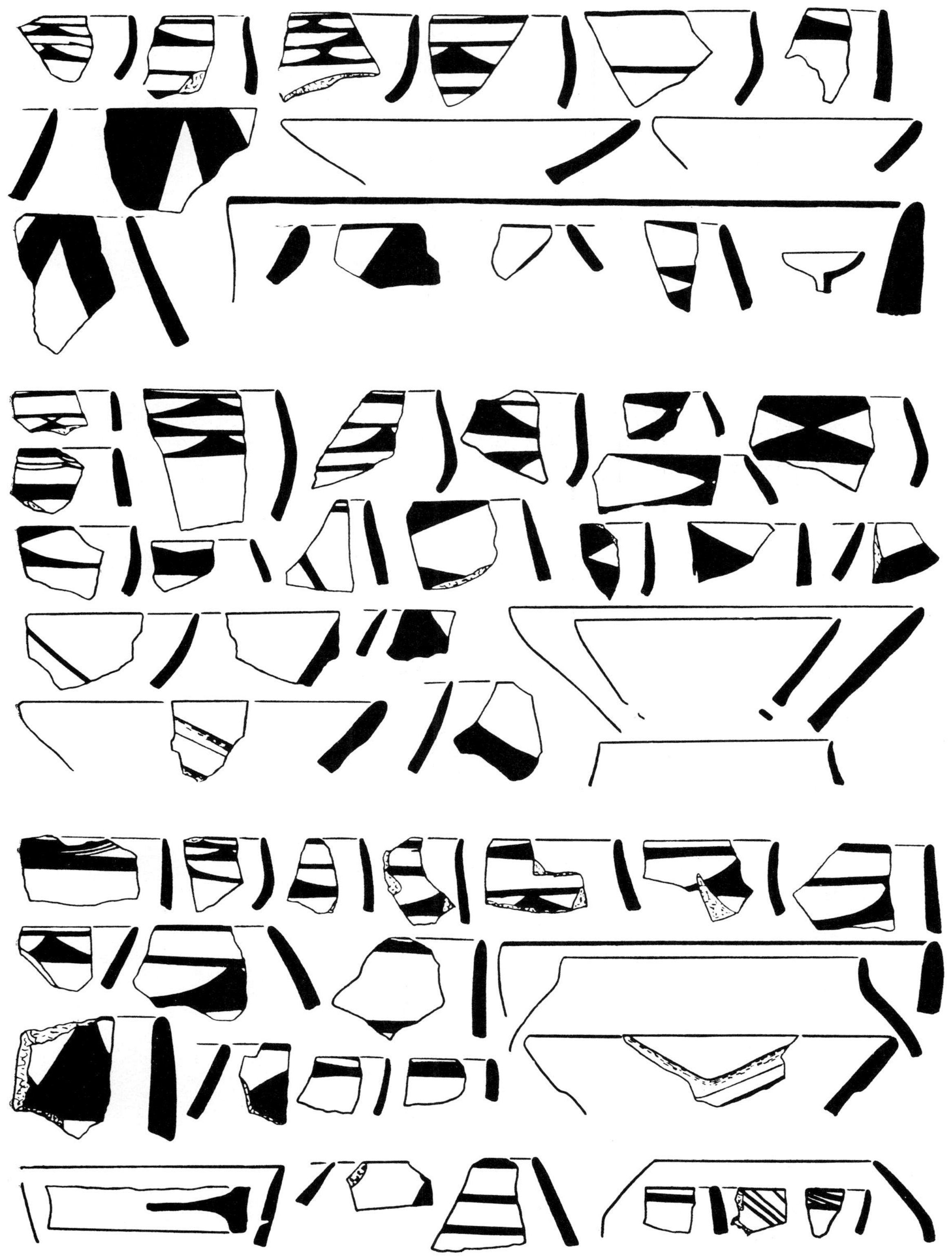

Trench of Excavation 11.

Excavation 1, horizon Altyn 10.

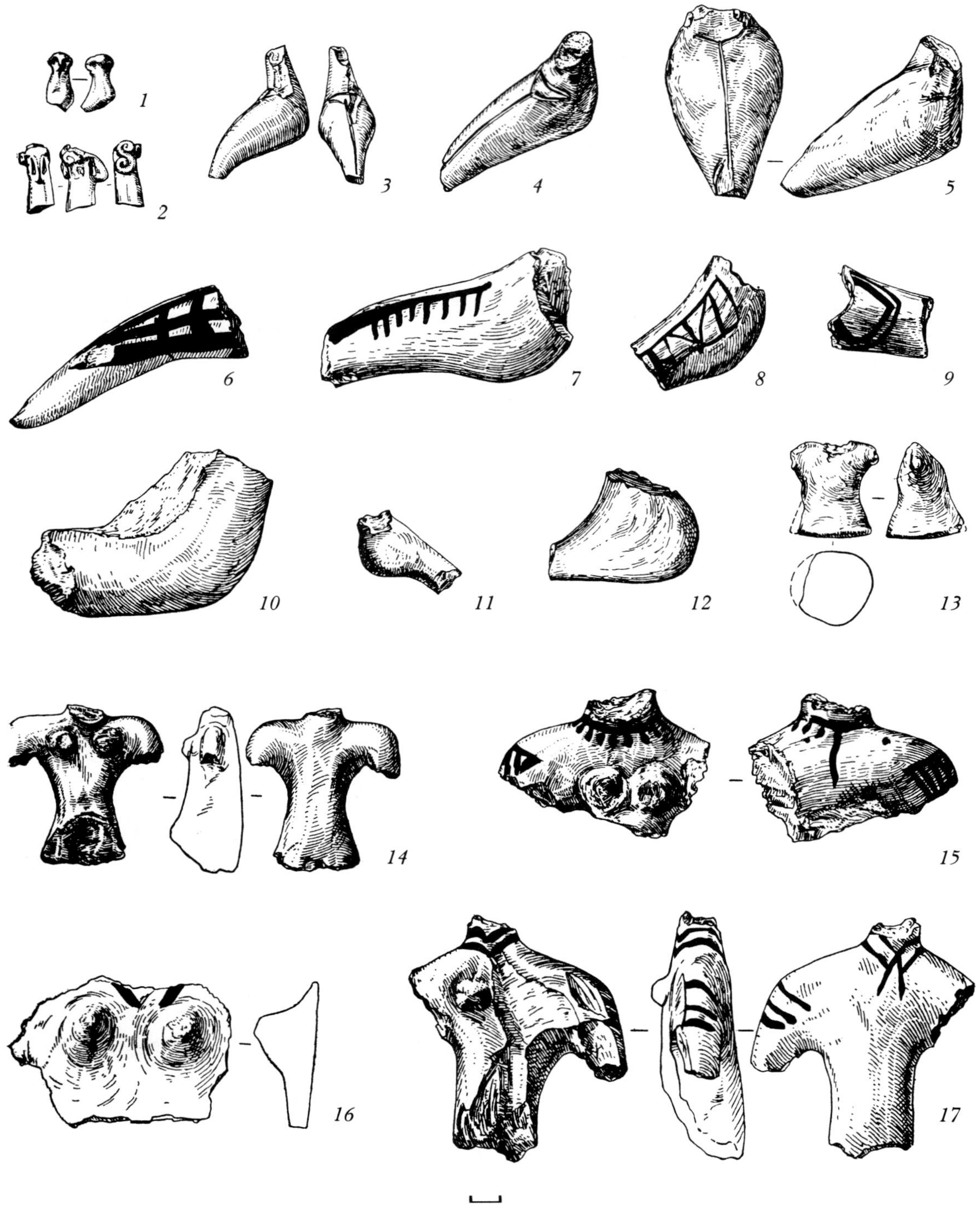

Items 1 to 12 and 14 to 17 are female statuettes; 13 is anthropomorphic. Item 1: *trench 2, 1st horizon*. Item 2: *trench 2, 3rd horizon*. Item 3: *trench of Excavation 11, Level V*. Item 4: *trench 2, 4th horizon*. Item 5: *trench 2, 2nd horizon*. Items 6 and 13: *Excavation 1, Level XXXVI*. Item 7: *Excavation 1, Level XXXIII*. Item 8: *Excavation 1, Level XXXVI*. Items 9, 10, 12, and 14: Excavation 1, horizon Altyn 13. Item 11: *Excavation 1, horizon Altyn 14*. Item 15: *Excavation 1, Level XXXVI*. Item 16: *trench of Excavation 11, Level XVII*. Item 17: *Excavation 1, horizon Altyn 10*.

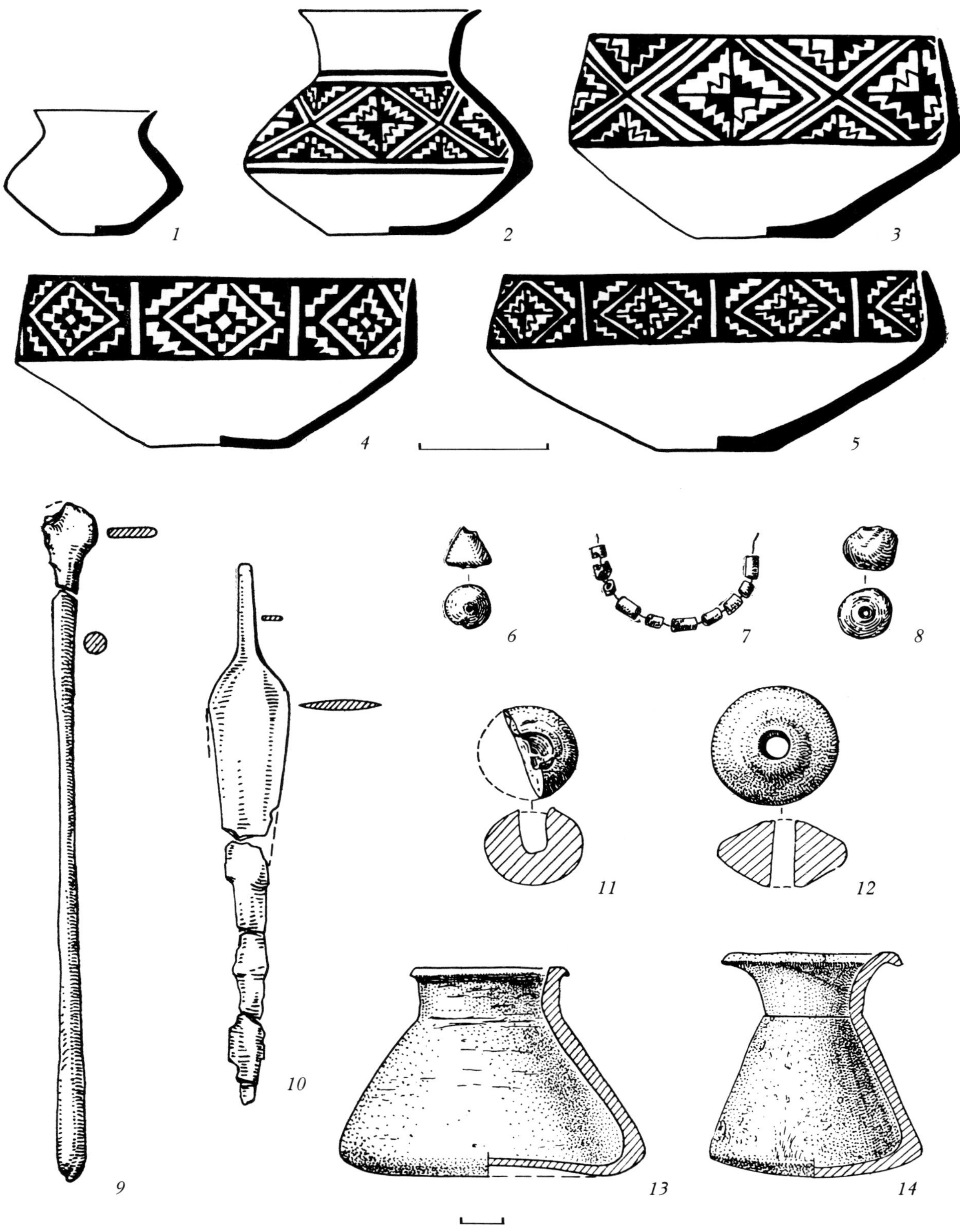

Excavation 1, horizon Altyn 10. Items 1 to 5: *painted pottery*. Items 6 to 8, and 12: *beads*. Items 9 and 10: *copper artifacts*. Item 11: *lid*. Items 13 and 14: *stone vessels*.

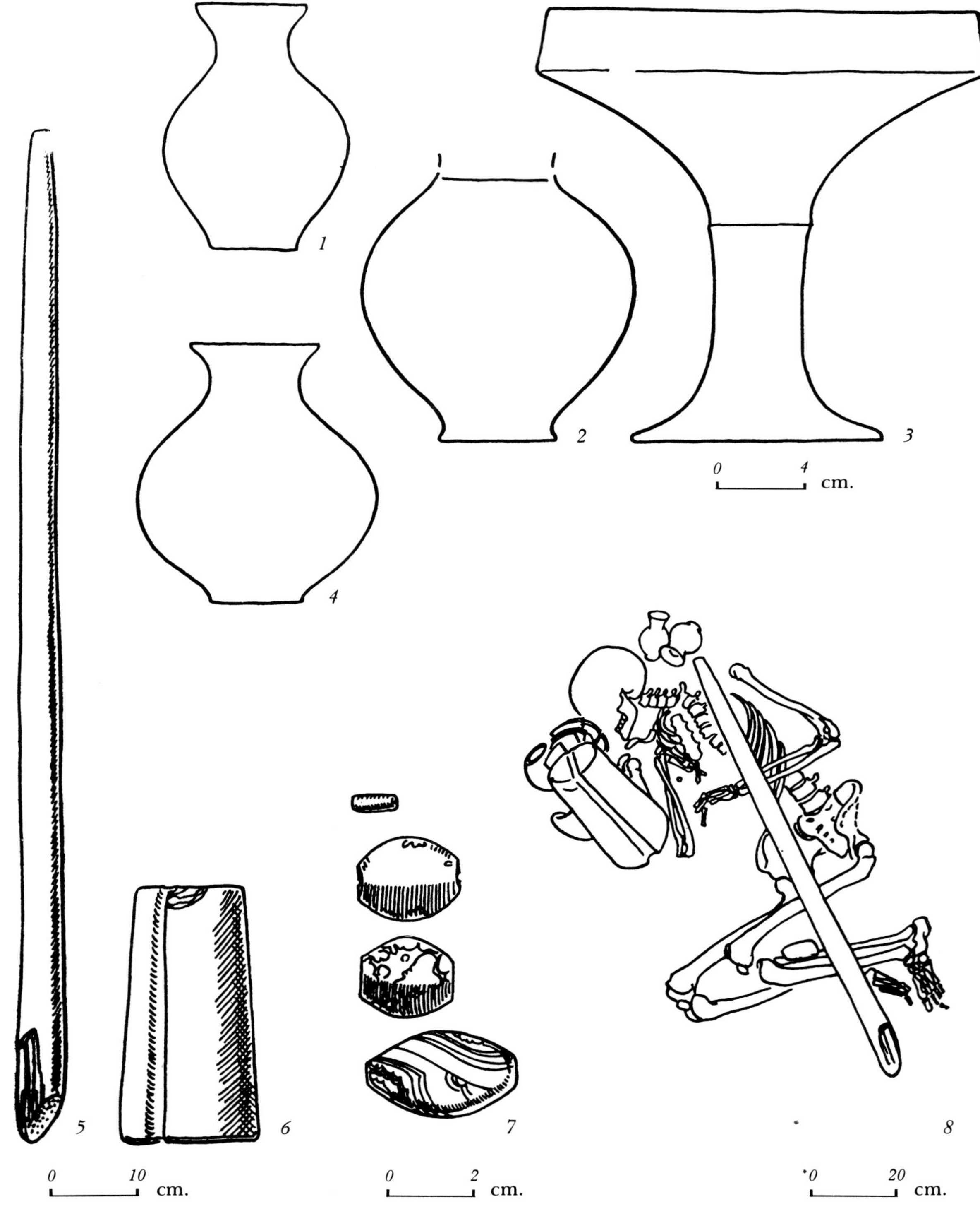

Excavation 9, room 110. Items 1 to 4: *ceramic vessels.* Items 5 and 6: *stone objects.* Item 7: *beads.* Item 8: *distribution of grave goods in the burial.*

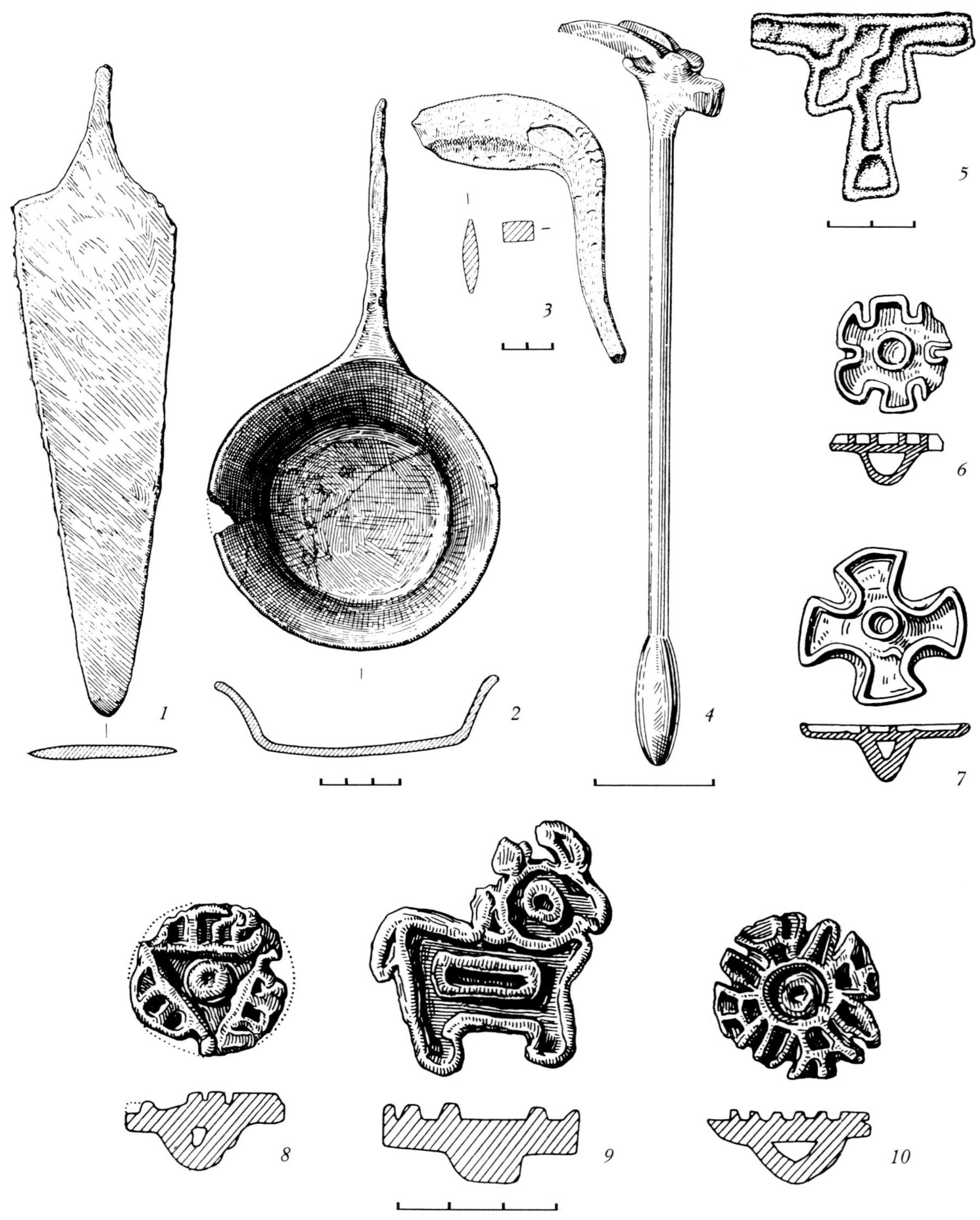

Items 1 and 2: *Excavation 1, horizon Altyn 2, burial 4*. Item 3: *Excavation 13*. Items 4, 6, and 7: *Excavation 10, burial 109*. Item 5: *Excavation 9, room 130*. Items 8 to 10: *seals from Namazga V layers (excavations of 1959-1961)*.

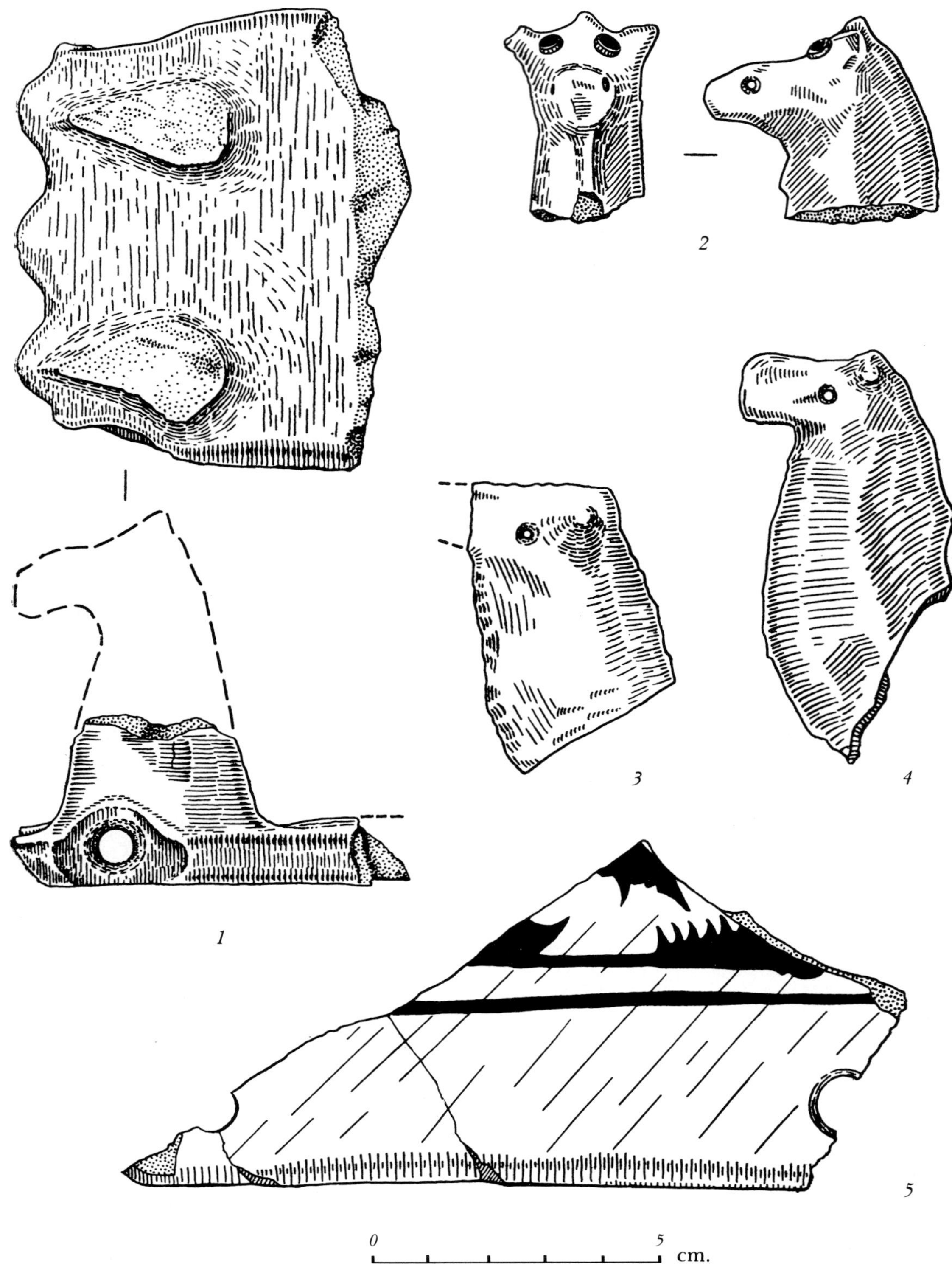

Item 1: *Excavation 9, room 37.* Item 2: *Excavation 7, lower horizon, courtyard B.* Item 3: *Excavation 9, room 37.* Items 4 and 5: *Excavation 7, lower horizon, courtyard A.*

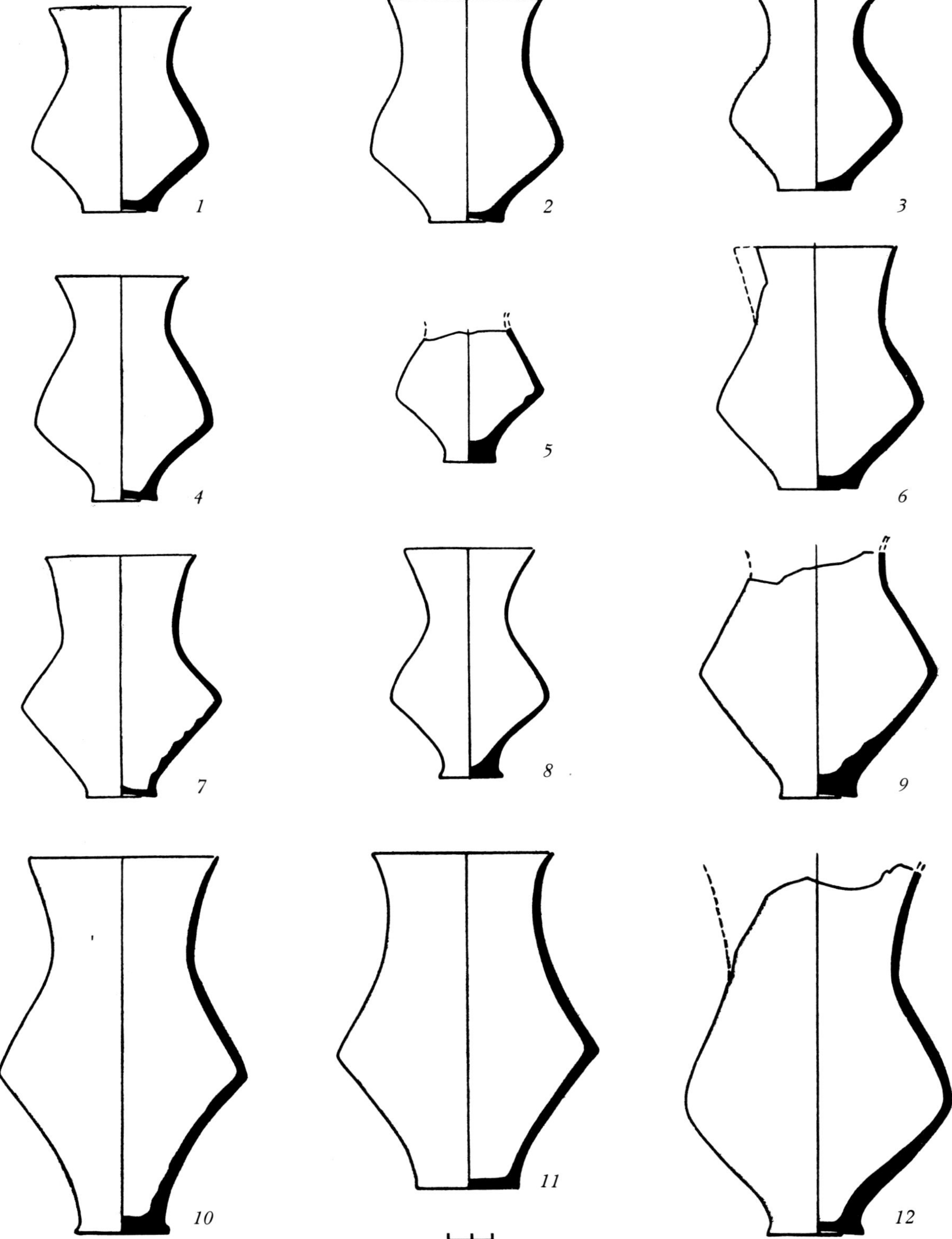

Item 1: *Excavation 1, upper horizon, room 12.* Items 2 to 12: *Excavation 7, lower horizon, room 32 (excavations of 1969).*

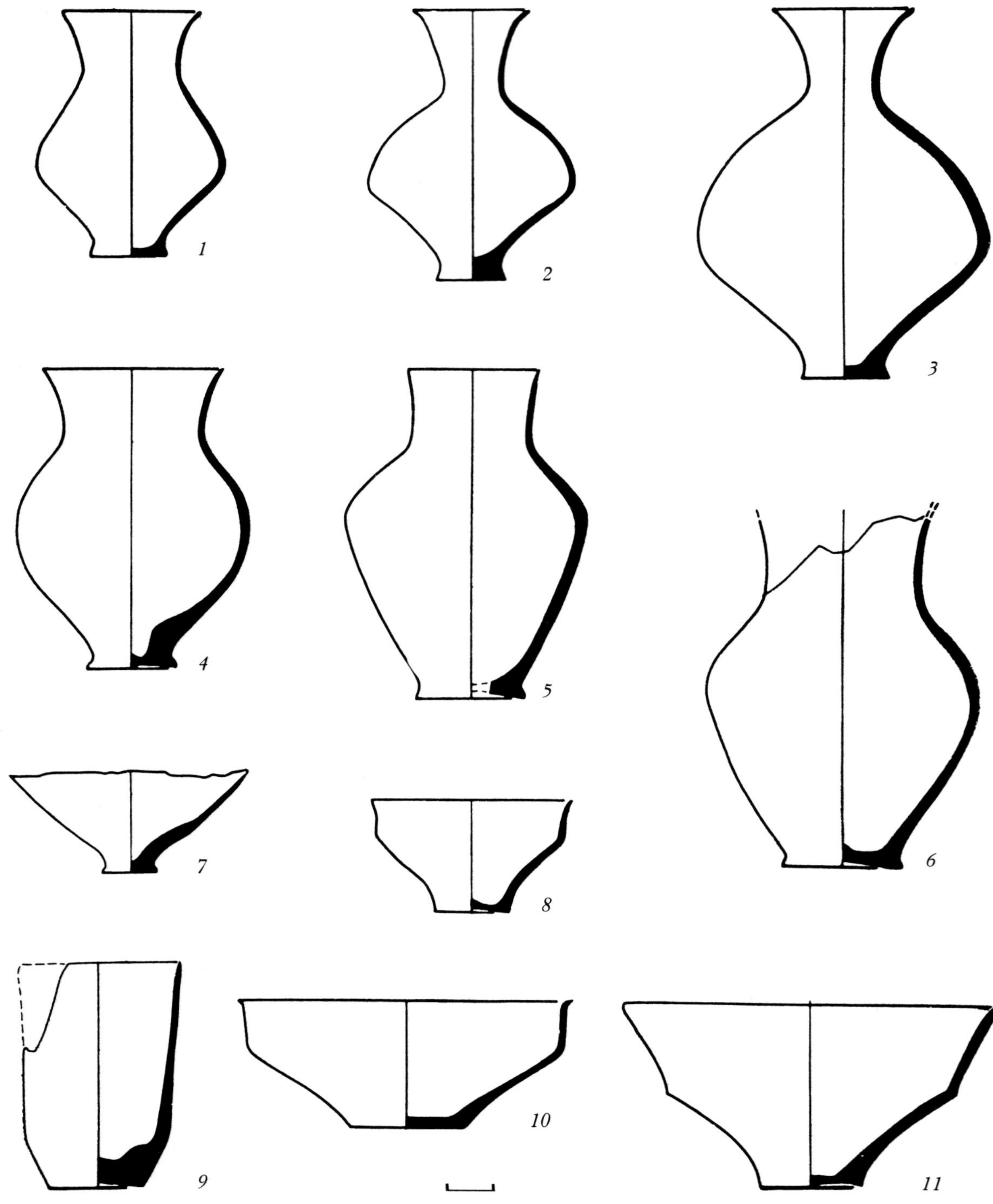

Items 1 to 3, 7, 8, and 11: *Excavation 7, room 32 (excavations of 1969)*. Item 4: *Excavation 10, room 3 (excavations of 1969)*. Items 5 and 9: *Excavation 9, room 5*. Item 6: *Excavation 9, Leader's House*. Item 10: *Excavation 10*.

Items 1 to 28: *Excavation 9, burial chamber 9.*

Items 1 to 11: *Excavation 9, burial chamber 124*. Items 12 to 17: *Excavation 7, lower horizon, burials 240-241*. Items 18, 20, 26, and 28: *Excavation 7, lower horizon, room 7*. Items 21 to 25, and 30: *Excavation 7, lower horizon, room 9*. Items 19, 27, and 29: *Excavation 7, lower horizon, room 10*.

Altyn-Depe excavations of 1972 and 1981. Items 1 to 3 are miniature "columns" from Excavation 9. Item 1: *burial 362.* Item 2: *locality 289, upper floor.* Item 3: *locality 329.* Item 4: *weight, Excavation 7, horizon 3, locality 7, sanctuary of the priest's tomb.* Item 5: *"mace," Excavation 7, horizon 3, locality 7, sanctuary of the priest's tomb.* Item 6: *weight, Excavation 7, horizon 2, localities 5 and 6.* Item 7: *miniature "column," Excavation 7, horizon 3, locality 7, sanctuary of the priest's tomb.* Excavations of 1984. Item 8: *stone vessel, Excavation 5, horizon 9, burial 828.* Excavations of 1983. Items 9a, 9b, and 9c: *stone vessels and statuette, Excavation 9, burial 813.*

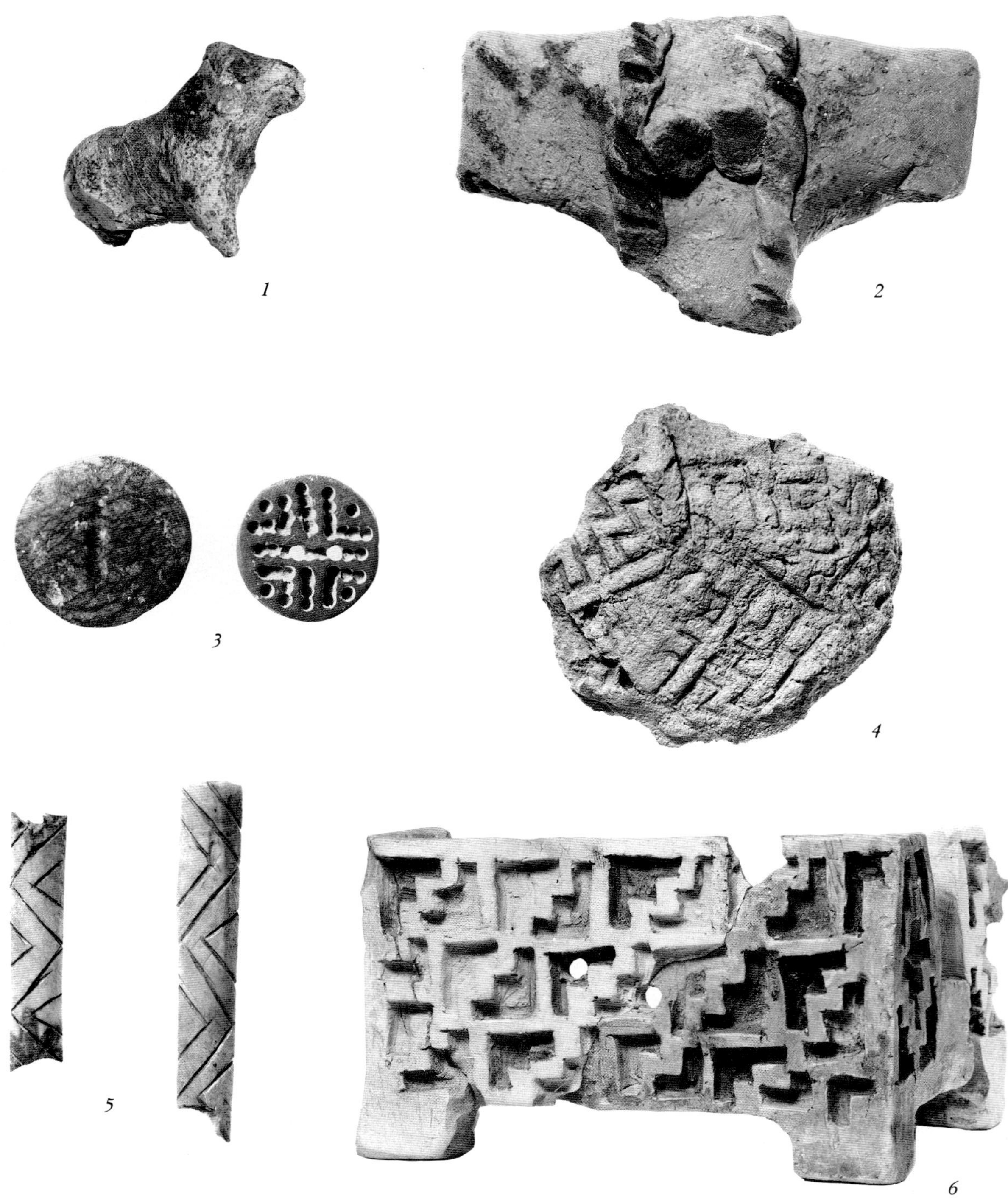

Altyn-Depe excavations of 1982 to 1984. Item 1: *clay, horizon 9, courtyard A*. Item 2: *terracotta, horizon 9, locality 12*. Item 3: *stone, horizon 8*. Item 4: *terracotta, horizon 8, locality 6*. Item 5: *bone, horizon 9, courtyard A*. Item 6: *terracotta, horizon 8, locality 20*.

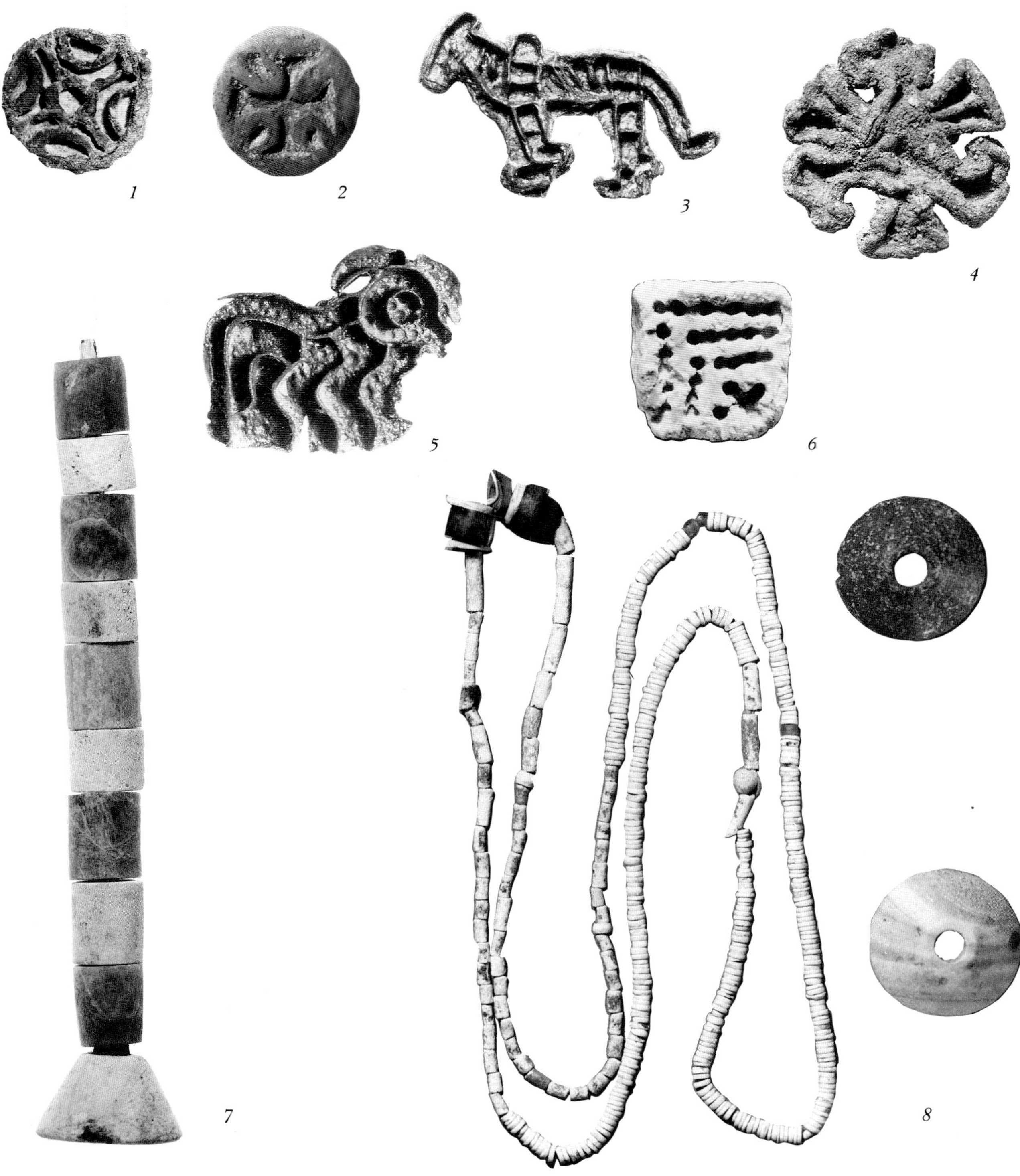

Altyn-Depe excavations of 1981. Items 1 to 6 are seals. Item 1: *bronze, Excavation 9*. Item 2: *terracotta, Excavation 9, courtyard R*. Items 3 to 5 are bronze. Item 3: *surface find on the Tower Mound*. Item 4: *Excavation 9, locality 254*. Item 5: *surface find on the Tower Mound*. Item 6: *Excavation 9, locality 331*. Item 7: *composite mace, Excavation 9, burial 695*. Item 8: *beads, Excavation 9, burial 705*.

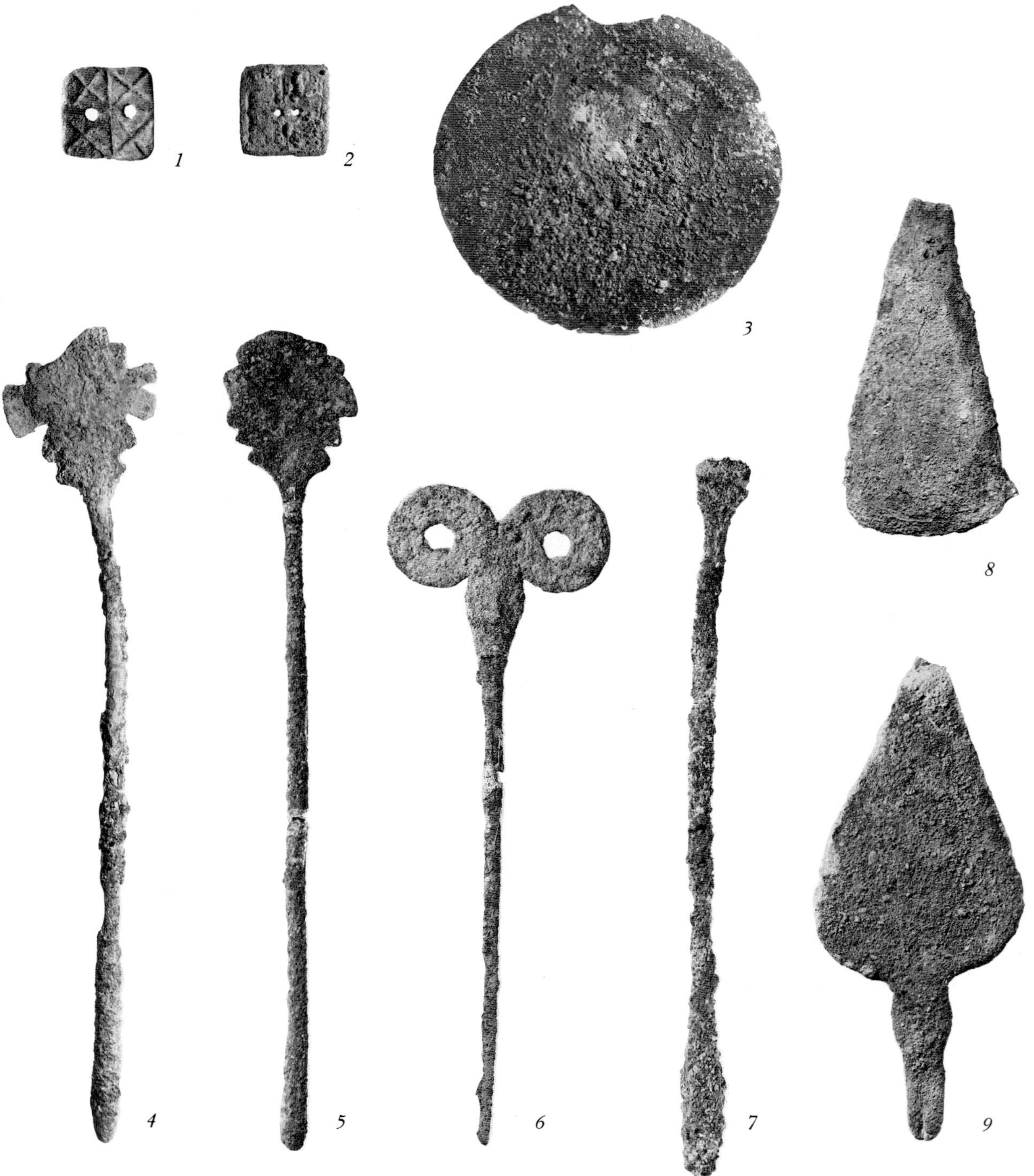

Altyn-Depe excavations of 1981 to 1985. Excavation 5. Item 1: *seal, bone, horizon 9, burial 843*. Items 2 to 9 are bronze. Item 2: *seal, horizon 9, burial 843*. Item 3: *brooch, horizon 9, burial 845*. Items 4, 5, and 7 are rods thickened at one end and splayed at the other (maces?). Item 4: *horizon 9, burial 845*. Item 5: *horizon 9, burial 828*. Item 6: *pin with double spiral, horizon 8, burial 736*. Item 8: *adze, horizon 9, burial chamber 3*. Item 9: *knife or dart, horizon 8, locality 29*.

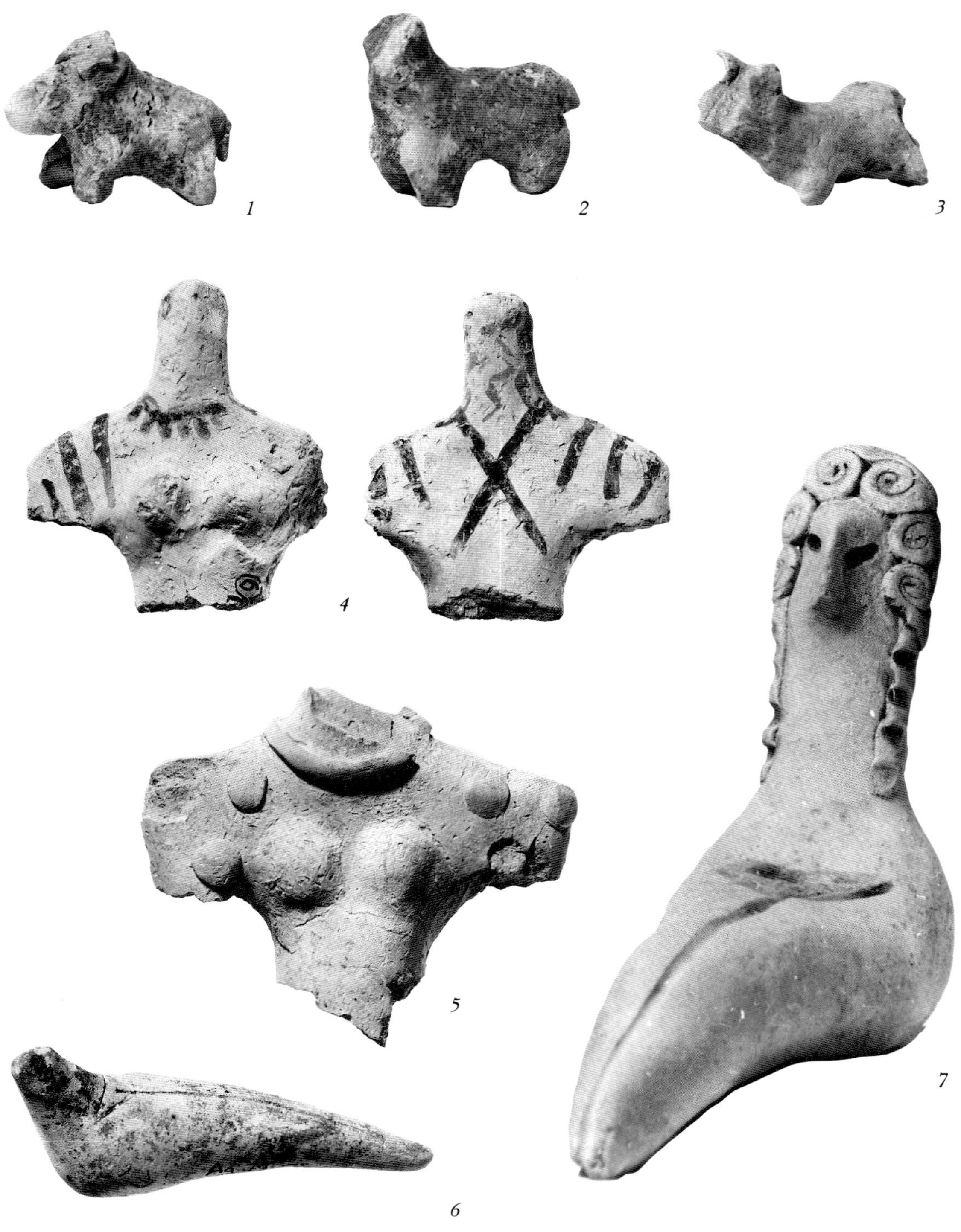

Altyn-Depe excavations of 1979 to 1983. Items 1 to 3 are terracotta statuettes of animals. Item 1: *Excavation 8.* Items 2 and 3: *Excavation 1, horizon Altyn 9.* Items 4 to 7 are terracotta statuettes of goddesses. Item 4: *Excavation 14, beyond the upper wall.* Item 5: *Excavation 8, layer 15.* Item 6: *Excavation 8, layer 14.* Item 7: *Excavation 15, burial chamber 2.*

Altyn-Depe excavations of 1981 and 1982. Excavation 9. Item 1: *locality 317*. Item 2: *burial 782*. Items 3 and 4: *courtyard O, burial 718*. Item 5: *burial chamber 321*. Item 6: *burial 721*. Item 7: *burial chamber 281*.

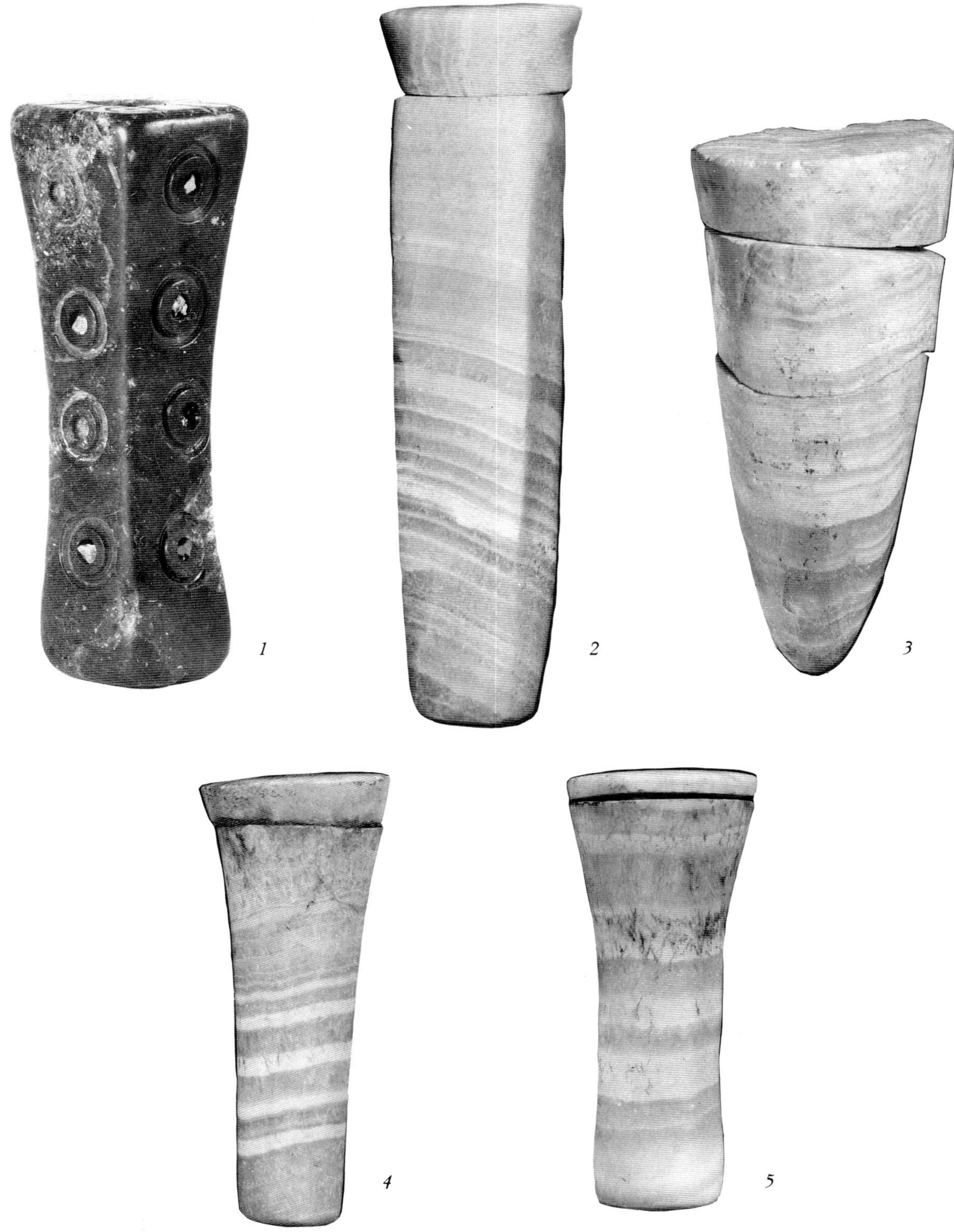

Altyn-Depe. Excavation 5. Item 1: *horizon 4, burial 728*. Item 2: *horizon 4, locality 44*. Item 3: *horizon 7, courtyard A*. Item 4: *horizon 9, locality 33*. Item 5: *horizon 9, burial 845*.

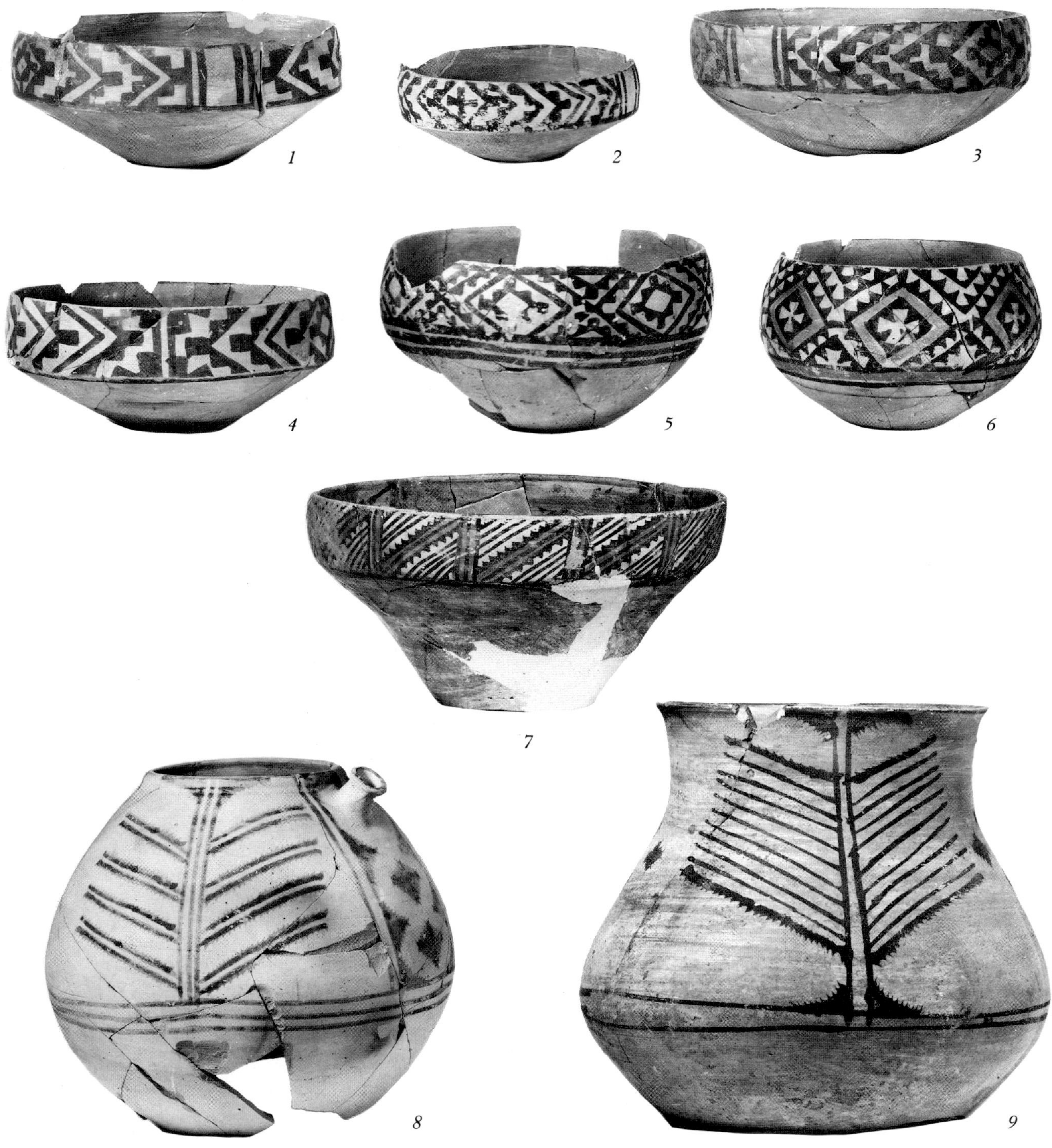

Altyn-Depe excavations of 1981. Items 1 to 7 are Late Eneolithic painted pottery. Items 1 to 6: *Excavation 15, burial chamber 2*. Item 7: *Excavation 1, horizon Altyn 9*. Items 8 and 9 are Early Bronze Age painted vessels from Excavation 5. Item 8: *horizon 4, locality 66*. Item 9: *horizon 4, locality 52*.

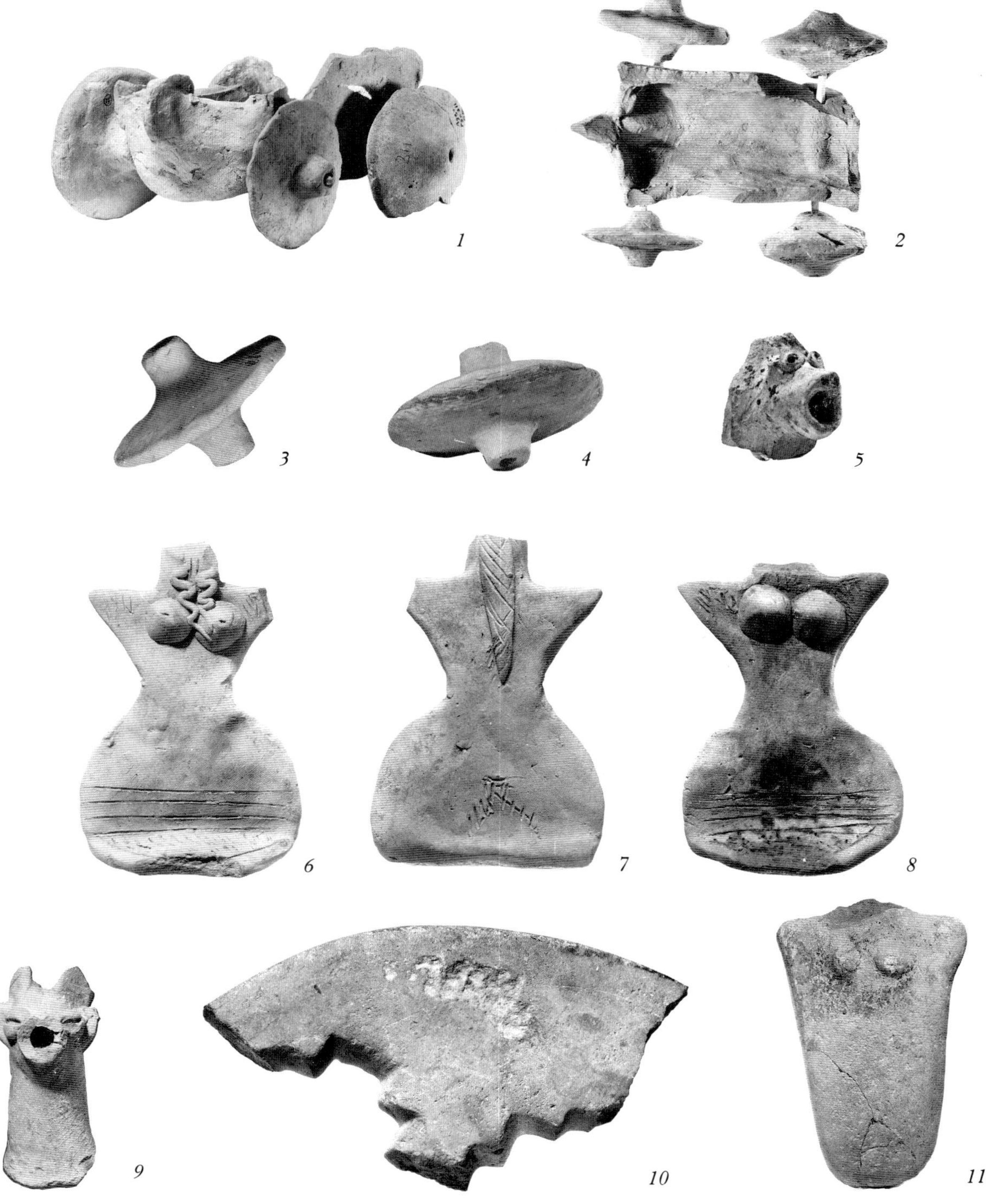

Items 1 to 9 are Middle Bronze Age artifacts from Altyn-Depe excavations of 1982 and 1983. Item 10 is a Late Eneolithic artifact from Altyn-Depe excavations of 1983. Items 1 to 8 and 11 are terracotta; Item 10 is stone. Items 1 to 9 are from Excavation 9. Items 1 and 2: *model of cart, locality 311*. Items 3 and 4: *wheels of cart model, burial 718*. Item 5: *zoomorphic spout, locality 329*. Items 6 and 7: *female statuette, locality 293*. Item 8: *female statuette*. Item 9: *zoomorphic spout, "Krasivaya" Street*. Item 10: *Excavation 5, horizon 1, fragment of stone weight*. Item 11: *female statuette, Ilgynly-Depe excavations of 1985, North*.